red robin

autobiography of r.e. davis

Order this book online at www.trafford.com/07-2657
or email orders@trafford.com

Most Trafford titles are also available at major online book retailers.

© Copyright 2008 Rodney Davis.

All rights reserved. No part of this publication may be reproduced, stored in a retrieval system, or transmitted, in any form or by any means, electronic, mechanical, photocopying, recording, or otherwise, without the written prior permission of the author.

Note for Librarians: A cataloguing record for this book is available from Library and Archives Canada at www.collectionscanada.ca/amicus/index-e.html

ISBN: 978-1-4251-5878-1

We at Trafford believe that it is the responsibility of us all, as both individuals and corporations, to make choices that are environmentally and socially sound. You, in turn, are supporting this responsible conduct each time you purchase a Trafford book, or make use of our publishing services. To find out how you are helping, please visit www.trafford.com/responsiblepublishing.html

Our mission is to efficiently provide the world's finest, most comprehensive book publishing service, enabling every author to experience success. To find out how to publish your book, your way, and have it available worldwide, visit us online at www.trafford.com/10510

 www.trafford.com

North America & international
toll-free: 1 888 232 4444 (USA & Canada)
phone: 250 383 6864 ♦ fax: 250 383 6804 ♦ email: info@trafford.com

The United Kingdom & Europe
phone: +44 (0)1865 722 113 ♦ local rate: 0845 230 9601
facsimile: +44 (0)1865 722 868 ♦ email: info.uk@trafford.com

10 9 8 7 6 5 4 3 2

Foreword

The vast majority of children are loved and well cared for by their parents or guardians. But for some, regardless of being given whatever they ask for, and being able to do whatever they want, this may not be enough! Petulance from the majority of these children is virtually unheard of, adults having given in to the child's slightest whim in return for harmony, thus avoiding tantrums.

Whilst many children are loved and cared for, it seems to be necessary for others to suffer hardship to enable the child to enjoy a happy lifestyle. In the majority of these cases the child realises and appreciates the efforts made by others, which in turn leads to a contented happy upbringing and understanding between all concerned.

A very small number of children are unwanted and uncared for, to the extent that the child must learn to fend for itself to survive. This autobiography is the true story of the early years of one of these children; brought up in a hostile environment and reliant upon nature's natural larder and wildlife for sustenance. The contents, which will shock and disillusion adults and children; will strengthen their appreciation of the loving and caring environment, which the author hopes they have been fortunate enough to experience.

Acknowledgements

In compiling my recollections of the events in my early life I would like to thank Amy Lucas who guided me in so many different ways and whom I admired greatly. Also Ellen Champkin, whom I always called Nan; if it had not been for her looking after my welfare I am sure I would not have lived through my childhood. Last and by no means least the help, support and encouragement from my wife Jean. God Bless them all.

red robin

Chapter One

On two occasions in the past there was total darkness: silence, no senses, and a mindless void. They could have lasted for a microsecond, or the whole of eternity, and surrounded me. I shall never know because I was oblivious to everything. The closest I have ever been to death; but survived, by waking. I retained the memory of past existence.

I vaguely remember the beginning was very different. It wasn't as dark and there was a very tiny spark of life. A glimmer of grey light filtered through the darkness above. From where I lay I knew there were high steps ahead, barely within reach. To the left and right these stretched endlessly and I could just make out their pale colour, great size and height. I was in a deep chasm, the only egress a climb to the top, into the greyness.

I managed to get to the first step, reached up, then held the edge and hauled myself onto the flat ledge. I did the same on the second and third, then rested. I looked up and sensed the darkness far above was beginning to fade away; a little more light was showing. I began to slide towards the edge of the step but crawled to the back and hauled myself onto the next and rested again. I knew there was something wrong; I shouldn't be sliding without reason. I didn't understand, although it happened four more times on the long exhausting journey to the top.

There was one more step ahead; everything above me was much brighter. I looked down into an impenetrable darkness then reached for the last ledge and heaved myself over the top. I was there. For a split-second in time, I didn't know where, but I was there.

I screamed out loud from the excruciating, uncontrollable pain filling my body then burst into tears. My arms and legs flayed, jerking like a stringless puppet. Though my eyes were closed, the brightness penetrated my eyelids and they kept on watering. Taking my first breath of air, then breathing caused the pain, and I knew I had been born. God had given me life.

Chapter Two

For many weeks I could only just lie and get stronger and accustomed to sound, light, my surroundings and relief from the pain, which had made me scream so much in the past.

I became aware of a man and woman in a small country house. They were older than another woman, who washed and fed me and with whom I slept at night. I remember one terrible night in bed when she held me with both hands so tightly I was unable to move. I was face down on top of her. She held my legs tight, my face between her breasts; my head pressed down so tightly I couldn't breath. As her hold tightened, I tried to move, but it was impossible. I began to weaken and fade into darkness but not of the life-giving type I'd experienced before. Suddenly, I was released from the oncoming eternity of darkness and oblivion as her tight grip loosened. The bed covers were pulled down and I gasped for air just in time to continue life.

Her whole body was shaking with emotion and, as she sobbed, the heavy tears ran down her face and dripped on to me. She kept on kissing me as if to ask forgiveness for what we both knew she'd intended to do.

Any affection for me didn't last very long; the deep fingernail wounds inflicted on my forehead became more frequent, the scars they left still visible until my late teens. Those on my head were never seen, always being hidden by hair. The unseen scars, within my mind, will stay forever.

The older man and woman knew something was very wrong and took over caring for me until a man in a car came to take me away. Dressed in uniform, his smooth dark hair was partly concealed on one side by his cap; he looked very smart, but sad and cautious. As he approached the younger woman who was holding me, he stared as if in horror. His mouth fell open in shock and disbelief when he saw the deep wounds on my forehead. Initially there was complete silence; then grasping me from the clutches of the woman he began shouting at each of the three in turn. My body shook with fear, while his shook with anger; the two women looked remorseful. Within seconds, red in the face with fury, he laid me on the front seat of a car. Then, while shaking his fist out of the window and still shouting, he drove a short distance onto a single-track country lane and onwards. I was too small to see through the car windows; only the tops of the trees were visible as we passed beneath them. After a while they disappeared from view and were replaced by the rooftops of buildings on both sides of the road, which eventually led us to London.

Chapter Three

I remember lying in a pram in the hallway close to the front door of the house where I was being cared for. Three or four families took it in turn to care for me but after several weeks I went to live with a couple called Kit and Bob in Brockley, a mile or two away. I had my own room, which they'd created for me, with a small bed and nursery-style wallpaper. They always cared for me as if I was their own son; and after a few weeks I thought I was.

The war seemed to get worse every day. Aeroplanes shot at each other fighting high in the sky and creating holes in the roof of the house; the bullets often passing through to embed themselves in the ceiling.

Tethered barrage balloons to stop aircraft flying low, floated across the sky like huge grey ears with a giant-sized nose, slowly bobbing and swaying in the wind. Bombs and incendiaries from some of the bigger aircraft started falling more frequently; the noise from the aircraft, the loud explosions and the anti aircraft fire sometimes deafened. Buildings blazed and rubble lay strewn over the roads and pavements. Masses of glittering sharp splinters of shrapnel frequently became embedded into exterior walls or lay shattered on paths and open spaces.

Air raid shelters were built and were frequently used. They were made of thick, corrugated galvanised iron sheets and dug about two feet into the soil. The excavated earth, sometimes with added concrete, was put on the top of the shelters, together with grass to retain the warmth and added safety and camouflage. For safety, most people would tolerate the cold and damp of a night in an Anderson Shelter rather than risk staying in a house but they were bland and uncomfortable to stay in for a long period; having only four bunks inside with metal straps fitted with a thin mattress to either sit or lay on.

Within a year I was taken to Mannings Heath in West Sussex to elude the continuing war. I felt distraught; I'd lost the first two people in my life who cared and acted as my mother and father and who's love I'd happily shared.

Chapter Four

The property, where I lived blissfully for three and a half to four years with my adopted Aunt Meena and Uncle Bert was a council house. Apart from a main bedroom, there were two very small box rooms, one of which I sometimes shared with as many as four other children. I stayed the longest of all; most of the others stayed only a few weeks or months. All were regularly visited by their parents, while the only person to visit me, very occasionally, was the man who took me to London. He was the one who ensured I was looked after, and had brought me to my new home.

The ground floor of the house was one large combined living room, and kitchen. On the hob of a large black iron cooking stove or 'range' stood an enormous old kettle always boiling; ready for making tea, or washing-up. The huge room was warm and cosy.

Everyone bathed once a week in a large tin tub, which was kept on the wall outside the kitchen door. It was placed in front of the range for warmth during the winter, with a curtain stretched across the room for privacy. Because so many kettles and pots of hot water were required to fill the bathtub, we all became accustomed to sharing the same water. Uncle Bert always bathed first, Aunt Meena second; I was third, the other children took it in turn. Whenever the bath water became chilled, the water in the kettle was normally hot enough to top it up.

The long back garden was the same width as the house and contained a fenced area where, dependent on the season, masses of vegetables grew. Throughout the year the homegrown produce, played an important part in helping to supplement the food rationing then in force.

The toilet, a tatty old wooden shed halfway up the garden, didn't have electric light, which was probably safer as the rain poured through the roof. Sitting in the cold wind with your coat over your head to keep dry was one thing; but it was quite another to be scared whenever the candle blew out and you imagined the large creepy looking spiders, which had been on the toilet walls, were now crawling over you. We were all very reluctant to go to the toilet during bad weather; but the warmth of the fire and sharing of beds was always welcome on the cold and wet winter nights.

One day, when a little girl had a visit from her parents, I asked Aunt Meena who my parents were, and why they never came to see me? She explained they were in the Royal Air Force and it was impossible to know where either of them was; and that being so young I'd have got confused if I'd been told before. She went on to tell me that everyone who'd looked after me in London, had been a member of my family, and that the man who came to see me occasionally, was in fact my father. She assured me that my parents would undoubtedly come to see me whenever it was possible and that they'd be sure to take me home after the war. I was by then, old enough to understand and I felt happier knowing I had a natural family of which I'd eventually become part.

I began spending a few hours each day at a small school in Golding Lane and began to learn how to understand and appreciate others, and what to expect of life, as I grew up.

Just past the school there was a Prisoner of War Camp mainly full of airmen. I used to walk to it frequently, being inquisitive and liking to talk and listen to those who could speak English. They seemed pleased to see me and talked about their homes and the families they missed. It was sometimes very sad, and I'd often notice a glint of sadness or a tear in their eyes.

Although I was only about three and a half years old, one British soldier, a prison guard, always jokingly called me Master Davis, as we walked around the barbed wire fencing together. All the prisoners told me they enjoyed my visits and chats, one presenting me with a hand-carved pistol operated by an elastic band, which fired matchsticks. It must have taken him hours to make and to me it was a work of art. I treasured it for ages until it was stolen by one of the boys when he left the house to go home to his parents. It saddened me; already I'd learnt the lesson of how considerate and kind some people can be, and how inconsiderate and horrible others are.

One summer's day in 1943 I got home from playing with my friends to be met at the door by Aunt Meena. She took me by the hand and said, "You've a visitor, it's not your Dad, it's a lady." We went inside where a woman wearing a smart jacket and matching skirt rose from a chair and approached me.

"Hello Rod. How are you?" she asked as she bent down and gazed into my face.

"Very well, thank you," I politely answered, marvelling at her prettiness.

Straightening, she spoke to Aunt Meena for several minutes, all the while holding my hand. When they'd finished talking she turned towards me and stroked my hair. Kneeling, as if studying every aspect of my face, she pushed the hair off my forehead revealing the scars. Putting her arms around me she kissed me on each of my cheeks, before softly whispering, "I've just come to see how you are. I'm glad you're being looked after. Goodbye and good luck!" Then, before I realised what was happening, she stood, and with tears in her eyes, she hastily and silently left. I followed her to the gate where she turned toward the main road and briskly hurried away. I shouted "Goodbye," then again, at the top of my voice, but she never replied, or turned or looked back. I didn't know who she was, neither did Aunt Meena, or so she said; it was just somebody who'd come to see me! I shrugged my shoulders, and wondered why she'd bothered, before dismissing any other thoughts regarding her visit.

The next day, as I stood watching Uncle Bert trim the front hedge, a Spitfire aeroplane came roaring out of the sky and crashed into Walder's Woods only a few hundred yards from the farmhouses opposite. It burst into an enormous bubbling ball of red, yellow, and golden flames with columns of dense black smoke. We watched, speechless, as the pilot swayed gently from side to side as he parachuted safely down; he was lucky enough to land next to the clubhouse on the local Golf Course!

In the afternoon I went towards the woodland where the aeroplane had crashed. A small gypsy family had been camping in the serenity of a field by the side of the road for the past two weeks; the customary green canvas roof covered their traditionally styled and brightly painted caravan. The brown and white carthorse that pulled it along stood by the hedgerow eating the grass and nibbling at the fresh leaves. The gypsies who made, and sold clothes pegs and saucepans to the local people before moving on to the next village, waved and exchanged greetings as I continued to where the Spitfire had crashed.

A small crowd of people had already gathered at the site, where the trees, set on fire from the damaged fuel tanks, were still burning. The remains of the aeroplane were almost impossible to make out, leaving nothing very much to see. Looking around I noticed there was something worth a second glance; the local Bobby. He stood out from the crowd, trousers tucked into his socks, wearing bicycle clips over the top. His belly was so big he could only manage to do up the two top buttons of his tunic; exposing his tight, bulging white shirt, only half of which was tucked under a home made plaited string belt. I almost laughed out loud at his comical appearance but couldn't hide my smile when he sent me away for my safety.

I walked home and as I was about to open the gate noticed the geese in the driveway of Swallowfield Farm opposite, had all started to waddle away. I looked closely at where they'd been squatting and noticed an enormous egg; I picked it up. It was the biggest I'd ever seen and still warm. The farm was so far up the driveway I decided to take the egg home. Uncle Bert was over the moon with it. "What a good meal it'll make, and what's more you'll have half for finding it and bringing it home," he said. True to his word I did get half, but it was the white half; he had the yolk! The quantity was fair, but the quality of my part wasn't.

It was a cold early spring morning and I'd been to the local shop to get some shopping. On my return Aunt Meena met me at the gate. She held me and said "Rod, this is the day you've been waiting for, your father's here; he's come to take you home to your mother."

Aunt Meena and I both wept a little while Uncle Bert looked very miserable as he and my father put what clothes I had into a small bag. I hugged my Aunt and Uncle, whom I'd loved so much for what seemed such a long time. It was like losing my mother and father for the second time; I'd never felt so sad. I kissed them goodbye and left, leaving them both looking forlorn. Neither they nor I knew that we'd never meet again. I still had tears in my eyes when Dad and I left; I was experiencing how it felt, to be heartbroken with sadness yet at the same time overwhelmed and filled with happiness.

Chapter Five

Dad and I never stopped talking all the way home; now in the small rural town of Dorking in Surrey, close to the countryside. He told me his name was Bernard and that he'd been in the RAF during the war. Mum had been in the Army, and although her name was Violet, she was always called Babs. He went on to tell me that Ellen, my maternal grandmother, who lived with us, would help take care of me. He also told me we had two young pets: a small dog named Wendy with long golden-brown and white hair and a curly tail. The other pet was a tomcat named Jet because of his smooth, short black coat, which glittered like the black mineral used for making jewellery.

Once in Dorking we drove along South Street until we turned into a narrow lane, which lead to a small yard where we stopped in front of the steps to my new home. Within a couple of minutes Dad, his hand on my shoulder, guided me to the two women waiting at the doorway. The younger of the women took several strides forward and put her arms around me, giving me a hug and kiss; then taking a step back gazed at me, as if in wonder, as she spoke. "Hello Rod, I'm your mother and this is your grandmother." She smiled, directing my attention with her hand, to the older woman. "It's been a long time since we were all together son, but we've got you back at last, and we'll never let you go again."

I could finally believe I'd been reunited with my real family. All the while we were greeting each other; Wendy sensing our excitement kept barking and running around in circles chasing her tail. Jet, remained half-asleep on the windowsill, but opened one bright yellow eye showing a thin black vertical pupil.

Settling into my new home made me feel happy, safe, and content very quickly. Was it all too good to be true, or was I a 'Doubting Thomas,' I asked myself.

I became a pupil at the local Powell Corderoy Infants School, a short walk away. Within a week I'd made a friend; we'd meet at his house and walk to school together. His mother always insisted I had a little breakfast each morning, for which I was grateful: it was as if she knew that at home my breakfast usually seemed to be forgotten; either that or I was too late for any.

One day during early May, my grandmother Nan and I walked along the short driveway, around the corner where Dr Bourne-Taylor lived, and onto a high embankment by some shops. It overlooked the bandstand across South Street, towards 'The Spotted Dog' public house. It was 'Victory in Europe Day' and there were masses of people celebrating: brass bands played and people sang and danced, packing the whole area with relieved and jubilant souls. Mum and Dad celebrated with the crowds for hours, well into the night. Nan and I walked home late in the evening, and I could still hear the band playing and the singing revellers when I went to bed.

During the last week of May, Dad told me that Mum and Nan would be operating a café each weekday. They'd sell food and drinks to the workmen building an estate of new homes at a place called Chart Downs, at the end of Deepdene Avenue. Dad explained the route I should take from school to the café; it was a long walk, taking about half an hour, but there was no other option.

When I left school to walk to Chart Downs for the first time, I discovered how far it was. I had to find my way from one end of Dorking, through the town centre, then along the fast main bypass of the town until I eventually reached the building site. When I arrived Nan always gave me a cup of tea and whatever was left in the way of food for my dinner; but once I'd finished that there wasn't anything to do except wait for Dad to collect us, as it was too far for Mum or Nan to walk home.

Despite any adverse weather conditions, I made the trip every school day for months. Eventually as the main buildings were finished, most of the builders left for other jobs and it wasn't long before the café was no longer viable, and closed.

In mid September, Dad informed me we'd be going to London for the wedding of his younger sister Jean, where I'd also meet a lot more of my relations. We left Dorking, to arrive in less than an hour at West Croydon and the home of Mum's sister Doss, her husband and son Ken. I was given a cup of tea and told to wait in the garden out of the way. Within half an hour, it was time to go; Nan would stay with her daughter and family for about a week then get the bus home.

Having said our farewells, we set off for Balham to Mum's other sister, her husband and their son. It was almost a repeat performance: I was greeted with a "hello"; given a cup of tea and a sandwich, and then told to keep out of the way while they talked. Then, within half an hour it was goodbye time again; I was bored!

It was very different when we got to Blackpool Road, Peckham and Dad's old home, where most of his family still lived. I met Dad's parents, his brothers and sisters, two more cousins, plus lots of family friends. Sent to sit on the stairs I watched the laughter, singing and dancing all afternoon and into the evening until everybody went home.

Wrapped in Nan's shawl while sitting in the back seat of the car on the way home, I thought of all the people I'd met. Although I tried to recall ever seeing, or meeting any of them before, I couldn't; not even my mother or grandmother! I couldn't understand why: I thought I had a good memory, certainly good enough to remember how and when my forehead was wounded.

Towards the end of the year, Dad told Nan and me he'd bought a plot of land in the countryside at a place called Ifold, near Loxwood in West Sussex. The nearest large town was Horsham. I knew the name well; it was near Mannings Heath, which brought back many happy memories to me.

On the Saturday Dad, having said he'd take us to see the land he'd bought, took us on our first visit to Ifold. We passed through the tiny village of Loxwood, then along the Plaistow Road. We saw a small shop called Ifold Stores, at the beginning of the Ifold area, in the middle of nowhere. Driving through the countryside we passed 'Foxbridge Farm' then stopped directly opposite a bungalow called 'Strudwick Farm.'

The land Mum and Dad had bought with the intention of building a bungalow, was covered with woodland made up of hazel, birch, and oak trees. Dad told us that firstly, he needed to clear enough of the land at the far end to make room for a large railway carriage; then he'd build a brick building on the back, comprising two rooms; a kitchen and a sitting room. He anticipated we'd only need the carriage while he was building the bungalow, which he thought would take two or three years.

Having surveyed the land, Dad drove us around the area. There were very few houses to see along the narrow lanes; it was mainly undisturbed woodland, the whole area being quiet and tranquil. Before returning home, Dad drove to Plaistow village; a tiny quaint hamlet as quiet and peaceful as Ifold.

Dad worked every weekend or weekday he could preparing the land and building our temporary home. In April he told us everything was ready and we'd be moving within the next two weeks; ten days later we moved to our new home and future in Ifold.

Chapter Six

It was a lovely clear spring morning; Mum sat in the front seat of the car holding on to Wendy. Nan and I sat in the back: I gently held and comforted Jet to relax him; there was no doubt he didn't like the drive. Nan had boxes of pre-prepared food packed around her feet and on her lap; once we arrived, she'd be too busy to cook anything to eat. In the boot of the small car were four five-gallon cans containing drinking water. Whenever needed, we'd get more from a communal well half a mile away situated by the side of the road at Spring Hill, on the outskirts of Plaistow village. It was used by almost everybody living around the area.

A small removal van, containing the furniture we'd be able to get into our new home had followed us from Dorking, through the attractive Surrey and Sussex boundary village of Ockley en route to Loxwood, then Ifold.

When we arrived at the plot, Nan and I were in for our first surprise. Part of the earth bank had been dug away and the ditch filled and levelled. We drove onto a driveway made up of stones and ballast, then past a five-barred gate, with a sign fixed to the middle of it, which I couldn't read.

Within seconds we saw that Dad had cleared the land, allowing ample space to position the railway-carriage and build our adjacent temporary brick home. It was, as he'd wanted. He'd left three or four large clumps of hazel trees, but the large oak trees had been cut down, sold, and removed. Later I learned the large piles of oak wood dotted about the land were the branches; sawn into four feet lengths and laid in stacks three feet high and twelve feet wide, these were called 'cordwood'.

Nan and I got out of the car and looked at each other. When we saw the large area of land compared to the size of the wagon our mouths fell open with disbelief, but we said nothing. I asked her about the strange word on the sign attached to the gate, which had now been propped wide open against the hazel trees at the side, where it was to remain. The word reads 'Vi-Bern,' she said. "Although we call her Babs, they are the first two letters of Mum's name Violet and the first four letters of Dad's name, Bernard reading 'Vi-Bern'; the name of your new home." I understood what was meant by the name, but thought it strange, and unfitting for a home in the country.

I carried whatever I could to the doorway of our new home, leaving it outside to be put away later. Wendy followed closely, watching me constantly as if waiting to be told she could go for a run. I smeared butter over Jet's paws and rubbed it in thoroughly, knowing he'd be able to pick up the scent trail to find his way home, should he get lost in the woods. Then picking him up, to hold him under my arm and with Wendy following, walked to the end of the roughly made path. She thought it was wonderful, sniffing at almost everything she found and giving out little barks of excitement. When I put Jet down he scurried off straight to the edge of the ferns covering the ground in front of the woods. He looked magnificent; his short black fur shining like mink in the bright sunlight.

Jet wanted to have a good look around his new home and prowling-ground. With his smooth, shining tail sticking straight up, he ran through the ferns, which although only half-grown were at least twice his height. They swayed, showing from their movement the direction he was going and then suddenly stopped. He popped his head up above the ferns, his big wide-open yellow eyes looking to see where he was. I watched his much slower movements, first to the left, then to the right. I knew he was confused and was getting his bearings. He'd soon learn I thought, and left him alone to enjoy his new environment. He must have felt a sense of adventure; I certainly did!

My new home was a guard's railway wagon in which Dad had installed two small bay windows. With the wheels removed, it had been placed in a level position near our boundary. At the back of the wagon Dad had built a brick building, the same size as the wagon, both in length and width. The only entrance door was at the end nearest to the path, under a lean-to that stopped the rain driving in on wet and windy days. There was plenty of room for storage; at the end of the lean-to, a large curtain made of sacking hung from the doorway to a small area containing an Elsan toilet. There wasn't any electric light, but unlike at Mannings Heath it had a tin roof.

The two removal men finished for the day and left after Dad paid them. I was told to wait outside while our new home was arranged, as I'd only get in the way of the work; it wouldn't take long.

It was a lovely spring day and getting warmer as the day passed. I enjoyed walking the land and the surrounding wood, but didn't want to go too far away in case I was called. Nearby, I found a large oak chopping block fixed into the ground only a few yards from the door with a hand-held long-bladed axe with a hooked tip, called a billhook, stuck in the top. Close by was a large pile of hazel sticks of different sizes all partly trimmed; I also I found some string which had been used for tying up the boxes we'd brought. Using the billhook, I cut a piece of hazel wood about the thickness of my thumb and about three feet long, and made a bow with arrows. I then practised shooting for what seemed long enough to make me a reasonable shot, or at least I thought so.

A wood pigeon roosted on a top branch of a chestnut tree by the side of the wagon. I tried to get as close as I could by creeping from one clump of bushes to the next; bobbing up and down each time I moved to see if the pigeon was still there. I got within range, took aim, and fired. I missed by such a wide margin, the bird didn't flinch, or even realise I'd shot at it! I decided not to bother wasting any more time with bows and arrows.

Nan came outside laughing. "I've been watching you," she smiled. "You made me laugh so much I'm going to nickname you Robin and that's what I'll call you in future."

"Why do you want to call me Robin?"

"Because you were bobbing up and down so much when you tried to shoot at the pigeon, you reminded me of the old rhyme called 'Robin a bobbin,' which goes,

'Robin a bobbin bent his bow. Shot at a pigeon and killed a crow.' You were flitting around like a Robin. Your initials spell the word red, so you could even be called red robin," Nan chuckled.

We both laughed at what was to become my family nickname for many years to come.

Waiting to be told I could go indoors, I left Nan sitting outside and walked to the front of the land and onto the narrow road. Wendy close at my heels continued sniffing at smells she'd never encountered before. On the bank at the front of the property I noticed a beautiful silver slow-worm lying on top of a mound of clay, basking in the warmth of the spring sun. It was about the size of a pencil and the reflection from its tiny scales made it shine like a mirror. It seemed to be unperturbed by my presence and just looked up at me, then slowly slid away into the dry, sun-bleached grass.

A little further along the bank, I saw five or six lizards sprawled out full length and motionless, their heads and necks all craned to look in my direction. Intrigued, I gently reached forward to pick one up and look at its beautiful autumn coloured markings more closely. I was completely unaware that a lizard was able to painlessly shed the end of its tail; to my astonishment, I was left holding only the wriggling tip, and could only watch as unharmed it joined the others as they slowly clambered into the tiny holes in the bank.

Chapter Seven

Half an hour later, Dad called for Nan and me to go indoors and familiarise ourselves with our new home. We went together, and looked.

The brick room which Dad had divided in half was square and the same width as the railway wagon. The first room contained two small paraffin stoves, which stood on top of a small oven. There were two tables; one with bottles of water, bowls for washing, soap, towels, and cooking utensils; the other, with chairs around three sides, was pushed against the wall. Other bits and pieces for cooking and general household effects were stored on shelves fitted to the bare walls.

Over the top of the door dividing the two rooms, a wooden shelf had been fitted, on the underside of which were two large hooks, each fixed a few inches from the end: for hanging ornaments, I innocently thought. I thought wrong; never guessing that what was to be laid between the hooks would bring me so much sorrow and pain, for so many years.

The only light in the room came from the window fitted in the guard's wagon. It shone through the wide opening between the two small rooms where we stood. This was the kitchen, dining room, and bathroom, all in one. For a moment or two it reminded me of my earlier life in Mannings Heath; but this room was only a fraction of the size. It was darker and colder; the thin corrugated tin roof set at a slight angle had no insulation, which made it vulnerable to the slightest sound of wind, and rain. Like the thin roof, the walls, built of a single thickness of bricks, couldn't contain much warmth during the winter.

The adjacent room in the wagon was a bedroom, with a standard sized double bed, cupboards, and wardrobe; there wasn't space for anything else. The bed was pushed against the partitioning which divided the wagon in half. Nan and I were told it was our bedroom and that I would sleep against the wall.

My memories went back to Mannings Heath again. I'd been in similar positions before and told myself I could handle the situation, but what about Nan? She was over the age of seventy, and I felt concerned about how she'd cope.

Lastly we were shown into the room next to the kitchen with the shelf fixed over the top of the doorway. It was a comfortable looking sitting room, containing armchairs and other general household furniture. Strategically placed, a large fireplace had been built directly opposite the opening to Mum and Dad's bedroom in the wagon. They never bothered to show us their room because it was the same as ours, or so we were told; there wasn't any mention of the room being kept permanently warm by the fire during winter!

We were told they had done enough that day and it was time to relax. When the kettle on the oil stove eventually boiled Nan made tea, and then went through the boxes to find the previously made sandwiches and some home-made cake. After we'd eaten we went outside so Dad could explain where the boundary lines of the land lay and where he was going to build the bungalow and garage, and dig the cesspit.

It was a lot to take in but all fell into place very quickly. I was told I'd be very much involved, as I'd be expected to get any building materials, such as bricks, concrete, etc. ready for Dad to use at weekends, or when he came home from work of an evening and it was still light.

The left side of the land had a chain-link fence running from the front edge to the back. Mum saw a young lady standing on a lawn at the back of an adjacent bungalow looking and waving in our direction. We introduced ourselves and chatted for ages; I didn't realise at the time that I'd met a wonderful person who'd hold my love, and respect for the rest of my life. Her name was Amy Lucas; she had a sister, Kathy, and together with their mother they spent a lot of time caring for their father, who'd been unwell for a long time. A few days later, when I waved she turned and waved towards the large French window at the back of the bungalow from where her father could see us. Instinctively I also gave a big wave towards the window. She smiled and thanked me, telling me how pleased it would make him. From that day onwards, although I couldn't see anybody, I waved every time I was on that side of the land.

The land to the right of the boundary contained four or five oak trees growing on the far side; near to the door of our home were the chestnut trees where I'd tried to shoot the pigeon and earned my nickname. The land was covered with a mixture of hazel trees, ferns, brambles and grass. The land at the back was exactly the same, except some ten times larger, with a clear fresh water stream running through the middle of it. In every direction, a carpet of primroses showed their flowers through the undergrowth. The young trees, shrubs and other plants growing in the bright sunlight were showing the first growth of coloured leaves and blooms.

Before it got too dark, I looked for Jet. He had vanished since I'd let him loose. By the time I gave up searching, Dad had lit the oil lamps, which gave off an unwelcome odour. We sat and listened to the wireless in the sitting room for about an hour when Dad told me Nan was tired and ready for sleep; because I was to sleep against the wall I'd have to go to bed first.

"Does that mean every night?" I asked.

"Yes of course it does, now go to bed."

I lay tightly pressed against the wall; leaving enough room for Nan, who came in a few moments later, blew the lamp out, put on her nightclothes, and then got into bed.

"There isn't much room is there?" I said.

"No not at all, but we're here, so we'll have to make the most of it. Are you pleased to be here?"

Immediately, without thinking, I answered, "No! Definitely not."

"Me neither," was her answer.

Between her gentle, quiet sobbing, she said. "Goodnight Robin, God bless, and don't forget to say your prayers."

Nan was still sobbing when I fell asleep.

Chapter Eight

Frequently during the night Nan and I found it difficult to sleep. We tried lying on our backs at the same time, to find there wasn't enough room in the standard sized double bed. Eventually we turned on our sides and lay back to back. In the main I was comfortable, although occasionally woke up stiff, from lying in the same position. Every time I woke I heard the sound of nightingales; their comforting song of high and low trills and full musical notes lulled me to sleep with an indescribable feeling of complete relaxation. The soothing warble of birdsong always helped me forget any worries.

The sound of the kettle whistling woke me and from where I lay I could see it boiling on the oil stove. I had the whole bed to myself, and wanted to stretch out and sleep but it was the first full day of my future life in Ifold so groggily I dressed.

Mum and Nan were sitting at the kitchen table. Nan gave me a cup of tea and some bread and jam she'd brought with us from Dorking. When I'd eaten my sandwich I asked if Jet had come home yet. Mum, sounding annoyed, told me he hadn't been seen.

Dad had been working outside on different jobs since early morning. He showed me the trestle bench he'd made to saw timber on, then demonstrated how to use a bow-saw, a large axe for chopping or splitting logs, and the billhook I'd used the day before. He told me the cordwood would need to be cut into logs every day, to fit the fireplace. His expression changed and he looked almost apologetic as he told me that the responsibility of ensuring there was always sufficient firewood would fall upon my shoulders. I was told to stack the wood under the lean-to so it would be kept dry, and to ensure there was always plenty. Dad was arranging to get a wood-burning stove, which would be constantly kept alight in the kitchen for cooking. I was horrified; it was a mega amount of work, as I could barely swing the heavy axe above my head. An hour later I'd discovered just how much strength and effort it took to keep only one fire alight.

From a large pile of various building materials and wooden boxes, Dad dragged out eight large curved sections of corrugated iron, which I recognised and remembered as the heavy galvanized corrugated sheets, used during the war to make the Anderson bomb shelters. "What are they for Dad?"

"These are for making a small stable Robin; we'll be getting a goat. Hopefully it'll save us buying fresh milk from Ifold Stores every day. We'll also get some chicken and with any luck we'll be able to sell some of the eggs," he answered, having called me Robin for the first time.

"That's a good idea Dad, do you need a hand?"

"Yes; it would be helpful if you could cut a couple of dozen thick hazel poles and dig them into the ground. Then I'll only have to fix the wire netting to make the chicken run, and make a hutch and nest box for the eggs."

Dad bolted the sheets of iron together, and stood them upright to make a shelter for the goat. Digging and fixing the posts into the hard Sussex clay was exhausting. Dad fixed the wire to the posts, and then made the gate to keep it secure.

The egg box and hutch were easily made from one of the large wooden boxes previously delivered. Within about three hours the stable, chicken run, and the chicken hutch were finished.

By midday, Mum and Dad had gone shopping to Loxwood for food and other bits and pieces, while, followed by Wendy, I went looking for Jet. I walked through the large wooded area at the back and over the stream, until I reached Chalk Road, calling Jet's name every two or three minutes. Covering as much ground as I could, I turned towards 'The Ride', a road at the back of the woods. I searched for nearly one and half-hours, but there was no sign of him.

The wildlife of Ifold was unbelievable. Never in my life, had I seen so many different types of creatures in their natural habitat getting on with their lives in such a contented and natural way. A song thrush was singing its head off; blue and great tits, in their colourful yellow, blue, and green plumage hopped from one tree branch to another, hanging upside down, and performing their acrobatics. A tiny Jenny wren, with its tilted upright tail, perched unconcerned a couple of feet away as I passed it by. A robin watched every move I made: it was as if he was trying to tell me I was trespassing on his territory and shouldn't be there. Within a day or so he felt confident he and his habitat were safe and felt comfortable enough to stay close and follow me about the land; frequently showing off and puffing up his bright red breast

With Wendy at my side, who'd amused me when I'd watched her splashing about in the stream, I gave up for the day. With the disappointment of not being able to find Jet foremost in my mind I went home feeling tired and hungry from the hard day's work.

At home Dad showed me how to change the accumulator on the wireless, which I would need to exchange every week at the Stores in Loxwood. He'd bought three Tilly lamps, and showed me how to fill, fit the mantles, and light them. They'd give far more light than regular oil lamps, and wouldn't be affected outside in rain or strong winds.

"At least it's better than when I was evacuated; we only had candles, and they kept going out in the wind," I commented. "Mind you, it's about the only thing which is better. The rooms here are much smaller, and there isn't much room in bed. I'll be glad when the bungalow's built. How long will it take Dad?"

"Just keep your opinions and thoughts to yourself," he said, without even looking at me.

I immediately regretted what I'd said and decided the best thing to do was to keep quiet for the rest of the evening.

Mum told me that, over the next few days that I should get enough logs stacked up to last for a couple of weeks. She said I should also have my last look for Jet, and asked if I'd put enough butter on his paws.

Nan interrupted and speaking generally to us all said, "I saw how much butter Robin used on Jet's paws. There was plenty and it was rubbed in so thoroughly I'd be very surprised if he couldn't find his way home from ten miles away."

I was glad Nan spoke up for me because I was beginning to feel a little uneasy and didn't want to be blamed if Jet was lost. I was feeling a little concerned at both Mum and Dad's attitude towards me that day, but everything seemed to be normal by the end of the evening.

I went to bed where the songs of the nightingales soon drifted across my thoughts and fell into such a deep sleep; I didn't even hear Nan come to bed.

Chapter Nine

The dawn chorus gradually woke me the next morning; it was bright and sunny, but nevertheless I felt downcast when Mum told me Jet was still missing.

A little later Dad drove me to various places to meet people whom I became accustomed to seeing over the next few years. We turned left towards Baker's Farm, opposite Chalk Road, then up a long steep drive verging a copse of hazel and silver birch. Huge white, free-range pigs rambled here; they were either busy rooting up plants or shrubs for food, or lying about in mud baths made when the ground was wet; others were lying on the dry clay.

We reached the farmhouse where Dad met Mr. Baker; I was told to wait in the car. They chatted for some time about the local area and residents before getting to the price of chicken. Within five minutes they'd agreed on the price of pullets on the point of lay, plus a regular supply of feed.

Travelling towards Plaistow we passed Ifold Cottage, on the border of Ifold, before stopping on the downward slope at Spring Hill to draw fresh clear, natural spring water, from the deep well. Dad filled the empty bottles and jerrycans we'd brought with us which would serve for three or four days. It was a long way to travel but there was no choice. He explained that he'd always get it, even if it meant walking all the way because of snow or icy conditions; I might be asked to help, but only if absolutely necessary.

I was taken into the shop on the corner opposite the Holy Trinity Church in Plaistow. It was tiny; no bigger than one of the rooms in the wagon at home. Then we returned to Ifold and the store there. In both shops I was introduced to the owners, enabling them to identify me whenever I went to buy anything.

Towards Loxwood, Dad showed me the house where Dr Vine and Dr Woods, held their surgery. Very soon we passed by the small village school, opposite the old and majestic St John the Baptist Church; then crossed the river, a tributary of the River Arun and passed the 'Onslow Arms'; then up the hill to the only butcher in the area. After I'd been introduced to the owner, Dad purchased some meat for our dinner and offal for Wendy, which was unusual as she was normally, only fed scraps and left over food.

We parked outside the post office, where I was introduced to the postmaster, his wife and their daughter Margaret. We crossed the road near the village pond and entered Loxwood Stores. It was here that I could exchange the accumulators; get bread and other provisions, bicycle parts and tools, clothing and haberdashery. Dad bought a few items before driving back towards Ifold.

When we reached Ifold Stores, Dad turned, passing the old Lodge House into The Drive, one of the narrow lanes surrounding the Estate. Halfway along the lane near the top end, I was shown a footpath; a short cut leading past a lake, over the river and then across the fields to Loxwood. He explained that it was the shortest route for me to use whenever Mum wanted shopping from the village. He showed me an old silo, and a tiny garage and workshop owned by a Mr Curtis and then we returned home.

I took the shopping and water indoors while Mum and Dad made another inspection of the site where the bungalow was to be built. Nan met me and pointed towards the goat stable. "Robin have a look over there and see what Wendy's eating."

At the sound of her name, Wendy looked up and I saw what looked like a fur glove in her mouth. I called her to me, then realised it was the hindquarters of a rabbit. "Where on earth did she get that from? She'd never catch anything in this dense undergrowth, certainly not a rabbit," I said.

"She got it from under the cupboard indoors. I saw her get it and run outside, but I didn't know what it was."

"How did it get there?"

"I can't imagine. She's hardly been outside since you went off this morning with your Dad." Nan replied.

We left Wendy gnawing the bones and went indoors quite befuddled, but determined to solve the mystery.

"It came from under there, Robin," Nan pointed at the cupboard.

I knelt and looked into the shadowy narrow space beneath the cupboard. Then as my eyes began to focus in the dim light I was able to see a dark shape in a corner at the back. Cautiously, I slowly slid my hand forward until I touched it. I could feel the fur of an animal and how it lay; it was warm, and breathing.

"I think it's a rabbit," I said.

"My goodness, surely not!"

I put my hand over the bundle of soft fur against the wall, and with a very slow movement pulled it towards me. To our amazement, out slithered Jet, curled up fast asleep.

"So that's where Wendy's rabbit leg came from. Jet must have caught it and brought it home. From the size of his fat tummy I'd have thought he'd eaten most of it himself; Wendy must have found what was left." I remarked.

I slid one hand under his head and front shoulder, the other under his back end, then put him on one of the chairs to finish his sleep. He opened one eye, as if to say hello, then curled himself into an even tighter ball, closed his eye and carried on sleeping.

Nan looked at me and smiled. "It's good to see him back home. I knew he'd be all right even though Mum and Dad had their doubts."

"I'm only too pleased and relieved he's home. I think I might have found myself in a spot of trouble otherwise Nan," I replied.

Nan and I walked up the path to tell Mum and Dad the good news and found them talking to Amy and Kathy Lucas. I waved towards the French windows of Mr Lucas's room while Nan broke the good news about Jet. Everybody was pleased, although Mum didn't appear very interested and after a few minutes changed the subject by reminding me to cut the firewood; I went off to do the work.

Watched by the friendly and inquisitive red robin, I cut kindling wood and logs, for over two hours, and then stacked them under the lean-to. By the time I'd carried enough indoors to last the evening, it was getting dark.

Because the oven was so small, and never got hot enough to roast meat, Nan could only fry, or boil food. Using the three kitchen chairs, the others had sat together and eaten their dinner and then gone into the sitting room while I'd been cutting the firewood. My dinner, which was always chosen by Mum, but generally cooked by Nan, consisted of mashed potatoes and one sausage and had been kept warm in the tiny oven. I was hungry, having eaten nothing all day.

Later, Mum told us that as Jet would always be able to catch his own dinner, it wouldn't be necessary to feed him in future. If he continued to bring something home for Wendy, it wouldn't be necessary to feed her either. I was certain she was wrong, but only time would tell; I'd wait and see.

The next morning, Dad and I went to Baker's Farm. The big white pigs kept up with us, walking along snorting and grunting, secure behind their fence as we strolled along the drive. Dad disappeared into a huge shed with Mr Baker. Within ten minutes they reappeared with four sacks; I was given two to carry, and Dad took the other two. It was obvious from the clucking that they contained chicken.

Dad carried something different. His sacks were half-full; there was no sound from inside, only a slight movement. That puzzled me. "What have you got there Dad?" I asked.

"Just wait until we get home, and you may be surprised," he answered laughing.

I released the young hens; of which there were six in each bag, into the chicken run and watched them run around flapping their wings and clucking their heads off, settling in. Dad up-ended his sacks at the same time and to my amazement and delight, out fell two geese.

"How about that?" He said, as I watched them gaggling and wobbling, stretching their long necks and wings.

"With the eggs from the geese and chicken, we'll all have plenty to eat, won't we?" I remarked.

Dad looked at me and replied, "I hope you're right, Robin. There will be some for us, but most will be sold, to pay for the fodder, for them and the goat, which will be coming this afternoon. At least we'll get some chicken eggs and goat's milk, free."

"I'm sure it'll be worth it in the long run," I said, "I don't like goose eggs anyway."

"Don't tell fibs," he smiled.

We closed the gate of the run and left the new arrivals to settle in.

When I'd had a drink of water, Dad gave me my next set of orders. "Walk along to Foxbridge Lane, leading to Foxbridge Farm. On the right hand corner you'll see a five-barred gate, which leads to Fox Cottage. Go through the gate, along the driveway and past the fruit trees: there's a large wooden building on the left. Take the small milk churn I bought yesterday and wait there for Mr Rose; introduce yourself and he'll give you some goats' milk."

"But you said we were getting a goat of our own Dad, and we'd have our own milk."

"It won't give enough milk for all of us; I expect you'll need to get an extra pint every day. Now, I told you before, just do as you're told, now go!" The look he gave me as he walked away worried me. I didn't think I'd said nor done anything wrong; he must have thought differently. I took the milk churn and walked off to meet Mr Rose.

Chapter Ten

Following the short walk to the entrance of 'Fox Cottage' I climbed over the gate, and walked along the driveway to the large wooden building. I stood next to one of the many chicken runs and admired a large pond, partly covered in beautiful water lilies, which were just beginning to flower. Swimming between them were some very large goldfish of various types, but mainly koi carp, and golden orfe. The pond had a few trees around the edge and with the cottage in the background it was wonderfully picturesque.

A man came out of the building towards me carrying a pail of animal feed in each hand, the buckets swinging behind each leg with every step. When he got closer I noticed his friendly smile and lined, tanned face, which showed he'd worked outside, in all types of weather, for many years. He was not a particularly tall man; about Dad's height but maybe just a little older.

"Excuse me, are you Mr Rose?" I asked.

"Yes, who wants to know?" He replied smiling.

I introduced myself and told him Dad's name and that I'd be calling for goats' milk, probably every day.

"Oh yes, your Dad told me a couple of weeks ago, I've been expecting you to turn up sooner or later."

He showed me the sheds where he kept dozens of chicken and half a dozen goats. Within a long bank at the edge of the woodland just over his boundary were masses of burrows, dug out by rats, attracted by the waste food from the adjacent chicken farm. He told me they did so much damage; he trapped as many as possible on his land.

Inside the goat hut he filled the milk churn chatting all the while; telling me I was welcome to visit to chat or mooch about the land at any time. I thanked him for his invitation and the milk and left.

At home, Dad told me the goat had been delivered. "Mum has decided to name her Judy, I can't imagine why," Dad said. "You can tether her out every morning, and bring her back in the evening for milking. You can deal with the chicken and geese at the same time. We've got all the animal food we're likely to need, so you can feed them all each morning when you let them out."

"What shall I do if it's pouring with rain, or its deep in snow Dad?" I asked.

"Let the chicken out just the same, but leave Judy in her stable until the weather gets better. Now then, I'll tell you this once, and once only; under no circumstances are you to collect any of the eggs, or milk the goat, do you understand?"

"Yes, but why?" I asked.

"Because I said so. Now keep your thoughts to yourself and do what you're told, unless you want a good hiding! I've never given you one yet, but it doesn't mean I won't."

"I haven't done anything wrong Dad. Nobody's ever threatened me before."

Having told me to follow, Dad walked to the chopping block and removed the billhook stuck in the top. We went to the nearest clump of hazel bushes where he cut a stick from a two or three year old growth. I watched as Dad cut the stick about three feet in length. Then having trimmed all the leaves off, and rounded off the ends, he swished the stick up and down and said. "Let this be a warning to you because it's what you'll get across the back of your legs, if you don't do as you're told. Keep your opinions to yourself, and no backchat, do you understand?"

"Yes Dad," was all I dared say.

Concerned and confused at Dad's attitude, I cut and stacked kindling wood and logs under the lean-to until dusk. Having checked the chicken and geese were in the hutch, I locked them up while they were still clucking and sorting themselves out. Then I brought Judy back for the night, and went indoors determined to keep quiet, to agree, and do all Mum or Dad said or asked of me.

As I entered the kitchen I was horrified to see the stick laying between the two large cup-hooks fixed to the top of the doorway opening into the sitting room. I couldn't miss it; it was in full view when I or anyone else walked through the doorway or stood in the kitchen.

While I'd been cutting the wood earlier, everybody else had eaten their dinner. I was left alone to eat my meagre meal, which had been left on the table getting cold. I could have eaten it twice!

During the evening Mum told me I'd be starting school next term, after the summer holidays; as these were only two or three weeks away it was a waste of time to enrol now. They again reminded me of my daily responsibilities; my latest, to check the post-box regularly for any letters. I was never to forget any of my jobs, was my firm warning. Dad told me I'd need to go to the Post Office at Loxwood in the morning to get a postal order to send off with his football pools coupon; I was to get cigarettes for Mum, plus two boxes of Swan Vesta matches for the fire and oil lamps. "But we only went there yesterday Dad; why didn't you get them then? It's about a two mile walk each way." I could have bitten my tongue for speaking without thinking, but it was too late!

Dad leapt out of his chair, stood upright and shouted. "Get outside and cut yourself a stick, you little sod. You've been asking for it, now you'll get it. Perhaps it'll teach you to stop your backchat, and do what you're told in future! Take the spare Tilly lamp, and cut a stick the same as the one I've put over the door. "Now do it!" he roared.

By the time I'd taken the lamp, collected the billhook, and walked to the edge of the copse, I was shaking. While cutting, then trimming the stick, I knew the emotional pain I was feeling far outweighed any forthcoming physical pain. I controlled the tears, which began filling my eyes, determined I wouldn't let anyone see them. From that moment onwards, although I couldn't control the odd emotional tearful eye, I could not, would not, and did not, ever cry again.

I tested the stick; to check it had the same whipping action as the one Dad had cut earlier. It was the same. When I went indoors and gave it to him, he showed it to Mum, who thought it was suitable. Then as instructed I placed myself in front of Dad with the back of my legs towards him. "This is no good," he said, flicking the stick, "it's far too thick and stiff. Go get another one and this time get it right!"

I went back to the copse, and cut another stick. It was thinner and whipped so much it would cut flesh, more than bruise. I didn't care; I wanted it over with as soon as possible. Dad had inflicted more pain on me by telling me to cut another stick than I could ever imagine. He couldn't hurt me any more: he'd broken my strength of mind without even touching me.

He took the stick from me, gave it a good examination, and stood up. "That's better: if you'd done this the first time, you'd have saved yourself a lot of pain. Now turn around!"

Nan turned and faced the wall; she couldn't bear to see what was about to happen. Mum, who didn't appear at all perturbed, watched each of the four whipping strokes on the back of each leg, behind the knee. The pain was excruciating, but I kept a straight, expressionless face. Dad broke the stick into four pieces, and then putting them on the fire, looked at me and said. "Perhaps you'll keep your opinions to yourself in future, and do what you're told without any backchat, now get to bed."

It wasn't long before Nan came to bed and concerned, asked me if I was in much pain. Trying to sound humorous, I told her the weals on my legs weren't as painful as the mental pain I had felt while cutting the sticks, particularly the second one. Telling her I'd feel better tomorrow, I wished her goodnight. As I turned over and faced the wall she whispered. "Goodnight, God bless Robin, and don't forget to say your prayers."

"I won't Nan, God bless."

Chapter Eleven

As dawn broke the following morning, and it was light enough to see, I dressed. Outside I fed Judy a bowl of bran; opened the chicken run and gave them mixed corn, leaving the gate open so they could run freely. The goat finished her food, and I tethered her at the edge of the woodland.

It was still too early in the morning to do much else, so with Wendy by my side, I crossed the land next to ours to a bungalow I'd noticed from the road while passing. Even though it was early in the morning a man was digging the garden. Having called 'Good Morning' to make him aware of my presence, I approached him. When we'd introduced ourselves, he told me I could call him by his first name, Eddie. He told me this was his second home, which he simply came to for relaxation, every two or three weeks. He'd arrived last night and enjoyed gardening and as it was the time of year to prepare for the following year, he'd risen early to get a good start to the day.

He asked if I'd keep my eye on the place while he was away, and told me I'd be welcome to any fruit or vegetables, which would be wasted if left on the plants to over-ripen or go to seed. I thanked him for his offer, telling him I'd look around the bungalow whenever I could.

We chatted for a while longer, before I walked home; only too pleased my long socks saved me from any embarrassment by covering the deep red weals from the beating.

Nan asked me if I was suffering much pain. I told her I was okay and had finished the majority of my daily jobs just as Mum gave me money to get the shopping from Loxwood. "There's no need to rush back as long as you're back in time to get the milk from Mr Rose," she said expressionlessly. "I want you to spend the next few days finding your way about so you'll always know where you are, and where to go when told."

She returned to the sitting room and I set off to Loxwood.

There were only five or six houses along the whole length of Chalk Road. As I was nearing the last one on the left a blind man came out from the old cottage, guided by a most unusual looking dog which was almost three feet high; the tallest I'd ever seen. Its long white and light brown smooth-flowing coat hung from its deep chest, almost reaching the ground between the long thin front legs. It was slim; almost streamlined, with a narrow head, long thin face and large brown protruding eyes. Its unusual appearance traumatized me; so that I felt a little frightened as it passed me so gracefully. I quickened my pace, concerned about the strange creature; and I glanced over my shoulder several times before turning along a short path to the footpath leading to Loxwood.

Passing an enormous grand old oak tree, I came to Ifold Lake. The morning mist still lay on the surface of the water as I walked to the edge to have a closer look. It was beautiful; branches from many of the trees at the water's edge hung down into the mist covering the surface of the clear water, with just the tips of the early-forming leaves still wet and dripping from the morning dew. Sunlight lit up the brown tips of the bulrushes sticking up out of the white mist at the far end of the lake and gently moving in the soft breeze. I stayed for a while enjoying the tranquillity and the comfortable feeling it gave me of belonging; of being at one with my surroundings. I didn't want to leave but eventually did, crossing the river at the narrowest part by the wooden footbridge, then going through a gate into the field that kept cattle from straying outside their boundary. A heavy weight had been fitted to a chain with one end fixed to the back post and the other end to the front edge of the gate: this was to ensure a speedy closing; it did, with a deafening bang, which could probably be heard at least half a mile away!

Passing the cattle in the large field, I came to the old dry canal and crossed over the bridge, then went through a farm and arrived in the centre of Loxwood. It was a long walk for only a few minutes' shopping. On the way home, I couldn't resist re-visiting the lake. It had only been half an hour or so since I'd left the water's edge, but the transformation was instantly noticeable. Sunlight was shining on the water and the mist had completely disappeared. Near to the middle of the lake there were whirls of movement on the surface where some large fish were moving and basking in the early warmth.

With a few slow majestic movements of its silver grey wings, a heron soared effortlessly from the bank at the far side of the lake and into the sky. Its neck outstretched to the front, its long legs to the back; it floated effortlessly away into the pale blue sky.

A few wild ducks and drakes quacked and made other sounds of excitement near the bulrushes. They were followed by two clutches of ducklings, splashing and cleaning themselves;

dunking their heads under the surface, and then stretching their necks in an upward position to allow the clear droplets of water to run down onto their backs. They were enjoying the beginning of the day. Full of wonder and contentment, I stayed and watched the glorious morning in Ifold gradually unfold, before continuing my walk home.

The only people I'd seen were the blind man, and five others in Loxwood; I hadn't even seen a car! It didn't matter because the cattle, the wild life, the beautiful lake and countryside, even the strange dog I saw, were far more enjoyable than staying at home.

Chapter Twelve

Wendy met me, wagging her tail, and giving a few little barks and whines. Nan told me Mum and Dad had gone to Horsham, for a few hours. "I noticed the car was missing; you'd have thought they'd have got the shopping in Loxwood as they went through, wouldn't you? It would certainly have saved me the long walk; how considerate of them!" I said sarcastically.

"I wouldn't mention it when they get home if I were you," Nan said, and changed the subject. "When I made fresh bread this morning, I also made some scones. They're still warm and you've had nothing to eat yet, so put some jam on a couple; they'll be nice and you'll like them, but whatever you do don't tell your mother."

Shortly afterwards I set off to get the goats' milk and waited at the pond for some time, without any sight of Mr Rose. I went to his cottage. Mrs Rose met me at the door, then having taken me to get the milk told me I wouldn't be seeing Mr Rose as he was working on the land, and she wasn't sure where he was or when he'd be home.

After I'd given the milk to Nan and followed closely by Wendy, I went into the woodland. On a few occasions I'd noticed the top branches of a very large tree towering above the hazel and silver birch trees. I made my way through the wood and over the stream towards the tree to have a closer look. I was surprised to find it was a beech, which like the chestnut trees near home, were very uncommon within the area. Its enormous girth and height overwhelmed me; the branches were far too high to reach and there were no footholds on the smooth silver surface of the trunk making it impossible to climb.

Looking between the branches towards the top, I saw sunlight shining through the leaves, which were in various stages of summer growth. The variety of colours reflected uncountable different shades; it was an incredible sight. Although nature's beauty is always here, I regretted I'd not taken more notice of its wonderful gifts in the past.

Behind me I gazed at the surrounding woodland, and was awe-struck by the mass of different greens and other colours. What a magnificent sight! Why hadn't I been aware of this glory before? I drank it in, and then again looked at the beech tree. Most of the smooth shiny bark at the base of the tree, and on the lower branches, had been engraved and carved with shapes or words but the bark had begun to grow over the scars, and fill with green moss. Looking closely, I was able to trace the shape of lovers' hearts with arrows carved through the top and bottom of them; the initials of the giver and receiver at each end, and the word 'loves', in the centre painstakingly carved with affection. There were also lots of other messages to loved ones.

Reading the other engravings took a long time; there were so many and quite a few had become unreadable through weather and age. I could tell by the engraving styles that they were nearly all done by different people, most of whom were soldiers. Some of them showed verses from the Ten Commandments, while others were sentences or quotations from the Bible. I had never realised before the love and concern people had for those they'd left behind. The tree was a living, beautiful and peaceful shrine, unintentionally created by soldiers who felt lonely and missed their loved ones while away from home during the war, and who needed personal comfort and peace of mind.

I sat on the clay base below the mighty tree. Wendy lay on her back close to the side of my leg, offering her tummy to be tickled, stroked or rubbed. The faster I rubbed her, the faster her back leg would jerk, up and down, as if she were scratching herself, holding her head back as far as she could in pure ecstasy.

We sat there for some time, before my thoughts turned from the servicemen who had been there before me, to myself. Just as some of the others had done, I considered my own personal comforts and peace of mind. I also wondered what Mum and Dad would expect of me in the future.

After a short time, I decided no matter what might be expected of me, I would do my best to please them, whenever possible. I vowed not to voice my own opinion, without thinking about their reactions first, and to do my utmost to avoid any more encounters with the stick. It'd been the psychological pain that had hurt most, even though my long walk to Loxwood had opened the wounds and made them bleed in places.

Ambling through the woods in the dusk, I decided no matter what had happened in the past and whatever might happen in the future, I wouldn't be moulded into a false person.

When I collected Judy and took her back to be milked, Nan came outside to say Mum and Dad were having their dinner; I'd be called when they'd finished.

Half an hour later after I'd locked up the chicken and geese for the night and cut some logs and kindling wood, Nan called me in. While I was putting the tools away before going indoors, Mum came outside to milk Judy. Neither of us spoke as we passed.

While sitting alone in the kitchen eating the only food Nan had been able to cook and keep as hot as possible on the small cooking stove, Mum returned. "As you've done what you were told and got the shopping, your father and I got you a present from Horsham. You can come into the sitting room when you've finished your dinner."

I sat in the sitting room, saying nothing, and stroking Jet who'd jumped on my lap. Dad looked up from the book about building regulations and groundwork preparation he was reading and said, "I'm glad you found your way to Loxwood because I want you to go again tomorrow." He looked at Mum then Nan, then at me, before continuing, "I've filled in the football coupon and I want it posted. I know you'd normally use the letterbox at Ifold Stores, but we need a recharged accumulator; the one we've got is getting low. Your mother also needs some other bits and pieces; she'll tell you what tomorrow."

Taking a large paper bag from the side of her chair, Mum said. "We bought you a blazer to wear at your new school so try it on, and see if it fits." I tried it on. It was made of a soft green material; it felt comfortable, and fitted perfectly. "That fits fine, now turn around and let me see the back," Mum said. As usual, my long socks had fallen down around my ankles, revealing the back of my legs and the red weals and cuts I'd received the night before. It went very quiet.

Breaking the silence, I told them about the blind man with the strange dog I'd seen. I asked them if they knew what kind it was. Nobody could say, and suggested it was probably an Alsatian or an Afghan. I knew both of those breeds, and it wasn't either of them. Dad said I'd either made a mistake, or it was a mongrel.

Mum asked. "Did you check the post-box before you went out this morning?"

"No, I didn't bother," I replied.

Mum glared at me." Why not? You were told to check for letters every day. How many times do you have to be told?"

"Mum, I didn't check because Sid the postman did his deliveries yesterday. He wouldn't be here today; he only delivers every other day, so I didn't bother."

"You clever little sod, are you asking for another good hiding? I'd have thought you'd have learnt your lesson by now," Mum shouted at me, "now get to bed."

Within a couple of minutes I lay in bed listening to Mum's raised voice telling Dad he'd been too heavy-handed with me the evening before and that the cuts on my legs were because the stick was far too thin. He agreed, saying next time he'd use a thicker one, about the same size, as I'd cut in the first place. He asked Nan to make sure my socks were pulled up; if they wouldn't stay up they'd need to have elastic fitted around the tops. Neither he nor Mum wanted anybody to see the weals. Their voices and the nightingale's song got fainter and fainter.

Chapter Thirteen

The next day after I'd finished my jobs, I collected Dad's football coupon, the accumulator, and getting the rest of Mum's instructions, set off for Loxwood. Three quarters of an hour later I'd visited the Post Office and the village stores so I set off for home with the heavy load.

When I'd crossed over the river, I walked along the edge of Ifold Lake. Jack the heron was there, standing in the water, stabbing at the fish he could reach from the edge of the lake. Then as I'd expected, becoming aware of my presence and with very little movement of his wings, he effortlessly soared into the sky.

A large rhododendron bush flourished at the edge of the lake with a mass of huge red blooms, which reflected in the clear water like a beautiful, glittering carpet. The splendour of it was overwhelming. Glancing upwards, I saw the transparent shapes of dozens of different coloured green leaves reflecting in the sunlight, as again the lake brought me peace and tranquillity. I hoped it would last.

About an hour later, as I was about to pass through the gate at home, I noticed lizards scurrying along the top of the bank. Moving very slowly I crept towards them then looking carefully saw the silver slow-worm in his normal position, curled up on the dry clay, serenely warming himself in the bright sun. Checking the post-box and finding nothing, I walked towards the wagon. Dad was tying string between pegs driven into the ground, marking out the lines of the foundations, which would indicate the size of the bungalow. I kept out of his way.

Later, as I walked along the path to get the milk, Dad called out asking if everything was okay. I shouted back it was and that I'd cut some more logs and fill the lamps, the heater and cooking stove with paraffin when I got back. As expected my answer put a smile on his face, as I hoped it would.

Nearing the end of the driveway, I saw Mr Rose was kneeling while hammering a small spike into the ground, by the side of the pond. "What is that for?" I asked.

"I'm fixing a dozen or so gin traps around the pond and chicken runs to catch the rats," he replied. They're attacking and killing my goldfish; they swim from one lily to another, and then when they're close enough to a fish they slip into the water, grab it in their jaws and swim to the bank to eat it."

"I'd never have thought they could do that. But surely they can't kill and eat a chicken, can they?"

"No, thank goodness, but they can take a chicken egg without too much of a problem. They can even gang up and take young chicks whenever old mother hen's not there to protect them. I'll keep all the chicken locked up for the next few days; it'll keep them safe from the gin traps."

"Well you do surprise me; I'd never have thought it,"

"Old Jack heron will be safe," he continued, returning my smile. "He's far too crafty to be caught by one of these traps. The only way to get him is to shoot him; I'll need to build a hide by the side of the pond, when the leaves on the trees are fully grown."

"Why do you want to shoot him? He's a lovely bird."

Mr Rose moved a few feet along the pond edge and started to fix another spike into the ground. "They may look lovely to you Rod, but they're also a terrible pest. Every year they cost me a lot of money by killing my valuable fish. They stand motionless at the edge of the water looking grand in their grey-feathered coats, until they've speared their prey with their long beaks and eaten their fill. They kill more fish than they can eat and leave them on the bank dead, or half-dead, which alone attracts the rats. They're pests I can assure you."

I fully understood and half-heartedly agreed with him, but before I could say anything he added. "They're thoughtless and do a lot of damage; but not nearly as bad as Charlie."

"Who on earth's Charlie?" I asked.

Charlie is the countryman's name for the fox, because he's a silly Charlie."

"I always thought he was crafty, not silly, Mr Rose."

"Oh he's crafty, make no mistake, but he's also very silly. Let me explain. If you had twelve chickens and Charlie the fox got into your chicken run, he'd probably bite the heads off all of them, but he'd only be able to take one away to eat. What he plans, is to return later in the night and take the others away and bury them for another day. Normally one of two things happens. Either, he's full up after eating so much, falls asleep, and forgets to go back for the others; or he'll go back two or maybe three times leaving the rest where he killed them. He'll bury the ones he's collected in various spots in the woods, but by the next day he'll have forgotten where he's buried them. That's why he's a proper Charlie. If he'd left the others alive, and only taken one, he'd have another eleven meals, wouldn't he?"

"Yes he would. I didn't realise he was such a Charlie," I said laughing.

"Now think about the loss of the eggs every day plus the loss of the chicken and their value," Mr Rose continued. "Unfortunately some people are no better; they may seem nice on the outside but are often unaware or do not understand the hurt or harm they do to others or themselves."

He asked me if I'd like to see old mother hen scratching and clucking about her clutch of two or three day old yellow fluffy chicks, showing them how to feed. I told him it would be a lovely sight to see them enjoying their new life and growing up in the warmth of the sunshine. He then asked me how I'd feel if Charlie the fox had also been watching them and suddenly rushed out from his hiding place and killed old mother hen and took her away to be eaten leaving the young dead chicks on the spot where he'd bitten their heads off.

It wasn't difficult to find an answer, and I told him I understood Charlie needed food to live, but nevertheless was a cold-blooded killer.

"Well now you know something about Charlie. Do you know how the heron got his name of Jack?"

"Yes I think so," I replied. "When I was evacuated, Uncle Bert told me they put their head back and upright to allow their food to slide easily down their long necks. When they do that, their standing position is in a straight line, from top to bottom, like a beanstalk. I was told they were called Jack after the children's story, Jack and the Beanstalk."

"Well your Uncle Bert was right. Next time you come for milk, and we've time, I'll show you how to set rabbit snares. Bright-eyes, as they're known are good to eat; especially in a warming stew during the winter, to keep out the cold."

When I got home I began my daily log cutting, under the watchful eye of red robin, perched on the pile of logs with a beak full of insects. Jet had caught another rabbit, which Wendy was noisily enjoying.

Within an hour Dad called me indoors where he told me he'd finished marking out the footings and the cesspit for the bungalow, and I'd be expected to help with the digging. Mum having readily agreed, he went on to tell me I was to spend time outside in future finding myself something to do, while the rest of them had dinner.

Chapter Fourteen

Discovering the woodlands growing into their full summer glory, the paths, mainly used as shortcuts, the lanes and surrounding areas of Ifold, made the following days merge into enjoyable weeks. The variety of people I met, most of who became my friends, have remained in my memory and made me appreciative of their friendship, both then and now.

The school summer holidays started, to the delight of the children who were free to play, or not do very much at all for the next six weeks; some wouldn't be so fortunate.

The sky was a soft light blue, with a bright golden sun as the days became steadily warmer. The ground cracked open everywhere with the sun's heat; it was possible to put your hand down the wide-open gaps into the yellow clay as far as your wrist. Ants and other insects had difficulty crossing the surface fissures; needing to climb down one side of the cracks then up the other side took them ages. If they'd been able to get across the gap it would only have been a few inches in distance, and seconds in time.

The evenings were cool and fresh with welcoming showers of rain most nights. The noise often woke us as it drummed on the roof of the wagon and flat roof of the kitchen. Despite the often-deafening noise, whenever it stopped I'd hear the heart-rending and comforting song of the nightingale.

Log cutting became less urgent, because of the summer warmth, although I'd built up a good stock during the weeks beforehand because the fire had to be kept alight to help with cooking or to keep food hot.

The primroses and wood anemones finished their colourful display for the year and masses of nuts formed on the hazel, chestnut and beech trees. Most of the fruit bearing trees and bushes lost their colourful blossoms and grew fruits, to be eaten fresh, cooked, preserved in jars or made into jam, to last throughout the winter months ahead.

Wild strawberries grew everywhere and large early-formed blackberries began to show on the bramble bushes in abundance. Due to the warm days and cool damp nights, the woodland fruit made a good feast at any time, supplementing my meagre home rations.

Mum and Dad knew the distance I had to walk, and the weight I had to carry whenever they sent me shopping to Loxwood. Occasionally they'd exchange the accumulator, or get Dad's football coupon postal order when they drove through the village. They could have done it every week, but as Mum often said; to send me shopping got me out the way.

One morning walking along Chalk Road, while on my way to Loxwood, two or three weeks before I was due to start school, I met two boys I'd never seen before.

They told me they were brothers with a family name of Howell. One was Desmond, the other, who became a life long friend, was David. They had three brothers and two younger sisters, and lived with their parents on the narrow track near where we stood. They told me their home was a brick and timber built temporary home, similar to the few other properties built in Ifold after the war. We talked for ages and to avoid any explanation I gave an edited version of my life, and the various jobs I was expected to do at home. When they told me their duties were shared with their brothers and sisters, I couldn't help feeling a little envious.

We were surprised that although we only lived four or five minutes' walking distance away from each other, miles from anywhere, they went to Kirdford School whilst I'd be going to Loxwood School in the opposite direction. They told me it was the same with some other children who they passed every school day. We agreed: to us it seemed a bit daft, but perhaps the Council, one day would change the situation. Eventually they did, but it took them about five years.

Having told them about the different places, and ways I'd found around the area, they told me of more paths, shortcuts and lanes, woodlands and two other lakes. They also told me that none of the local landowners would object if I went onto their land, but a few of them would at least want to know who I was.

They said to call at their home any time, and providing they'd done their jobs we could go bird-nesting, swimming in the river, fishing, or generally mooching about. Having told them I liked the idea, we said our brief farewells, and I continued to Loxwood, looking forward to our friendship.

On the way home I rested at Ifold Lake and sat on the edge dangling my feet in the water; enjoying the warmth, not only from the sun, but also the beautiful sight of nature's unspoilt beauty.

In the water there were several smooth, black-looking objects sticking upwards out of the lakebed. I pulled one out; it was oval in shape and opened down the whole of one edge. Revealed was a white, pink and orange body attached to a glittering pearl shell that within seconds closed tightly, locking inside its glowing and secretly held beauty. It was a large, freshwater swan mussel, almost as big as my hand. I'd seen smaller ones when Uncle Bert had taken me fishing to a lake near Horsham. He'd told me they were good bait for all types of larger fish.

I decided there and then I'd try to make myself a rod, a float and some fishing hooks. I could then fish the lake, and the river, to try and catch anything edible I'd be able to cook over an open fire. A good idea!

Miss Lucas was in her garden when I passed, and being one of the most pleasant people I'd ever met, we talked for about half an hour or so. I told her about the two brothers I'd met, the lake, and all the different places I'd found, and those I'd been told about still to be discovered. She always seemed to be interested and understanding, asking me various questions and my opinions.

At home the car had gone and neither Mum nor Dad were to be seen. "Where have they gone Nan?" I asked.

"Shopping; and before you ask, yes they could have got the shopping and saved your trip to Loxwood. They asked me to tell you to cut more logs, and get the goats' milk from Mr Rose." Nan put her hand on my shoulder, and continued, "keep your opinions to yourself Robin; otherwise you know what'll happen. Now sit down and I'll make you tea and a cheese sandwich, but don't tell them you had their cheese, and try not to get cross."

She was right: there was no point in getting annoyed. The best thing to do was to say nothing.

Chapter Fifteen

When I reached the edge of the pond I noticed most of the branches of one apple tree had been pulled down and staked into the ground. Hazel sticks had been woven between the gaps forming a leafy curtain across the front and sides closest to the pond. Seeing the opening at the rear side and the three-legged milking stool, tucked away between the leafy walls I realised it was the hide Mr Rose had made to act as cover for getting a shot at Jack heron.

Mr Rose came out of the large shed carrying a bundle of rabbit snares and striding towards me. "Hello Rod, I'm just off to set these rabbit snares in the field. If you've got time, come along with me and I'll show you how it's done."

"Yes, as long as I get home to finish all my jobs before it gets dark," I answered walking with him towards the woods and field.

We passed several small pits dotted around the woodland, which were parts of the old clay workings from years before. Despite the long hot summer, nearly all the pits contained water and appeared from their natural dark colour to be quite deep. Most were encircled with hazel bushes and shrubs, their saplings growing or just laying on the surface. Some contained moorhens, which at the sight of us, ran across the water flapping their wings, nodding their heads and making noisy screeching sounds, trying to frighten us away and protect their privacy.

We continued through the dense wood and undergrowth until we reached the edge of the field. "This way Rod; we'll start at the top end, working down both sides until we run out of snares; the ten or twelve I've brought should be enough to give us a good meal with a few to spare," he said, striding up the field. "The more of the pests we catch, the happier the farmer and I'll be," he added as he glanced around.

I was a little surprised at what seemed to be his almost bitter attitude and asked, "I know they're good food, but they're not very much of a pest; are they?"

"Oh yes; they'll strip whatever bark they can from my fruit trees, and rose bushes, killing them all. I'm sure you know they'll completely destroy your vegetable garden, given a chance, leaving nothing at all. This field was planted with wheat last year; when it started to grow the shoots were soft and tender. The bright-eyes had a feast, by eating a strip around the edge of the field about eight-yards wide. The farmer reckoned he lost about three acres of wheat."

When we reached the edge of the field, he knelt where the grass stopped and undergrowth started. "Now look closely and I'll show you where, and how to fit the snare." I crouched by his side, as he continued, "If you look closely you'll notice a small tunnel coming out of the undergrowth, into the field. Can you see that?" He said pointing at the hole in the bush.

"Yes," I replied looking along the field at a few others we'd passed.

He pointed to where the bright-eye would sit in the undergrowth checking if it was safe to venture out into the field. When he felt secure, he'd hop from his hiding place leaving flat patches in the grass where he'd landed, every few inches apart. The place to fit the snare was over the top edge of the undisturbed longer grass causing the bright-eye to hop into the snare headfirst.

Taking his hook-bladed pocketknife, he cut a thin, short twig from a branch, and then cut a slot into one end, making a sharp point at the other. By fixing the twig under the wire loop he'd formed it was held upright in the centre of the run. He then cut a larger branch to which he tied the other end. Having pushed the branch into the edge of the thicket he said. "The reason I've not tied the cord to a stake is because when a bright-eye gets caught, it'll be in the open and easily seen by Charlie. Any fox would make easy work of digging the snare up to have a free meal. If you tie one end to a branch the rabbit will be able to drag it into the thicket far enough to be able to hide, but easy enough for us to find."

Mr Rose fixed another four snares before letting me try my hand at doing some. He had six left and, under his instruction, I fitted them all to his satisfaction.

We returned to his cottage where I sat outside while he went inside returning with two large chunks of bread and cheese, two home-made pickled onions and a tin mug of goats' milk. I couldn't believe his generosity and kept thanking him while we sat on a pile of logs and ate a good and filling meal. I hadn't eaten cheese for weeks and now found myself feeding on it for the second time in one day. It was very welcome, and unexpected.

Mr. Rose took the mug he was drinking from away from his mouth then, looking at me closely, as if to check my reactions said. "If you can get here about eight o'clock tomorrow morning we'll go and see what we've caught. If there are three or more, then you can have one as a reward for your first catch. When we get back I'll show you how to paunch and skin them ready for cooking."

"Well it's a job that has to be done and I'd appreciate you showing me how to do it. I'm sure Mum and Dad would be pleased if I was able to catch dinner."

"I'm sure they would be," he smiled.

"Later on tonight if we don't get too much of a shower, I'll sit inside the hide I built, by the edge of the pond. Old Jack heron's been about a lot in the last few days. He's done a lot of damage, so he'll have to go I'm afraid."

"It seems a shame for such a beautiful creature, but like Charlie, for all the damage they do, I suppose, they've got to go," I replied, feeling sad.

Changing the subject I told him about the lake I'd seen on the way to Loxwood, where I often stopped to enjoy the peace and rest from carrying the heavy shopping home.

"Yes, it's certainly a tranquil place. I've only ever seen it once as I've no reason to go there for anything," he remarked, drinking the remains of his goats' milk.

"When I went through Ifold a few days ago, I saw a blind man near the end of Chalk Road, with a very strange looking guide dog. It really was very odd looking; it was tall and thin, with a long flowing coat of hair. Mum and Dad think it must be some kind of a mongrel."

Mr Rose chuckled to himself. "That was David with his dog which is a very special breed. It's called and sounds like Borzoy, but it's spelt with an I, not a Y at the end, in other words, Borzoi."

He spelt the word out to me so I fully understood, then looked across the pond and surrounding land while he was thinking and said. "The dog first came from a country called Arabia. Then it travelled to Russia where it was crossbred and used for hunting. It earned the name over hundreds of years as the Russian wolfhound. When it first came to this country it became one of the favourite breeds of Queen Victoria and other royalty. It's a very protective and intelligent dog which can kill intruding and unwelcome animals in a split second."

He laughed out loud. "That sounded good didn't it? I only found out myself a few weeks ago. Somebody I know went to Horsham Reference Library, looked up the type of breed it was, and told me."

"Now, do you mind if I ask you something Rod?"

"No of course not, what is it?" I replied.

"Well," he said, "over the past weeks you've been getting a nice deep suntan. It suits you but because of the change in your colour, it's made the scars on your forehead more prominent. Mrs Rose and I have noticed them before, but can't fathom out what type of accident you had to cause them. What happened?"

I couldn't answer his question and remained silent. Within a few seconds I said I had to leave. Thanking him for a nice afternoon and the food, I stood and asked if I could still come over the next morning but walked away before he could answer. "Yes of course you can," he answered softly, "I'm sorry Rod, and I hope I haven't upset you." I didn't answer, or turn around.

We didn't have a mirror at home so I was unable to see the scars engraved on my forehead. Upset and unprepared for any remarks made or questions asked, I felt annoyed with my parents for not telling me the old wounds were so visible.

Chapter Sixteen

Dad was at the far end of the land near the chicken run where he'd driven wooden stakes into the hard ground and fixed sheets of corrugated iron to them forming a large square. I told him about the rabbit snares and that we might have one for dinner tomorrow; he seemed pleased.

"Good luck," he said; "now go indoors and tell Nan, so she can decide what vegetables she'll need to get ready for a possible rabbit stew tomorrow; then I want you to help me finish making this pigsty."

"Yes okay, but I didn't know you were a getting a pig Dad?"

"Neither did I, until your mother had one of her bright ideas this morning."

Having told Mum and Nan we might have rabbit stew, Mum said that because I was being useful, she'd ask Nan to cook me something special for dinner. I could hardly believe my ears. Then she went on to tell me they had been to Billingshurst to buy various tools and on the way back they'd purchased a young weaner pig, which would be fattened for Christmas.

Returning outside, Dad promptly sent me to cut ferns to make a bed for the pig, in the same way I did for Judy every week. We went to the lean-to where he kept all his tools and other bits and pieces and he showed me the new tools he'd bought, saying they'd make my life a bit easier.

There was a heart-shaped spade, which he explained could be driven into the hard ground with less effort than a standard type. It was a tool I'd become accustomed to using over the following years for digging out the roots of the trees and bushes, which had been felled, filling in the holes and enabling the land to be levelled. I also used the spade to dig foundations for the bungalow; the cesspit and mixing the concrete, or cement required at various stages of building. It didn't make life easier for me!

From a sack in the corner he took out a long-handled tool; it looked like a pickaxe with a wide blade at one end. "This is a mattock," he informed me, and continued, "its common name is a grub axe, because it's mainly used for grubbing out weeds and roots, but it's also very useful for digging into hard clay: you'll certainly need it."

Taking hold of it and feeling its unbalanced weight, I remarked. "It's very heavy; I don't know if I'll be able to manage it."

"Of course you will," he said, "you're an up and growing strong young man; you'll get used to it in no time, you wait and see."

I said nothing. The biggest shock for me came next: It was a woodman's large single-handed crosscut saw. I hadn't noticed it leaning against the wall behind me. Dad took it and held it upright. It was longer than I was tall, the enormous sawing teeth over one inch in depth. To operate the saw I'd need both hands to grip the large handle. There was nothing I dared say: Dad had already decided I'd be able to use all the tools he'd bought.

While helping with the rest of the work to complete the pigsty, the little red robin on the roof of the wagon silently watched me. I thought, perhaps the reason he wasn't singing might be because he understood how I despaired of the heavy work expected of me. Although I learnt to control the new tools within a few days I didn't foresee that the shafts would be worn smooth and shiny by my hands over the coming years. The sweat and pain; the blisters, not having time to heal, would often break open to bleed from the cracks in the open wounds, eventually becoming hard thick corns at the base of every finger.

We worked on the pigsty until it was finished; Dad went for his dinner, whilst I cut more ferns for bedding, before finishing my daily jobs. Then having walked to the car, I opened the door and sat in the front seat, where I was able to adjust the interior mirror, and look at my forehead. The thin skin of the eight or nine shiny, pink scars running from my hairline to my eyebrows showed up more than usual against my sun-tanned forehead. Apart from wearing a cap, or letting my hair fall at an angle, forwards and sideways to hide them, I could only wait for them to gradually fade away with time.

I sat alone at the kitchen table as Nan cooked my special dinner in anticipation of having rabbit stew tomorrow. She cracked an egg into the frying pan while I sat at the table with my back to the doorway. I didn't want to sit in full view of the punishment stick, hanging from the top hooks.

Nan put my dinner in front of me. It was an enormous plate of mashed potatoes with a fried egg on top, one and a half sausages, and incredibly it was covered with grated cheese. I couldn't believe my eyes; I'd been given the best meal I'd had for weeks and weeks. Inwardly and silently, I almost shook with laughter. Mum thought this would be my only meal of the day. She also thought it was special, because of the cheese I'd been given. Nan thought it was my second helping of cheese that day, and felt happy for me, but they were all wrong. It was my third, and the best!

I gave Wendy, who was sitting at my feet looking up at me for food, half a sausage; Jet couldn't have brought anything home for her. I knew she was hungry. When I'd finished and washed up, Mum called me into the sitting room where she sat back in her chair, folded her arms and said. "Now pay attention to what I'm about to say. On Monday you start school at Loxwood. As it'll be your first day, your father will take you in the car, but after that, you'll have to walk. It's not too far and should only take you three-quarters of an hour at the most. Whenever we need shopping, you can either go on to the shops at Loxwood, or call in at Ifold Stores on your way home. Do you have anything to ask me?"

"Yes Mum, what day is it today?"

"Today's the last Tuesday in July; you've nearly a week left before you start. There'll still be plenty of daylight left to do your jobs when you get home from school, particularly at this time of year," she said, with her arms now resting on her lap.

"If it's the end of July Mum, we've passed Midsummer's Day and my birthday. I was eight wasn't I?"

"Yes you were," she replied, "but we couldn't think of anything to get you, so you'll just have to wait until next year."

I said nothing but wondered why she hadn't told me. If nothing else I could at least have been wished a Happy Birthday.

Mum said Dad would be looking for work, as we couldn't begin the first stages of work on the bungalow, until planning permission, which was only a formality, had been confirmed.

If Dad worked for the rest of the summer and throughout the winter, they'd be able to save money for materials to use on the bungalow. Mum had decided to join the local Woman's Land Army Office and Training Depot based on the Plaistow Road, next to the sports field.

"When I finish school, I'll still have time to do my jobs and help Nan. The only problem is Mum, in the winter, when it gets dark at about four o'clock in the afternoon, I won't have time to help Dad, will I?"

"If you're told to help that's what you'll do. Now I don't want to hear any more about it, is that clear?"

"Yes Mum I'm sorry."

From her stern expression I decided in future, not to speak until she spoke to me.

I was allowed to remain in the sitting room, but after an hour or so of having been ignored, I was getting up to leave when, unexpectedly, Mum spoke to me. "I'm pleased you learnt how to set snares today; did you learn anything else?"

"Yes, I told Mr Rose about the strange dog I'd seen with the blind man. I also told him we didn't know if it was a particular breed, or a mongrel. He told me the breed of dog was called a Borzoi; it was crossbred in Russia from Arabia and---."

"Shut up and stop there you little sod," Dad shouted loudly, glaring as he leaped out of his chair and stood directly in front of me.

Wendy dashed out of his way with her tail between her back legs and bolted into the kitchen. Jet who'd been fast asleep suddenly woke and dived under a chair for safety.

Nan looked at the floor, while Mum showing signs of a smile, just stared at me.

"Are you trying to make us look fools, or idiots, in the minds of others or are you just stupid?" He paused, took a deep breath and continued in an angry and loud voice that frightened me. "Of course we knew the bloody dog was a Borzoi. The only reason we didn't tell you was because we thought you wouldn't understand."

He stopped shouting at me, turned his back, and sat. He looked at Mum, who was smiling, then at Nan, then back to me. He didn't like the fact I'd found out about the dog, and it was obvious neither of them liked the idea I knew, and they didn't.

"You've been building up for a good hiding for the past few weeks, and you're going the right way to get one, so just behave yourself."

"But I haven't done anything wrong Dad!"

"Right that's it, you've gone far enough. I've just about had enough of your backchat.

Now get outside and cut yourself a stick." He stood up from his chair again, grabbed me by the back of the neck, then marching me outside yelled, "and don't be long."

I took the billhook from the chopping block and walked to the woods. My emotions were overwhelming; I hadn't done anything wrong to deserve this punishment and couldn't think why it was necessary.

Having trimmed the thicker stick, I stuck the billhook back into the block and went indoors to face Dad. Nan was in the kitchen waiting for me, and putting her arm on my shoulders, she whispered in my ear. "Don't worry, Dad won't be giving you the stick. I reminded them both you'd be suffering enough now by just cutting it; what's more, they shouldn't forget you could be getting tomorrow's dinner. It didn't seem fair as far as I was concerned," she added. "In the end they thought I might be right, so they've decided to leave it for today and see what happens."

She looked at the roof, and putting her arms upwards said. "For goodness sake Robin, please catch some rabbits tomorrow."

Muttering quietly I said, "I'd better go in; they'll be waiting for me."

I gave Dad the stick, and then turned my back towards him. He pushed me away and stood the stick in the corner by the side of the fireplace. "Think yourself lucky I don't give you a good hiding, because that's what you deserve. Nevertheless I've decided to give you one more chance to behave yourself. Don't let me see you again tonight, otherwise you'll be for it, now get out!"

Followed by Wendy I went outside taking a deep breath and considering myself lucky that Nan had spoken up for me. Dusk was falling as we walked to the roadway and sat on the dry clay bank to watch the small black, wide-winged bats gliding, dashing and diving, searching for insects. Spellbound, I watched the activity in the darkening sky while listening to the heart-rending song of the nightingale and the enjoyable tweeting of red robin perched on a nearby branch. The oil lamps indoors were lit and glowed through the windows and open door; it was time to go in. When I'd drunk the mug of milk Nan had left for me, I slipped quietly into bed and immediate sleep.

Chapter Seventeen

Next morning I was up at first light. As usual there wasn't any chance of breakfast, but a mug of tea. Having completed my morning jobs, I was on my way to see if I'd caught any bright-eyes, desperately hoping I had.

Mr Rose and I met at the edge of the pond where, tied to one of the branches at the top of an apple tree hung a sight never to be forgotten. It was Jack heron, which he'd shot during the night. The bird, at least six feet long, had a wingspan almost twice the width I could reach.

Mr Rose, turning from gazing across the water and lilies, briefly pointed and said. "He sat in that big old oak tree at the top of the woods all night. Then this morning, at about five thirty, he swooped and glided to the waters edge, thinking he was safe, but he was within shotgun range." He paused momentarily. "It was a clear night, and from where he was perched, he could see Charlie sniffing around the chicken coop quite undisturbed. Several rats were scurrying about, hoping if he turned up they'd get a meal from the fish he'd leave. All this made him think everything was clear and safe. It was his last and fatal mistake. He didn't reckon on me being in the hide watching his every move."

"What about Charlie and the rats? I suppose you couldn't do anything except sit and watch them; I bet that was annoying, wasn't it?"

"Yes, too right it was; they were within range but I didn't want to frighten Jack away. I can shoot Charlie another night, and put gin traps down for the rats, any time. Now then, let's go and see if we caught any bright-eyes, and whether you've earned your dinner for tonight."

We walked to where we'd set the snares. The first one was undisturbed, as was the second, but the third was missing. Mr Rose smiled, and putting his hand into the undergrowth slowly drew out the branch with a bright-eye firmly attached to the other end of the snare. I was shown how to apply a rabbit punch; it was a quick and painless end.

We checked the other two runs and caught one more. He was pleased and told me two out of five was quite good. He picked up the two rabbits and the five snares, then walking off said. "Now it's your turn, let's see if you've got bright-eye for dinner tonight."

Half an hour later while on our way back to the cottage, he kept repeating out aloud, the same words; "I don't believe it, I just don't believe it. How could you do that, I only showed you what I knew, I'd never have thought you'd have done that. What did you do?"

Laughing at him I proudly said, "I only did as you showed me; perhaps you shouldn't be such a good teacher, imagine how I'd feel if I hadn't caught anything at all!"

"But to catch four out of six is unbelievable Rod: I've never caught as many myself."

"It must be beginner's luck," I said smiling. "It was my birthday last month; perhaps it's a late present, I probably won't be so lucky next time."

During the walk back we laughed and joked most of the time. He explained the technique he used for paunching and skinning.

When we reached the cottage, Mr Rose paunched and skinned four of the rabbits in no time at all keeping the giblets separate as a meal for Wendy; the coats to be cured, and then sold at a later date. Then, taking a closed knife with a wide curved blade from his pocket he passed it to me. "Be careful, this is a pruning knife and it's as sharp as a razor. I'll show you how it's used for pruning and grafting early next spring, but for now let's see how you get on dealing with these bright-eyes."

Although the job took me longer than expected, I was told I'd made a satisfactory first attempt. Having been told half the secret of paunching and skinning was to always use a sharp knife, I was then told the knife I'd used was a present I could keep, for doing a good morning's work. It was a wonderful gift. The handle was carved out of cherry-wood; it had a slight bend enabling the sharp hooked blade to be closed away in a safe position.

I was so delighted, I repeatedly thanked him, asking was he sure I could keep the impressive and useful tool.

"You've earned it," he said, whilst wrapping up two of the bright-eyes and giblets in some brown paper. "Keep it with you at all times; you never know when you may need it. It's a very important piece of country life; you can bet when you want it, you'll be only too pleased you've got it with you."

I put the two parcels into a carrier bag, and set off towards home, collecting the goats' milk from the shed on the way.

Checking Eddie's house I found everything was locked up and quite safe. Then as I'd been told I could, I helped myself to some carrots, onions, and two parsnips for Nan to put into the stew.

Before going indoors I went to the pigsty to check if the weaner had arrived. It had, and I smiled to myself when I realised that the small saddleback lying stretched out, fast asleep in the morning sun, had settled into its new home with ease.

When I got indoors I gave Nan all the food I had. She looked inside the bag and whispered, "thank goodness Robin, you've done well; you've also saved your bacon if you know what I mean."

"Yes I've been lucky, like I was last night, thanks to your help."

Mum and Dad were pleased when they saw what I'd brought home, although they couldn't have been half as pleased and relieved as I was.

Having told Dad I'd seen the piglet, he gave me instructions to feed it; one half-bucket full of bran each day, which he'd put under the lean-to, in the dry with the other animal feed. I was then told I'd be going with him to buy a stove from a disused army camp near Plaistow, which would help with the heating and cooking in the kitchen.

Chapter Eighteen

We very soon reached the edge of Plaistow village, where we turned left towards Kirdford, past the Mission Hall, and 'The Bush' public house. We drove about another mile, and then stopped at the partly demolished, disused army barracks.

After Dad had spent a while talking to one of the men, and they'd concluded their business, we crossed the camp to a pile of stoves, beds, window frames, and other bits and pieces which had been piled up for sale.

The stove was cylindrical and stood about three feet high with a flat top on which was fitted a solid iron, removable ring, from where it was stoked. Dad told me that because it stood on four short fat legs with an engraved top resembling a tortoise shell; it was not surprisingly called a 'tortoise' stove. It would certainly be good enough for our kitchen, as it'd previously been used to heat the whole of an army barracks. When the stove was loaded into the boot of the car along with various pieces of large tin pipe to make up the chimney, we set off to get some fresh spring water on the way home.

Dad pushed the heavy stove in the wheelbarrow, while I carried the metal pipes into the kitchen, where we were met by the lovely smell of rabbit stew gently cooking.

"My goodness Robin, that smells delicious; perhaps you should go rabbiting every day," he said standing the stove about a foot away from the back of the room. Mum came into the room, smiling with approval at the stove, while Dad marked the wall at the same level as the smoke outlet of the stove, where he intended to knock a hole for the chimney to go through.

After looking at the wall I asked him why he'd marked the chimney hole so low. Taking the hammer and chisel from his toolbox he looked at me blankly, then taking a deep breath, said sarcastically: "What do you think I'm going to do? I'm going to make a hole for the chimney to go outside; the smoke has to go outside doesn't it? Or do you think we'll just fill the room with smoke, and then open the door to let it out. Are you stupid, or what?"

I was shocked by his change in attitude and the way he'd spoken to me. He'd involved me in his work and been in a pleasant mood all afternoon. I'd asked a sensible question, and was expecting a logical answer. If I was wrong, I'd apologise, but I wanted to find out why. "We all know the chimney gets very hot Dad, so why put it on the wall outside and lose all the heat? If you fix it to the wall inside, it'll help keep the room warm in the winter and help dry the washing, if we put up an indoors clothes line."

"Shut up you little sod," Mum shouted; "how many times do you have to be told to keep your opinions to yourself? You don't know what you're talking about; now get outside and consider yourself lucky you haven't got a good hiding."

I watched as Dad, his back to me, let the hammer and chisel slip from his grip, dropping onto the floor with a thud. He turned and glanced at me, then looking at Mum said, "the little sod's right; get him out of my sight before I do something I'll regret later."

Wendy, aware something was wrong, followed close behind me as I left as quickly as possible. Within seconds I could hear the sound of raised voices and felt sorry for Nan. She'd had nothing to do with the situation, but was left as the go- between. She'd have to agree with both of them, or try to avoid saying anything. Better still, she'd need to come up with a plan acceptable to both of them.

Sitting under the beech tree I tried to fathom out what I'd inadvertently said to annoy them. What had I said that was so wrong? The more I thought the more I became convinced my suggestion was sound. Dad's idea wasn't; he'd embarrassed himself in front of us and what's more he knew it.

Sitting there, in the peacefulness of my special place gave me inner comfort; which helped me relax with contentment. With Wendy at my side, I sat half upright against the great tree dozing off every now and again for a couple of minutes. We enjoyed the tranquillity of the surroundings for over two hours. Before going home I read again several of the engravings cut into the tree; they made me wonder at the love and caring thoughts some people had for others and how it must feel.

Miss Lucas was in her garden and I called out to her as I walked towards the fence to meet her. As usual she was pleasing and easy to talk to. I told her about the rabbits I'd caught, which Mr Rose called bright-eyes; the pig Dad had bought and the tortoise stove from the old army camp the other side of Plaistow. Having told me she regularly went to the old Mission Hall we'd passed, she offered to take me with her if ever I'd like to go. Little did either of us realise, I'd join her on Sundays whenever I could, and thankfully, within my mind and soul be able to join God every day of my life.

It started getting dark, and having a couple of jobs waiting I wished her goodnight, to which she replied softly, "goodnight and God bless Robin."

I turned, looked at her, then smiling said, "thank you; Nan says that to me every night along with; and don't forget to say your prayers."

"Well don't," was her sweet and short answer.

"If I do, it's because I've fallen asleep as soon as my head hits the pillow," I smiled.

When I'd finished my jobs, Nan was waiting for me at the doorway. She put her hand on my shoulder as we went inside, where she pointed with one of her bent arthritic fingers towards the wall, and speaking softly so as not to be overheard by Mum or Dad in the sitting room said, "Just look at that; its what we've been waiting for, and thanks to you Robin, we've got it. What's more I've also got three clothes lines; not one or two, but three!"

Looking past Nan, I was dumbfounded to see that Dad had fitted the tortoise stove close to the wall, and fitted the chimney up the inside, allowing the heat it gave off to remain within the kitchen. Nan told me she'd cooked the giblets I'd brought home. Some she'd fed to Jet, the rest were wrapped up for me to give to Wendy who followed me outside while sniffing at the bag of fresh food.

When I returned indoors a few minutes later, on the table was a pudding basin, full to the top with thick rich brown gravy covering a generous helping of the fresh rabbit, carrots, parsnips and potatoes with two slices of home-made bread. I sat with my back to the sitting room door and ate the best dinner I could ever remember. Then I went into the sitting room to see if there were any repercussions from my suggestions about the stove or Nan's tasty rabbit stew.

There was complete silence for a long time; the stick I'd cut the day before was still standing in the corner. Eventually Dad looked up from reading his building book. "We'll be lighting the new stove tomorrow, so you'll need to cut more logs in future, do you understand?"

Knowing they were waiting for me to say the wrong thing, I replied, "There are plenty of logs for this fire Dad. In the morning I'll check if they'll fit into the new stove. If they do I'll cut some more and if they don't I'll cut a load of new ones and make a separate pile. I'll make sure there'll always be plenty of each."

Dad stared at me, as though looking for some weakness, then said, "Good; when you've finished, look around the area for some replacement wood. The timber we've got for logs won't last forever; you'll probably need to find some more one of these days." He looked down at his book, casually adding, and "don't forget to have a good wash down on Sunday evening for school on Monday. Now, as you've got a full tummy from the dinner you brought us, the best thing for you to do is to go to bed." Feeling relieved that everything seemed okay I quickly left the room.

Chapter Nineteen

The next morning I checked the size of the logs against the new stove. They fitted perfectly, and using the new long and heavy woodman's crosscut saw, I cut a large pile of logs, which I thought would be sufficient to last until the end of the following week. To my dismay they didn't, lasting only half the time I'd expected.

When I'd finished my jobs, I cut through the woods to Chalk Road and the pathway leading to where David Howell and his family lived. I told him I was going for a mooch and asked if he'd like to come. We walked along the road leading to the top end of Ifold, passing under overhanging trees until, through a gap between the branches of a large group of oaks, we came within view of the old silo. Built of bland concrete blocks, the tall unattractive shape, stuck out above the woodland on the horizon, dominating the whole of the surrounding area.

At the silo we looked inside and saw disused piles of rotting, vile-smelling silage. There were iron rails fixed to the outside wall from the bottom for many feet to the top and partly covered for safety reasons. We decided it was worth taking a chance to climb on them to the roof to look at the view.

It was very unsafe: several of the iron rails had become loose and we had to check the safety of each one as we climbed. We found most of the concrete blocks on the top edge had crumbled away due to the past years of severe winter conditions. Carefully we got ourselves to the top, but the tin roof and wooden ceiling had mainly rotted away; it was very dangerous. One slip could have been fatal, but we agreed the fantastic view of the area laid out before us was worth it! Later, when we'd both taken a deep breath having reached ground level again, we agreed it'd been a little scary but we wouldn't be frightened to do it again, although we never did.

We walked on past an old wooden shed, which had been treated with creosote so many times over the years it'd turned black with stain and age. In Hogwood Road David introduced me to Frankie Brooks who lived at the end of the short road at the start of a footpath through the woods to Ifold Cottage. We walked along the long narrow footpath, emerging at the old cottage on the corner of The Ride, another small lane, which always appeared deserted. For the remaining few days of the holidays, Dave and I became good and trusting friends.

All too quickly it was Sunday. I'd kept up with my jobs at home and stayed in Mum and Dads' good books since we'd had the rabbit stew. Whenever I checked Eddie's house and garden and because I normally felt the need for more food than I got at home, I filled up with fruit and vegetables, before they over-ripened or went bad.

As we couldn't ever get enough hot water to be able to use a tin bath, I washed myself down in the kitchen during the evening, ready for school the next morning.

Chapter Twenty

The morning came and I felt a little uneasy about going to a new school. It would be my third, as was my family! I knew without doubt, there'd be other schools in the future.

When I got back to the kitchen from doing the regular jobs, Nan had been able to boil some water. Then, having washed and changed into fresh short flannel trousers, socks and shirt and put on my new blazer I was ready. Dad and I walked to the car chatting about the hot weather and how long it would take me to walk home. Our reckoning of about three quarters of an hour, each way, was correct.

We arrived at Loxwood close to the river bridge on the edge of the village. He parked in the entrance of St John the Baptist Church opposite the school, and we went into a classroom to meet Miss Botting. She was one of the teachers; Miss Rees was the headmistress. I wasn't expected to stay and following my introduction was ushered out to meet the other boys and girls, leaving the adults to talk.

Soon Dad departed, leaving me feeling a little uncomfortable in my shirt, tie and blazer. All the other boys simply wore short trousers with an open neck shirt. Within seconds I'd put my tie in my blazer pocket, which I hung up in the classroom.

Before classes had even begun I'd made several new friends. Two of the boys told me if I walked across the field almost opposite, then along the track towards the dairy buildings everybody called Turpins Farm, I'd cut quite a lot of time off my journey home. They said the correct name of the farm was Headfoldswood Farm, but the name was seldom used.

Miss Botting rang the hand-bell; playing stopped, and about thirty of us went into the classroom. By the time the dinner bell rang we hadn't done any lessons, but had got to know each other and where each lived. We were each given a small bottle of milk, which was drunk with sandwiches brought by the majority of the children. There were three of us who didn't have anything to eat, each of us saying they'd eaten a good-sized breakfast and weren't hungry; I wished it were true.

After school, I walked towards home cutting across the fields Bill and Tommy had mentioned; then through a large herd of Friesian cows grazing on the dry grass stubble covering the unploughed areas of the large fields. At the farmyard I went into the dairy where I introduced myself to the head dairyman; having explained I had to walk to school I asked permission to cross his fields. He told me to ensure I closed the gates after me and telling me his name was Dick he showed me around the milking parlour.

"Try this," he said, pouring a large tin beaker of fresh milk.

"Thanks Mr Dick, I'll be only too pleased to."

"There's no need to call me Mr Dick, just call me Dick! When there are only two people together, it's obvious whom you're talking to, so why even bother to say their name. It's different if there are more than two of you. It's also often a waste of time, stopping work or whatever you're doing to look at the person you're talking to."

"Yes, you're right," I agreed. "I never thought of it like that before. Why waste time, and why bother using their name when they know you're talking to them. Thanks for the milk, and for letting me cut across your land. Oh, by the way, why do they call it Turpins Farm, and not Headfoldswood Farm?"

"Because my second name's Turpin, and I don't want to hear any jokes," he laughed.

"Ok Dick Turpin," I smiled, "I promise; thanks for the milk and see you tomorrow."

I reached home, hungry and tired. Nan made me a homemade jam sandwich, so thick that despite being the first thing I'd eaten all day, it gave me the strength to keep going with my chores.

School days soon became a routine as I became reliant on the small bottle of milk at school; the gratefully appreciated beaker of fresh milk from Dick at Turpins Farm every afternoon, plus the sandwich Nan always had ready for me when I got home. It was all I had until I sat alone in the kitchen of an evening to eat whatever dinner I was given.

Chapter Twenty-one

At the end of my first week at school, while playing the game of tag, Tommy accidentally grabbed my blazer pocket as I passed and pulled it off, tearing the material. I knew I'd be in trouble when I got home and Mum found out; but there wasn't a thing I could do about it.

During the evening I plucked up the courage to tell Mum and Dad about the accident I'd had with my blazer. Mum went mad; no matter how much I apologised or whatever I said, they were both determined I should be punished for not being more careful.

"Get outside and cut yourself a stick, you little sod. You were lucky to get away with it last time, but not this!" Mum shouted.

Being called a little sod always meant trouble. I looked at Dad, hoping for some form of comfort, but there was none. The last thing I wanted to do was to cut my own punishment stick.

Dad picked up the unused stick from the side of the fireplace and broke it in half.

"This one's no good," he said, "go and cut a fresh one!"

Because my pruning knife would cut just as well as the billhook, I walked straight out to the woods. Naturally, whenever I was hit with a stick it hurt, but the stinging from the wounds would only last about two or three hours; that wasn't too drastic for me. What hurt most, was the anguish I suffered when cutting the stick.

It was while I was selecting an appropriate sapling that I suddenly had an idea that would put an end to the poignant pain forever. It was so simple I smiled to myself. "Why cut them one at a time; why not cut three or four?" I muttered aloud, then instinctively looked around unnecessarily thinking someone might have overheard. Dad would never know and I'd save myself a lot of heartache. All I'd have to do was to walk into the woods, collect one of my ready-cut sticks; trim each end, to make it look freshly prepared, and then simply take it to Dad. It'd be painless.

When I got indoors, I handed Dad the stick. Normally I'd be feeling upset and be unable to hide my feelings: it always gave them a sense of control and power, which was obvious from the slight smile of satisfaction, particularly on Mum's face. This time was different; the expression on her face was of disbelief and shock, when I simply said. "There you are Dad; I'm sorry I was so long getting it but I wanted to be sure it was the thickness you wanted."

I turned around to face Mum; I watched her face, my back towards Dad, making it easy for him to hit the back of my legs without getting out of his chair. Each of the strokes hurt a great deal and it took all my willpower not to even flinch. Neither of them smiled at the other; they just looked at me hoping and waiting for a sign of sorrow, but they were out of luck. It never came! I glanced towards Nan and in a calm, controlled voice said, "I'm going outside for the rest of the evening so if I'm not in when you want to go to bed give me a call and I'll come back straight away."

As I left, Mum and Dad were still sitting in their chairs, gawking at each other with their mouths partly open in disbelief that I hadn't shown any signs of distress. They weren't to know that I'd taken the first step in avoiding a lot of heartache. They were completely unaware that I'd won a small battle for myself; my only worry was that perhaps I should have appeared more upset and hurt.

Passing through the kitchen, I saw Nan's needlework basket on the table from which I took four of the spare pins from the inside of the lid, and then went outside. Placing the top end of each pin into the vice fitted to a bench at the end of the wagon, I bent the pins over a large nail, shaping them until they became half-round, with each end at a slight angle from the other. Then, using the smooth side of a broken brick, I carefully fashioned the end of each pin to a needle sharp tip. Tying a length of string to the thick end of each one, I then stuck the sharp tips into a small piece of wood, and rolled them up. I'd made my very own fishing hooks and line. All I needed was a rod and float, which I'd cut at the water's edge from a hazel bush. I knew one slice of Nan's bread would do nicely as bait, but if there wasn't enough I was prepared to go without. If my idea worked, it would not only be beneficial for me, but also for Wendy and Jet.

As there was still plenty of daylight I walked along the lane as far as the Foxbridge Farm entrance where four empty metal churns for the next day's milk were still sitting on the specially made wooden bench awaiting collection and refilling. A little further along the road, past the farm entrance, there was a muddy track leading into the middle of a mixed hazel and birch woodland. Having been told a charcoal burner lived and worked in the wood, I walked up the track to meet him.

He was standing by the side of an old wooden caravan. A shed on the edge of a small clearing contained several rows of tightly packed sacks. Four large thick black rubber objects marked 'Wing Fuel Tanks' partly overgrown with brambles, made me wonder how they'd ever ended up in the middle of woodland.

I saw a large mound of what I thought must be wood, buried under a layer of clay and wood ash slowly smouldering with the white wispy smoke seeping out through the small holes at the top. It was where he made the charcoal. I'd noticed some on the floor of the shed. It was black, and looked very brittle, mainly very thin, about the size I used at school in Dorking for drawing and sketching.

When I'd introduced myself in a proper way, I told him we were almost opposite neighbours and Mr Rose had been kind and helpful to me. He looked wide-eyed, directly into my face, saying nothing and I realised he'd been staring at me, in silence ever since I met him. I didn't feel comfortable in his presence and increasingly bothered. Something in the back of my mind told me something wasn't right, and I didn't like it; without a second thought I called Wendy to my side, then feeling very uneasy and without even saying goodbye, left quickly, never to return.

The stinging at the back of my legs had eased by the time I approached home where I saw Amy and Cathy Lucas in their garden and spoke to them until it got dark.

"Goodnight, God bless Robin, and don't forget to say your prayers," I heard Amy say as I walked away. "By the way I forgot to tell you, your little red-breasted namesake has been flying about from pillar to post every day this week looking for you all the while you were at school."

I turned and looking at their smiling faces called back, "I think we both missed each other. Good night, God bless."

They were both such pleasing people; I wished everybody could be the same. I found out later in life that people's kindness and understanding varies considerably; often because some people are so thoughtlessly self-opinionated, they wrongly pre-judge others.

Nan was sitting at the kitchen table knitting a shawl. I told her I'd be going fishing in the morning, and she laughed when I told her how I'd made hooks out of the pins. I ate the sparse meal Mum had left for me and went to bed

Chapter Twenty-two

Taking a few Swan Vesta matches, I carefully wrapped them in pairs, head to tail into my handkerchief to avoid them accidentally striking against each other and catching fire. They very soon became part of the standard kit I carried at all times.

I set off through Ifold, along the canal, until I reached Loxwood Stores. I saw dozens of accumulators the same as the one I was carrying, lined up on the floor, all marked with different names on their attached labels. I'd never imagined there were so many and asked the man behind the counter why. I was very pleasantly surprised when he casually told me, "Well, instead of bringing the used one into the shop every week, for a freshly charged one, like you do, I'll exchange it by dropping a fresh one off at your home later this morning. I do the same every Saturday for all my customers when I deliver the groceries and other provisions; providing your parents agree of course."

I made the decision without hesitation and just hoped it was acceptable to Mum and Dad. "Yes please," I answered, "I'm sure it'll be okay; you deliver to us every Saturday anyway." I then thought about what I'd said and added, "the only problem is, what will happen to me if you forget, and don't bring it? Your shop closes at lunchtime and I wouldn't be able to replace it. You've no idea of the trouble I'd be in."

"Don't worry about it, or give it a second thought," he replied. "I promise you it'll always be delivered. I've never let anybody down yet, not even if the van breaks down; you'll get the accumulator one way or the other. I've even resorted to a tractor and trailer in bad weather conditions."

His reply convinced me I'd made the right decision, particularly when I thought of how much time and effort I'd save, especially during the oncoming cold winter months.

On the way home, I noticed the water level in the river was so low only a trickle flowed along the muddy bottom. As there wasn't any point in trying to fish in the shallows, I walked the short distance from the footpath to Ifold Lake.

Making my way through the brambles along the narrow unused path, a snake slithered across the surface of the shining clear water to my side and across the path only a foot or so in front of me. At first I thought it was a common grass snake, I'd seen several before near home, but upon looking closer, I realised it was an adder. I'd only seen one before, and not wanting to get too close, stood motionless, waiting for it to slide into the undergrowth before quickly going to the far side of the lake.

A Jack heron stood motionless at the edge of the rushes. He'd become accustomed to seeing me; aware he was perfectly safe he scarcely looked in my direction. A small cluster of moorhens scuttled off temporarily out of sight, followed by several ducks half flying and scurrying away while the majority of the others continued making various loud quacking noises while splashing about and dunking themselves in the clear reflective surface of the lake.

An opening between a group of trees and bushes at the waters edge, close to the lilies, was wide enough to allow me plenty of room to fish; it was ideal.

I cut and trimmed a long thin hazel pole to use as a rod, then tied the length of string line and home-made hook to the end. Using a pinch of bread as bait, I got myself into a comfortable position and very gently flicked the line. From what my Uncle Bert had taught and shown me, I knew the lake was teeming with hundreds of fish called rudd, which often fed on or near the surface. They were the fish to catch if my plans were to succeed.

The string line floated in mid air, then breathtakingly, seemed to stop before very slowly moving downwards until, caught in the light movement of its own draught, it drifted like a feather onto the clear silk-like surface. The bait floated motionless for no longer than a couple of seconds before silently disappearing in a whirl coming from below the flat calm water. The line gently lay in round loops on the surface but now started to straighten out. I felt the slight tug on the tip of the rod, and knew I'd hooked a fish. I drew it under the water surface to stop it splashing about and alarming any other within close proximity; I judged from its weight and strength, it would take at least another six, or maybe eight the same size to make my plan work successfully.

It was the most colourful rudd I'd ever seen or could even begin to imagine. The shiny silver body reflected in the sunlight showing its golden and red fins and the tail wiggling franticly non-stop, was a deep orange with red edges.

My plan had begun to work but what should I do? It was a dilemma; Wendy and Jet were normally hungry. Jet not only had to find his own food, but also hunt for Wendy whenever he could. I was also in need of much more food than I was given at home. I didn't want to kill such an attractive fish but fished on. Several of my catch fell off my home-made hooks, but I decided I wouldn't give up until I had enough.

Once I had enough, I cleaned them, and then protected myself from the heat of the sun by sitting in the shade of a large oak tree. I made a small fire from dry grass and twigs and cut two forked sticks and placed one at each side of the fire. Then threading a long thin twig through the fish I placed each end into the forked ends of the sticks. Within a short while I'd cooked and enjoyed a large healthy meal.

I took the remaining fish, wrapped them in some waxed paper and placed them inside my shirt. I dowsed the fire with water from my cupped hands, cleared up the area and went towards the footpath.

From nearby I heard loud screams of delight mixed with the sound of giggling and splashing water. Wondering who, or what it could be, I crossed back over the bridge then, turning left, walked along the riverbank to a big old ash tree, close to where the noise was.

I found a few of the boys and girls from school together with two or three others I hadn't met. They were all splashing and playing about in a large pool, which despite the heat of the summer, hadn't dried up and still contained enough water to reach chest-high. It took little encouragement from them before I'd stripped off all my clothes and jumped in with them. Within minutes, we were splashing about; soaking each other with the large sheets of water we produced by flaying our arms across the clear surface of the river.

We didn't realise that not only were we enjoying ourselves, but with the soft clay oozing between our toes, we were cleaning our feet and our bodies at the same time. It was thoroughly enjoyed by all of us; so much in fact that we'd frequently meet during the warmth of the summer, just for a good soaking, and to wash. None of us ever thought of it coming to an end, but it did as we grew into puberty; although it was all part of growing into adulthood, in a way we regretted it, but the innocent happy times would remain with us forever.

Chapter Twenty-three

About an hour later, Dave and I walked home with Michael Simms, another boy who became a good friend. Michael lived in a white brick bungalow on the Plaistow Road, midway between Chalk Road and Ifold Cottage. Opposite his entrance was an oak tree I'll never forget due to the nesting pair of nuthatches, who would repair the entrance hole to the nest with fresh clay every year.

It was mid-afternoon when I got home; hoping above hope the accumulator had been delivered. If it hadn't I'd be in serious trouble as I'd be unable to get another until Monday after school. The decision to have it delivered was mine, and mine alone; I knew I'd only have myself to blame if it hadn't arrived.

Keeping my fingers crossed for luck, I went into the kitchen, half expecting to hear the sound of Mum screeching at me. There was silence; not a sound to be heard, except the faint grunting from Nan who was dozing in the heat of the afternoon. What I saw next made all my worries disappear in a flash. On the table, polished and shining, with a large label tied to the thin handle was the accumulator. I gave a deep sigh of relief and smiled to myself; I was safe, thank goodness!

Leaving Nan dozing, I quietly slipped outside, where I fed Wendy the surprise meal of the fish, which within a few seconds, she had hungrily gulped down. Jet was nowhere to be seen, but knowing he'd be about sooner or later, I left him a good-sized meal in the shade of the bench where he'd be bound to find it when he got home.

Not wanting to disturb Nan by cutting logs, I decided my first job would be to get the milk for the weekend. A short while later, having found Mr Rose in the big shed and exchanged greetings he asked, "Have you put any snares down today Rod?"

"I haven't any snares to put down," I answered, "it's a shame really because I've seen loads of bright-eyes on my way to school every day, and there are masses of them in the large field opposite Keepers Cottage, and almost everywhere you look." I then said. "I've had an idea and would like to ask you what you think. If you say no, I'll understand."

"This idea of yours obviously involves me, so let's sit down while you explain what it's all about," he replied, with a big smile on his face.

When we'd made ourselves comfortable on sacks of chicken and goat food I began. "If you'll lend me two snares, I could set them on my way home from school, and check them every morning on my way to school. I'll give you the first bright-eye I catch in exchange for the loan of the snares: I'd take the next two home because there are four of us to feed; the next two I'd sell to Mr Sopp the butcher. I've heard he pays good money for them and what's more he paunches and skins them himself, which means I'd still be clean for school. Then I'd start again until I've saved enough money to replace your snares with new ones from the village stores."

"It's an idea Rod, but there's one thing you've forgotten!" he said shuffling his feet into the dry dusty clay, and looking very pleased. Then turning his head towards me in an enquiring manner asked, "What would your Dad say if you asked him to buy a few snares? So anything you caught would be his; your dinner wouldn't cost anything and you could still sell the rest."

"I'm sure he'd say no! I'd like to snare some first to prove it worthwhile."

"Good thinking. Now listen to me, and don't interrupt; just do as I tell you," he said. "You have the first two bright-eyes each week; you can sell the rest as and when. If I need one I can always set some snares myself. Now go to the back of the shed but don't take two snares, take three. Then go to the field opposite Keepers Cottage, walk down the right-hand side, pick yourself some good runs and set the snares as you've been shown. Tomorrow morning check them, and continue doing that until your Dad buys some for you. Don't forget to collect your milk; I'll see you later in the week. Good luck!"

He turned to walk away, as I asked, "What if the farmer catches me? I don't know who owns the land, or where the boundaries start or finish, I could get myself into trouble."

"The bright-eyes we snared last week came from the same farmer's land as the one you're going to, so don't worry. He lives at Foxbridge Farm and owns most of the land around here; he's a nice chap who'll always help you if he can. You should go and introduce yourself when you've time; his name is HRH Prince Tomislav of Yugoslavia. He and his brother Prince André took over the farm when they escaped after Germany invaded their country during the war; they've been very welcome here ever since. When you do meet, you can call him Prince Thomas, or even Tom, he doesn't mind. Most people call him Tom."

Having gathered the snares, and putting the goats' milk near the gate to collect later, I set off. The field was enormous, and edged each side by hazel woods; the bottom contained a small stream with a narrow hazel strip separating the next field.

There were so many rabbit runs; I hardly knew where to start. Within fifteen minutes I was quite pleased with where I'd set them, and was on my way home.

As I walked into the kitchen, Nan looked up from ironing the weekly wash, which had dried in the heat of the sun. "I've cooked some Spam, potatoes, and peas, with rice pudding to follow for your dinner; it's the best I could do I'm afraid. Your mother didn't leave much for you; it's in the oil stove keeping warm, for whenever you're ready!"

"Never mind Nan, I've already had something to eat."

"Good, I shan't ask you what it was but I'm pleased for you," she answered with a smile, "what's more, I'm glad the accumulator arrived! Well done, it's a pity your parents didn't arrange it ages ago. Mind you after what happened last night, I'm sure you'll be all right for the next few days. Mum and Dad can't understand what happened; they can't stop talking about your lack of concern or feelings after being given the stick last night. I must confess you certainly didn't show any emotions. Now go and finish your jobs, while I finish off the ironing; by then I'll have your dinner ready and Mum and Dad will be home," she quietly said, giving my shoulders a squeeze.

Nan, who stayed in the kitchen with me while I ate my dinner, said Dad would be taking her to Horsham on Monday morning to catch the number 316 bus to East Croydon. I was pleased for her when she said she'd stay until Friday, for a well-earned rest with her daughter Doss, and her family.

"Unfortunately I'll have to wear my slippers during the trip," she smiled, "I'll take my shoes with me, to wear later."

"Why on earth will you have to wear your slippers?" I jokingly asked.

Her answer was simple, and so obvious I should have realised beforehand. "Because my fingers are so swollen and painful with arthritis I'm unable to use the scissors to cut my toenails, and I can't get my shoes on. Even if I soften them in warm water, I wouldn't be able to bend down to cut them. I'm getting to be a bit of a wreck Robin! That's what happens when you get old."

"We can't have you going to London in your slippers Nan! If Mum won't cut them for you, I shall! Now then let's get a bowl of hot water, the scissors and a towel."

After half an hour of soaking in warm soapy water I was able to make a decent job of cleaning, cutting and scraping away the hard skin, off Nan's feet. She must have thanked me a dozen times; I could tell from her face, she felt the relief.

Nan had only been in the sitting room a couple of minutes before Mum called me to go in. Gingerly I entered the room; she stared expressionlessly at me. "Nan tells me you've made a good job of cutting her nails and trimming the hard skin off. That's good, you can cut mine tomorrow; then we'll see how good you are."

"He'll do no such thing!" Dad firmly said. "You may not be bothered to cut your own mother's toenails, but at least you can cut your own! I'll hear no more about it, and that's that."

Concerned I might have caused an argument, or bad feeling and certainly some embarrassment, I quickly changed the subject telling them I'd put three rabbit snares down, that I'd borrowed from Mr Rose and would check them in the morning. Then making an excuse to go outside, I kept out of the way until bedtime.

Chapter Twenty-four

In the morning I checked Eddie's place and found him there. We talked for a while and I told him I'd taken some soft fruit and vegetables. "That's okay with me," he said. "I just enjoy growing them; it takes my mind off other things. You take whatever you want Rod; it's a way of saying thanks for keeping your eye on the place. I expect you've had your breakfast; I'm going indoors now for mine before I leave, so I'll see you in about three weeks time."

We said our goodbyes and I continued on my way wishing I had indeed had breakfast! I found the first and second snares untouched. Not too good I thought, but when I checked the third one, it was missing. It didn't take long to find where the rabbit had dragged it into the thicket, about six feet away; as far as the attached branch would allow.

I paunched skinned and jointed the rabbit, feeding the giblets to Wendy who'd been sitting at my side waiting patiently. After taking the rest indoors to Mum, who seemed quite pleased, I set off to find Dave or Michael.

Within half an hour the three of us were walking along the stone lane leading to Hogwood Forest, when we came to a field I was told belonged to a Mr Mepham, nicknamed the Goat Man. He lived alone in a shed, around which he kept an enormous herd of goats, which supplied the majority of families in the area with probably the only milk available to them.

Very soon we'd passed the tiny chicken farm where Sid the postman lived, then a lovely old period cottage, similar to Keepers Cottage, where the owner kept dozens of pigs, which he reared for market.

Continuing our walk along the edge of Hogwood Forest we very soon came to a dirt road called The Lane. None of us considered the name very apt, because in winter, the deep tracks would fill with water and it would become very muddy and unusable. We jokingly decided a name like 'Boggy Track,' or 'Mud Trail,' would have been more appropriate. A short way along The Lane we met Ernie Honeyset who was a friend of Dave's elder brother Arthur; Ernie had two sisters and a younger brother, Douglas. They also lived in a wooden building as most people in the area did, but being a long distance away at the top end of Ifold, we only met very occasionally.

When we'd almost reached the end of The Lane, we stopped opposite the closed gates of a small brick and wooden property called Three Oaks and watched a dozen or so turkey and duck scratching about the yard. It was where one of my classroom mates, Tommy Bachaus lived who, like myself, also had a long walk to school. Although it became a stopping off place to see Tommy whenever I was in the area I would certainly never have guessed I was standing in the exact spot where at a much later date I'd load my catapult, with what I thought was a lump of dry clay, and fire it at Douglas Honeyset, hitting him over the top of the right eye. Unfortunately and completely unbeknown to me, the piece of clay contained a stone, which split his eyebrow wide open. He'd held the wound closed to stop the blood running into his eye and down his face, before going home to be comforted by his two sisters, when they'd finished shouting and calling me names.

Almost half a lifetime later on a trip down memory lane I passed through Loxwood and stopped at the Onslow Arms for an early evening pint of King and Barns Festive Bitter. At about eight o'clock, I thought I'd finish my pint off, and get on my way home to East Sussex. I swigged the last drop and was about to leave, when the door opened and a slightly younger man than I, walked in. Having ordered his pint of bitter he stood by my side and exchanged greetings. We instantly started chatting to each other; the more we chatted, the more we drank, and so it went on, and on. Later in the evening and several drinks more, I told him I knew the area, and that I'd lived in Ifold, being educated locally, whenever I was permitted, at Loxwood School. Having told me he was a local man, and had also lived in Ifold we laughingly introduced ourselves formally.

He didn't recognise my name at first, but when he told me his, I knew exactly, who he was; I was speechless, and a little taken aback to say the least.

"What's the matter Rod, are you alright?" He said looking concerned.

"Yes I'm okay thanks, I remember you now," I answered then continued, "the scar over your eye, do you remember how you got it?"

"No I've no idea at all, it's been there ever since I can remember; it's never bothered me, I forget it's even there. Why?"

"Well Douglas, I remember you now, and your family, better than you may think. I can also tell you exactly how you got that scar."

"Well nobody else seems to know; as I said it doesn't bother me. But if you know, you may as well tell me. How did I get it?"

"I did it; it wasn't intentional, but I did it outside a place called Three Oaks owned by the Bachaus's." I then went on to explain exactly what happened, and how sorry I was.

"I told you Rod it doesn't worry me in the least. Now stop feeling sorry for the two of us and get that drink down. It's my round next, so let's have the next one with a drop of scotch, cheers mate!"

We enjoyed the rest of the evening; having such a good time that neither of us could drive so we slept in our cars waking up with hangovers. In the morning the Landlord invited us into the kitchen and we were given a free, very welcome home-cooked English breakfast!

An hour later, Douglas and I shook hands and said goodbye, hoping we'd meet again one day. We never did.

When Dave, Michael and I passed Tommy's place we walked on to the small garage near the old silo. Mr Curtis who owned the tiny garage containing one solitary petrol pump, had erected two large bird cages, which stood at least eight feet high and six feet square each containing a very large owl.

On the floor of each of the wire-framed cages were several regurgitated food pellets; each one containing the bones, fur, and other body waste from their meals. From the amount of them scattered around the floor the birds were obviously well fed. I knew the one nearest to me was a fully-grown barn owl by its white face and breast; the wing and back were a lovely freckled light-brown colour. When the wings were closed, its white face set with large round black eyes was its main visible feature. On the gate was a small sign with the word Moses written upon it; we agreed it was a strange and unusual name for a bird.

I didn't know the other type of owl, until Michael told me it was a tawny owl, a common breed throughout the area. It sat on its perch looking sad, frequently turning its head to the left or right and looking behind as if checking it was safe. Its plumage was a light brown with light and dark vertical streaks running down the whole length of its body from the front to the back; it was certainly an attractive looking bird.

Having my jobs at home to do and having agreed we'd all done enough talking and walking about for the day, we set off, passing the silo to Chalk Road. Before long we'd said our farewells at the appropriate places, and went off in different directions.

At home, Dad told me I'd have time for a mug of tea before starting the jobs he wanted me to do. There was no mention of food; I was only too pleased I'd had the hazelnuts and apples I'd picked earlier in the day.

With the mattock and spade I spent most of the afternoon grubbing out some of the many hazel roots still left sticking up out of the hard clay; then a couple of hours sawing and stacking piles of logs and kindling wood getting ready for the winter.

Later my watchful friendly red robin, fluttered off to roost for the night, and then followed by Wendy my other close companion I went indoors for whatever dinner Nan was able to give me. It was sausage, mashed potatoes, and some fresh home-made bread, which I spread with a special treat of Bovril. It tasted good and it was filling; causing me to sleep soundly, facing the partitioning, without moving all night, or so Nan jokingly told me the next morning.

Chapter Twenty-five

Giving Nan a kiss on the cheek the next morning, and wishing her a good rest while she was away at her daughter's, I left for school.

Later, I passed through Turpins Farm towards the four large trees growing near to the edge of the main Loxwood road, midway between the school and Plaistow Road junction. I found they'd shed a few round green hard fruit I'd never seen before. The fruit grew in abundance on three of the trees, while the fourth had none at all: I had no idea what they were.

During the week Bill, who'd become one of my schoolmates, introduced me to his two older sisters, Pauline and Pearl and their friend Margaret, whom I'd met before at the village Post Office. There was another Rodney who came to school with his two sisters, Winnie and Connie. By the time I was about ten years old, I think I must have fallen in love or had a crush on all of them at some time or other but was always too shy to tell them. I couldn't help envying most of my new schoolmates a little for the friendship and care they could all share with their brothers and sisters; let alone to have help with the workload.

When I set off home that afternoon I called in to see Dick the dairyman and receive my welcome beaker of milk. He realised my appreciation and often asked me if I'd like another; I always thanked him, but although it often wasn't true I always told him I'd had plenty.

I mentioned the four large trees I'd noticed; one of which only grew leaves, while the other three grew the strange green round balls, which I assumed were the fruit.

He laughed and said. "Don't you know what they are?"

"No, I've never seen anything like them before! What are they?"

"They're walnuts. I can't eat them with my teeth, but you're more than welcome to them," he said. "Break them out of the soft thick casing they're in, but be careful because the moisture inside will stain your hands black, and it's very difficult to get off. Inside you'll find the large nut; the best way to crack them open is by crushing two of them together in your hands. They've got a very tough shell but that's the only way it works when you're out in the country." He walked to the door of the dairy with me and added, "I'll be in that field next week; whilst I'm there I'll sort the walnut tree out so it'll give a good crop of nuts in the future. I've been meaning to do it for the past couple of years; you've just reminded me! I'll do it next week."

"How will you do that? Surely you can't just go up to it and tell it to grow some nuts," I remarked, with a smile.

He saw the funny side of what I'd said, and chuckling to himself replied, "No, not quite Rod, but there's an old country saying which I've never known to fail yet. I'll tell it to you." He bent forward and looked me full in the face, nodding and wagging his finger to emphasise every word as he said in a very slow manner, "Woman, child, walnut tree; the more you beat them, the better they be."

He stood upright; pushing his cap back to scratch his head and almost blushing he said. "It never fails with a walnut tree;

some children may deserve a clip around the ear from time to time, but I certainly wouldn't try it on a woman, not if you know what's good for you."

When I'd finished my chores Mum and Dad had already eaten their dinner of rabbit stew. It smelt mouth-wateringly good and had been slowly cooking all day. Mine was left in the saucepan on top of the tortoise stove. When I took a spoon and tasted it before tipping it into a basin, I realised Mum, who hardly ever did any cooking, had forgotten to add any salt. Breaking a small chunk from the hard salt block, I sprinkled the grains over the stew to bring out the flavour. Then cutting myself two slices of bread, I sat down to eat my dinner, my first meal of the day.

When I'd emptied the saucepan into the bowl I sat and stared with exasperation. The stew consisted of about four spoonfuls of vegetables, the rib cage and the two small front legs of the rabbit; about two mouthfuls of meat in total.

Mum and Dad had not only eaten virtually all the vegetables; they'd also eaten the two large back legs, and the whole back of the rabbit between them! There should have been plenty for the three of us. I hungrily ate what little I'd been left within a couple of minutes. The bones were far too small to give to Wendy and Jet, who'd been sitting at my feet waiting for any leftovers; they looked equally disappointed.

Dad called me into the sitting room, where he told me that to enable Mum to carry water from Spring Hill; he'd bought her a pushbike, fitted with a large basket on the front. He'd be starting a job within the next week and wouldn't be able to fetch the water on most days. Mum would use the pushbike daily as she'd be starting work with the Land Army and wouldn't be here when I got home from school every day.

When he told me what time they expected to be home, I suggested that, if it would help, I'd milk Judy and collect the chicken and goose eggs. At this proposal Mum went into a rage and shouted, "No certainly not! I don't trust you. You'd take a quantity of the milk, and eggs to mix an egg and milk drink. The answer is no! I don't want to hear anything more about it. Do you understand?"

"Yes Mum; I was only trying to be helpful. I'm sorry."

"Well don't even think about it, now get out."

Sitting in the kitchen I wondered why Mum would say or think such a thing of me; after all I was only trying to be helpful and considerate. In the quietness I overheard Dad half-laughing tell Mum there wasn't any point in buying snares, all the time Mr Rose was prepared to let me use his. I thought he was being less than fair. Then, considering I'd caught their dinner for nothing, and the amount I was given to eat, I was encouraged to make a decision, which would certainly affect us all, one way or the other.

The next day, when I went to collect some goats' milk, I took the three snares Mr Rose had lent me and gave them back to him, thanking him for the use. When he asked me why I'd returned them, I lied to him, saying Dad had given me the money to buy some from Loxwood Stores. He seemed pleased, but said nothing, and I knew from his reaction he wasn't too sure of what had really happened.

During the evening, after eating the cold food Mum had left on the table for me, I sat by the stove with Wendy listening to the sound of the wireless, coming from the next room. After an hour or so I was surprised when Dad came into the room and sat at the kitchen table with me. He started by telling me he realised I was upset with what Mum had said, but that she didn't mean it and I should forget it. He then suggested I should go into the sitting room, and give her a kiss to make up.

"No! I've done nothing wrong," I blurted out, not caring what he'd say or do, "I'll never milk Judy or collect the eggs, even if you were to beg me to, so don't worry. I've also taken the snares back to Mr Rose because I'll never catch another rabbit and bring it home for you. Now if you want me to cut a stick, just say so."

Initially he looked dumbfounded but it was obvious he knew why I'd made such a decision. His attitude changed in a flash as he bawled at me, "what do you mean, you've taken the snares back. You had half of the rabbit to eat for yourself didn't you?"

"Yes," I replied quickly adding, "Uncle Bert gave me half a goose egg once; that wasn't a fair and equal half either. I never took him any eggs home again, and I'll never bring home any more rabbits for you."

I didn't care what I said, because it was true and I was prepared to face any punishment he might give me. I waited for what he would say next. It was only a moment or two before he went red in the face and bitterly said. "You've deserved the stick for what you've said, and you can bet your sweet life you're going to get it. But not right now, I'll keep you waiting until I'm ready! Anyway, I don't want you going to school with weals on your legs, otherwise everybody will know what's happened."

"It doesn't really matter Dad, everybody I meet very soon finds out for themselves. They always look."

He rose from the table saying, "You wait until I'm good and ready; I'll tell you when. Now get out, or go to bed."

I knew I'd shocked him by being so outspoken and voicing my views. He was wrong and knew it and he'd decided to punish me, and told me so. Nevertheless I knew he was so astounded he couldn't bring himself to do it, right there and then. Most important of all, we both knew I was right, and he'd probably have made the same decision as I had.

When he'd left the kitchen, I tried to listen through the thin wall at what they were saying to each other. I knew it was about what I'd said, as I could just hear part of the conversation, and then the wireless was turned up so I couldn't hear anything. I went to bed.

When I got back from school on Friday, Nan was already home, cooking dinner, and washing last week's laundry, which as expected hadn't been done. She told me the rest had made her feel much better; what's more, she'd had a real bath and hot or roast food every day. I felt pleased for her, and jokingly told her she made me feel a little jealous.

"Your Mum and Dad are out already," she said. Then from the front pocket of her apron she took a bar of milk chocolate and a very small tin. "Don't let anybody see the chocolate; eat it when you're alone. The small tin once contained 'Benton' snuff; it'll be ideal for keeping your Swan Vesta matches safe. Your cousin Ken gave it to me for you, with some plasticine to put inside; it'll hold the matches in a firm and safe position. I'm sure you don't need telling."

Nan knew what I used the matches for, and I carried them with me everywhere I went for several years to follow. The amount I carried with me, was enough to light at least a dozen or so fires for cooking various food I trapped, or caught.

Chapter Twenty-six

The following week, Dick had ploughed and prepared the large field from the farm entrance, along the length of Plaistow Road, up to the main junction by the pond. Two of the other farm workers, and half a dozen women, worked for about four days planting out rows and rows of various types of winter vegetables for the market, or for cattle food during the winter months.

At the end of the week on the way home from school I noticed the non-fruit bearing walnut tree had been terribly scarred and half the bark on one side had been completely ripped off. When I saw Dick a little later at the dairy I mentioned what I'd seen. "You won't believe it now, but you just wait and see the large crop of nuts we'll get this time next year, he answered. "I scraped the bark off the tree by driving tight to the side of it with the large spiked iron wheel of the tractor; that's what you call a good beating."

"I though you meant you beat them with a stick," I said.

"No, you need to beat seriously; an axe will do if you haven't got a tractor" he went on. "By the way, you can start collecting the nuts from under the other trees now; they're ready to harvest. Eat whatever you want; you can save some here if you don't want to take them all home, they'll last for later in the year."

"Thanks, I'll start from next week," I answered drinking the last of my milk.

"There's something else you can do as well," he said; then after a short pause continued, "as you've probably noticed, we've finished planting all our winter vegetables. Keep your eye on them growing and when they're ready for eating, you can help yourself. Just remember they're for you to eat, not take home."

He thought for a moment then said, "When you leave the farm, you turn right towards Ifold, then down the slope over the brook, right?"

"Dead right," I smiled.

"Then you pass a large field on your right?"

"Yes, the gate's on the right the other side going up the slope," I answered.

"Good, although they're not quite ready yet, within a few weeks or so, you can do something for both of us. This time you can take something home for your efforts, providing you don't eat them all before you get there," he said smiling.

Not having a clue, or being able to imagine what he was talking about, because there certainly wasn't any fruit growing at this time of the year, I looked at him and said, "eat what?"

"Mushrooms; big, wild field mushrooms. Raw or cooked they're lovely; I can't wait to smell them frying, I can even taste them now." He was almost drooling as he spoke. "Right," he said as if coming back to reality, "when they're ready, which will be soon, I'll leave a carrier bag here for you every day. When you've had your milk, take the bag, and on your way home, go into the field and pick any mushrooms you want; that should please your Mum and Dad," he said smiling and roughing up my hair. "Then on your way to school, go into the field and half fill the bag for me and the other dairymen.

There's always fresh ones every morning so pick as many as you want, until they've finished. Now be on your way, and have a nice weekend," he said, as he walked off.

By the time I'd reached home the temperature had dropped slightly and rain was falling quiet heavily. It was the beginning of my first winter in Ifold. Due to the clay beginning to soften with the rain, Dad told me I'd be able to use the mattock and spade to begin digging out the foundations for the bungalow. When I got home from school I had to dig out the foundations during whatever daylight hours were left, weather and other jobs permitting. Dad was working and didn't get home until the evening by which time it was dark.

The heavy wet clay, which stuck so tightly to the spade and mattock, took twice as long to remove as it took to dig a spade full. I worked virtually every school day, even if it was for only half an hour; hoping every day I'd get a decent-sized meal and that because of the heavy work I was doing, Dad would forget about giving me the stick. I knew I'd just have to wait and see. The portion size of my meals didn't increase and I realised Dad was determined not to forgive and forget, but to find any excuse to give me the stick because of the embarrassment he'd caused himself. I didn't have to wait long.

A few days after starting the work, when I got home from school, Mum gave me a ten-shilling note and told me to walk back to the stores at Ifold and buy her ten Players Weight cigarettes. I sighed and must have looked displeased as I said, "I only walked past the shop twenty minutes ago; you've cycled past it on your way to and from your day at the Land Army. Could I use your bike please? It'll save me the walk, and I'll be there, and back, in a fraction of the time."

Her answer was short, and to the point. "No you can't; if you can ride the bike to Ifold Stores, you can ride it to Spring Hill and fetch the water in future."

She gave me a sideways glance and added, "Well, what do you want to do?"

I knew I'd have to go, but as I didn't want to give myself another job replied, "I'll walk; I think the bike's far too big for me anyway."

I ended up getting her cigarettes; nevertheless Mum told Dad what I'd said as soon as he got home. That was excuse enough to tell me I was to cut myself a stick when I'd finished all my jobs and before it got dark. I collected and gave Dad one of my previously cut sticks. It stung my legs terribly, but I wouldn't show any sign of distress at all. Dad however showed signs of bewilderment due to my apparent lack of concern. It must have confused him more than I realised, as the punishment I'd normally received for no apparent reason, become less frequent. It was only every three or four weeks, just to keep me in line; or whenever it was thought I'd done something wrong.

Chapter Twenty-seven

I'd had so many walnuts every day from Turpins Farm that I started to save some in the dairy for later in the winter, when there'd be a shortage of fresh fruit.

One morning within a couple of weeks of the start of autumn, I noticed the first of the mushrooms, which had grown during the night, and told Dick the good news. Later that afternoon when I'd finished my milk, Dick took two carrier bags and decided to walk towards Ifold with me, to look at the mushrooms for himself. Within five minutes we'd climbed over the old five-barred gate of the field to have a closer look to see if any were ready for picking.

What a pleasant surprise we got! The further we walked into the field, the more there were. Masses grew out of the soft green grass. Some had been knocked over by the cattle; some were small and still growing, while others were as big as saucers.

"Right," he said, "pick what you want to take home, and remember to add a few extra ones to eat going along. Like I told you the other day, they're good and tasty even when raw; in fact I'm going to have some now, I can't wait."

"I think I'll join you; I've never eaten them uncooked before," I said, picking one up, peeling off the skin, and eating it slowly, feeling a little uncertain of what it might taste like.

He raised an eyebrow, and waiting for my response, just smiled and said, "well then, what do you think?"

"I think they're lovely; it's the first time I've ever tasted them raw, but they're so nice it certainly won't be the last," I answered, peeling the next one ready to eat.

"Good, I'm glad you like them. Now don't forget what I told you," he said, passing me the bag and wagging his finger at me. "Half-fill the bag for me every morning, not forgetting a few for yourself, to eat on the way to school; you can leave them up at the farm for me to collect later. The empty bag will be there for you to collect every afternoon, when you get your milk; then you can pick some more for yourself to take home. You can keep on until the mushroom season has finished."

"Okay," I said, and then looking up at him asked, "when will the season finish? Does it last very long?"

"Well, it's hard to say. It all depends on how much rain we get in the next few weeks, to keep them growing. It's been another very dry summer this year; that's why they're a little late, but the heavy rain in the past week or two has suddenly brought them on." He hesitated for a moment. "It could be four or even six weeks! The last thing we want is a frost, that'll finish them off completely. We'll have to wait and see. I expect the rain has also made the toadstools grow. We don't really need them both at the same time."

"Toadstools; what on earth are you going to do with them?" I asked, unable to hide my surprise.

"You think these field mushrooms taste good, cooked or uncooked, don't you?"

"Yes I certainly do," I replied.

"I'll be driving around the farm on Saturday morning, feeding the cattle and checking the fencing. If you can get here at a reasonable time, I'll take you with me. If they're ready, and they probably will be, you'll have some fungi, the taste and flavour of which you've never experienced before." He looked up the field as he finished talking, at the masses of different-sized white caps of the field mushrooms laid out before us in the damp grass reflecting the light from the breaks in the clouds.

"Goodnight; don't forget to pick your dinner and I'll see you in the morning."

"Goodnight and thanks. I'll have yours with me in the morning," I replied as I started half-filling the bag.

I ate five of the large mushrooms on the way home and wondered what Nan would do with the rest of them. There were seldom any spare eggs; if there were Mum or Dad normally ate them. I thought how nice it would be to have something like chips, tinned Spam, or corned beef, with perhaps some tinned beans or peas and fried mushrooms, providing there was enough heat left in the tortoise stove.

Having shown Mum and Nan what I'd got, Mum half-laughing said, "you must be a mind-reader Robin! Dad's got so fed up with not being able to have a fry-up; he's come home early with a Primus stove he's bought. He'll be over the moon when he sees what you've got. Well done; it's a good old fry-up tonight, and to hell with it all, we'll even have some fried eggs."

I could hardly believe my ears; I'd had a good feed of milk, walnuts and mushrooms and was feeling a little more content and happier than usual. My friendly red robin must have sensed my mood by staying close to my side, singing his head off while flustering around me watching while I did my jobs.

I was sawing logs to add to the already large pile for the winter stock when Dad came home. He walked down the path carrying a five-gallon fresh water can in each hand, stopping when he got level with me. He looked and sounded in a reasonably good mood telling me to fetch the other can of water from the car.

Putting the saw down immediately I simply replied, "Yes Dad, right away."

"Good," he replied, "and while you're there, have a look at the foundations I've been digging this afternoon; you'll be very surprised."

He couldn't have done very much digging, I thought, because the trenches were full of water, which had been unable to drain away due to the dense heavy clay.

When I got there, what a surprise I had. Dad had somehow managed to get a large double-handed pump. By using the pump and removing all the water from the trenches, he'd been able to dig out one side of what was to become the kitchen area.

"You must have worked hard to get all that done, in one afternoon." I commented to him when I'd taken the can of water indoors. "Getting the pump was certainly a good idea Dad."

"Well you may not think so later, because you'll be the one using it most of the time. You simply prime it with a bucket of water first, and it's ready to use; you'll be able to manage it without too much trouble. Make it your first job every weekend, if the weather looks kind. It'll probably take you about half an hour initially, although it'll take longer the more clay we remove between us during the week and weekends."

He hadn't glanced at me once as he'd given his instructions, but looked directly into my face as he changed the subject and said, "Thanks for the mushrooms you brought home, they'll go down well. Your mother tells me you'll be able to get more, next thing you know it'll be a rabbit, I hope."

"No it won't be, it never will be, and you know why," I said.

The silence that followed seemed to last for ages; the atmosphere in the room changed becoming a heavy burden; nothing was said and his face showed no expression. Eventually Dad spoke. "Okay, you've stuck to your guns; you've made your own decisions, and stuck by them. That's all right. From what I can tell lately, you're able to stand on your own two feet. That's good, but just you remember, if you do anything I think is wrong, you'll still get the stick. You do what you're told to do, and when you're told. No backchat and keep your opinions to yourself. Do I make myself perfectly clear?"

"Yes Dad, perfectly."

Nan looked from Dad to me. She looked a little confused, knowing nothing about my disagreement with Mum and Dad over the small amount of rabbit I was given for dinner, while she was away for the week. Trying to do the best thing, she changed the subject. "Talking about rabbits, Jet brought one in this morning, but I couldn't reach what he'd left from under the cupboard. Would you get it out Robin and give it to Wendy? It's the best bit, the two back legs, and the back. That only left the small rib cage and front legs; Jet certainly didn't have much for himself. Perhaps he wasn't very hungry."

Nan didn't realise that she'd 'hit the nail right on the head,' so to speak. What she'd so innocently said was so apt I could barely stop myself from smiling. Mum and Dad stood speechless, glaring at Nan then at me, then each other, their faces showing their embarrassment and guilt.

"I'll do it now Nan. She'll enjoy that, see you later on," I said, retrieving the rabbit and getting out as fast as I could.

"I'll give you a shout as soon as your dinner's ready, so don't go too far," Nan called after me.

Once outside, I ran over and waved toward Mr Lucas's window and Amy came to talk to me. I told her about the field mushrooms and said I'd bring some home for them during the week. She was pleased with the idea and thought her mother or sister would probably make a meat and vegetable stew and add them to it. "That would be lovely; tasty, rich and very much appreciated by all of us," she said clasping her hands together.

"Robin, dinner's ready in about five minutes, don't go far," we heard Nan call.

"You'd better go, otherwise it might get cold. See you soon, bye for now," she said, then as expected adding, "Good night, and God bless."

I instinctively repeated the same to her as I went to eat my special dinner.

Nan had used the new Primus stove, which was sizzling away on the side table. I watched her in awe as she put a fried egg on top of a pile of the first chips I'd seen for months. There were the lovely fried mushrooms in their rich brown juice, corned beef, fried Tomatoes and baked beans. What a meal, and what a lovely smell! Dad came out of the sitting room and passing by me, towards the outside door said, "that was a lovely dinner; I can't remember when I last had such a good fry-up. I hope you enjoy yours as much as I enjoyed mine." I knew from his pleasant attitude and the tone of his voice, he didn't bear any animosity towards me.

It rained heavily during the night so with sensible footwear I walked through the fields on my way to and from school. I'd worn my plimsolls throughout the summer; they'd been ideal, but now they'd be put away until next year. I had a choice of what to wear; smooth black shiny Wellington boots, with an almost flat sole, which I knew, wouldn't give much grip and certainly weren't strong enough for the amount of work and walking I was expected to do. Like the other boys at school, I couldn't wear the dull grey-coloured strong, adult-type Wellingtons with the large heavy grip on the sole; they were only made for feet over the size of thirteen. My feet, like most of the other boys, were only a size ten or eleven. The other footwear was a strong pair of lace-up leather boots, with steel tips on the toes and heels. I didn't think twice about which ones I'd wear; it would undoubtedly be the leather boots. They were strong, comfortable and would last right through the winter, maybe for two.

Neither did we have an alternative to wearing short grey flannel trousers; there wasn't any other length, or type we could expect to get. Boys didn't wear long trousers until the age of eleven years old; even then they were still made of the dull grey flannel material.

Every school day I picked mushrooms twice, leaving some in the farm and taking some home. By the end of the first week I'd given half a bag to Amy Lucas, half a bag to Mr Rose, and over a full bag for us at home.

Chapter Twenty-eight

On Saturday morning, having finished my jobs, I was at the farm by eight o'clock and looking forward to learning about edible toadstools. When Dick arrived on the tractor and I'd helped him load several bales of hay, he drove to the far side of the land and along the riverbank almost as far as Ifold Lake. I opened bales of hay before unloading them for the cattle as we went along.

Within twenty minutes he stopped at the edge of a wooded area. "This is normally a good spot for toadstools, or fungi; I've collected some from here before."

"Toadstools I've heard of before, but I've never heard of fungi. Can you eat them or are they poisonous as well?" I asked.

"Well," he said, pointing towards a small group of plants, "see those growing there, with the long thin white stalk, green cap, and wide, white gills on the underside. Do you think it would be alright to eat them?"

I looked at them for a moment or two then answered, "well they're definitely toadstools and I wouldn't fancy eating them. There's something about them; they don't look very nice."

"You're right. You shouldn't eat them. They're also known as fungi, both the names are correct. The ones, which grow out of the ground, are usually called toadstools, and the ones growing on the bark of trees are usually called fungi. That's what I was taught anyway."

"That's easy enough to remember, but I expect the hard part will be learning which you can or can't eat," I said.

"You'll be surprised how many are safe to eat; it's easy to remember, even though you may not think so. You simply look for the markings to avoid and you can't go wrong."

We moved a little deeper into the wood where Dick frequently stopped to look about the ground and up the trunks of large trees. After a while pointing up an oak tree he said. "Look up there. Can you see those fungi, growing on the side?" Looking upwards several feet, I saw a large cluster of very dark blue, almost black, shell-shaped plants, each with pale cream coloured undersides. There were dozens of them, all growing tightly together, forming a great mass. "Yes I see them okay; they look awful, I don't think I'd like to eat any of them," I said answering his question.

"Well you can; they're called oyster mushrooms, and taste even better than the field mushrooms. There's no mistaking them from any other type of fungi; they're safe to eat, and they grow all year round. I'll come back when all the others have finished and collect some. They're my wife's favourite, so I'll be in her good books," he laughed.

"There's a large beech tree near home," I said while still looking at the fungi, "it's got the same type as these growing out of the side of it; trouble is, just like these, they're too high to reach. The tree's impossible to climb because the first branches are out of reach."

"That's no problem; I'll tell you how to get them down, without climbing the tree," he said, giving me a gentle pat on the shoulder.

"What do you do, cut a long stick, and knock them off the side?" I asked.

"No, don't do that, you'll damage them. Get yourself a long piece of string, or fishing line, and tie a weight, such as a lump of wood, or stone, to one end. Then throw it high so the line slides down between the fungi and the bark of the tree." He flicked his arm upwards as if demonstrating how it was done. "The rest is easy," he said, "simply take hold of the two sides of the string or line hanging down and give them a gentle, but firm tug; the fungi will be sliced from the bark of the tree and fall to your feet, it's that simple"

As we continued walking through the woodland Dick said, "you've got some fishing line to get the oyster mushrooms off the beech tree, haven't you?"

"No I haven't," I answered, "I was going to ask to borrow some of the string from the bales of hay. That's if you don't mind."

"You told me you went fishing, whenever you could. What am I supposed to believe you catch them with if you haven't got any line? I suppose you haven't got any hooks either. Am I to believe you or not?" He inquisitively asked.

"It's the truth," I told him, feeling ashamed he thought I might be lying. "I use a length of string, and a hook I made from bending a pin I'd sharpened to a needle point, and I do catch fish. I wouldn't lie to you about that," I paused, thought for a moment, and then said, "I'm going home."

"Wait," he called out as I turned to walk away, "I'm sorry, I didn't mean to upset you. I said it without thinking, and I was wrong; can you forgive and forget?" He walked up to me and putting his hand on my arm said, "You okay?"

"Yes of course," I answered with a hidden sigh of relief.

"Good for you. Now let's forget all about it."

We walked along the side of the brook towards the river, until we came to a very large mound, completely out of character with the rest of the surrounding land. It was so steep and high it wasn't natural and could only have been man-made. We both instinctively quickened our pace, hastily striding on to the next clump of trees. Everything around us fell silent, as we experienced a strange feeling deep inside which neither of us could begin to explain. Although Dick must have passed the hillock on many occasions, he'd never mentioned it. It was as if it was taboo, as neither of us ever discussed the strange experience we'd encountered, with anybody else.

Within a few minutes of walking through the woodland Dick called out. "There they are; that's what we're looking for; I was beginning to think we wouldn't find any!"

I walked to his side to see what he was so excited about. There were a few dirty brown-coloured toadstools sitting on a thick bulging stem. They were of various sizes, each with a dull green spongy underside; all looked so uninteresting they were barely worth a second glance. "What on earth are they?" I asked, "I've seen a few before, in the woods near home. You can't eat them can you? They look horrible!"

"They're called ceps, or penny bun. Unfortunately, they only grow in the autumn. The taste is unbeatable; they're so good there's no comparison, nothing. I've even heard people in Europe have killed each other for them. Like most of the edible wild mushrooms you can hang them up to dry, and have them during the winter. All you need to do then is put them in soak; they'll soften, and swell up to their original size," he said, then suddenly added, "they're good, trust me, they're very good."

Picking one up and looking at it closely I said, "You can't really make a mistake with them either, can you? They're so different from any of the others."

"Well you can if you're not too careful" he said. "Don't bother picking them if they're flat or thin on the top; if they're green, if they go blue when damaged, or have a narrow stem. Keep to the thick and same-coloured ones, the same as you're holding, and you won't go wrong."

"I see what you mean; there is a difference. I'll help pick some with you; there aren't very many, but by the looks of it, enough for the two of you. I'll get some for myself on the way home, no problem, now I know the difference. I saw some on the edge of the woodland, close to the side of the road only yesterday, they were exactly the same," I said, smiling and feeling happier with myself.

We picked all we could find, and then strode off towards the tractor to make our way to the farm.

Thanking Dick for what I'd learnt and for such an interesting morning, I took another brown paper carrier bag and went on my way to collect field mushrooms, and the first ceps I'd take home.

Chapter Twenty-nine

"Looks to me as if you've got a big load of something or other there Robin," Dad greeted me.

"Yes Dad, I've also got what Dick told me are the best wild mushrooms you can eat; I've brought some for us to try. I've also got some ordinary ones I'll give to Mr Rose when I get the milk."

When I walked up to him and showed him the ceps, he smiled as he lightly shook his head and said, "well your Mum and I won't be trying them, that's for sure! You won't get me eating toadstool, and if you do, and get stomach pains or even poisoned, it'll serve you right."

When I got indoors I emptied the ceps out of the bag onto the kitchen table. I didn't hear Nan come up behind me, until she startled me by loudly saying, "where on earth did you get those beauties from?" She paused, her mouth half-open while smiling, "I haven't seen any ceps since I was a youngster, and they're about the best you can get. They're so good, anybody who knows anything about them, normally keeps it a secret where they were found. You'll never, ever, be able to buy them from a shop. Can you get any more before the season ends?"

"Yes, I know several places. There's quite a few more in the same place as these came from," I answered, then added, "I even saw some this morning on the land where I tethered

Judy out for the day. All I have to do is check if they're the right ones."

Nan having asked me to get as many as I could, told me she'd hang them on lengths of cotton, to dry for the winter. She could understand Dad and probably Mum not wanting to even try the ceps, because they'd both been brought up in London and didn't appreciate some of the country ways. "Mind you," Nan laughingly said, "not that it's harmful, but they'll always eat mushrooms, which grow in, or around cow dung, or piles of horse manure stacked near the farm stables. Edible mushrooms, toadstools, and fungi only grow on nature's natural pure fertiliser. It takes years and years to rot the dead leaves, grass, and undergrowth, to eventually become rich and good soil for all plants." She thought for a moment. "Then again," she added, with a big smile, "it's not a bad thing they don't want the ceps, not when you think about it Robin, it simply means there's all the more for us. I may not get many thanks from your mother, for all the work I do, but at least you've given me an unexpected treat. These will certainly bring back fond memories of my childhood."

"I always thought you were a Londoner, Nan. I didn't realise you knew anything about the countryside."

"Oh yes. Before my family moved to London, I spent most of my childhood in the countryside," she told me to my surprise. "You didn't know that, did you?"

"Well I am surprised; I didn't have a clue Nan."

"You'll know more one day Robin, more than enough."

"Yes, I expect so." I didn't give a second thought to what she'd said as she passed me a few mushrooms for Mr Rose. "Thanks, I'll take these to him now, and get the milk at the same time."

As I walked around the sheds to find Mr Rose, the bright summer sun of earlier in the year, was now a pale and watery round light, just visible in the pale grey sky, between dark clouds. From its position, I knew it was close to mid-afternoon. Wearing only a thin V-neck jumper over my shirt, I felt the chill of the autumn breeze and quickened my pace to keep warm. Almost all the leaves of the hazel trees had either turned a bright yellow, or a golden-brown. Many falling from the branches were lifted by the light breeze and floated around, in various directions, as if looking for somewhere snug and comfortable to settle down for winter.

Being unable to find Mr Rose, I guessed he'd be at his house, and went towards it. As I passed the pond, I noticed all the lily leaves, which normally floated on the surface like large, green shining dinner plates had turned a pale dull faded green, with brown edges. A few beautifully coloured koi carp and golden orfe swam just under the leaves, nudging into them trying to loosen the edges to nibble at. I looked towards where the hide had been built earlier in the summer and noticed old Jack heron; its wings still sticking out, swing gently in the breeze, hanging from the apple tree as a warning to others. There were quite a few gin traps set and ready to operate, scattered in various positions around the sides of the pond; the rats would certainly try to eat the corn laid to lure them into the traps.

Mr Rose must have seen me coming up the driveway because he was standing watching me from the porch.

"Here's your milk Rod; you look cold. How are you, and what have you got in the bag?"

"I'm fine thanks, and I've got a surprise for you. I hope you like them; I picked them about two hours ago. Nan says they should stay fresh for at least four or five days as long as you keep them cool." I passed him the bag saying, "if you like them, could you empty the bag and give it back please?"

He looked inside and his face lit up as he said, "mushrooms, lovely and fresh, thanks Rod. We'll enjoy these for breakfast tomorrow," he continued, as he tipped them out onto the table, "I'm not so sure about only breakfast though; there's enough here for dinner as well, for at least two days. Well done and thanks again!"

"That's okay; I'm only too pleased you like them. I took some home when I first found them during the week. I've given some to Miss Lucas and some to you, that means we're all happy," I said, and then added, "Dick the head dairyman at Turpin's Farm said I could have them. He also told me I could have some edible toadstools and showed me different types, and which are okay to eat."

"Well, I certainly don't want any of those, thank you very much," he laughingly said. "I've heard some are very nice, but I don't know anybody who eats them, or knows anything about them. I've never tried them, and I don't think I'll start now, thank you very much all the same."

We laughed with each other, and said goodbye; then having collected the milk and empty bag, I set off home smiling to myself at what Nan had told me, of the way some people, whether from the town or country, react to the thought of eating toadstools.

Dad, who was still working on the foundations, called out to me as I walked along the path, "I've had enough for today, so I'm packing up. When you've taken the day's logs indoors, I want you to saw as many as you can until dinner time; we can't have too many for the winter."

Within an hour, Nan called me and I went indoors to find her clearing up the kitchen table. "Your Mum and Dad won't even try the ceps; they've told me they want proper mushrooms. That's good in a way, because like I said earlier, it means we've got all the ceps." Then pointing towards the table she said, "sit yourself down while I finish cooking your dinner, then you can tell me what you think of your first ceps."

She'd certainly planned a special treat for me. There were two thick slices of bread, which she'd covered with baked beans, all buried under a large pile of fried ceps. As I popped the strange food into my mouth, for the very first time, Nan closely watched every move, and expression I made. The flavour was certainly unusual; it was lovely. I tried another, and then another, until Nan, showing an enormous grin said, "I don't think you like those Robin, do you?" I don't think you'll like the fried egg either; in case your mother comes out I've hidden it under the beans!"

"They're fantastic; I've never tasted anything so good before. I'll definitely get a load more of these while I can, particularly as you can dry them for the winter."

I told her all I'd learned about the oyster mushrooms and how good they were supposed to be. I wasn't surprised when Nan told me she knew them, even where they grew and how to dislodge them. What did surprise me was when she described in detail another edible one called a chantarelle; I agreed to pick as many as I possibly could before the season ended.

"I'd have thought by now, somebody, somewhere would have written a book with diagrams showing and describing all the different types of edible wild mushrooms, toadstools and fungi; there are dozens, and dozens of them," Nan said looking thoughtful.

"I'm not so sure Nan. If someone does write a book about them one day, you may be sorry because everybody will be picking them, and there won't be enough for us," I laughed.

Thanking Nan for my special dinner, I went outside to finish my jobs, where my friendly red robin immediately met me and began singing his head off. Somehow or other he seemed to know the type of mood I was in, and whether I'd had a good or bad day. It was uncanny; if I'd had a bad day, he'd sit close watching me, giving the odd little chirp every now and then. If I'd had a good day, he'd be in full song, while fluttering around. At times like this, Wendy would watch what was going on, first looking at me, then at red robin, with her head cocked to one side, looking very confused.

Chapter Thirty

When I asked Mum if I could go wild mushrooming, she realised it would be food for Nan and I, and readily agreed, telling me she thought we were both quite mad. Taking the road towards Ifold Stores, I stopped where I'd picked the ceps the day before. Walking into the woodland a little further than previously, I completely filled the large bag to the top with the younger and more succulent ones.

I went straight home and emptied the great pile onto the kitchen table. Nan was speechless, but her face told me enough. Without a word being spoken between us, just big smiles, I headed off towards Ifold Lake to see if I could find any chantarelles near the top end, where the water was very shallow and covered with trees growing through the surface. It was a natural hide for the many different types of waterfowl that nested without any disturbance or fear from predators. Between the water's edge, and the field, which was the boundary of Turpins Farm, the strip of land, which was about thirty feet in width, contained masses of chantarelles. Within five minutes I'd filled the bag, while laughing aloud with joy.

At home for the second time that day I emptied the bag of chantarelles onto the kitchen table; Nan couldn't believe her eyes; she was so pleased, "Where did you get them? No don't tell me, oh my goodness we're certainly in for a feast." Nan put the flat of her open hands onto her cheeks and half-crying and half-grinning with happiness said, "I do hope your Mum and Dad don't want to try these, I think they're the best!" She couldn't withhold a laugh any longer and neither could I.

On Monday morning, I collected a bag of mushrooms for Dick and left them in the dairy as arranged, then continued to face what was to become the worst day at school I'd ever experienced.

During the morning break, there was a visit to the school from the Council dentist; there was also a nurse. Every one, without exception, had their teeth inspected, and almost all of us had to undergo fillings. There were no painkilling injections and the foot-operated drill was so coarse and slow it broke parts of the tooth away, bringing tears to the eyes of many. I had four fillings, but all four teeth were so badly filled, each one had to be extracted within three years. We were told to brush our teeth at least once a day to avoid any problems in future, but nobody said they did, or would. Every one of us had seen a picture of a toothbrush, but no one said they owned or had ever used one.

Next it was the turn of the nurse, whose nickname we were told by Miss Rees, was Nitty Nora. Her first job was simply to look at your hair, and scalp; then she'd dust your head with a fine powder, which she rubbed vigorously into your skin. We were told it was a precaution against any fleas and nits we might have, but none of us did!

We all agreed it hadn't been a good start to the week. Most of us had suffered pain, but it was soon forgotten when we joked about Nitty Nora and the flea and nit powder. At least we hadn't done any schoolwork; nothing at all except messing about, chatting, climbing trees or playing.

As usual on the way home, I popped into the dairy and was met by one of the dairymen. "Hello Rod," he said, "Dick's taken the day off; he's gone shopping in Horsham with his wife and won't be back until tomorrow. Help yourself to some milk, and the empty bag hanging on the door; I've got a lot to do, I'll see you later."

"Thanks," I answered, "See you in the morning."

Alone with Nan, I was able to have a mug of Bovril, and a home-made blackberry jam sandwich. "You've got a slice of Spam, peas, boiled potatoes and ceps for dinner, with bread and butter pudding for dessert. How does that sound?"

"That sounds good to me," I said, looking at the dozens of wild mushrooms stitched through the base of the stem, hanging from lines of cotton close to the tortoiseshell stove to dry. I'd never seen anything like it before; I was amazed! "It must have taken you ages to thread all those Nan," I commented, full of admiration.

"Not so long," she answered, "you picked the good ones like I asked. None of them had the fly, I just trimmed them, threaded them with a needle and cotton and hung them up; it didn't take long at all. Just remember; pick what you can, when you can, and while the season lasts, but for goodness sake do all your other jobs first. Only collect any mushrooms when you've done everything else, and when you've got time."

About an hour later I'd finished my jobs and as expected was digging the footings, when Mum came home on her bike; Dad followed half an hour later. It began to get dark, so I went indoors and sat in the kitchen. Mum came from the sitting room and standing at my side said, "damn it Robin, I had so much on my mind I rode past Ifold Stores and forgot to get some cigarettes. You'd better go and get me some. Put your coat on otherwise you'll get soaked; it looks as if it's about to pour with rain any minute."

I didn't want to cause myself any trouble or get the stick; I just wanted my dinner and to go to bed; I was tired. Nevertheless, with very little choice I could only say, "yes, okay Mum."

Dad appeared in the doorway separating the two rooms; anger clearly showing on his face. He glared at me, and I knew instinctively trouble was coming. "You just stay there," he said, "don't move, and keep quiet!" Unexpectedly he turned to Mum, and still glaring and obviously very cross, he shook his finger in her face and said, "I can't believe what I just heard you tell Robin to do. If you want cigarettes that badly, go and get them yourself. Surely you don't expect him to walk all the way back to Ifold Stores, in this weather, just because you forgot to get your cigarettes, do you?"

"No of course not," Mum lied, "I've probably got enough to last me until the morning anyway," she answered. Then looking at me, to avoid Dad's glare, said, "I'll make do and get some more tomorrow."

Within a few seconds they were both back in the sitting room. Nan and I, virtually whispering to each other, agreed the best thing I could do was to keep out of their way and discreetly avoid contact with either of them for the next two or three days, unless it was absolutely necessary.

The next morning, due to the heavy rain, I had no choice but to wear my raincoat. It was a double-breasted gabardine, which had a wide belt, wide collar, and was so long it came down below my knees. I put on my Wellingtons and my old school cap, and then lifting my collar to help keep dry, set about doing my jobs before setting off to pick Dick's mushrooms on the way to school.

Later, during the day at school, everyone was told they'd be expected to collect rosehips, to be used for making cough mixture, and acorns for planting to grow oak trees. This we were told should be done daily over the next three weeks on the way to and from school, or at weekends. I felt a twinge of concern at the thought of yet another job, even more so when Miss Rees took four of us aside into her classroom. Gradually I began to relax as she explained we'd be excused from making any collections of rose hips or acorns; she was aware of the long walk we had every day and the amount of work we were expected to do at home. We were all thankful and smiled as we all breathed a sigh of relief at the same time!

When I got to the dairy later in the afternoon, one of the dairymen approached me. "Dick's asked me to give you a message as he is working on the far side of the farm. He'd like you to continue collecting the mushrooms, whenever you can. Take whatever you need for yourself, and don't forget to have your milk every day. He'll see you on Friday, when he gets back."

Within half an hour I was home; soaking wet, but nevertheless with my bag of mushrooms. There was little point in going indoors and getting dry, so I got on with my jobs regardless of the weather. I could easily avoid having any conversation or eye contact with Mum or Dad; that I could control, but I couldn't control the rain.

Chapter Thirty-one

On the Friday, as I left school, it stopped raining, and the clouds parted revealing the pale sky for the first time that week. I reached the dairy and went inside where I saw Dick and the other two workmen chatting to each other. They were all laughing and joking, when one of them beckoned me to join them. He was a huge man who, when I reached where they stood, bent down, looked me in the face, and then still smiling said, "your mate Dick's back, as you can see, and what's more, he's got something for you."

I looked at the three smiling faces, and then rubbing my tummy while pulling a pained looking expression, I jokingly remarked, "hello Dick. It's nice to see you back again, but I do hope you haven't got any mushrooms, I don't think I can eat anymore."

"Better than that," he said laughing. "I think what we've got for you, you'll like even more; it'll last longer as well!"

He reached up to a nearby shelf and took down two pieces of polished bamboo, both about three feet long. Then passing them to me said, "we all know you like fishing. We're all too busy to go nowadays, so we've had a sort out of our old tackle which we thought might be of use to you."

I looked at the canes, which made up a two-piece fishing rod. I was dumbfounded. It had two brass ferrules, for strengthening and fixing the pieces together, and a total of four eyes to pass the line through, and a shaped cork handle to hold it by and for fixing a reel. It was brand new. I was lost for words and unable to speak as the other workmen emptied the contents of a brown canvas bag on to the small table.

There was a small fishing reel, completely full of line and ready to use; a small tin of special grease, to smear on the line to make it float; two goose-quill floats; a tin of split lead shot, an assortment of hooks, and an army billycan.

"These are all brand new," I heard myself say, "they've never been used, you've bought them, haven't you?"

"I'll speak for the three of us," Dick answered. "We know you haven't got any fishing tackle, or a rod, except for your name, that is," he joked. "The billycan is just in case you light a fire while you're fishing one of these days, and decide to cook some fish or moorhen eggs while your waiting for your catch; you never know. We're all grateful you save us time and trouble by getting the mushrooms for us. Anyway, consider it our way of saying, 'thank you'."

My mind was turning over, and over; surely they hadn't given me this magnificent gift just because I picked mushrooms for them. I was a little confused and wondered why they'd been so kind.

"If you ever fancy boiling any eggs, the best and easiest ones you can get to eat are the moorhens'," the smaller man said. "You'll undoubtedly get wet feet collecting them, but they're worth it in the long run. What's more, they're easy to cook; simply lightly boil them for a minute or two in your billycan. Moorhens usually lay about twelve eggs; when the hen bird's laid six eggs, you can safely take two. When she's laid eight, you can take three, and so on and so on. The hen won't realise what's happened, because she can't count; she'll simply keep on laying extra ones. Mallard and magpie eggs are also good," he added, "you can do the same with them, but they only lay between eight and ten eggs each. Just remember to make sure the eggs aren't addled."

I was still trying to think of a way of thanking them when Dick smiling, and waggling his finger said, "there are three more things you should know, okay?"

"Okay with me," I said, smiling back at the three of them.

"Right then! Number one: you've now got some fishing line so you'll be able to get oyster mushrooms at any time, okay?"

"Yes I can, and will, thanks to all of you."

"Number two: try fishing in the river, there's loads of gudgeon in it. They're easy to catch and taste as good as rudd, they're lovely."

"Okay," I answered, "I'll try it; I've never given it a thought before, but it sounds a good idea." I was baffled; I'd never mentioned cooking, or eating any fish I'd caught. What made him think or say that, I wondered? Had I unsuspectingly been seen? Or had they put two and two together? Suddenly my thoughts were brought to a halt as passing me a small khaki canvas bundle, he continued, "and this is number three. It's an army gas mask bag. It's ideal for putting your bits and pieces into, including any wild mushrooms or fishing tackle. We all use them for work every day to keep our sandwiches and Thermos flask in; so will you one day, I expect, but until then I'm sure you'll find a use for it."

"I don't know what to say," I stammered. "Thanks very much, you've all been very kind."

"That's alright; just remember if you ever need any help in the future, all you need to do is ask. Now get off home; try your new rod if you get a chance over the weekend, and don't forget the mushrooms on Monday. We'll see you next week."

We all raised an open hand to each other for a brief second as a farewell gesture, and went our different ways.

When I got within a few yards of home, I crept through the woodland to the big beech tree. Leaving the fishing tackle and the bag at the foot of the tree, I quietly sneaked unseen to the back of the lean-to near the kitchen door. Taking a rusty unwanted sheet of corrugated iron, I returned to where I'd left my fishing tackle. Then, choosing a suitable hiding place tucked all my newly acquired gifts away between some ferns and covered them over with the corrugated sheet for protection from the weather.

Eventually, I came to terms with why the farm workers had shown me so much kindness. Because Mum and Dad made very few friends, I was uncertain if they'd ever understand the bond of friendship, which existed between the farmers and me, or indeed the friends I'd made with many of the locals. I felt certain hiding my gifts, until the time was right, would be the best thing to do, if indeed the time would ever come right.

Chapter Thirty-two

The next morning was bitterly cold, and while doing my jobs I noticed the pig had become very lame in its hindquarters. Not having time to stop then, I decided I'd make it a priority to have a closer look as soon as I had time. Dad told me he'd be out until lunchtime but he'd be working on the bungalow for the rest of the weekend.

By the time I'd done most of my chores, Dad had gone. I looked at the lengthy trench, which had been dug for the foundations. To my horror, it was half-full of water, which I knew I'd be expected to pump out before he returned.

When I'd finished two hours later, in addition to the existing blisters on my hands, caused by the rough shafts of the grub axe and spade, I'd worn three more very large ones on my hands. The two on my right hand had burst, so I tore the skin off, allowing them to dry and heal without any delay. I burst the tight, bubble-shaped blister on the left hand with the tip of my knife; then as before, removed the skin allowing the wound to dry and harden naturally. I knew they'd crack open, but they'd heal quicker.

When everything was done, and I'd inspected the pig's leg closely, I realised how much he was suffering. I had to help, if I could, but how? Who could I turn to? Then the possibility of where I'd get help came to mind. Walking quickly to the foot s Hill, I turned onto the track towards Hogwood, ьed dozens of goats, then on past Sid the postman's home, until I reached the small pig farm. The farmer, who'd been cleaning out the sties, stopped as I approached him. We'd seen each other before, but apart from passing greetings, we'd never talked together. Having introduced myself I explained the reason for my visit was because of my concern about our pig's back legs.

After explaining the problem, he told me the best way to give it some relief, was to rub horse oils into its hindquarters three or four times a week. I told him my Nan rubbed horse oil on her hands to ease arthritis. He smiled and said if I used it generously I couldn't go wrong. He then told me if I ran out and couldn't continue the treatment, he'd always help if he could. He was undoubtedly a decisive, helpful and pleasant person, like so many country folk I'd met. After a brief chat, I thanked him for his help and set off for home.

Within twenty minutes I was gently massaging the back end of the pig. It lay, eyes closed, grunting and squeaking with relief from the pain. The sounds it made got quieter and quieter, until all I could hear was deep breathing. Then after a short while the breathing faded away until there was complete silence; I looked to see what had happened and realised it was fast asleep! Then it began to snore, and even my laughter didn't wake it up.

The next morning when I was able, I collected my new fishing tackle and went to try it out in the river, but it was in flood and the flow was much too fast to even try. I gave up the idea and tried my favourite spot on Ifold Lake. When I'd almost made up the tackle, I smeared the special grease on the line to stop it sinking. Then I fixed two of the split shot just below the quill float, adding extra weight to cock it upright and to enable me to cast further. I found if I unwound a few yards of line off the reel and made sure it didn't snarl up on the grass or other plants, I could cast a great distance further than before. I hardly ever missed catching a fish on the new purpose-made hooks; whenever I struck it was fantastic! It didn't take long to catch enough rudd for me, with ample to take home to give Wendy, and Jet a good meal. I lit a small fire and lightly cooked the fish, for the first time in the billycan; they were the best I'd ever done.

Because of the early dark nights, and the hard sharp frosts that would form ice around the water's edge, it was to be the last fishing I'd be able to do at Ifold Lake for several weeks.

After I'd hidden my fishing tackle close to the beech tree and got home, I noticed Dad hadn't done any more digging on the foundations. I'd wasted my time working so hard to pump them out; I didn't mention it to anyone, and it was never mentioned to me.

The weather got steadily colder each day, and the bitter wind felt as if it'd cut right through clothes and skin. Dad found another job for me by showing me how to drain the radiator of the car every evening after he'd got home, just in case it froze up. The frost got thicker and thicker each night, making everything as white as snow; but not my uncovered bare knees, they just went blue with the cold. Fortunately, because of the wide openings leading to each bedroom in the wagon, the fire and the tortoise stove indoors kept the whole place as warm as toast, day and night.

Mum only went outside when it was absolutely necessary: the eggs still had to be collected, and Judy had to be milked, but I was never asked to do it. Mum knew I'd refuse, even if it meant I'd get the stick.

Although there was a boiler that heated the big old iron radiators at school, they barely got warm. The whole place was so cold everyone kept their coats on all day. If they were wet, we'd either wear them, and stay damp all day, or take them off, hoping they'd dry by home time, but we'd be cold all day.

Two weeks before Christmas we had to make paper chains, pretend presents, and decorate a Xmas tree. It was all good fun for the girls, but the rest of the boys and myself thought it was daft, and a waste of time; we knew they'd only be up for a couple of weeks, before being taken down, but we had to do it.

On the last day of school, when we all broke up for Christmas, I called into the dairy for the last time that year and to wish everybody a Merry Christmas. All four of us chatted, telling each other what we'd be doing. It all seemed very much the same as normal; the farm still had to be run, the cows had to be fed and milked each day, and I still had all my jobs to do at home.

"I'm not very happy about it at all," I said.

They all gave a quick, concerned glance to each other, wondering what might be wrong. Dick frowning a little said, "what is it you're not very happy about Rod?"

I put a big smile on my face to ease any concerns they had. They were all eager to hear my answer; they didn't know what to expect and couldn't hold back giving me a half smile. "Well, I had to make paper chains at school this week, and didn't like it. I told Mum about it, and now, I've got to make some for the sitting room when I get home; I should have kept quiet."

They all gave a sigh and shook their heads, as if feeling sorry for me. The smaller of the men chuckled and said. "Well if that's the only thing you don't like, it's not too bad is it?"

"But it's not, it's worse; they've taken the pig away this week and he comes back today or tomorrow as smoked joints and bacon. I spent hours rubbing the poor old thing's legs with horse oils so he wouldn't suffer and now he's gone."

Dick shrugged his shoulders. "Well you've got to eat, and that's what they're for, so try not to think about it."

"I'm not thinking about it, I just hope its nice tasty bacon. I'd really love some; I've not had any for ages, and it really would be a treat" I laughingly answered. "That's not all I'm not very happy about. The mushrooms have all finished; I used to enjoy those, as we all did. Then there are the walnuts, I've eaten the last of them, and they've all gone now. The river's in flood, Ifold Lake's frozen over, so I can't go fishing and to top it all I've got to go up to London with Mum and Dad next week to take some of the bacon to their families as a Christmas present. That'll really be exciting!" I added sarcastically.

We all laughed for a while, and then wishing each other luck, I went home.

Sitting on the gatepost looking as if he wanted to scold me, was my friendly red robin. I felt sure if he could have spoken, he'd have told me off for being late home, causing him to wait for me in the freezing cold dusk. I walked along the path to be met by Wendy, who was always pleased to see me. She must have had some effect on red robin because he suddenly appeared from a bush a couple of feet away singing his little head off. On the face of it everything looked good; I had ten days off school, and all I had to do was my jobs every day, or anything else I was asked.

Christmas Eve arrived and we were due to set off to London in the morning. Judy and the chicken were to be locked up for the day; I was to feed them just before we left. It was one of my jobs, and they'd be fed plenty I decided.

The trip to London was exactly the same as before. I was told to say, "hello," and "goodbye"; otherwise to speak only when spoken to, and to sit in the kitchen and keep quiet. For me, the best thing about the day was the large sandwiches I was given; a different one every visit we made. The best of all was at my Gran and Granddad's where I had two thick slices of bread and beef dripping, with lots of thick brown jelly. The worst thing about the day was when we left Nan with Mum's sister Doss for Christmas. She wouldn't be home until the first working day of the New Year.

I sat in the back seat of the small car going home, with Nan's rug wrapped around me for warmth. I was cold but not as cold as I was when we got home and found the fires had gone out; it was freezing cold. Mum and Dad had eaten well, and went to bed to get warm. Knowing even after I'd lit the fires it'd be a while before the place warmed up, I went to bed shivering. Tomorrow was Christmas Day.

Chapter Thirty-three

The bed was cold, and the heat that would normally have been given out by the two fires, had disappeared through the thin walls and ceiling. I'd curled up like a ball with my knees under my chin for most of the night trying to keep warm. During the summer months, I'd lain in bed baking hot from the continuous heat of the fires and the warmth of Nan's body.

Mum got up and I heard her put the kettle on for tea. Then putting her head around the corner of the wagon opening into the bedroom said, "good morning Robin, Merry Christmas; now get yourself out of bed and light the fires. Then you can open your presents."

Not expecting any Christmas presents, I was surprised at what Mum had said. I got out of bed, dressed as quickly as I could, and set about cleaning the fireplaces out and emptying the ash outside onto the path so that we didn't tread mud indoors.

I collected the firewood from under the lean-to, and then lit the fires. I remember Dad telling me before, should we have been able to use coal or coke, the tortoise stove would have kept alight. As I re-lit the two fires I wished we had, but it didn't take long to warm up, and by the time I'd finished my jobs all four rooms had heated throughout.

The unexpected Christmas presents were a big surprise to me; I didn't realise Mum and Dad had collected them during our visit to London. In particular, I was pleased with my new clothes, which would help keep me warm during the winter months. There were socks, short trousers, and a Fair-Isle 'v' neck pullover. It was a kind thought, but I'd have appreciated it more if it had been long-sleeved with a high neck. To top it all, there was a large special bag containing a box of dates, sweets and chocolate for me with a note that read, 'don't eat them all at once, see you soon, Merry Christmas, love from Nan.' There was even a packet of Spillers biscuits for Wendy and Jet.

Dad told me because it was Christmas, we could have chicken for dinner as a special treat. I was to catch the one suspected of stealing eggs from the others, even though I thought I'd deterred it by trimming the tip of its beak. When I'd caught it, Dad called me over to where he was standing by the side of the chopping block, close to the small stable where Judy was housed. She was still inside, but her head was poking over the low door, watching our every movement.

"Hold the damned chicken still Robin; try to stop it wriggling about while I do the business." He took the head of the bird in one hand and stretched it over the chopping block. In the other hand he held the billhook.

The thought of what he was going to do made me shudder. "You can't do that Dad, it's not right! Do it properly for goodness sake." I quickly said, not thinking of his reaction.

"What do you think I'm going to do? If we're to have chicken, this has to be done doesn't it? It's the only thing to do," he remarked shrugging his shoulders.

"Yes of course" I answered, "but not like that Dad. You wring its neck, painlessly, and then you pluck, and draw it. I've seen it done many times before."

Dad released his grip and I was left holding the whole bird again. He smiled at me and sticking the billhook back into the chopping block said, "I've never owned chicken before, or seen them killed, but as you seem to know what to do you've just talked yourself into a job, so get on and deal with it; good luck!"

He was right: I'd learnt another good lesson in life, and one Dad had been trying to teach me for ages; to shut up, and to keep my opinions to myself!

"When you've finished come indoors and you can have some breakfast for doing it. Then before dinner I'll take you down to Loxwood and you can buy me a pint of beer as my Christmas present." What he'd said was a surprise, but what he said next wasn't. "You won't get any breakfast or go to Loxwood with me if you don't let Judy out; she was shut up all day yesterday, and you've forgotten all about her today."

"I haven't forgotten her Dad; I've fed her as normal but left her shut up because she wasn't milked yesterday and needs milking soon. If she isn't, she'll be in a lot of pain," I said, then added, "I'm sorry but I thought you'd be aware of that."

"Oh! Yes of course," he lied as he walked away, "I'll tell Mum now."

When I'd finished the unpleasant job with the chicken, and started to clear up, I noticed my friendly red robin watching me. He hadn't sung a single note. For some reason, which I couldn't understand, I felt guilty, and a little embarrassed at what he'd seen me doing.

When I got indoors, Mum didn't seem very happy and told me she would cook the chicken, but if I wanted the giblets for

Wendy and Jet boiled, I should do it myself. There were much more important things to do, such as milking Judy. Dad had reminded her: I knew they'd both forgotten to do it.

My breakfast, the first for months and months was on the table. It was a large soup plate full of porridge, a tin jug of goats' milk, and a packet of lump sugar. I pulled a chair up to the table and sat down to eat. Pouring the milk on top, I added four lumps of sugar, and tried to mix it all together. It was stone cold; the milk floated on the top and the sugar wouldn't mix into the solid lump. I tried to eat it, but it was awful and I couldn't. I spooned off and drank the milk and sucked the lumps of sugar. I gave the porridge to Wendy who gulped it down. Mum never knew!

By midday Mum had given me a half-crown piece to buy Dad's Christmas drink for him, and told me I could keep the change. I'd never owned any money of that size before; it was an enormous amount and worth a small fortune to me. I gripped it tightly in my hand and thought how lucky and rich I was!

A little later, with me sitting in the front seat, Dad and I set off in the car for our trip to Loxwood. "You don't very often get the opportunity to sit in the front seat Robin; it's the second time in as many days. What's more, it's the first time you've ever owned a half-crown piece; you must be feeling pleased with yourself I'll bet. It must be Christmas!"

"Yes Dad, I do," I said looking out of the window and remembering a time when he'd been concerned and caring for me, always having my best interest at heart; those days seemed a lifetime away, probably never to return. I told myself that even though it would be difficult, I shouldn't feel self-pity, or sorry about the past; it wasn't a good thing to do. Anyway it was Christmas-time and I was going out with Dad to buy his present and despite his inexplicable mood swings over the past months he was in a good mood today, and so too should I be.

When we got to the 'Onslow Arms' I gave Dad the half-crown piece; it was warm and left a deep indentation in my hand where I'd been holding it tightly. He took it from me, and noticing the mark it had left he said, "don't worry Robin, I'll bring you the change, and you can bet you'll own lots more of these in your life, you just wait and see."

The weather had changed; there was a clear blue sky and the cold wind had dropped. I stood under the porch, which stopped any wind and rain from driving through the cracks of the doorway into the pub. Dad brought me out a glass of ginger beer and a packet of Smiths crisps, which I sprinkled with salt from the small blue bag inside. I stood there enjoying, watching and listening to the sounds of the river. The water level had dropped to half its normal height as it raced along at a tremendous speed. It made a thunderous roaring noise, which could be heard the distance of two fields away as it uncontrollably gushed through the open floodgates, and poured down, into the large deep whirling pools many feet below at the old Brewhurst Mill.

Within an hour, with four pence change, left from the half-crown piece in my pocket, we were back in the car on our way home.

Dinner took ages to cook, but when it was ready Mum told me she could only get two meals on the table at the same time; I'd need to wait until they'd eaten theirs. When mine was ready I'd be called.

I took the uncooked giblets outside followed by Wendy; I gave her the large neck, which was a good meal on its own, a square of chocolate and some of the biscuits Nan had bought. I looked at her tummy; it was like a small barrel, not surprisingingly I thought, with what I'd just fed her, plus the porridge she'd eaten earlier. It would only result in one thing for her this afternoon; a good sleep!

Jet came running at my first call. I gave him all the giblets, some biscuits and chocolate; he also had his fill. I was pleased, because it was difficult for him to catch food at this time of the year and he'd need to be fed, whenever possible.

I waited about for another twenty minutes to half-hour before I heard Mum calling out that my dinner was ready, and on the table. Getting back, as quickly as possible, I could hardly believe my eyes. There was an enormous meal steaming hot; there were two complete chicken wings and lots of slices of the breast, stuffing, roast potatoes and different types of vegetables, all covered in thick brown Bisto gravy. I never realised Mum could cook so well!

The sitting room door was closed, so I called through the thin wall, "thank you very much, it looks lovely."

Dad raising his voice for me to hear answered. "That's all right," he called, "you've earned it today; just enjoy it, and don't make a noise when you do the washing-up. We're going to have a doze for half an hour or so."

I didn't know what he meant by saying I'd earned it; instinctively I looked up towards the top of the doorway at the stick. It was as if it was laying there waiting for me, but I didn't care. I sat down at the table near to the stove for extra warmth and ate a good and filling meal. When I'd finished I stayed sitting at the table for some time. I was so full I could hardly move, and I dozed for about half an hour.

When I awoke it was getting dark. I lit the Tilly lamps, washed-up then went outside and did all my jobs before emptying the car radiator in anticipation of an overnight frost.

When I got back indoors I could hear the snoring through the wall. Having cleared up the best I could I waited until about eight o'clock; they were still asleep. With nothing else to do I went to bed.

On Boxing Day it took Dad and me from dawn until dusk to clear the last of the hazel stumps from the land. The next job would be to cut them up for firewood, and stack them up to dry under the lean-to.

Every day for the next week we worked hard digging out the foundations for the bungalow. When the day came for Dad to return to work, I was left to continue alone. The blisters on my hands caused by using the water pump had begun to heal, but now had broken open and bled. New large swellings had appeared, shining and stinging the insides of my thumbs and fingers; they were caused by the amount of gripping and chafing they'd received on the wooden handles of the tools I used. Only when I went back to school did they begin to heal. Mum never returned to the Land Army.

Chapter Thirty-four

As I passed through Turpins Farm for the first time in three weeks, I noticed how much the winter cattle fodder had grown over the last month or so. Most of the kale, and sugar beet was fully-grown, and large enough to be picked.

A little further down the field, I passed countless rows of sprout plants. The upright green stalks with small leafed tops were almost waist high. Masses of tightly packed, round-shaped growth had formed on either side of them; they looked young and tender, almost ready for picking, a huge job for the merchant who'd buy the whole crop. The green tops, and sprouts, would be reaped and sold separately at various vegetable markets, and shops within the area.

Everything was the same at school. A few of the children talked about the presents they'd received, while most of us just played or climbed trees, waiting for the bell to ring. We all thought the first job we'd have to do would be to take the Christmas decorations down, but we were wrong. It was to be our second job. The first was to listen to Miss Rees tell us what most of us had for our special Christmas dinner, and what presents we'd received. I found out most of it was true; she was a terrible gossip and nothing was kept private. Her plan was to involve us all in joint conversation, and it worked. What she didn't know she would ask outright, in front of the whole class; we relished every moment listening to the answers, never considering the embarrassment, or in some cases, the jealousy it caused.

When it was home time, and just before we went our separate ways, I asked Tommy how Miss Rees knew so much about us all. He'd been going to Loxwood School from the age of six; I thought if anybody would know he would.

"It's very easy: I used to wonder the same," he replied, "then I realised nearly all the other kids live in, or close to the village; they do don't they?"

"Yes, almost every one, except about five of us," I answered.

"That's right," he said, and then continued, "everybody within the area, including Miss Rees, normally gets their shopping in the village. You can imagine how much chatting goes on when she meets the parents."

"Like the old saying, 'talking the hind leg off a donkey,'" I jokingly said. "I hope she never meets and has a chat with my parents."

Tommy looked down at the grass verge where we were standing. Then shaking his head gently said, "oh it's too late for that; she knows exactly how far you walk to school, all the jobs and work you have to do at home, what your Mum and Dad do during the week, the amount and type of wild stock you have. Miss Rees will even know what and how much food your family eat every week."

Dumbfounded, it took me what seemed forever, to say, "how could she? It doesn't seem possible."

"Simple, it's so simple," Tommy replied. "I bet your Mum gets most of the weekly shopping from Loxwood Stores; you do most of your jobs on a Saturday morning, at the same time the deliveryman arrives with the order."

"Yes, but what has it to do with Miss Rees? I don't understand," I muttered.

Tommy smiled in response. "The delivery man, he's a terrible gossip. He doesn't stop asking questions, never misses a trick, so to speak. I've been told he's very polite and friendly; people like talking to him, to catch up with the latest gossip. He's probably the only person they've seen all week; he just talks, and listens. He likes his customers, and they like him."

"Well, there's nothing wrong with listening, or talking to anyone, providing it's the truth, is there?"

"No, not at all," he replied, bursting with laughter, but putting his hand up in front of his mouth to hide the embarrassment of his two broken front teeth, "not at all, but when it's Miss Rees. Can you imagine it?"

"My goodness yes," I said, immediately joining in his laughter.

"Mind you Rod, if the weather's very bad, or it gets dark earlier, she sometimes lets us go home before the others. We didn't have to collect the rose hips and acorns a few weeks ago because she knew exactly how far we have to walk every day, and what work we have to do when we get home."

"So generally speaking, all the gossiping between the two of them does us a favour," I said.

"Yes, I suppose if you look at it that way, you could even say she's kind." He shook his head as he was thinking. "I've never thought of it like that before. Anyway, see you tomorrow." We both set off home our different ways; Tommy along the old canal bank, as far as Ifold Lake, and from there he would head towards the silo. I walked across the field towards the dairy.

When I met Dick and the other two farm workers, my first reaction was to greet them and to ask if they'd had a nice Christmas. They didn't appear very happy with what I'd asked, and the look on their faces reminded me that every day is the same for the farmer; milking, feeding, and other work still has to be done regardless.

On a table by the side of the doorway I noticed a whole sprout plant cut off at the base. All the growth on its sides and top remained intact. A large round sugar beet as big as a man's fist lay by the side; it looked like a swede, except that the thick skin was a dark brownish red. The roots had been cut off short and the top leaves had been trimmed down leaving enough to hold for ease of carrying.

The smaller of the men walked to the table, then turning to face me said. "We all had our fill of these sprouts earlier on, but we've saved these for you to try. Have you ever eaten them like this before?"

"No never, not raw," I answered. "Cooked yes, but never sugar beet. At least I don't think so."

"Well, you don't know what you've missed," Dick remarked, "we'll show you. What's more there's plenty, so if you fancy some at any time, just help yourself."

"They're good; the only way to find out is to try them. We wouldn't eat them if we didn't like them." The other two men, each chewing a mouthful, nodded their heads in agreement with Dick. There wasn't much choice left to me; I put one into my mouth and chewed. It only took me a second or two to taste and appreciate the flavour; they were good!

"These are lovely," I said, "they're almost the same as cooked ones, but harder with a stronger taste. They really are nice." They all seemed pleased I liked them.

I was then shown how to split open the hard stalk by striking it repeatedly on the top of the nearest gatepost. When it had been smashed open it revealed the best edible part of all; the core! There was no doubt in my mind; it really was the best bit. The pale green lengths stayed firm but broke into short pieces as it came out of the hard stalk. It was like biting into a carrot, it would often snap off between my teeth, but was nicer, rich in proteins, and much better for me.

Dick smashed the large sugar beet open in the same way. It took two hard strikes and broke into large lumps; the inside was firm and pale orange in colour. Not only was it good to eat it was also full of protein; not surprisingly, it was good fodder for the cattle and other farm animals during the cold winter months.

"I've got to go and do my jobs before it gets dark. My Nan's been away much longer than expected, but thank goodness she comes home today. She's being collected by Dad from Horsham, I hope."

"Yes, you'd better be going," Dick remarked, "we could be in for some snow pretty soon, so best if you make for home. Don't forget you can take some sprouts, or whatever, whenever."

"Thanks I will; they all taste so good I'll get some for my breakfast on the way to school tomorrow."

Thanking them, I was about to leave when the big man said, "I'm going to Ifold Stores, I'll walk along with you. We can keep each other company."

After we'd walked a few yards, I was striding out at twice my normal speed. It was the only way I could keep up with him, as being such a big man his normal strides equalled two of mine.

Before reaching the stores I noticed a few flakes of snow float to the ground. They settled for a moment or two without melting. Looking upwards I couldn't see any clouds; the sky was a dull grey.

"How did Dick know it was going to snow," I asked, "there isn't a cloud in sight?"

"That's easy; there may not be any clouds but what colour is the sky?"

"Grey; it's grey all over. Just like it is when it rains," I answered.

"Not quite. Look closely." He stopped walking and pointed upwards. "Now look up there and I'll explain, then you'll know for next time." It was almost an instruction. I stopped and did as he'd said.

"It's all one thick, dark, dull grey solid mass. There's no lightness yet there's no blackness. Not a breeze or movement to be felt or seen. It's very low and dense and gives the impression of being very heavy. The reason is because it's full of snow. What's more I'm sure we'll get plenty tonight."

"How on earth do you know all that?" I asked, wondering if he was right.

We'd almost got to the end of our journey together when he asked me a question, which made me stop dead in my tracks with surprise. He walked on a few more paces before he realised I'd stopped, and then stopping also he looked back at me. The expression on my face made him frown and re-consider what he'd asked. He thought he'd upset me: he hadn't; it was the unexpected question that shocked me.

"You're not upset are you? If you are I'm sorry. I didn't mean to"

"No, but when you asked what name I preferred to be called, Rod or Robin, I was a bit shaken. Only my family ever calls me Robin. How did you know I had a nickname?"

"My wife told me; it's not a secret is it?"

"Of course not; I was just a bit shocked that's all, because I've never told anybody. I wonder how your wife found out."

"It may have been from somebody in the village, or your parents may have said something at one time or other." He stopped talking; I could see him thinking. It was his smile that told me before he did. "But then again, we have all our shopping delivered from Loxwood Stores every week. It was probably the deliveryman; in fact I bet it was; I'll tell you about him."

My smile matched his as I said, "there's no need; I found out only today, but thanks anyway." We talked and joked for the rest of the short distance to the stores. He went inside and I continued on towards home in the light falling snow.

It was while walking along eating the last sprout that I realised how lucky I'd been. I received supplements of various foods. Whether given freely by others, or helped by nature, I'd been able to eat wild or cultivated fruit and vegetables; nuts, mushrooms and fish during the summer and autumn months.

I had thought winter would be my hardest and worst time: I'd worried about not finding anything extra to eat, but thanks to my friends at Turpins Farm I needn't have worried. I was feeling a little more content as I strode on. It'd soon be getting dark. The snow kept falling, getting heavier and heavier. I turned the collar up on my gabardine raincoat; it wasn't rain or windproof, but it was all I had!

Chapter Thirty-five

Before I went into the kitchen, I kicked my boots against the side of the lean-to, and gave my coat a shake to remove most of the snow. Once inside, I knew Nan was home and had been for several hours. All the dirty clothing, which had been left since she'd gone away, was washed and hanging up to dry. The largest saucepan we ever used was simmering on the tortoise stove. It was half-full, and gave off the wonderful smell of a meat and vegetable stew.

After Nan and I had greeted each other and chatted for a while I told her I'd noticed Judy was still tethered out and that she must be wet through and freezing. "I wonder why Mum hasn't brought her in." I commented.

"Goodness knows Robin, but then again, it doesn't take much working out does it?" She answered, shrugging her shoulders.

Before I could say anything Mum, who must have overheard Nan and me talking came into the room and told me to fetch Judy in and dry her off before milking in case she was wet; then to take the torch and get extra milk. She then asked Nan to get her dinner ready for about ten minutes time when the milking was done. Dad would have his when he got home. As usual I was to have mine when all my jobs were finished.

It stopped snowing during the night and in the morning there was what looked like a white carpet four to five inches deep over the ground. After dressing I put on a pair of socks, and pulling them as high as I could above my knees, I folded them over the tops of my Wellington boots to stop the snow from falling inside and making my feet cold and wet for the rest of the day.

As I opened the door to go outside, my friendly red robin startled me as he unexpectedly quickly fluttered across in front of me from under the lean-to roof where he had been sheltering overnight. Wendy dashed past me to be first outside where she frolicked in the snow. It came up to the top of her legs but she didn't care, and she loved it, jumping about with delight. Jet had other thoughts; he slowly sneaked forward until his front paws came in contact with the cold snow. Then, lifting his tail bolt upright shook his whole body, turned towards me and darted between my legs, and back indoors. He knew being curled up in the warm would suit him more than going out in the cold. At least he had a choice, I thought.

Scraping a clear area near their hutch, I laid extra food and eggshell grit down for the geese and chicken and left them locked inside the run for their own safety. It was the best thing to do. I'd seen Charlie's footprints around the edge of the fencing and knew he wouldn't be killing for the fun of it today; he'd be on the prowl for food at anytime; day or night. I gave Judy extra food, hay, and straw; there was no point in tethering her out for the day, not in the snow-covered land and woods.

Nan told me Mum had got up while I'd been outside, and had gone back to bed. Dad wouldn't be able to get to work in these weather conditions. Nevertheless as it was impossible to do any work about the place I was to get to school, if I could. I sat at the table and had a mug of hot Bovril to warm me up.

Shortly after I set off I felt something in my pocket. Taking it out, I wondered what on earth it could be; I certainly never put it there. Opening the small package I was full of curiosity; then I realised what it was, and how it got there. It was a fish-paste sandwich. Thanks Nan, I thought as I bit into it, you made sure I got breakfast today; it'll do me a treat

The narrow road was completely covered in crisp white snow; it almost reached the top of my boots and crunched, leaving deep footprints with each step I took. The only tracks I saw in front of me in the flat, undisturbed crisp surface were those of a few deer or the ones Charlie made when he'd crossed the road during the night or early morning.

The silence seemed unnatural; there wasn't a sound to be heard, no matter how hard I listened, nor the sight or indication of a bird anywhere. The clouds were still dark and heavy, and again everything was still; not a movement. It seemed very strange at first, but I felt quite relaxed and comfortable within the atmosphere and began to enjoy the peace and tranquillity.

There were two people inside Ifold Stores, with lots of footprints around the entrance. A tractor was parked outside; I looked at the tracks the big tyres had left, they were the only tracks in the road, and came from the Loxwood direction. From the side of the road where I'd stopped, I realised it was the one I'd ridden on with Dick at the farm. The smaller of the dairymen was the driver and as he came out of the stores he offered me a lift to the farm. They all seemed surprised to see me, saying they didn't think I'd be at school due to the bad weather. I made a joke by telling them I was tough and if they thought this was bad weather, they should wait until winter got here, then they'd really know what it was like. I wouldn't have dreamt of telling them I'd had no choice.

Dick told me they were going to hook up the trailer to the tractor and feed the cattle with hay and sugar beet. They were in the large field down near the church and river and if I wanted a lift to climb on. I ended up getting my second lift of the day, saving about twenty-five minutes walking.

Chapter Thirty-six

There were no more than twelve other children at school. They all lived within a very short walking distance and like the dairymen couldn't understand why I should walk all the way to school in this weather. Miss Rees told me three times she would have understood if I hadn't shown up. By one o'clock it was snowing again and getting so heavy we were all sent home. I was taken aside by Miss Rees as we were leaving. "I want to speak to you Master Davis," she said, loud enough for everybody to hear. "I don't want to see you again in this school until the thaw sets in, do you understand." She looked very cross. "Now get off home while you still can, and remember what I've told you."

"Yes Miss, thank you," was all I could say.

Thinking about what she'd said to me, as I walked across the fields towards the farm, made me wonder what Mum would say when I told her. I could only hope the snow would stop overnight and have thawed by morning. The farm buildings were empty; the cattle had been brought in from the field and put into the two large barns for shelter. Everybody had gone home but as usual, a beaker of milk had been left on the table for me.

Through the falling snow I could only see a short distance in front of me; it got deeper and deeper. I was glad when I got home where I was surprised to find the evening supply of logs had been stacked by the side of both fires. Dad had brought them in during the morning; he'd done the job for me! All I had to do was to lock up the chicken hutch; nothing else could be done outside.

While Mum and Nan listened to the wireless for the rest of the day, Dad read his building book to help with the work needed on the bungalow. For no apparent reason, I was allowed into the sitting room, where I sat whittling fishing floats from some of the kindling wood. When I'd made half a dozen or so, I painted them bright colours to make them attractive. As it was a water-soluble paint, I knew it would wash off as soon as they got wet; nevertheless, it kept my mind and hands occupied for an hour or so and I was pleased with the result.

Not a word had been spoken all evening by anyone until, having sat in silence for two hours or more I spoke generally. I began by saying I'd met and been told quite a lot about Dad's family, but I knew nothing about Mum's, except Nan was her mother and there were two sisters. I asked about my grandfather, where they all came from originally, where they all lived and worked, and how Mum and Dad had met. The reply was quick and cold, as if rehearsed many times. "Never mind about your grandfather or where Nan or I came from, and never mind about how or where your father and I met. It's not important; you'll find out everything you want to know, all in good time."

I wouldn't give in, even though I knew my questions would get me into trouble; I had to know. They'd answer some of them surely. I took the chance, and told them I remembered my early life and Dad collecting me and taking me to London. I asked why, and then told them I could recall most of what had happened, but I didn't tell them how much I could remember. I told them of several of the families I'd stayed with for short periods of time; then described all I remembered about the bombing and about Kit and Bob, the two people who had loved and cared for me and whom I thought were my parents.

I explained why I then thought Aunt Meena and Uncle Bert were my parents, and had done so, until told otherwise. I asked why Dad had hardly ever visited me and why, Mum never did. There was a very long silence, which seemed to last forever.

Eventually Mum answered. "It was during the war: it was all done for the best and the only thing that could be done at the time; now shut up! That's all gone and forgotten; I never want to hear another word about it."

Dad, who I knew had been pretending to read his book, looked at me and quietly said, "your mother's right; we did all we were able, at the time. We're all happy now, so just think yourself lucky. Now forget the past, and only think of what the future could bring."

I looked towards Nan, maybe for some sign of understanding, or comfort. She remained looking down; there was nothing she could do, or say. Even though Mum had turned up the sound of the wireless, it was overcome by the loud noise of Nan's metal knitting needles clattering together with great force; I could see and hear her frustration. I sat staring at the logs burning on the fire, the flames licking the inside of the black soot-covered brick fireplace. I thought of the past; I'd been happy. I thought of the way I was cared for now, and I wasn't so happy. Then as Dad had told me, I thought of the future. It made me shudder.

I never would have believed that, in the not too distant future, all the questions I'd ever wanted to ask would be answered. One day, quite unexpectedly and without any consideration for my feelings, I was casually informed of the most devastating information about myself I could ever imagine. Within minutes almost everything in my past began to fit together, eventually becoming crystal clear.

Chapter Thirty-seven

It snowed every day until the end of the week, getting lighter and softer every time. Apart from various animal tracks, the only other clearly visible signs of movement were those of a few carthorses or tractors with iron-spiked wheels. There was no doubt in my mind that neither was being used for work on the land, but simply as an effective means of transport to and from the shops.

Ifold Lake hadn't frozen over: the temperature had remained above freezing, and soon the weather turned milder. I was often able to see small openings in the higher and lighter grey clouds, revealing pale blue sky. The light shining through the gaps reflected like glittering water on the smooth white snow. It was possible for me, on several occasions during the week, to catch fish from the lake by using only a baited hook tied directly to an old piece of string line. It was a length I'd used on many occasions before but fortunately hadn't disposed of when given my fishing rod.

It felt comforting and peaceful sitting around my little wood fire under the big old tree, even though surrounded by snow. Cooking my catch and keeping warm, it reminded me of my favourite place; the big old beech tree near home where I'd enjoyed so many happy hours.

The thaw set in on Friday night and the melting snow dripped from the trees and bushes non-stop until midday on Sunday. By Monday it had gone, and everything was soaking wet. The footpaths turned into mud tracks, as did a lot of the lanes around the area. Dad had laid down two narrow flat metal paths; they were lengths about eight feet long linked together and had large holes pressed into them. He'd placed them the width of the car wheels apart, from the edge of the road, onto the land. On their surface I could see the mud from the tyres making me realise their usefulness and importance. Dad told me later they were called 'Marsden Matting,' and were used by the Army to help lorries and trucks drive over stone or sandy beaches without getting stuck. They'd also make it easier to get the car and delivery lorries through the mud and on and off the land.

I knew as soon as the sun peeked through the clouds that everything would be back to the normal routine; and it was. Wandering about for a few hours a day with Dave and Michael, sadly came to an end, but it'd been a good and enjoyable rest for us all.

Because we still had plenty left in reserve, there was no need to cut any logs or kindling for over three weeks. Instead, Dad instructed me to make a start on digging the cesspit out of the hard clay, several feet away from the back of the bungalow. The guideline size of the surface area had been marked out; it needed to be nine feet deep and nine feet wide by twelve feet in length. Any water I pumped from the bungalow foundations was to be channelled into the hole and would be stored, as if contained in a metal tank, by the hard yellow and blue clay. He then told me it would be held there ready for use in mixing the cement and concrete we'd need for the foundations and brickwork.

Dad put his hands in his pockets, then looking directly at me said. "All you've got to do is remove half the topside, to about four feet deep; that'll be big enough to hold all the water for our needs. It needs to be done by the beginning of spring. I'll help you whenever I can, but you'll be the one doing most of it I'm afraid. Don't worry about the rest of the cesspit; it'll be finished at a later date."

There was complete silence for a moment or two, then in a voice no louder than a whisper he added, "one way or the other, I don't care how, we must get the main brickwork started this summer."

As he walked away, I thought he might be concerned with the workload facing him. I knew what my involvement would be, and I was worried. Nevertheless, when Dad and I had worked or been out together in the past, I recalled he'd often been considerate and understanding towards me so, even though I didn't have a choice; it might be a good thing for me if we did work together.

I felt a half-smile take shape on my face. I realised I was in the position of being able to tell my own father not to feel sorry, or sad for himself; it wouldn't make the situation any easier. Instead he should get on with the job and try to forget any problems; I knew that turning them over and over in your mind would only make them worse. I would have loved to tell him, but I didn't dare.

Dad and I worked shoulder-to-shoulder, weather permitting whenever we could. My work was to break the clay open with the mattock, while Dad shovelled it up and out of the hole away from the sides. The first blisters appeared on his hands the second day. I'd used the mattock over a thousand times before in the same way as using an adze for splitting logs. The skin on my hands had become tough and hard with many corns; they wouldn't cause me any problems at all. I'd learnt to perfect my timing down to a split second and only a small amount of energy was required to use all the tools to the best advantage.

Dad's blisters burst, eventually turning into hard corns. He never mentioned them once; I thought perhaps he'd realised that if he had, I wouldn't have felt sorry for him, in fact I might even smile. He told me how pleased he was with all the help I gave him. I asked if I could have extra food to help keep my strength up; taking the opportunity, I reminded him of all the other work I had to do. He told me he'd mention it to Mum which cheered me up immensely; whether he did or not, I never found out, but nothing changed.

Chapter Thirty-eight

Earlier in the year I'd been very concerned about where I'd be able to find another supply of extra food during the hard winter months. But there hadn't been any cause for alarm because my friends at Turpins Farm had solved the problem for me. Now it was fast approaching springtime and all the remaining sprout stems and sugar beet had been fed to the cattle; there was nothing left. New growth was beginning to show in abundance on the walnut tree Dick had damaged so severely, and I realised there was some truth in the rhyme he'd told me about the woman, the child, and the walnut tree.

There weren't any plants I could eat, nor were there any bird's eggs at that time of the year; fish seemed to be the only answer, but I could only catch them once or twice a week.

When I thought of bright-eyes I realised it would be impossible to catch and cook them during the week. But if I could catch them and then sell them, I would be able to use the money to buy extra food from Ifold or Loxwood Stores. Because of the excuse I'd made before, I didn't want to ask Mr Rose if he'd lend me his snares; I knew he'd agree but would ask me why I'd changed my mind and I knew it would embarrass me too much to tell him. Instead I thought of another idea, and hoped it would work.

It was three days before I saw Dick and the other two dairymen together. I knew what I wanted to ask them, but I needed to be successful in explaining my idea to get them to agree. I started by telling them about the amount of bright-eyes I'd seen most days around the perimeter of the large field where I'd picked the mushrooms which we'd all enjoyed so much in the early autumn. They all agreed without hesitation.

"Well, if you all enjoy a rabbit dinner, why don't we catch some?" I said, hoping my question sounded casual, as I wished so hard for an agreeable and definite answer.

Dick answered me within seconds. "We've only got two snares between us; we're not much good at catching them. Goodness knows it's not for the want of trying, time and time again. We seldom bother any more; it's not worth the time and trouble. Occasionally we bag one with the gun but we're just too busy. We'd like to very much, but we can't."

As pleased as I was with what Dick had said, I knew everything depended on what I was to say next. I put one hand behind my back and crossing my fingers for luck said, "my friend Mr Rose taught me how to set a snare and all he knew about catching bright-eyes, paunching, and skinning. I could catch them for you; I've done it lots of times."

The big man sat himself on a milk churn, then folding his massive arms, grinned at me and almost laughing said. "Well my little friend what are you going to get out of all this? Do you want to take the odd bright-eye home for yourself?"

"No I don't think so, but I could use your two snares to catch them. Maybe set them on my way home every day, and make any collections each morning. If you think it's fair, perhaps I could have every fourth one for catching them." They watched me as I moved towards the table and took my drink of milk.

"If you say okay, I won't be taking any home; instead I'll sell them to Mr Sopp the butcher. He'll pay me one shilling and six pence for each one and I won't need to paunch or skin them first. It would be difficult anyway, ending up a bit smelly before I went to school."

Dick looked at the other two dairymen. There seemed to be some kind of silent communication; time seemed to stop. It was important to get approval, and I believed all the while I had my fingers crossed, I had a chance.

"Alright then; you can do it, but don't sell your bright-eyes to the butcher, we'll pay you the same price for them. Now then, when do you want to start? And what are you going to do with the money you may earn?"

They'd accepted my idea! "I'll buy some chocolate or sweets, and I'll start today, on my way home," I said, partly telling the truth, then adding, "there's one thing you should know."

Dick looked at me, and as he spoke I saw a deep enquiring frown on his forehead. "Oh dear me!" What should we know then Rod? You'd better tell us," he joked.

"Well," I said, "during the summer months of June, until the end of August, the does normally give birth to between three and seven kittens each month. If at any time they have, or show any sign of bearing their milk, or I see any kittens at all, I shall stop setting the snares immediately. I don't want to kill them; I'd much sooner leave them alone and give them a chance throughout the summer. They'll have enough to cope with from Charlie, badgers, stoats, weasels and crows all trying to feed their own young." I made a further excuse by saying, "it means there'll be more for next year anyway." The smaller man nodded his head in agreement. "Quite right; it's a shame a lot more people don't think like that, well said. Now, I'll get the snares for you, because it's time we all went home, and you've got to set them yet."

Dick laughed. "It's nice to think you're so considerate, I'm sure we all approve but," he paused and then said, "cats have kittens, not rabbits, you're wrong there!"

"I don't think so, not from what I was taught," I said. "Cats do, yes; so do rabbits, and so do ferrets; they're all called kittens."

"He's right Dick," the smaller man said, "I'm sorry to tell you, but I've also heard they're called kittens."

Dick smiled and shaking his head laughingly said, "I don't believe it! Here we have a young country boy, who can set snares when us old country boys can't. He knows when or when not to set them, and tells me the young are called kittens. It's all too much for me I'm going home. Well done, good luck with the snares, and we'll see you tomorrow."

As I climbed over the gate into the large field, at least a dozen bright-eyes bolted for cover, flashing the white danger sign of fur under their scut. So great was the effect, the whole area in front of me cleared within seconds. Their runs were almost everywhere around the edge of the field so that I didn't know where to start. Nevertheless once I'd made a start it only took a few minutes before I'd finished.

When I got home Mum, who would have normally been sitting in the other room in front of the fire at this time of day, was in the kitchen waiting for me. She looked concerned, and so did Nan.

"Where on earth have you been? You should have been home ages ago."

I didn't dare tell her where and what I'd been doing. "I just went for a mooch. Why is something wrong?" I asked.

"Yes; Jet's been under the cupboard since coming home early this morning. It doesn't matter what we try or do, he won't come out. He left a trail of blood on the floor when he came in; it was pouring from his front leg, and he's covered in it. For goodness sake try to get him out." Mum sounded very concerned, then looking at me as if asking for help, added, "when Nan or I try to put our hand in under him he spits, hisses, and claws at us. You try and get him out, we can't!"

As I knelt down in front of the cupboard to try and draw him out from underneath, I noticed the scratch marks on the back of their hands; they weren't deep wounds, they were only given as a warning to keep away. I hoped I'd be able to get Jet out, and treat his wound; I felt his cold body curled up into a ball against the back wall, and putting my arm slowly over him I could feel him shaking. He kept silent; the only movement he made was the lightening of his body, as I slid him out to where I could see the damage.

All the fur, skin, and most of the flesh on his front left leg had been ripped off down to the white smooth bone. It hung loosely from the first joint, and completely covered his paw, like a small shredded sock hanging inside out. I knew the skin, about two inches in length, which had covered his lower leg would need to be cut off; otherwise it would turn gangrenous and he'd surely die.

Mum and Nan look at each other horrified and speechless. "What shall we do? It looks terrible; how do you think he did it?" Mum asked.

Looking up at her from my kneeling position, I couldn't stop myself answering sarcastically, "I don't know how Jet did it Mum; or as you might say, it's all in the past, only think of the future. All I'm concerned about is how to help him." Then looking at Nan I spoke quickly, "will you help me?"

"Yes of course I will. What do you need?"

After a moment's thought, I said, "I need Mum's small sharp nail-scissors, and the big ones; the wooden medicine box, some clean strips of rag, some brown paper, some string, and some plain cardboard."

Mum who'd remained silent asked, "Is there anything I can do Robin?"

"Yes Mum; I need a bowl of warm water, and a cloth to clean the wound. I also need a dry cloth to put over Jet's head for a minute or two. I'll also need your help to hold him still. Is that okay with you?"

She didn't answer, but started to do what I'd asked of her.

When everything was to hand, I laid him on the table and gently bathed his leg. It was a mess; there were long deep scores on the bone and the muscle running the whole length from the leg joint, down and parallel with the sinews to his paw. Fortunately no bones were broken, but most of the flesh had been torn away. The bleeding had stopped, and while he was gently being held, I was able to clean the whole area. Then I carefully trimmed off the two or so inches of stripped hanging skin up to the very edge of his thick pads. When I'd completed cutting it off, I laid it onto a piece of paper where it looked like an open-ended fingerstall cut from a black fur glove.

The next part of the job was the worst. I covered him with the towel and Mum and Nan gently but firmly held him down on the table by his three good legs, while I soaked the whole raw wound with iodine. He wriggled and tried to free himself from the stinging brown antiseptic; I knew it was painful but the wound needed to be sterilised and it was all we had. When I'd finished, I gently held him under the towel for a moment or two, until eventually he gradually began to relax. I covered the wound with Germolene, and then wrapped the badly damaged leg in strips of cloth, which I covered with brown paper to help absorb any extra ointment. Then making a cone shape from the smooth cardboard large enough to cover the whole leg, I loosely tied it up under Jet's chest and tummy. He had no choice; being unable to walk he could only rest and allow the wound to heal.

I'd done all I could for him; now it was a case of waiting. Nan laid an old pillow by the stove and gave him a bowl of milk. It didn't take him long to settle down after his ordeal. It was as if he knew we'd done all we could to help him.

I realised he'd been looking for food and accidentally got caught in a gin trap. I knew from where. Jet had ripped and torn the flesh and skin off, by tearing his leg free from the iron jaws that held him so tight. The pain must have been excruciating, much worse than the hunger pains, which were the main reason for him being caught in the first place. Mr Rose probably wasn't aware of what had happened; it certainly wasn't his fault so I decided not to mention anything about it.

Chapter Thirty-nine

The next day while talking to Mr Rose I learnt he'd found a gin trap had been tripped and snapped shut with a small amount of black fur caught in the metal teeth. He'd guessed it was Jet's but as it was such a small amount he thought he'd probably escaped with only a fright. After I'd explained it was quite a serious wound we agreed there was nothing we could do; Jet was simply looking for food. We both knew he'd been unlucky, and he'd only kill to eat. Most other cats, would capture, play, torture and seriously maim small creatures; watch them suffer, then when they got bored would kill, simply for the fun of it and take the prey home as if to show off. Mr Rose told me that all animals throughout the world that killed other creatures for food would only do so when hungry; their prey would be completely safe at other times. There were only three murderous animals he knew of: the fox, who in the main was just a stupid Charlie; he wasn't as bad as most domestic cats, but far worse than all, was man. He can kill for all the same reasons but he is the worst because he's the cruellest of them all. He plans to kill for excitement; for the pleasure of watching the misery he has caused and the control over life or death of what are normally defenceless and often harmless animals.

Jet started hobbling around the kitchen within three days; he was definitely getting better. I took the cardboard splint off his leg leaving the bandage on. I knew he wouldn't try to gnaw it off because he didn't like the unpleasant taste of the Germolene ointment. He was over the worst and I took the bandage off completely five days later, once the flesh had become firm and he could lick the wound clean himself. Being fed regularly, his leg healed quickly as he got stronger each day.

Every day after school I fixed snares for bright-eyes at Turpins Farm. Most days I caught one, sometimes two. Dick and the other two dairymen were pleased; I was grateful, as I didn't have to do anything except catch them. During the week I was occasionally able to buy a bread roll, a meat pie, or chocolate. Jet and Wendy were given all the giblets but I withheld the meaty necks, which during the week I'd cook for myself. Nobody ever knew.

The half of the cesspit Dad wanted dug out to hold hundreds of gallons of water for mixing the concrete was completed by the early spring. He was pleased with the result of the hard work we'd done; digging out the last of the foundations only took another month or so. We then had to wait for the fine weather of late spring to settle in before the concrete work could start.

As the buds began to form on his fruit trees, Mr Rose showed me how to graft new shoots from one tree branch onto another. He'd previously cut various types of plum and apple shoots, soaked them in water and wrapped them in paper, which he had hung down his well to keep cool. He showed me how, and where, to cut the end off an established but small branch and gently slice into the bark without damaging the wood. Using my pruning knife, he showed me how and at what angles to make a slanting cut and trim above and below the buds of last year's shoot, or bud-wood, which he called a scion. Then carefully lifting the bark he inserted the scion under the bark onto the branch to make a perfect contact, like a foot into a shoe. Then they were bound together with raffia and the whole area was covered with a wax. He told me we'd made a crown graft. Next he taught me how to make a difficult bark graft. I thought it was the better of the two because it was quicker, easier to do and very neat. Over the following days we grafted different types of plum scions onto plum trees, as well as various apple scions on to apple trees. He told me most would grow; he already had a dozen or more fruit trees with up to five different fruit on each one. He explained how it could be done a slightly different way with roses. He had done it many times before and although it would take up to three years before they were fully established I'd be able to see some of the results this summer.

When I eventually found the right time one evening, I told Dad what I'd learnt. He seemed interested and suggested it could be a way of earning extra money. He said that not many people could do it, and as a part-time hobby the experience might come in handy; perhaps when we've got some rose bushes or apple trees I'd practise on them.

Then changing the subject completely he said, "by the way, your friend Michael came round to see you. Apparently he and his Dad are going ferreting tomorrow morning and if you want to go with them be round his place by eight o'clock; he said you can take Wendy with you if you want to."

"Would it be okay Dad, or do you have something you want me to do?" I asked.

"You can go if you want to" he answered. "You've worked hard with me for several weeks and you've behaved yourself;

I've not had to give you the stick for a while. I'm glad of that because my hands are so bloody sore, it would have hurt me more than it hurt you."

We looked at each other and smiled.

"Good I'm glad," I joked, "now you know how it feels."

He smiled. "I thought you might do, you little sod." Then changing the subject said, "I suppose there's no chance of you bringing a rabbit home if you get one, is there?"

"No Dad, no chance at all," then quickly I added, "I'm only going to watch and help."

He knew exactly what I'd meant.

My friendly red robin was under the lean-to when I went outside in the morning. He and his mate had decided to build their new nest in the gap on the ledge between the wall, and the roof. It was an ideal spot; it was safe and dry, and close to the chicken food; neither would be concerned about anybody passing them closely to go in, or out, of the wagon. They seemed identical in size; their bright red plumage trimmed with a light brown back and wings and white underside was the same and they both had tiny black shiny eyes, and a pointed beak. The only way I could tell the cock bird from the hen was because he was the cheekier and came within a few inches of me. He sung almost non-stop, collected most of the twigs, soft feathers, hair and moss to build the nest, and kept other robins or intruders off their territory whenever necessary. Neither of them ever left their territory and no other robin ever entered it. The hen was in charge of building the nest and sitting on the eggs to hatch once she'd become broody and laid them. He had an easy time once the nest was finished; all he did was to watch what was going on, eat, sing, and then help feed the hungry chicks after they were hatched.

Chapter Forty

With time to spare, I was about to set off for Michael's place when Nan called out to me. "You may be out a long time today, so your Mum's asked me to make you a sandwich to take with you. Have you got time to wait?"

"Oh yes Nan, definitely yes. Thanks very much," I said.

I was given an enormous cheese sandwich, which was put into a paper bag with two pickled onions. In the back of my mind I wondered what had made Mum so considerate, but didn't care; she'd had a nice thought.

By the time Wendy and I reached Michael's I'd eaten half the sandwich and both pickled onions; they were good and filling and set me up for any work I might need to do during the day ahead. I was invited into the kitchen where I sat at the table; it must be Wendy's and my lucky day I thought. I was given a mug of tea and she was given scraps of meat.

Michael's Dad told me I was to call him by his name, which was Frank. As I hadn't been ferreting before he showed me everything we'd need, and explained how they were used. First there was a wooden box with an opening at the top, fitted with a leather strap for ease to carry over the shoulder. He opened the box and inside was two cream-coloured ferrets with small bright pink eyes and long slim smooth bodies. They were so beautiful and perfect the sight of them took my breath away; I was speechless. There was a third one in a separate compartment from the others, which was exactly the same but with slightly darker fur. They stood up and put their heads over the sides of the box, sniffing at the air with little pink noses and looking around all the time. Frank explained the two light-cream ones were the females called gills, whereas the slightly darker one was the male called a hob. There is another one, which is sometimes used, called a polecat, he told me, but he didn't use them.

He put his jacket on and picking up the box said, "right, I'll take the ferrets. Michael, there's some sandwiches, two bottles of tea and the nets in the canvas bag by the door, you take them. Rod you take the spade, just in case we need it; but I hope not. I'll tell you more on the way; it's going to be a nice day, so let's go."

Wendy didn't stray further than five feet from my side as we walked up the road. At Bakers Hill, we headed towards Hogwood; then up the mud track through the hazel wood leading us towards the top end of Ifold and the old silo. Michael had been ferreting with his Dad before and knew the general procedure. I didn't know anything about how it was done at all and listened to every word Frank said, as he explained what we'd do and the hopeful results we could expect.

Halfway along the track we came to a grass clearing with a bank running along its edge. We left the path and followed the bank along the grass until we came to a small rabbit warren containing ten or more burrows. From the canvas bag Frank took out the nets used to cover the holes; they were about two feet square with a cord threaded between the holes of the nets around the edges. Attached to each cord was a wooden peg for pushing into the ground to keep them in place. When we'd covered all the visible holes, we searched around the area looking for additional small burrows used only as emergency escape holes and partly buried under dead leaves, dried grass, or ferns. Frank explained they were called pop holes, and were used by the rabbits when there was danger underground from ferrets or stoats.

When everything was in place, Frank slipped one of the gills down a well-used burrow and we waited. Within a few minutes we heard the thumping sound from underground; the bright-eyes warning signal to the others of danger. Within an hour, eight had dashed out of the pop holes, and had been caught and entangled within the nets.

"Well, I think that's about all we'll get from this warren; now we've got to wait and see if I've fed the ferrets too much, not enough, or just right" Frank said, as he walked away to start collecting the nets.

"What does he mean Michael? Fed them just right!"

"Well Rod, if they've been overfed, they'll be tired and will curl up with the bright-eyes to keep nice and warm, then fall asleep. If they've been underfed, they'll eat as much of the bright-eyes as they want, then fall asleep; but if they've been fed just right, there's nothing for them to do, so they'll come out by themselves."

Michael gave me a mournful look and added, "if she doesn't come out, we'll have to dig her out; it'll take ages, so keep your fingers crossed she does."

I paunched all the bright-eyes we'd caught, then for ease of carrying, cut and crossed the back legs. I ate the remains of my sandwich, after which I was given one of theirs and a swig of tea before the ferret slipped out of the burrow and we were able to set off to look for another decent-sized warren.

Further along the bank we came to a single burrow, which we could see, from the paw marks in the entrance, was in regular use. We found four pop holes, which we covered with the nets, and Frank slipped the second gill into the hole. Within half an hour we had three more bright-eyes; everything was completely silent, and we waited for the ferret to come out. Nothing happened, so the hob was put down the hole to flush her out. If he couldn't flush her out, we'd have problems I was told. Within ten minutes he slipped back out; he kept on being put down again but kept returning alone. He couldn't get her to come out, she remained down there, and we could only wait.

Half an hour later Frank told us he didn't think the gill was going to come out for a long time yet. So we took it in turns to dig until we could reach her. Fortunately the ground wasn't solid clay, as it was at home, and we were able to dig and remove the soil without too much trouble. Each time we changed over from each other Wendy would dive into the hole and unwittingly help us by scratching out the loose soil left in the bottom of the trench. We were quite surprised when Michael, digging about three feet down, came across the large root of an oak tree that was growing about twenty feet away! As we were working at an angle of about forty-five degrees, we dug over the top of the root and onwards towards the centre of the burrow.

When it was my turn, we agreed I should clean and widen the sides of the trench as it was beginning to narrow. Wendy, who was behind me, scratching the soil out between her back legs must suddenly have decided to have a closer look at what I was doing. As I drove the spade downwards to clear the side and cut through some small roots, Wendy suddenly stuck her head around the side of my left leg between the spade and the large oak root. Fortunately I missed her head by a fraction of an inch, but caught the top end of her ear between the sharp edge of the spade and the tree root. There was one almighty yelp; then silence as she carried on scratching at the soil as if nothing had happened. I knew it was a nasty wound as I could see the tip of her left ear hanging and swinging from side to side. It was only held on by a small amount of skin still intact on the thin edge. Within seconds there was blood spattered over the side of the trench, and down the side of her neck and front leg. I dropped the spade, picked Wendy up and stepped up onto the flat ground to inspect the damage.

Kneeling down, I had to hold her tightly, as she was wriggling, whining, and panting with excitement to get back down the trench to scratch out more soil; her bright pink tongue was hanging out twice its normal length and dripping with sweat. Her ear didn't seem to bother her, as the three of us looked at the damage. From about half an inch down from the very tip, with the exception of about one-quarter on the thinner backside, the whole width of ear was completely severed. We agreed it couldn't be left just hanging, and it would be impossible to stitch it together. In any event we didn't know of any vets in the area. I couldn't bandage it up because she'd scratch it off within a few minutes; therefore only one choice remained; it had to be cut off cleanly, otherwise it would never heal and would become infected.

I'd need to make a quick, clean and straight slash, and use both hands to hold the ear steady. Frank very gently, but firmly, held Wendy's body, while Michael stroked her head to comfort her. Opening the curved blade of the pruning knife I held the two separated pieces of ear together and slipped the cutting edge between the two up as far as the attached edge. I knew the blade was as sharp as a razor, because I regularly honed it with Dad's very fine Carborundum stone. It only needed a flick of my wrist, and it would be over. Without looking at either Frank or Michael I concentrated on what I was about to do, then quickly said, "ready?"

They were both about to answer; one was about to answer, "ready," the other, "yes," but before they could, the slash was made quicker than the blink of an eye, and the tip was off. Wendy was left with a shorter ear than she'd had which now ended in a perfectly straight line.

Within seconds she was back down the trench scratching at the soil as if nothing had happened; we all breathed a sigh of relief and carried on digging. An hour or so later we'd dug down to a depth of about three feet and Frank lay in the trench to put his arm inside the burrow. "I can feel the bright-eye and I've got him. I think we're there at last", he said, looking up and smiling. He stood up and stepped out of the trench. "I'll give her two minutes and because she's alone, I bet the ferret follows." She did, very soon afterwards and was put back into the box. We put the soil back into the trench and let Wendy, whose ear had stopped bleeding, and who showed no concern following her ordeal, enjoy herself by helping in her own way to back-fill.

We were walking along the edge of the bank separating the hazel woodland from the grass area, when Michael suddenly put his arm out to stop us; put his finger to his lips to quieten us and pointed ahead. We looked towards the spot he had pointed out, and there sitting upright was a large bright-eye. Frank put his hand into the canvas bag and withdrew a catapult, and a large shiny ball-bearing. I'd used a catapult before but I'd never seen one made with square elastic; they'd always been made from a strip cut from a car inner tube. Frank signalled us to remain still. He slowly crept forward then stopped when he was in the right position to have his shot. Lifting the silent weapon he took aim, by simply looking at the target with both eyes open. The elastic stretched over a foot, he paused a second and released the shot. It travelled silently - so fast, all I saw was the bright-eye keel over.

Michael and I walked over to him; we were both amazed at his accuracy, and he was smiling as he said, "well lads we've worked hard digging; Wendy's lost part of her ear and we can't carry any more. It's been a good day, so let's go home."

Chapter Forty-one

About twenty minutes later we were back at Frank's house. Michael returned the ferrets to their wire-fronted boxes while Frank hung the bright-eyes in the scullery. Michael's Mum slid the steaming kettle onto the range, which was the same as the one used in the kitchen by Aunt Meena.

Frank gave me a bowl of warm water, a piece of clean rag, and bottle of iodine to clean Wendy's damaged ear. She sat quite unconcerned as I gently washed the wound and cleaned the side of her face and leg. The bleeding had completely stopped, but I could see the damage caused by the blunt edge of the spade. I knew it would become very sore, within the next twenty-four hours.

Michael's younger sister Jenny gave Wendy a bowl of milk, and after a few more meat scraps she was dozing by the side of the stove. Frank kept bees at the bottom of the garden and we all sat at the large kitchen table, with a mug of tea and a honey sandwich, talking about the day's events. I asked about the catapult, and told them I'd never seen one like it, or as powerful! Frank explained it was made from special elastic. Michael had the same, he told me, and one day he'd show me how to make one.

"Well, Wendy's going to be okay, that's one thing; what's more, she's got enough giblets to last a couple of days, she's earned them," Frank said. "Now what about you Rod?"

"What do you mean; what about me?"

"We've done well today, especially after all the digging we did and catching thirteen bright-eyes. As a small reward I want you to take two home with you."

"No; definitely no!" Then realising I'd answered much too quickly and abruptly, I felt embarrassed and hastily added, "thanks very much anyway."

"What on earth do you mean; no? Doesn't anybody at home like them?" He said.

"Yes I think so, but no; I don't want to take any home with me, thanks all the same."

"Okay, you're the boss," Frank said. "I'll sell ten of those bright-eyes for food without any problem at all. I've got an idea; tell me what you think, okay."

"Okay," I answered.

"I've got some of the special square catapult elastic in the shed. I've also got a well-shaped half-round ash crotch to give a perfect aim and grip. I've also some old soft leather to use as the shot holder." He returned my smile as he added, "what do you think so far?"

"There's nothing else I dare to think, is there?" I asked.

"Oh yes there is," he joked, still smiling. "I'll make it for you now, as a way of saying thanks for your help; it'll only take ten minutes or so. When you take it home you must also take a jar of my home-made honey. Is that a deal Rod?"

"You bet your life it's a deal; it's better than anything. Thanks very much."

Michael and I watched as his Dad cut, shaped, and whipped the ends of the elastic around each end with a strong thin fishing-line material. When he'd finished, it was the best catapult I'd ever seen. I was surprised how small it was, fitting in my hand and pocket perfectly.

We all had another mug of tea, and I told them about Jet's bad luck at being caught in the gin trap; how a lot of the muscle in the lower part of his foot had been damaged but his limp would hopefully get better as he got the strength back. I said it wasn't anybody's fault, but we now had two injured pets and I didn't know how Mum or Dad would react to what had happened today.

"If you explain what happened, and that it was unavoidable, they'll understand won't they?" Frank asked.

"I'm not sure; there's no way of telling, I'll have to wait and see," I answered.

"But it wasn't your fault; it was Wendy's own fault being over-excited" Michael said.

"Yes I know and so do you! But they will remind me I was responsible for her."

Frank looked at me and said. "I'll tell you what we'll do. We'll walk back home with you and explain exactly what happened. Wendy's alright anyway" Frank said.

He must have read the horrified expression on my face and realised how much trouble it could cause me. "Why not take a couple of bright-eyes home; I'm sure they'd be pleased?"

"They would be Frank; but no, I'll only take the honey. Thanks for the catapult; it really is an unexpected surprise. My first day ferreting was terrific; I've really enjoyed myself and would like to come out with you both again one day, if you've no objections, that is!"

"Of course you can. I'm going to explain to Michael about all the different birds in the area very soon; you're more than welcome to join us, so if you'd like to come along I'll see you then. Good luck!"

Having told them I'd like to, then thanking them again, I set off home. We were about half way when Wendy began carrying her head slightly one-sided. I knew the bruising was coming out; it'd begun to swell and the ear was beginning to feel heavy. There was nothing anybody could do.

Dad was levelling the ground a few yards inside the front gate and stopped me as I said hello and went to walk past. Wendy went straight indoors.

"While you're here, I'll explain the next job we've to do Robin." He paused for a moment and then continued, "all the materials should arrive tomorrow some time. There's a lot to do, and it's going to take a long time, so listen carefully." He sounded as if he was apologising as he spoke, but I knew he wasn't.

I looked towards the end of the plot of land and saw Mum walking our way. She didn't look annoyed or angry and she wasn't shouting; I guessed she hadn't seen Wendy's ear. As she got closer she looked at me and said, "what on earth have you done to Wendy?" My heart almost stopped with fright; she knows, I thought. What's she up to?

"Why, what's wrong?" I heard myself say.

"Well," Mum answered, "she came in; I heard her have a drink and the next thing I saw was her curled up into a ball, fast asleep on her blanket."

I gave Mum the honey and told her it was a gift from Frank and he'd made me a catapult for my help during the day. She seemed pleased, then spoke to Dad for a while before going back indoors. Wendy must have been so tired after her busy day she'd had another drink, before lying down on her left side. Mum couldn't have seen the damaged ear. I was safe:

I knew it'd only be for a short time, but I was safe for the time being.

"Now then, as I was saying, listen carefully to what I tell you," Dad said, as he sat on the edge of the water pump. "Tomorrow, fingers crossed, we should have a twenty-five gallon drum delivered. I want you to position it close to the end of the Marsden Matting, and make sure you fill it every day with buckets of water from the cesspit. It'll be for mixing the concrete on the two large sheets of metal which are also being delivered." He paused, beckoning me to sit on the side of the wheelbarrow, before continuing. "We should also get two full loads of ballast, a full load of sand plus a ton of cement in hundredweight bags. There'll be five thousand sand-faced bricks, which I want stacked up as soon as you've got time. What do you think so far?" He asked.

I took a deep breath and then puffing-out my cheeks, gave a deep sigh and answered, "I don't think that's all Dad; there's more to come isn't there?"

"Yes there is," he said. "Every day the weather is dry, I want you to thoroughly mix fifteen shovels of ballast with three shovels of cement and leave a large hole in the middle for me to add the water, turn it over and lay it to form the foundations, when I get home."

"Wow it's going to be hard work Dad; but I shouldn't have to carry the water in a bucket from the pit to the tank every time, because I'll turn the pump around the opposite way and draw the water from the pit, directly into the tank. It'll save a lot of time and hard work."

"Good idea Robin! Now, if you do it before your other jobs, I'll be able to make a start as soon as I get home. If I'm late or it rains, you can cover it over with some corrugated sheets and I'll use it the next day."

It was early evening and Wendy was still asleep when I decided to tell Mum and Dad about the accident to the tip of her ear. I didn't want them to find out for themselves. I started by telling them about the ferret staying down the burrow, how we dug the trench and how the mishap occurred, and that Frank, Michael's father wanted to come home with me to explain how Wendy became over-excited and that it wasn't anybody's fault!

Mum leaped up and dashed into the kitchen. Within a few seconds there was one almighty scream, "Bern, Nan, Robin come here quickly!" Dad and Nan got up straight away and went to see what the trouble and fuss was about. All I could hear was Mum shouting, "look what the little sod's done! He's cut her ear off, the little sod. Robin get in here now, you wicked sod."

I waited a few moments, and then went into the room expecting trouble, but not what was to happen next. For the first time ever, Mum hit me; it was across my face with such force, my top lip split open. Nan put her arm around me, and then looking directly at Mum said, "I'm sure it was an accident Babs. He wouldn't do Wendy any harm; he's so fond of her. It must have been unavoidable as he said. Perhaps we should have listened to Michael's father, and let him explain."

"I don't care what the little sod says, just look at my Wendy!" I was surprised to hear Mum say 'my Wendy.' Normally she didn't care about her at all, or even bother to feed her; now all of a sudden she was 'Mum's Wendy.' She changed her stare from Nan to me and between almost clenched teeth said, "I entrusted her to your care, you did it, therefore it's your fault. Now go and cut yourself a stick. Your father's going to give you a good hiding. If he doesn't then I shall, you little sod."

I tried my best to explain time and time again, but no matter what I said, Mum wouldn't listen

I walked into the woods and collected a ready-cut stick, then trimmed the ends as usual. Being previously cut they'd always helped in the past to ease the mental and physical pain I would have to endure. This time it didn't work as before, as under Mum's orders, Dad spared me no mercy.

Chapter Forty-two

The next morning, Mum came into the kitchen, looked at my calves and said, "you won't want the teachers and the other children to see the weals on your legs. They'll know you've been misbehaving one way or the other, so keep your socks pulled up all the time to save yourself any embarrassment."

"I'll try, but none of the other boys have their socks pulled up; we all have them down. They'll all know why, if I pull them up. Don't concern yourself; I shan't feel embarrassed in the slightest, I'm not the one who should."

Nothing more was said, but Nan gave me a wink as I walked out.

Later in the afternoon, after I'd set the snares and reached home, I noticed the building materials had arrived. Very soon I'd be starting another big job, but the first thing I had to do was check the condition of Wendy's ear. The swelling had gone down, and the wound had dried out completely along its whole length; it seemed to be healing nicely. She appeared to understand what had happened to me and made a fuss every five or ten minutes, no matter what I was doing. I got changed into my old clothes, while Mum completely ignored me. I thought she might have felt a little embarrassed after what I'd said about my socks earlier in the day.

I left all my normal jobs until later, as instructed, and made a start on the new ones. Dragging the iron tank as close to the ballast as the water pipe would allow, I reversed the pump inlet and outlet and filled the tank to the top. It didn't take very long to get the fifteen shovel-loads of ballast on to the two six feet square metal sheets; it was much easier to move than the heavy wet sticky clay. When I'd added the cement, I mixed it all together as instructed and left it ready for Dad to add the water to make the concrete. Fortunately the deliveryman had neatly stacked all the bricks; he'd done it instinctively when unloading the lorry and it certainly saved me a lot of work.

Nan gave me some corned beef, with a large pile of vegetables for dinner, followed by a chunk of bread covered with Frank's home-made honey. I'd only just finished when Dad walked in; the first thing he did was to greet Nan and ask her if Wendy was well.

"Yes she's fine, has been all day; she's been outside with Robin since he got home. No problem at all Bern, forget all about it."

Dad looked down at Wendy who was sitting close to me and leaning against my leg.

"Wendy, come here," Dad said.

Wendy completely ignored Dad's command and remained unmoved.

"Wendy get here. Now!" Nothing happened; it was as if she'd gone deaf. "Get here. Now!" Dad repeated snapping his fingers.

Wendy still leaning against my leg looked up at me as if asking to stay where she was.

I put my hand on her head, and then giving a gentle push said, "go on, there's a good girl."

She crouched low, as if she'd done something wrong and slowly crept forward. When she'd got midway between the two of us, she stopped and looked back at me as if waiting for me to call her back. "Go on there's a good girl, go on," I said pointing and encouraging her towards Dad.

Wendy slowly crept forward until she reached Dad's feet, then stopped and sat.

Dad reached down and gently held up her ear for inspection. After a moment he stood upright and looking directly at me, said in a low tone, "you're lucky; it seems to be drying out and healing quite well. Keep your eye on it, and keep it clean, then she should be alright."

"She'll be okay Dad!" Then speaking a little louder I added, "won't you Wendy?"

Hearing me say her name, she spun around, took three quick paces and leaped into my arms and began licking my face. Dad and Nan looked at each other and laughed.

"I think she's more like your dog, Robin, but don't tell your mother I said so!"

"I noticed you'd mixed the ballast and cement, and filled the water tank. Any problems?"

"No not really Dad, except I couldn't move the bags of cement. They're far too heavy for me to shift. The deliveryman stacked the bricks; it saved me a big job. The tank and the metal sheets for mixing on were no problem, and the ballast is so much lighter than the heavy clay, I can manage a full shovel-load at a time. No problem at all." I answered.

"Good, how long did it take you, to make the mix, from start to finish?" Dad asked.

I thought for a moment, and then replied, "well to refill the tank, then to add three of cement to fifteen of ballast, then to mix it by turning it over and over about four times. To do the job properly; about half an hour, maybe a little longer."

"If you can do it every day the weather's fine, we'll finish all the foundations and have the brickwork up to damp-course level by autumn; that'll be fantastic."

Dad turned to Nan and asked, "where's Babs?"

Dad didn't expect the answer he got from Nan. "She's in the other room, she's not in a very good mood, I'll tell you now."

"Why on earth not; has Robin done something wrong and upset her again?" He looked at me, while waiting for Nan's answer.

"No Bern! He hasn't done anything wrong; neither did he yesterday when you gave him the stick over an accident." There was a harsh accusation in her voice and I'd never seen her look or sound so angry.

"Oh my goodness, what is it then?"

Nan's tone mellowed as she quietly explained the reason for Mum's mood. "Babs couldn't cover the deep weals you inflicted on Robin yesterday; his socks wouldn't stay up; therefore everybody at school has seen them and guessed what happened. She wasn't very happy about that, I can tell you."

"Oh bloody hell!" Dad muttered.

"Wait until I tell you what happened next," Nan continued. "Babs decided to get the bus to Horsham and buy him some new long socks that would stay up; she was determined it wouldn't happen again.

"Well, she must have been in a really strange mood to get the bus," Dad commented.

"That's the trouble," Nan said, half smiling, "she didn't get it. Let me explain: we all know the last bus in the morning is at ten o'clock, and the first in the afternoon is at two o'clock; that's a four-hour gap. Okay so far?"

Dad and I, a little bewildered, looked at each other and both answered, "yes."

Nan directed the rest of the story at me. "Mum left in good time to catch the morning bus, and then waited for over one and a half hours. Apparently, somebody came along on a bicycle and told her that the next bus wouldn't be along until four o'clock. She told them she knew and that she was waiting for the ten o'clock bus, but it was now over an hour late."

"Well what happened? Did she wait any longer or come home?" Dad enquired.

"Promise you won't laugh if I tell you; remember she'll be able to hear you from the next room."

"I don't think it's a laughing matter, Nan," Dad sounded cross.

"You will do," Nan smiled and continued, "Babs came home after waiting for ages. She was in a terrible mood; I couldn't even speak to her. It was much later, after she had calmed down that I eventually found out what happened."

"What did you find out?" I asked.

Nan looked at me, and then at Dad, then silently giggling said, "she was told the bus was on time one hour before she got there because the clocks had gone forward by one hour on Sunday. We didn't know, did we?"

Dad cupped his hands over his mouth to silence the spluttering of his laughter before calming down and jokingly saying, "can you imagine Babs stomping and cursing all the way back home? I'll bet she's in a foul mood!"

"She was still cursing when she eventually got home," Nan smiled. "Babs is asleep in the armchair Bern, and before she wakes up, I should tell you Robin's in trouble yet again. She believes he'd have heard from school about the clocks changing and not told her and that's why she missed the bus."

"I didn't Dad; I didn't have any idea at all! Like most of the others, I was an hour late. Even Miss Botting didn't know; she fell asleep when the news was on the wireless and missed it, or so she said! Anyway, I didn't know Mum was going to Horsham until Nan told us both a few minutes ago."

"It's not your fault," Dad said. "I didn't know either until I got to work. I'll sort it out with Mum. Meanwhile I suggest you get lost for a while Robin. Go for a meander or a mooch or whatever you call it; do something for an hour or so."

With Wendy close at my side, I walked through the woods to Eddie's place. I hadn't realised he'd been down over the weekend and started work on his garden. He'd cleared all the old foliage away, pruned the roses, dug the vegetable plot over and reinforced the netting to keep the bright-eyes out. He'd worked hard.

Within five minutes, I was sitting under my comforting beech tree with Wendy lying at my side. Completely relaxed, I didn't give the past twenty-four hours a second thought. I'd learnt to forget painful and sad thoughts; it only made the suffering last longer. I always tried to remember the good things that would make me smile. The sad things would often make me feel like shedding a tear; I was glad I could no longer cry.

From the natural country sounds and the warmth of the evening air, I knew spring had arrived. I heard the squeaking of the bats as they darted and tumbled about the sky. Nightingales sang day and night all through the year, but now seemed to have all joined in singing together; it was a wonderful chorus. There was a loud shrilling scream that sounded like a human baby; it was repeated by another, then another; my blood felt ice cold and I shivered as Wendy leapt to her feet. I would have been terrified if I'd never heard it before and didn't know what it was. It was late this year, but I knew it was the mating call of the vixen seeking out a dog fox to mate with for the summer. For the honour of winning the vixen's favour it could result in a terrible fight between two males that could last all night, often resulting in the death of the loser.

Wendy was eager to find out what was going on, but because I knew we'd never get close enough to see them and it was beginning to get dark, I went home knowing Mum would be in a better mood once Dad had spoken to her.

Chapter Forty-three

The sky was clear and the temperature had risen considerably, even though it was only half past seven in the morning of the last Saturday in March. I'd filled the water tank and mixed the dry ballast, which Dad was turning into the first batch of concrete for that day.

Wendy had given me a small problem the first week her ear began to heal; it must have itched so much that she couldn't help but scratch it for relief; then it would bleed a little, and she'd shake her head spraying small drops of blood everywhere. Mum and Dad very soon found an answer to that problem; I was made to wipe all the spots off the wall or furniture. But it didn't matter any more; she was okay now. Jet still had a very slight limp, but it was getting better each week and he was able to hunt again. The fur on the lower part of his foot had grown back snow-white, looking out of place against his jet-black fur. It may have looked odd, but at least it would remind him to be more careful in the future. I was pleased they were both well and healthy again and felt sure the giblets I was able to get from Turpins Farm most days had helped considerably.

Hearing Dad call, I turned and looked towards him. He was with Frank, Michael's Dad whom I hadn't seen arrive; he beckoned me towards them. I began walking, wondering what was going to happen and hoping Frank hadn't said anything to Dad about the bright-eyes he'd offered me to bring home the day we went ferreting. If he had mentioned it, Dad and I could be very embarrassed. As I got close to them Dad said, "Frank's got something to ask you!"

My heart sank, wondering what on earth he wanted to know. "I'm taking Michael out for the day, and wondered if you'd like to come along with us?" He asked.

"Well, yes, but where are you going?" I replied.

"Up to Hogwood," he answered, "there's a lake where I'll take him fishing for part of the day. On the way there and back, I'll teach you about bird-nesting. Now then, would you like to come along with us?"

"Yes, definitely, I'd love to, but I can't. I told Dad I'd help him today."

"Don't worry about it," Dad said, "you wouldn't be able to mix concrete all day any way; its very tough work and it'd half kill you. You've been working hard, so have the day off, and enjoy yourself. Why not take Wendy along, if you want?"

I couldn't believe my ears; I hadn't done anything different to make Dad so considerate. I wondered why, as I answered, "thanks Dad, thanks Frank, that's great; do I need to take anything with me? Anything at all?"

"No, just yourself." Frank responded. Then looking at Dad said, "I'll be taking a pile of sandwiches and drink with us; there'll be plenty enough for Rod, if that's alright with you Bern?"

"Yes sure, that's okay with me, have a good time; send him home in one piece Frank and by the way, thanks."

Within twenty minutes, the three of us were walking along the track leading to Hogwood. All the wild birds had finished building or repairing their nests for the year and were about to lay the first clutch of eggs; some had already started. We found one thrush was broody and sitting tight; she wouldn't move.

We'd walked a short distance, past the old cottage owned by the nice pig farmer, who'd told me the year before about using horse oils on our pig, when Frank exclaimed in quite an excited voice, "that's what I've been looking for, now we'll be able to catch some really good fish."

Michael and I looked at each other wondering what the fuss was about. There didn't seem to be anything special to look at: on the left of the track was the beginning of the pine forest, and on the right, a thin strip of land covered with fern, hazel, and birch.

Frank opened his bag and took out a small garden spade, a small bottle, some cotton wool and a tin. He walked half a dozen paces into the wood and beckoned us to follow, then told us exactly where we were to stand, and not to move away from the spot. I was told to hold Wendy close to my side and not to let her run about. Again Michael and I looked at each other in amazement; what was he up to? He poured a clear liquid from the bottle onto the cotton wool until it became soaking wet. Then he tossed it onto the ground a few feet in front of him. Exactly what was happening became clear as we watched and listened while he explained.

"The liquid I've used is called Thawpit and because you're both downwind from where I've placed it, the gentle breeze is wafting its fumes towards, and around you. As you know by now, it gives off a strong smell similar to cleaning spirit. Now look where I've put the cotton wool; it's by the side of a small hole in the ground, which is the entrance and exit of a wasp nest. Once they get the slightest smell, they become completely paralysed for about ten minutes or so. By the time they wake up I shall have dug up enough of their grubs for fishing, and we'll be gone!"

As the wasps came out of their underground nest, they crashed onto the ground fast asleep; even those returning to the nest crashed down all around us. Michael moved from his safe place, where he had been protected by the smell of the Thawpit, to the side for a closer look; within seconds he called out in pain, as he was stung twice on his face. Frank looked up from his digging and smiling to himself I heard him mutter, "it takes some people longer to learn than others, I suppose!" He finished collecting enough grubs and filled the tin. They were similar in colour and shape to maggots except they were at least five times longer and fatter; an ideal fishing bait.

Frank gathered his bits together and said, "we should move off as quickly as possible before the wasps wake up; they'll be in a filthy mood and could possibly swarm on us if we stay close to their nest."

We set off again along the track but hadn't gone far before Frank stopped, and opening his bag took out another tin. Handing it to Michael he told him, "inside you'll find some Ricketts Blue. Wet your finger and rub some of the powder on, and into the stings; it'll take most of the stinging pain away."

Michael did as he was told and almost immediately said, "Well I don't care what I look like with these blue spots on my forehead Dad, but the pain's gone already, thanks."

We checked almost everywhere for birds and their nests; in the woods, bushes and hedgerows; anywhere different species of birds would build. Frank seemed to know so much about them all and told us he'd test us later, on our way home, to find out what we'd learnt during the day. Michael and I knew we'd forget most of what we'd previously learnt.

We walked further than Michael and I had done before, then turning right, we passed through narrow woodland into a field that bordered our first view of the lake. Following Frank, we skirted the water's edge into a second field then came to a brick built dam fitted with an old oak sluice-gate. The length and width of the lake were about the same as Ifold Lake; there were groups of tiny bubbles floating to the surface and small fish making whirlpools and sucking sounds as they fed from unsuspecting insects, which skimmed across the surface. From what I could see, that was about all the two lakes had in common; the water was muddy, there weren't any birds to be seen or heard, not a bulrush, attractive tree or bush in sight. Nevertheless it was peaceful and comforting, and contained its own kind of silent and unseen beauty.

Frank, who'd been fitting his fishing tackle together, broke my thoughts as he said, "the whole lake is man-made and fed from water that trickles through the pine forest. It was built and used for the old Glass Furnace in Hog Copse; but it's all long gone now." He sighed, and then muttered, "you'd never believe it now, but that's progress I suppose."

"Arthur, one of Dave's older brothers, told me there was a lake near to Ernie Honeysett's place called Taymounds Lake; is this the one?" I asked.

"Yes it is, and he's right." Frank answered. "There aren't many people who know; almost everybody calls it Hogwood Lake, but it's really Taymounds."

Frank fitted a small goose quill float and two lead split shots to his fishing line. Then, gently hooking a fat wasp grub under the skin onto the tip of the hook, he cast it out into the water, adjusting the tension of the line until the tip of the float stuck upright on the surface of the water leaving the bait on the bottom at the exact depth. The three of us watched and waited in complete silence while Wendy stretched herself out against the wall, falling asleep almost immediately.

Within five minutes the float suddenly disappeared under the surface and the line streaked out. Frank stood up and by putting his finger to stop any more line from going out, it tightened, pulling the tip of the rod into an arch shape; a fish was hooked and the battle was on to get it into the landing net safely.

It was a beautiful tench of about four pounds in weight, covered with hundreds of minute pale olive green scales and with tiny bright red eyes. Frank told us to feel the thick slime covering the body, explaining the slime was thought to contain a healing property for other fish. No matter what kind of fish it might be, if it has a wound, of any type, and rubbed against the slime of the tench, it would be cured. It wasn't surprising it was often called, 'The Doctor Fish.'

By early afternoon we'd all taken turns at fishing and to our delight, each caught something, either rudd or trench. Michael gave us the biggest surprise of all by catching a young small and beautiful mirror carp. Frank told us despite all the times he'd fished the lake before he'd never seen one there.

When we stopped for the day to have something to eat and drink, Frank opened a bag and we all drank the warm sweet tea from a quart size bottle. It was good. Then he gave us each a bag containing sandwiches; thanking him I looked inside and could hardly believe my eyes. In the bottom of the bag was a banana; I hadn't seen one since I lived in Dorking! I knew I'd eat it! Then I looked inside the two large sandwiches and my mouth fell open with delight and disbelief. I thought of Dorking again; one was filled with peanut butter while the other contained lemon curd. Frank had even remembered biscuits for Wendy.

We sat at the water's edge eating and talking, until everything had gone. Then after putting the tackle away, cleared up and set off to spend most of the afternoon bird-spotting and learning about their nesting habits.

Chapter Forty-four

As we passed through the last field before entering the woodland we stopped, looked, and listened to the joyful trilling, and unmistakable flight song of a skylark, which appeared as a tiny dot, high in the sky. We walked a few paces further and saw another rise from the centre of the field and hover only just above the treetops. It wasn't singing; instead it stayed in the same position, and seemed to be watching every move we made. "Keep on walking until we get into the woods and I'll explain what the birds are doing," Frank said, "I'm sure you'll find it interesting."

Just inside the woods we sat on a large old fallen oak trunk. Wendy sat at my side, leaning against my leg looking at Frank with her head on one side as if, like Michael and I, she was also waiting for him to begin his explanation about the birds. We all noticed her and laughed.

He spoke softly, while we sat in silence. "When we were seen by the cock bird which was the one singing and hovering on high, it would have sounded a warning note to its mate who would have been sitting on the eggs in its roughly-made nest. As skylarks don't hop like most other birds, she would have left the nest and walked or run a considerable distance before flying off, which would confuse any intruder as to the position of the nest, which could contain eggs or young defenceless squabs. A magpie, jay or any crow, except a rook would certainly eat the eggs, or the young squabs; they kill dozens every year. Nevertheless they have to feed, and no very young birds of any type are spared from them."

Frank pointed towards the skylark. "She's getting lower and lower; she'll be down in a minute, and then on her way to the nest, keep your eye on her as she pops her head up."

Then with the gentleness of a soft summer breeze, she gracefully opened her striated brown wings and floated like a feather onto the soft primrose-strewn grass. We stood on the large tree trunk to get a clear view and watched. She ran, very fast, as Frank had told us she would and stopped every few feet to pop her head up looking for any possible danger. When she had stopped and looked around seven or eight times, she did it again, but this time in the same spot; we waited a moment or two and she did it again, she hadn't gone any further, she was at the nest.

We walked directly to the last spot we'd seen her but had only got half way there before we saw her flurry of wings as she took to the sky. Being careful not to accidentally step on the nest, we found it tightly pressed against the side of a large tuft of grass. It was hardly what I expected to see; barely a nest at all, simply a small pile of dry grass lying on the ground hidden by the green overhang from the tuft growing by the side. Frank moved the long lengths of grass to the side revealing four thumbnail size eggs lying close together within a small dip in the centre of the nest. They were an off-white colour; covered with brown freckles, spots and specks, a wonderful sight. Michael and I stood looking at them in wonder while Frank told us the hen bird normally lays five eggs, two or sometimes three times during summer. Covering the nest as it was before he said, "the skylark's a clever little bird; it knows the magpie will search the area where it lands, so it builds its nest a long distance away. Since they were first put on this earth, the magpie still hasn't worked out where the skylark builds its nest; good job too, but a shame for most other birds. Well I wonder what else we'll find today! There was a nest right under your noses while we were waiting in the woods a few minutes ago. Let's go and have a look."

We went back to the old oak tree trunk where we'd been sitting. Frank said, "there's a nest very close to this spot; you both missed it before, but now you know there's one here, see if you can find it."

Michael and I looked everywhere we could think of. Up the trees and bushes, on the ground, in the brambles but we couldn't see any sign of a nest. After a while, completely beaten we told Frank we'd given up. He smiled, then took four paces to his right and pointed to a spot within an inch of the green moss growing near the roots of the old oak tree base on which we'd been sitting. We went to his side and looked; to our amazement we noticed a few odd hairs and tiny feathers that seemed to be growing out of the moss; almost hidden near the top end was a tiny hole, which we realised was the work of art of a wren. The nest was so well camouflaged; I could have walked past it a dozen times without realising it was there.

The nest was dome-shaped and built mainly of moss interlocked with tiny, dry leaves, grass, hair and feathers. Frank told me to carefully feel inside; lined with down, it was soft and warm. I felt a lot of eggs and gently wiggled one up the inside and out through the small opening. It was white, faintly speckled with red and brown spots, and no bigger than a small garden pea.

"Little Jenny-wrens are only about three and a half inches long, that's why the eggs are so small; but nevertheless she lays a clutch of between five and twelve each brood, that's not bad aye! Right, that's Jenny-wren dealt with; let's move on and find out more about the nests we saw this morning."

Once we got back onto the stony main track, we walked along the edge of the pine forest towards home. We passed the wasp nest, which he'd dug up earlier and were within a few yards of the old cottage when Frank stopped. He pointed to a tiny, tightly packed, basket-shaped moss and twig object hanging from the thin branch of a pine tree, and said, "that's the nest of the beautiful olive and bright yellow-coloured, gold-crest. They nest during May and June, when the hen will lay its tiny red and brown spotted eggs. You may think little Jenny-wren is the smallest bird you've ever seen, but the gold-crest is a gem amongst them all; it's the smallest bird in Britain. Mark my words, once you've seen one you'll never forget it."

Frank taught us about the different materials various birds use to make their nests; the shapes, colour and amount of eggs each type lay, and where they build them. The most difficult of them all to identify were the great-tit, the blue-tit, and the coal-tit. They make their nests the same shape, with the same type of materials, the eggs being identical in colour and markings with the only difference being the size.

We were looking at a wood pigeon's nest made of twigs and nothing else. It was flat, plain and simple; woven between three or four branches it contained the two pure white eggs, which was the usual number laid. Feeling a slight nudge on my arm, I turned to Michael and asked, "What's wrong?"

"Nothing," he answered looking behind me and laughing, "but despite what happened to her last time we were out, it seems Wendy's got the bug for digging."

Turning to look I could only see the back-end of Wendy sticking up out of a hole she was enlarging and digging at furiously. "Wendy come out of there! Get here. Now!" I shouted. She reluctantly backed out of the hole she'd dug, then sat, looking at me and puffing and panting, with her tongue hanging out and dripping with sweat. I looked at Frank, then at Michael, and said, "you can tell from a glance she's enjoying herself, but after what happened last time I dare not take the chance of another accident happening. I'm surprised Dad even let me bring her." I added.

As we started to walk home, Frank gave a small cough to clear his throat and half smiling said, "I knew he would, after I told him what happened."

"I told Mum and Dad it was an accident; I told them exactly what happened, but they didn't believe me. I still got a good hiding for nothing! Again."

"Yes I know. He told me you were a little sod; you hadn't thought, therefore it was your fault, so he gave you a good hiding, which he said you deserved. Well Rod, I told your Dad it could have happened if I'd been using the spade, or Michael, or even if it had been him! It couldn't be avoided; it could have happened to anyone. I even told him you didn't deserve any punishment, and I'd never laid a finger on Michael." Frank smiled again and added; "I suggested it would be nice if he let you come out with us, and to bring Wendy."

"You didn't mention the amount of bright-eyes we caught, and that you offered me some to take home, did you Frank?" I asked feeling a little concerned.

"No, Rod."

"Oh, thank goodness for that! I don't know what he might do if he knew." I said, relieved.

"Actually, as it happens Rod, before I could say anything more, he told me even if I'd offered you some to take home you would have said, 'No thanks.' He explained you told him some time ago you'd never take any home again. It was a matter of principle on your part; and you'd stuck to it. He told me he'd wish you'd change your mind but he was proud of you for keeping to your word."

I thanked Frank for telling me what Dad said, and felt much more contented. I also thanked him and Michael for such an interesting day out. Then as I was about to set off home Michael asked, "will you start collecting eggs Rod? If you do we could start together and perhaps do some swaps with the other boys at our two different schools."

"I know most of the other boys do," I answered, "there are so many different types of birds and eggs I don't think it would do any harm. Yes okay. It's strange really; we all seem to collect something at some time or other. Boys living in towns can't collect eggs, because there aren't any; only cigarette cards or stamps. We can't collect cigarette cards or stamps, because there aren't any, only eggs. Daft isn't it?"

"Right," Frank said, "now you two have sorted that out we'd best be going; we've all got our jobs to do, so we'll see you soon Rod. Good luck!"

"Thanks again; it's been a lovely day, I've really enjoyed myself. I'll see you first chance I get," I said as I walked off.

Chapter Forty-five

Mum and Dad were standing talking and looking at the work Dad had done. I noticed Mum's bike leaning against the pile of bricks. The large basket on the front was loaded with bottles and cans of water; she'd obviously been up to Spring Hill and filled them at some time because Dad had been busy all day mixing and laying the concrete. She wouldn't be in a good mood.

As I got closer, Mum shouted at me, "is Wendy all right? You haven't hurt her have you?"

Dad looked at her sternly and answered her for me. "Of course he hasn't! Leave the boy alone; he wouldn't hurt Wendy on purpose, I know that much."

Yes; but only because Frank had told him, I thought.

"He'd better not," she replied looking directly at me, "now tell me what you've had to eat while you were out today Robin."

I explained exactly what I'd eaten and how good it all tasted. I shouldn't have; it was a big mistake. Mum told me I'd had sufficient for the day, especially with the richness of the banana, so I certainly wouldn't need any dinner. There was no point in telling either of them I was hungry, and I'd like something to eat because it wouldn't make any difference. Mum had decided and that was final.

I asked Dad if he wanted me to help him with anything in particular but before he could answer, Mum interrupted, "you can do something for me. I've almost run out of cigarettes, I shall need you to get me five Players Weights. It's Saturday afternoon and the stores at Plaistow and Ifold will be closed, so you'll need to go to the Post Office at Loxwood."

"Why didn't you get some this morning, when you went to Spring Hill to get the water?" Dad asked her, looking very inquisitive.

"I had so much on my mind, I forgot all about them until now," she answered.

I knew she was lying. It was more likely she was annoyed with me for being able to go out for the day and take Wendy, when I was expected to have been working. Dad knew about Wendy's accident, but Mum still didn't, and was determined to make me suffer.

I looked at their watchful faces alternately, then speaking directly to Mum said, "do you think five cigarettes will be enough Mum, or shall I get ten just in case?"

"I said five, didn't I? That's all I need! Now get five. How many times do your father or I have to tell you to do what you're told, and keep your opinions to yourself? Now go and get the money from Nan and get on your way."

When Nan gave me the cigarette money, I told her what Mum had said about my dinner. Nan told me she'd already been told not to get anything for me; Mum had already decided I wouldn't need anything else. "I hope you'll be alright during the next two weeks Robin. You haven't forgotten I'm going to stay with your Aunt Doss, have you?"

"No I haven't forgotten Nan. You deserve a good rest; you work much too hard!" "Don't worry about me; you'll be surprised how well I've learnt to look after myself!"

After taking the short cut to the Post Office, I purchased the five cigarettes, and then checked how much of my own money I had. Guessing Mum might need more than five cigarettes before Monday, I found I'd sufficient money to buy the same again, plus two fresh bread rolls to supplement my dinner. I didn't think twice about making the second purchase; if Mum decided tomorrow morning she needed more cigarettes, the extra five I'd bought could save me a long walk.

When I reached and crossed the wooden bridge over the river on my way home, I turned left and walked around the edge of Ifold Lake and headed towards the far end. It didn't take long to find what I was looking for; half-floating and half woven among the leafy branches at water level, almost hidden from sight by an overhanging tree, was a simply constructed mallard nest.

The branches and leaves from the small trees, growing through the shallows darkened the water that trickled from the stream inlet. I slipped my boots and socks off, then waded to the nest. In a cluster, lying in the centre, partly covered by dry rushes, were nine very pale green eggs, much larger than any chicken's egg I'd ever seen. I took two of them for myself. I knew the duck wouldn't miss them, and could lay as many as twelve. Placing them into the water I checked to see if they'd sink; only then I knew they weren't addled. I waded to the bank, replaced my socks and boots, then without having seen or heard anything of the duck, or drake went on my way having completed an important part of what I planned. To protect the eggs, I positioned them inside my shirt together with the packets of cigarettes and the bread rolls. Both my hands were left free which as normal allowed me to practise with my catapult while walking along.

Closer to home, I placed the eggs, one pack of cigarettes, and the bread rolls inside a biscuit tin I kept with my fishing tackle and other bits and pieces, inside a large old disused badger set dug into a high clay bank. Everything inside was hidden from sight, and protected from all weather conditions. It was ideal, and no further than five yards from either the beech tree or the cool, clear stream.

When I'd walked the short distance home, I went into the kitchen where Mum and Dad were sitting, eating their cooked dinner. It smelt good, but I knew there wouldn't be any for me. Mum told me to leave her cigarettes, then to do my jobs. It was her way of telling me to keep out of the way.

Within an hour I was sitting under the beech tree with Wendy puffing and blowing while she dozed. I eagerly watched the steam rise from the fresh stream water in my billycan as it balanced on the bricks surrounding the small fire I'd made. The motion of the gently boiling water moved the two duck eggs from side to side as they cooked. A few minutes later, having emptied the boiling water away, I peeled the eggs and destroyed the shells by burning them in the fire. The bread rolls, even though dry, and the two large hot duck eggs, made me a good healthy and filling meal.

Dad stood watching me the next morning while I mixed the first batch of concrete of the day. Mum walked over and stood with Dad smiling to herself.

"I'm sorry about this Bern," Mum said, "but I thought I had ten Players Weights. I can't find them! I've looked everywhere. Robin will have to go up to Plaistow and get me some, it's the only place open on a Sunday morning, I'm sorry."

Dad was furious; the colour drained from his face with rage, and he clenched his fists until the knuckles turned white, and the veins on the back of his hands swelled up to twice their normal size. He looked at Mum with the same angry stare I'd received from him on several occasions in the past. I knew he'd wait until I'd gone before saying anything to her. As he looked at me, I could feel his embarrassment. "Go and get some money from your Nan; ask her to make you a sandwich, and tell her I said it was okay. Then go and get your mother's cigarettes; don't rush, I'll see you in a couple of hours or so."

An hour later I was sitting on the bank of Ifold Lake having caught twelve or more rudd to feed Jet and Wendy, and myself. The mallard had already laid one replacement egg; I was pleased; it meant I could have more, when needed.

By climbing two oak trees, and wading into the lake, near a large reed bed, I collected a total of ten magpie and moorhen eggs as additional food. Keeping them separate, I placed them between layers of grass inside my bag for protection, and then set off towards home, pleased I hadn't needed to go for Mum's cigarettes; instead I'd been able to help myself in advance, for a few days at least. When I reached the beech tree, I removed the cigarettes from the tin and replaced them with the eggs. I put the fish inside the bag and then hanging it on a branch safe from any predators, strode home along the road as if from Plaistow.

When I got indoors, Mum and Dad were sitting at the kitchen table eating their lunch. I knew Dad had finished all the work he'd be doing that day. I reached into my pocket for the cigarettes to give to Mum, when for some inexplicable reason I stopped myself. Thank goodness I did! If I hadn't stopped, I couldn't begin to imagine the trouble I'd have got myself into; maybe it was partly to do with the sharp tone of Mum's voice as she almost convincingly said, "I'm sorry Robin, and I completely forgot it's against the law for shops to sell anything except food and essentials on a Sunday. I'm so sorry you had a wasted trip. Never mind, I found the cigarettes I thought I'd lost. Keep the money you've got, and get me some cigarettes tomorrow. Why don't you go out with Dave or Michael for the rest of the day? You've deserved it, but don't forget to be back home in time to do your jobs."

Half an hour later I sat watching the fish I'd caught slowly cook in the billycan over my open fire. I'd kept one slice of bread from my breakfast, to make a sandwich. Both Jet and Wendy had picked up the scent of the fish when I'd first got home, and were now sitting eating the little treat I'd brought them. Simply watching them gave me a feeling of contentment.

I remembered the different things I'd been able to do over the past few days and smiled to myself. Then I thought longer and harder; the result made me burst out with laughter! Even though nobody could hear me, it was so loud I instinctively put my hand over my mouth to quieten the noise; it made me feel silly.

I was about to have my second good meal within two days: I had enough eggs to last several days; I hadn't needed to walk to Plaistow; I'd been able to feed my two pets, and I still had five Players Weights left over for next time. I felt as if I'd won an enormous battle! And the feeling it gave me inside was good.

By cutting in advance, the sticks Dad would use to beat me with; I saved myself a lot of misery. It'd worked so perfectly: getting the stick only stung; it meant nothing else to me. Now I began thinking of something equally rewarding! Could I afford to buy two or three packets of cigarettes in advance? If so, I'd save myself miles of walking and overcome the unpleasantness of both problems I often had to endure. Now there's a thought! But, could I afford it?

Chapter Forty-six

After school the next afternoon, and crossing the fields towards the dairy, the thought of Nan being away for the next two weeks reminded me I'd only have the food Mum gave me. I knew it wouldn't be sufficient to keep my strength up. I'd made allowances for a few days but I'd need to get extra for the second week.

The main thought on my mind was how I'd get the money to buy extra cigarettes for whenever Mum would need them. Unlike most of my friends at school, I was never given any pocket money; therefore as usual, I'd have to earn the money somehow or other. Because it was the beginning of the breeding season there wouldn't be any money for about two months from the sale of any bright-eyes. It was too late in the season to earn any money grafting or pruning, even if somebody needed it done. I couldn't think of any other ideas, and temporarily gave up the thought.

As I entered the dairy, all three dairymen were hosing down the milking parlour and clearing up for the day. Dick saw me first and waved. Then calling out he said, "ah; just the young man I've been waiting for; stay there, I'll come over."

As he came closer I smiled and asked, "I haven't done anything wrong, have I?"

"No;" he said, "at least, not that I know of anyway. I just want to ask if you'd like to work next Sunday and earn some money for yourself and some farm provisions to take home for your Mum and Dad?"

I thought for a moment and then replied, "yes please, I'd like to, but I'll have to ask Dad first, as he let me go out bird-nesting last Sunday. I was very surprised; it was like a special treat. I normally have to help by mixing the concrete; I don't know if he'd let me go out again. What would I have to do? And how long would it take? He's bound to ask."

"Well Rod, every year at this time, three of the local farmers get together and have a Magpie Shoot. We do it to keep the magpies down, because they do so much harm to other birds. It normally takes us all day to clear the three farms of the pests. Everybody gets well fed and has a well-earned day off work. We take it in turns to organise the shoot, and it's my turn this year. All the birds that are shot must be picked up and not left in the field or woods; someone has to do the picking-up, as it's called. Each of us pays, if not with a few pence each, then with something from the farm. It could be anything but it's normally provisions of some sort or other. I've decided you can have the job if you want it."

"Thanks Dick, that's nice of you; and as you can guess, if I'm going to get fed, and earn some pocket money as well, my answer is definitely yes! When I ask Dad and he finds out I could be bringing something special home to eat I'm sure his answer will be yes as well!"

"Good; when can you let me know?" Dick asked.

"I'll be able to let you know tomorrow," I answered. "I'll ask Dad as soon as he gets in this evening. Thanks Dick."

Going home, I wondered if Dad did say okay and I could go on Sunday; would I get enough money to buy extra cigarettes and food? It would certainly solve a big problem in more ways than one.

I could hear my friendly red robin tweeting and chirping loudly and out of tune. I soon realised it was a noise made simply to attract attention to his continuous acrobatics; flitting and hopping between one of the hazel trees, on to the gatepost, then the gate. He was very excited as he hopped from one place to another in front of me as I walked and he led the way, checking all the while I was following. We reached the pile of logs I'd stacked under the lean-to by the side of the kitchen door.

I stopped at the entrance as he fluttered upwards to the ledge just under the roof, where he stood proudly by the side of his nest. He fully expanded his brilliant red breast as if showing off. Then, as if pointing with his head and shiny black eyes, he directed my vision towards the top of the nest.

I looked closely; there were five, bright yellow, diamond shapes, sticking upright on what seemed to be thin grey stalks. They all swayed together from side to side at the top edge of the nest and from the five closely huddled shapes came varying, continuous loud sounds like high-pitched squeaking. This was the reason for his excitement; no wonder! I thought he was showing off and he certainly was, as he proudly showed me the first hatch of robin squabs he and his mate had been able to produce for almost a year. He'd need to work very hard for hours every day to feed and care for the chicks. I smiled at him and couldn't stop myself saying. "Well done robin. Good luck!"

After I'd changed out of my school clothes in preparation for starting my jobs, Mum came into the kitchen from the sitting room. I knew as soon as she spoke, from the expression on her face and the look in her eyes that she'd only just woken up. "You can make yourself a mug of tea if you want. Don't expect me to wait on you like Nan does. After your father's got home, finished any work on the bungalow he wants to do and we've had our dinner, I'll call you. You've got potatoes, peas, and corned beef."

I knew it would be stone cold by the time I was called. Yuck! How awful, I thought. Nevertheless I was hungry and needed to keep my strength up, so I'd eat it.

I made myself a drink, and then having gone outside followed by Wendy passed the small rubbish pile at the back of the wagon, where I noticed Mum had discarded a small amount of waste during the day. That was unusual; she'd never done it before. I was the only one to put the rubbish out, and burn it.

On the very top of the pile lay a tin bearing the famous name of "Tate and Lyle Golden Syrup." I'd never seen one indoors. Where did it come from? Had it been kept hidden from me? Mum had finished the honey Frank had given me the first week; had she finished the tin of syrup today and didn't think I'd find the empty tin? Or did she put the tin on the rubbish pile knowing I'd find it, but wouldn't dare say anything? Whatever the reason, somehow it didn't seem to be right. I felt ridiculed.

Dad noticed I'd finished the dry mixing of the concrete when he got home and was stacking the logs I'd cut. "How long before you finish with those?" he called out to me.

"Not more than about ten minutes," I answered, "then I'll start on my other jobs. Is that okay?"

"No, do, those later," he replied. "I know its heavy work for you but I'd like you to add the water to the concrete and start mixing. I want an early night, so I'll get changed, then have a quick cup of tea and take over."

At my age and size it was hard, slow, painful and exhausting work but I managed to finish as Dad arrived. I knew he'd be pleased with what I'd managed to do, but would he give me Sunday off to work at the magpie shoot? I'd only tell him I'd be paid with home-cooked farmhouse food, plus other farm provisions to bring home; I decided not to mention the possibility of money.

He looked at what I'd done. Then expelling the air through his lips from tightly puffed-out cheeks said, "well done Robin! I didn't expect you to mix it all! Don't do it again, you're too young, and you'll hurt yourself. Now then, off you go!

Oh! By the way," he added, "next Sunday I'm going to try my hand at brick-laying on the corner where the sitting room will be, and down the side to the kitchen wall. During the week I'll make up some spot boards about three-foot square for putting the cement on. Then on Saturday I want you to stack about thirty or forty bricks between each board ready for use. We'll soon see how I get on."

"If I were to do that on Saturday, would you want me to do anything on Sunday Dad?" I asked; hoping his answer would be, No!

"Why?" he asked, "you don't expect another Sunday off, do you?"

"Well it's like this Dad," I started to explain, but within a moment or so he smiled and said.

"Get to the point Robin; I don't want to stand here all night listening to a cock and bull story of why I should give you the day off."

It was obvious he was in a reasonably good mood, so I simply told him what I'd been asked to do, and the type of food I could expect as payment. At first I thought he'd never answer. It was ages before he said, "yes all right then, but this is the last time until I say otherwise. Okay?"

"Okay Dad and thanks."

"Don't say anything to your mother. I'll tell her. Now get on and finish your jobs, I'll see you after I've had dinner. Remember what I said. I'll tell your mother."

I walked directly to the rubbish pile and took the empty syrup tin from the top. I'd made up my mind exactly what I was going to do with it. I didn't relish being made to feel a fool. I headed to the spot in the woods where I'd tethered Judy earlier in the day. Then after gently stroking her neck and ears I knelt down beside her and removed the lid from the syrup tin and milked her into it until it was half-filled with her rich warm milk. The quantity that Judy produced each day varied and the small amount I'd taken wouldn't be noticed.

When I'd finished, I placed the tin aside and took Judy back home where I fed her bran and food pellets as usual. I strode back through the woods and collected the half-full tin of milk, before heading towards the comfort of the beech tree. Taking three of the magpie eggs, and then cracking them into the milk, I replaced the lid of the tin and shook it vigorously for several minutes. The combination of the eggs, milk, and the syrup, which was left clinging to the inside of the tin, produced a tasty, sweet and nourishing drink.

By the time I was called for dinner, I was convinced it was intentional that I should find the empty syrup tin, but I didn't care. I wasn't upset any longer; instead I'd been able to benefit from it. I smiled to myself as I wished I had the nerve to ask Mum for another empty syrup tin tomorrow.

Another small but important lesson I'd learnt in life. To make the most out of whatever you get. Unfortunately the most I could make out of my cold dinner was to eat it, and be grateful.

Chapter Forty-seven

On the way home from school the next day, I found Dick and told him I'd be allowed out for the day on the Sunday. He was pleased for me and gave me full details of what I was expected to do.

On the Sunday, during my walk to Turpins Farm for my first shoot, I recalled some of the past few days' events in an effort to take my mind off the day ahead. All week I'd been looking forward eagerly to this day and hardly thought of anything else.

I recalled the afternoon we were taken from school to the Sports Fields for the first time that year. We soon realised there weren't enough boys to make up two sides to play each other in a game of either football or cricket. All we were able to do was to have a kick or knock about. The girls had the same problem with their chosen sport of stool-ball, but they were a little faster and smarter than us and explained to Miss Rees that although they couldn't play football or cricket, the boys could play stool-ball and make up for the girls' lack of numbers! We weren't very happy about it; none of the boys liked the idea of playing the game and felt embarrassed. The girls knew and couldn't stop giggling at us. When they saw the look on our faces, most of us were pacified with a kiss on the cheek, a smile, or a kind word or two of encouragement.

I had never been kissed before unless it was a farewell or a greeting, and never by a girl. Connie not only gave me a kiss but she also put her arm around me. It gave me a warm, and cared for feeling throughout my whole body. Nevertheless, like the other boys I wiped the kiss away, as if it were awful. I couldn't help blushing but turned away in case someone noticed. I never objected to playing stool-ball again!

My thoughts were distracted by the sound of a tractor approaching from behind me along the lane, but there was another noise I couldn't make out. I listened hard. A tractor and trailer rounded the bend and it was then I realised the noise was voices; many voices, talking, some excitedly, others laughing.

As the tractor drew closer I realised there were about eight men in the trailer all of whom I'd met at some time or other during my various trips around Foxbridge Farm. We'd either waved at each other across a field or we'd had a brief chat after I'd thanked them for a lift; I'd often jumped on to the back of the tractor or trailer as they'd passed, and had always felt safe, and comfortable in their presence.

The tractor slowed down slightly, and as I knew where they were going, I leaped aboard to their encouragement and greetings. I'd barely had time to scramble aboard when all the dogs leapt on me; some with long tails, others with little short stumps, all furiously wagging. Steaming hot, dripping wet tongues licked and soaked my face, arms and legs in greeting. We all laughed as I struggled under the mass of their excited and wriggling bodies, to stand upright.

Within ten minutes we arrived at Turpins Farm, to be greeted by Dick with the other two dairymen and three others who I'd seen working on the farm on previous occasions.

The second tractor and trailer containing another eight men, each with one, or in some cases two dogs, arrived within minutes. It was from Headfoldswood Farm, which was owned by Captain Moore. Dick had previously told me the Captain wouldn't be coming to the shoot himself because he considered himself a gentleman farmer, and didn't believe he should mix with his workmen. I realised I'd learnt another lesson in life; this time about self- importance, particularly when a little later I realised that the man who had driven the tractor from Foxbridge Farm was in fact HRH Prince Tomislav. He worked hard with his men, treated them as equals, and preferred to be called simply Tom, or Prince Tom, by everyone.

Most of the men hadn't seen each other since the last shoot, but they were all friends and within no time were laughing and joking as if they'd only met yesterday. Even the dogs were friendly and seemed to get on well together, despite the differences in size and breed.

All the Jack Russells and spaniels had dock tails, or handles as they were called; essential for pulling them out of burrows, safely and painlessly, should they ever get stuck. This was a virtually painless operation consisting of a nick through the skin between the bone joint of the tail, while young pups. The other dogs were collies plus a few mongrels, generally known as a 'Heinz 57' breed. They'd all be working dogs, and in most cases would have proved themselves and become the farmers' trusting and loyal friends.

Each man had either a game bag, or a half-sack tied each end, hanging from his shoulder on one side and an open unloaded double-barrelled 12-bore shotgun hanging over his arm the other side. I carried a full size sack to put the pick-ups in.

When the excited dogs were at their masters' side and everybody was ready, we set off towards the first long strip of woodland separating the two large fields which ran from the road, along the side of the stream and down to the river boundary.

The men divided themselves into three even groups. One group went into the woodland and started to walk through the whole width flushing out any birds. The men in the other two groups spread themselves out along the side of each field towards the middle; it was a simple and efficient method of covering the flight paths.

No matter which side of the woodland any magpie or crow appeared, it would be within range of at least three gunmen, known as 'the Guns'. All they needed to do was to close the pre-loaded shotgun; switch the safety catch to the 'off' position; point the gun at the target, judge the distance and speed by keeping both eyes open and then, pressing the butt firmly into the shoulder squeeze the trigger. No magpie or crow escaped.

Each dog appeared to delight in being the first to get to the scene and retrieve the quarry, which it took directly to its master. It saved me a good deal of walking and searching; all I needed to do was to ensure nothing was missed, and retrieve the pick-ups. When they'd cleared the selected areas, fourteen pests had been shot; the guns had probably saved the lives of over a hundred squabs.

Headfoldswood Farm, the smallest of the three, was bordered on one side by Headfolds Wood and the road to Plaistow on the other. Only one side of the farm could be worked; everything had to be flushed out from the dense woodland. Working their way through the dense bushes and ground cover, from one end of the farm to the other, took about two hours; it was much harder work, but the results were just as rewarding.

By early afternoon, we were all sitting in one of the barns at Foxbridge Farm eating the food Dick had brought for us all. I was treated and offered the same as everybody else. I chose home-made bread rolls, cheese and ham; we all drank refreshing cold sweet tea.

Whilst eating and drinking, we couldn't stop ourselves watching and laughing at the Jack Russells playing and mock-fighting each other. They were a mixture of smooth and broken-coated. Some had normal length legs; others were short and dumpy. Their expressions, yapping and antics relayed their happiness. Like most Jack Russells they all had different characters; they were as funny as clowns to watch, yet could be serious and extremely intelligent.

Foxbridge Farm was the largest of the three; it was completely bordered by the gigantic Headfolds Wood on one side, and apple farms that spread for miles at the top end. The insect life within the woodland and within the enormous orchards made it a haven for small birds to feed, but because of this it also became a haven for their deadly enemies, the magpie and crow.

During the three hours we spent working the land, I noticed four crows flushed from the woodland. They flew within range of at least five of the guns; any single one could have shot at them but nobody bothered. The birds, quite unperturbed simply flew away.

Later when we'd finished and returned to the barn, I asked Dick why the four crows I'd seen hadn't been shot. He explained they weren't crows but were harmless rooks; they looked the same and it was difficult to tell them apart from a distance. However, you could always tell the difference at a glance. It was simple he told me; if there are only one, or two, they're crows, but if there's more than two, they're rooks. They very often flock together and build their nests in the same group of trees, hence the name rookeries. On the other hand, he told me, crows were very different; they were very much loners! Unfortunately because of their situation, and through no fault of their own, some people become the same. I knew exactly what he meant.

When I was walking home from where Dick had dropped me off, I began to feel the heavy weight of the contents of the sack I'd been given for my day's work. The coppers I'd been given were bulging from my pocket; I knew I'd been rewarded very well indeed and I'd really enjoyed the day.

Chapter Forty-eight

A short distance from home, I turned into the adjacent woodland and settled myself on an old tree root out of sight of the bungalow to fully inspect everything I'd so generously been given. I opened the sack and, as instructed, very carefully took everything out and laid them on the ground one piece at a time. I couldn't believe the unexpected sight in front of me; my mouth fell open with delight. If this wonderful spread was normal home-made farmhouse produce I liked the idea of living in a farmhouse!

I marvelled at the sight of a pudding basin completely filled and covered with a cloth, tied at the top and trimmed around its contents which had a note attached explaining it was a freshly-made steak and kidney pudding ready for cooking. There was a large cake covered with chocolate icing, plus half a dozen smaller ones with a glazed half-cherry on the top as well as a large bag of bread rolls, six large lumps of bread pudding, six duck and six chicken eggs, half a leg of home-cooked ham and a brace of wood pigeons. There was also some bacon, a string of onions, and several jars of pickled fruit and jam, plus lots more.

Having counted the money I'd been given, I very soon realised there was not only enough to purchase several packets of cigarettes; there was also sufficient to allow for any change

I might need to bring home. Under a cluster of ferns I placed the required amount of money to buy two packets of cigarettes. I put the rest of the coins close to the tree where I'd sat, then did the same with the box containing the six chicken eggs. I carefully placed the rest back into the sack, with the exception of the brace of pigeons, which I hung high overhead, on the branch of a hazel tree, gently swinging in the light breeze.

Wendy must have picked up my scent and ran to meet me as I passed through the gate. We made a fuss of each other until she smelt the other dogs; she sniffed my socks, then my legs and her tail stopped frantically wagging; she stood up on her back legs, then leaning against me with her front paws, sniffed and snorted at my hands and arms. I could almost read her mind and I instinctively knew she was asking herself. "Where's he been? Where have all the others come from? What's he been doing, and why couldn't I have gone?" Wendy's bewildered and thoughtful expression showed clearly on her face until we reached the log stack outside the kitchen door.

One of the red robins was sitting tightly on its nest protecting the squabs, while the other was probably foraging for insects and grubs to feed them. Jet lay curled up fast asleep on top of the logs ignoring the fact he was no further than eight feet away from the red robin's nest. His left leg dangled over the side. Although the fur at the tip of his badly injured front paw had completely healed, it seemed strange it hadn't grown black again, but remained snow-white. From where I stood, I could see his tummy was full. There were plenty of young bright-eyes about at this time of the year, and he wouldn't have had any problem in catching them; he'd been well fed and was fast asleep.

Through the partly open kitchen door I noticed several dirty plates left on the table. I realised Mum and Dad had eaten their main meal of the day, and they'd undoubtedly be in the sitting room fast asleep. There wasn't any food prepared, or cooked for me, as Mum would have assumed that what I'd eaten during the day would be sufficient. For fear of waking either of them, I quietly cleared the table and carefully laid out the contents of my sack before going back outside.

The first thing I did was to look at the brickwork Dad was going to do. It looked good, and there were enough bricks to cover the length where the sitting room was to be, up to damp-course level. He must have felt very pleased with himself; so much he'd even cleaned, and washed the tools he'd used.

A short time later, after I'd collected the money I was to use as change, the chicken eggs, and the brace of pigeon, I reached the beech tree and sat for a while. I'd walked a long way during the day, covering the edge of most fields on each of the three farms. I lit a fire; then rolling up some chicken wire, I laid it up to the half full line inside the billycan. After quenching my thirst, I filled the can to just under the half-full level with clear fresh stream water, and then rested it across the bricks of the fire to boil.

I placed the money and eggs inside my store tin for whenever they were needed. I fetched one of the pigeons from the hazel branch where I'd left them hanging; as the birds hadn't been plucked or drawn they would be perfectly all right treated as game meat and allowed to hang for two or three days. I didn't bother too much with the bird; I simply drew it, trimmed it and then to save time, I skinned it; in all it only took a couple of minutes, there wasn't any mess and the waste was burnt. Using my penknife I cut the bird in half lengthways then placed the two halves in the billycan. They lay just out of the water on the wire rack I'd made. I fitted the lid and sat down.

Wendy, as usual, got herself comfortable by leaning against me. As she expected, I put my arm around her and cuddled up, while we both patiently waited for my pigeon dinner to steam cook. She knew she'd get something or other if at all possible. I was pleased she'd forgotten, forgiven, or realised she was unable to do anything about the other dogs I'd met!

It didn't take long before the steam began hissing from the small gap under the lid of the billycan. Dinner wouldn't be long! It was a warm evening and there were still a couple of hours of daylight left. I sat back and relaxed in the peacefulness and warm comforting feeling which seemed to radiate from the beech tree. I turned and read some of the extraordinary phrases and messages carved on the trunk. Then looking up through the pale green leaves reflecting like tiny mirrors, I thought again; this really was a very special place!

I recalled Dick telling me that through no fault of their own, some people during their lifetime could unwittingly become 'loners.' I'd previously realised, how easily it could happen; sometimes I'd feel left out of things when I saw the happiness and feelings shared between most families. They were fortunate, but how many of them realised it? I always felt happy for them and was never concerned for very long, because I enjoyed meeting and talking to people; it was natural for me to learn how to mix. But I'd also learnt how to become completely independent. It was easy to overcome loneliness and sometimes it was even enjoyable. Importantly, I realised that failure or success mostly depend on the confidence you have in yourself, or whatever it is you do.

Carefully removing the hot lid, I tested the pigeon with the tip of my penknife; it was ready for eating. I positioned it on the lid to cool and then removing the wire rack, carefully placed one of the chicken eggs in the hot water to hard boil. I removed the two pigeon legs; they were small with only a little meat. Wendy watched every move I made, while the saliva dripped from her tongue in anticipation of something to eat. I knew how she must have felt as I fed her and removed the thick and, surprisingly heavy breasts from the carcass. I could hardly believe how tightly packed with beautifully flavoured meat they were. By the time I'd eaten them, plus the boiled egg, on top of what I'd eaten during the day, I felt bloated. Wendy had also eaten sufficient; her tummy was bulging and I knew I wouldn't need to worry about her!

I cleared up and went home, knowing I had enough food to last a week, plus what I'd brought home. I'd even earned enough money not only for Mum's cigarettes, but also for some urgently needed size 16 and 12 fishing hooks.

Mum and Dad were in the kitchen when I got there, inspecting the food I'd been given. They both smiled at me; they must be very pleased I thought. Dad immediately asked if I'd be going to any more shoots and that I could always go again, particularly if I were to bring more farmhouse produce home. He told me everybody must have been pleased with what I'd done; he and Mum certainly were.

Mum cut three slices of the chocolate cake. We each had a slice, but in addition, I was given a piece of bread pudding. Mum told me I'd probably had sufficient to eat all day and wouldn't need anything else; in any event, she wasn't going to start cooking for me at that time of the day. I was glad I'd had the foresight to keep the eggs and pigeons for myself!

Chapter Forty-nine

Mum and Dad enjoyed the duck eggs and bacon; they ate them all for breakfast within the first two days. I'd have thought there'd have been enough steak and kidney pudding for the three of us, with the chocolate cake for afters. But I was wrong; all I saw were the dirty plates.

I didn't see anything of the bread rolls or the small cakes; nevertheless, by the end of the week, I'd been reminded several times that nobody except me had eaten any of the bread pudding; I'd also eaten most of the ham. It was true, even though I'd barely been given enough each day.

Every day that week I was given the home-cooked ham; with cold boiled potatoes, pickled onions, and a piece of bread pudding. I'd enjoyed my daily meal for the first four days, but after a week of the same thing every day I was pleased when it was all finished. I thought myself lucky I'd kept the pigeons and eggs as extra food; I should have kept more but at least they helped. At first I thought it was wrong to look after myself first, but later when I reconsidered the situation, I decided it was a good job I had.

Dad and I started work early on the Sunday morning. I reminded myself that, the chance of going anywhere or having any time for myself during the evenings or weekends, except perhaps on Sunday afternoons, would be out of the question until all the concrete for the foundations had been poured and the brickwork could be started.

Twice within the next three days, Mum told me to get her cigarettes; neither she nor Dad ever realised how much I enjoyed going! The first time, I simply made the collection and sorted out the change from the tin hidden close to the beech tree. Then I collected some mallard eggs from Ifold Lake and caught myself a fish dinner. On the second occasion I made the collection the same as before, but not until I'd enjoyed some time with Dave. Both of my parents would have been furious if they'd known my little secret. I'd have been in deep trouble and Dad would have been even more enraged if he realised that whenever he caned me, it was with a previously prepared stick.

A week later, I'd mixed the third batch of concrete and Dad was spreading it into the footings, when Mum arrived, and quietly started talking to him. It appeared to be a serious conversation; I was a little concerned because they kept looking towards me. Eventually Mum called out, "Robin come here, I want speak to you."

"Yes Mum, what is it?" I said as I reached her.

"As you know, Nan comes home tomorrow, thank goodness," Mum said smiling. "I've boiled as much water as possible and put enough into the half-size tin bath for washing our clothes, and also filled the big basin for washing-up our dinner things. Your father says you can help me clear up the wagon so it's clean and tidy for when Nan gets home."

"Okay Mum, saves me mixing the concrete," I replied looking at Dad, "sorry Dad."

"I always rest on Sunday afternoon," Dad reminded me, "so you won't be helping me any more today anyway; certainly not by the time you've cleared the mess up indoors."

Mum always made me clear up whenever Nan had been away. Dad and I knew if I didn't clean up, Nan would have to do it when she got home; neither of us would allow that. Dad was annoyed and it showed on his face. I felt the same, but dare not say, or show it.

Using the large scrubbing brush and washing board, I knelt on the ground outside and washed and scrubbed two weeks' worth of dirty clothes. Then, wringing them out and hanging them up to dry, I realised the ironing would now take priority. These clothes were all we had to wear and ironing would be Nan's first job.

By the time I'd washed all the crockery and cooking utensils; generally tidied and cleared up, and swept through the four small rooms, Dad had finished his work for the day. When Mum had prepared and cooked their dinner, I was told mine would be potatoes with grated cheese and farmhouse pickles. It would be my first meal of the day and be on the table for me at teatime.

Fortunately I had three mallard eggs left; and was soon sitting under the beech tree, where I'd boiled them, eaten two and given Wendy the third. They certainly made me feel better while I waited until my evening meal.

I wasn't surprised to find Nan ironing the large pile of clothes when I got home from school the next day. We'd both missed each other very much, which was obvious from the way we kept on chatting; we were like best mates, who trusted and would do anything, for each other.

Chapter Fifty

For several weeks the only chance I had to see and casually mooch about with Dave or Michael, was when I was told to get cigarettes; fortunately it was quite often! What would normally have been spare time was fully used working on the foundations; it was hard work for me and seemed to go on forever.

On the third week of June we finally finished and Dad was able to start the brick-laying. It wasn't such hard work stacking the bricks and mixing the cement, compared to mixing the concrete. Dad was delighted with the results we'd achieved. He was so pleased with me I felt sure he'd remember my birthday on the 24th; it was only a few days away. The day arrived, passed, and nothing was said. I never bothered looking forward to birthdays again. Nevertheless the foundations were finished and the worst was over. At least I thought so; how wrong I was!

When school broke up for the summer holidays, I often had time during the week to go out with my mates. I always enjoyed spending time learning or chatting with Mr Rose and Amy Lucas but it was essential I should always have finished stacking the bricks, and to have mixed any cement, for when Dad got home of an evening.

When I met Michael one day in mid July he asked me if I'd like to help him separate the honey from the wax combs his father would remove from the beehives. I thought it would be a good idea, as I'd never seen it done before. Neither of us envied Frank the job of collecting the honey. Even though the bees had become drowsy from the dense smoke he'd puffed into the hive, it was necessary to protect his hands and arms with long gloves. He wore a hat with a large brim, from which hung very fine netting over his face and neck, to protect him from bee stings.

On the kitchen table were basins and bowls of every description. I was shown how to remove the wax surface from the honeycombs, then to hold them upright over the bowls to allow the honey to drain out. When each receptacle held sufficient, Michael's Mum filled jar after jar with the sweet, smooth golden nectar, giving me two of the jars to take home. Michael and I sucked the combs smooth for any honey left inside. We should have realised when we'd had enough and stopped; we did realise it eventually, but far too late, and felt quite ill!

The weather was getting hotter by the day. One morning I was enjoying myself laughing and splashing about with friends in the river. Occasionally despite the noise of our shrieks of laughter, the loud bang of the gate slamming shut on the footbridge indicated somebody was passing. We always waited a few moments to find out if it was one of our friends. All inhibitions had been forgotten or dismissed by everyone, as enjoyment and companionship took priority over everything.

When we'd finished playing about and said our farewells, I headed towards the silo. It was clearly visible sticking up high above the surrounding trees. After I'd passed it, I noticed the two owls perched inside the cages. Their eyes were closed, and they didn't show the slightest sign of any movement. Definitely night owls, I thought. Leaving them in peace, I continued a few yards further along the lane.

Tommy, who was close to the verge and front gate, was hacking at the long grass and tall weeds with a sickle. "Hello Rod; that's funny! I was only thinking this morning; I must come and see you within the next few days."

"Why Tommy; it must be important if you're prepared to walk that far?" I jokingly said.

"Well it is really," he replied, "I remember you telling me how you got your fishing rod, and you thought your Mum or Dad wouldn't understand, do you remember?"

"Yes, of course. Apart from Dick and the other dairymen, you're the only person who knows I've got one."

"Well, why don't you say I gave it to you as a goodbye present; they'll never know. That's why I wanted to see you; to say goodbye, and suggest the idea of the rod." He sounded a little hoarse and upset as he spoke.

"Thanks, that's a good idea," I said, "but what do you mean, to say goodbye?"

Tommy and I sat on the soft grass bank. Then he explained his family had fled to England from Poland at the beginning of the war when Germany invaded the country. The family was of Jewish descent and would probably have been killed if they were caught. Tommy explained that most of his family had escaped to Canada and now his parents had been given clearance to emigrate and join them. He and his family would be leaving Ifold within the next ten days.

When we said our final farewell, we were both happy for the fresh start they'd deservedly been given for a new life with the rest of their family, but were both upset because we'd become friends who would undoubtedly miss each other.

I ambled along the lane until I reached Hogwood and was about to pass the main track leading into the woodland when I heard a sound I'd heard before, but couldn't remember where. It puzzled me, so I slowly and quietly walked along the track until just around a bend there was a sight I'd never seen before, or would ever forget. What I saw was the very reason for the area named Hogwood.

Wild boars were softly grunting as they rooted up the dry foliage in search of tender morsels of food. There were five large ones at least waist high and ten, or more others. Four or five were half-grown; all the rest were weaners, no larger than a small dog. The smaller ones couldn't grunt; they simply made a funny little squealing noise. I had to be careful, as the large boars would be very heavy and could easily rip me open with their two long lower teeth which grew upright, protruding like tusks, from their lower jaw. Being able to partly hide behind a tree, I watched them enthralled. They were thinly covered in a mixture of light brown to black hair; it grew longer around the jowls, ears, chest and the hindquarters. Slightly lighter hair grew in narrow rows along the sides of their bodies from front to back. Apart from their bright shiny black eyes, horned snouts and dark hairy faces, the most noticeable thing about them was their tails. They were longer than I'd expected; straight, and hairy, more like a dog's tail than the corkscrew shape of most pigs, and swished from side to side continuously.

They were fascinating and I watched them for five minutes or so. Then they saw me; with their bellies wobbling from side to side, they rushed off in the opposite direction, loudly grunting and squeaking. Two of the large ones slowed down, then turned to look at me; I thought my heart would stop beating when I thought of the damage they could cause. They seemed to glare into my eyes with disgust at being disturbed; then to my horror they charged towards me! I knew by their size, weight or tusks alone they could probably kill me. I was worried and concerned for my safety; the branches of the pine tree I'd partly hidden behind were far too high to reach and I couldn't climb the tree for safety. Then to my amazement they both stopped only feet from me! Grunting and puffing at each other face to face, it was as if they were saying, 'why are we bothering?' They looked at me; grunted again, then trotted back to join the others. I ran out of the woodland in what must have been record time.

In spite of being safe, and back on the stony track heading towards home, I walked at a far quicker pace than normal. I realised I was still a little scared and made myself slow down. How lucky I was to see such a rare sight! The strange grunting and squeaking I'd heard, together with the sight of their fat wobbling bellies and bottoms as they trotted off brought a smile to my face and I chuckled aloud.

Reaching the small pig farm, I saw the owner sitting in the shade; he must have been working in the heat and was taking a rest. As he mopped sweat away from his forehead, other beads dripped from the tip of his nose. The heat was ideal for sitting and resting, but too hot for working in. Stopping for a short time to exchange greetings, I told him about the wild boars I'd seen. I was surprised when he told me he'd never seen them in all the years he'd lived there. He knew they lived in the woodland, because he'd seen their tracks in the mud, and heard the loud noises they sometimes made at night. He was pleased they seemed fit and healthy and didn't harm me.

We chatted like a couple of old women, as he put it and it was a good half-hour before I set off again.

Halfway along the track I saw a magpies' nest built high in an oak tree, which grew on the edge of a small uneven field, where pigs at sometime or other, had completely cleared the area. There were pits and mounds, where their strong snouts had ripped out tree roots. On some of the mounds patchy grass had grown; others were covered in sun-baked clay and clumps of root lay everywhere.

I crossed the field to the oak tree and looked up between the branches at the nest. I wondered if it contained eggs that I could have for a meal, but I never found out. The nest was high and the branches that held it firm and safe were so small they were no larger than twigs; one glance and I knew it would be unsafe to climb.

Disappointed, I walked back to the edge of the field. Reaching a grassy mound, I sat and putting my hands behind me leaned back, placing them on a clay mound to support myself. As my right hand went down onto the mound I felt a slight movement and a light flick on the inside edge of my wrist. I casually glanced over my shoulder out of curiosity. What I saw horrified me!

For a fraction of a second it remained attached to my wrist. Then slowly, it uncurled itself from the top of the mound, sliding slowly, smoothly and silently into the grass. The light-grey colours with black round spots on the side, the 'v' on the head and the zigzag markings on its back, which covered the length of the slender body, set off a panic alarm which repeatedly shouted adder! Adder!

Chapter Fifty-one

I leapt to my feet, then turned to look at the adder; it had slipped away unhurt, silently and without a trace. The mound had a smooth flat clay surface in the middle, which had been worn level where the snake had lain curled up sunbathing on many occasions before. Completely unaware of what I was doing, I'd placed my hand on the creature while it slept. Startled, it had reacted instinctively: we'd both had a shock, but mine was undoubtedly the greater!

I knew I'd have to act quickly and get help from a doctor. I'd heard on several occasions that people had been known to die from the poisonous venom of an adder bite. I'd also heard I must cut deep across the bite to make it bleed freely, and then suck hard to draw the poison out and be sure to spit it away. It's the only thing to do and should be done as soon as possible.

I didn't hesitate; opening my pruning knife and left-handed, placed the razor- sharp tip onto one of the snake fang marks, in a line with the second. I didn't think about any pain; the knife was so sharp I shouldn't even feel it. When my wrist, the blade, and the fang marks all lined up together, I pressed down and away. It was all over painlessly within the bat of an eyelid. I sucked as hard as I could to clean the deep wound until it was almost white and had virtually stopped bleeding.

I'd pressed the tip of the knife down a fraction too hard and as I'd drawn the blade through, the two fang puncher marks the tip had hit my wrist-joint bone and twisted to form a deep cut the shape of a horseshoe, which left a scar for life. I wrapped the wound with my handkerchief; it was more like a piece of dirty rag, which I only used to stop any bits and pieces from falling out of my pocket.

I glanced across the lane at the goat farmer's property. Like many other homes around the area, it was only a temporary building made from weather boarding and corrugated tin. He owned a pushbike, but not a telephone. He'd be unable to help me. Heading back towards the pig farm I passed the only other property in the lane; it was the smallholding belonging to Sid the postman. He had the Post Office delivery pushbike, and a horse and cart, but again, no telephone. He wouldn't be able to help me either; I kept walking.

When I reached the pig farmer he looked hot and was sweating again, working in the sun clearing out one of the occupied sties. Pushing an enormous saddleback sow to one side he stepped out closing the gate behind him. I noticed the sow was so large; she could easily have crushed the farmer's legs against the wall of the sty causing him serious damage without even realising it.

The farmer sat down in the shade and wiped the sweat from his face again. "I thought you'd gone home," he said, but before I could answer he must have noticed the handkerchief I'd tied tightly around my wrist. "What have you done to yourself, you daft thing?" he smiled.

I explained what had happened and exactly what I'd done. He sat listening, his mouth open as if in horror and disbelief. "My goodness, at least you've got rid of the poison; well done! I haven't got a telephone," he said, "get in the pick-up; slowly, don't rush, just take your time. I'll get some clean cloth, and get you to a doctor." While I got into the Morris pick-up he quickly fetched some clean damp cloths from his house. Within two or three minutes we were on our way.

As we passed my home we both looked to see if the car was there. "It looks as if your Dad's still at work, so we'll keep going. By the way I know your name is Rod, mine's George, I thought it was about time you knew what to call me, okay?"

I was pleased he'd told me, "Yes, and thanks for your help George."

We passed Ifold Stores and continued until we reached the junction with the Loxwood road. He turned towards the village, then almost immediately into a driveway. It was the surgery, and the home of Dr Vine. Even though I felt quite well, George made me walk slowly into the waiting room and sit down. Dr Vine who was off-duty was found in the garden and came in immediately George called him.

The three of us went into his surgery, where he removed the cloth; then looking closely at the wound said, "well it looks as if you've kept it clean enough; two or three stitches should hold it, but it doesn't look quite right. Tell me young man, exactly what did you cut it on?"

Looking at the wound I simply answered his question as I withdrew the knife from my pocket and opened the blade, and handed it to him. "My pruning knife, doctor."

"This is filthy; it's not only used for pruning is it?" He asked inquisitively.

"No," I muttered; then proceeded to tell him about cleaning, and gutting the fish, all the various paunching and skinning I'd done, Wendy's ear, and lots more.

"And you've never cleaned it once, I'll bet." He paused as if thinking for a moment, then added. "I'll have to give you a tetanus, and a penicillin injection; serves you right, perhaps next time you'll clean the knife. Now then, how did you cut yourself in the first place?"

I had a feeling I'd be in for another ticking off, but as he had to be told I said. "I didn't see it at the time, but I accidentally put my hand on to an adder. I think it was sunbathing and fast asleep; anyway it bit me."

He stopped inspecting the wound and stood upright. "What did you do then?"

"I did what I had to. I cut where I'd been bitten, so the poison could run out with the blood. I then let it bleed for a little while. After a few moments, I sucked it hard until it was almost white and stopped bleeding; then I wrapped it tight and found my friend George who brought me here."

"You did very well; you should be pleased with yourself," George said smiling.

Dr Vine suddenly sat down heavily. He stared at the floor motionless; his mouth was slightly open and I could hear him breathing. George and I looked at each other wondering if we should say something. After a while he lifted his head; he looked at George, then me. I knew only too well what anger sounded like and was able to sense the tone in his voice as he said, "almost everybody thinks the same as you, but let me tell you, it's the worst thing you can possibly do."

"I thought I was doing the best thing," I said.

"I thought so as well," George added.

"With venomous bites or stings there are four things you should never forget. Never cut it or make it bleed. Never try to suck any poison out. Never tie it tight or apply a tourniquet. And never cover or put a bandage on it. You've done everything wrong! Take your shirt off and lie on the couch; I'll see what I can do." He turned and spoke to George, "you will be staying won't you?"

"Yes of course, I'll wait and take him home," George replied.

I'd never been to a doctor before and found it all very confusing, particularly when he took my blood pressure, listened to my heartbeat, and looked inside my mouth and ears. After a few minutes he lifted my arm and said, "despite doing all the wrong things, I think you'll be alright. You're young and fit; that'll help. You could do with some spare weight because you're all muscle; normally that would be a good thing, but not in this case."

"Why not?" I asked. "If I'm fit, and strong, surely that's a good thing isn't it?"

"Normally yes; but because this type of venom attacks the muscle system, you'll soon begin to feel very weak. You'll need plenty of rest; all you can get for at least a week, maybe two. The symptoms could take as long as two days before they show."

He directed his attention to George and spoke softly and quickly, repeatedly asking him if he fully understood. George confirmed what he was told by repeating everything word for word. Then turning to me he said, "I shall write a note for your parents. Your friend will give it to them when he takes you home shortly. I shall give you an anti-toxin vaccine now; it's all I can do, its all there is. Hopefully you'll get well in no time at all. My colleague Dr Wood will pop in and see you for the next few days."

The doctor gave me the injections I needed and told me, "you can go home now but you must remember; there'll be a marked swelling and blackness to your arm; it's expected. You'll probably feel drowsy and dizzy and you may feel sick;

hot one minute and cold the next but don't worry. If anything else happens tell your parents to get in touch with me straight away. You will get very weak; it's most important you get complete rest. Keep still, and calm, there's nothing else I can do. There's one more thing you must do though."

"What's that doctor?"

"Clean your bloody knife!"

Within a few minutes, after thanking him for his help, George and I were on our way home.

Chapter Fifty-two

On the way home, George asked me if I was still feeling all right.

"Yes, I feel fine thanks to your help. In fact I don't feel any different than usual; a little hungry maybe, that's all."

"You must eat to keep your strength up; what did you have for breakfast?"

"Nothing; I never do, but I'll have plenty for dinner, you can bet on it." I tried to sound truthful and convincing and he believed me. "I'll be okay; thanks anyway."

"Something's troubling you, I can tell," he said as he glanced at me quickly while changing gear. "What is it?" He looked thoughtful then added, "is it the bite?"

"No," I answered, "I can't even feel it; there's no problem with the bite at all."

"Well, what is it then? Tell me," he insisted.

I paused knowing he'd keep on asking until he got an answer. "Oh, It's nothing much," I casually replied. "One of my jobs is to stack the bricks and mix the cement for Dad of an evening. He'll be home now, and it hasn't been done. He and Mum will be going mad. They'll probably think I'm out enjoying myself and have forgotten. As if I possibly could; I never have yet! It's the last thing I dare do." I could have bitten my tongue. "I shouldn't have told you about all that George.

Please forget what I said and don't say anything when we get home, or I'll be in worse trouble."

"I've forgotten what you said already, so don't worry. I expect their bark is worse than their bite anyway; it is with most people! Anyway, once I've spoken to them, and they've read the doctor's note, they'll understand why you haven't been home. You'll be okay, don't worry."

I wished he were right. My main concern was Mum or Dad's frequent mood swings and aggressiveness. I knew only too well, it wasn't a case of their 'bark being worse than their bite.' Their outbursts were like claps of thunder directly overhead; so loud it often seemed to shake my brain. It was frequently followed by what I could only describe as a sudden flash of lightning, which struck in the form of a hazel stick.

George never realised I'd experienced both. If I had a choice of either, it would certainly be the, 'bark and bite', never the 'thunder and lightning.'

When we got home George explained everything he could. Dad read the doctor's note and everybody fully understood exactly what would happen once the symptoms began to show. Nan made me comfortable by putting pillows and cushions on to an armchair for me, and placed a spare blanket on the floor at the side, in case I felt cold. Wendy thought Nan had put it there just for her, and immediately settled down comfortably.

Mum and Dad stood outside talking to George. When Dad realised he was a pig farmer he promptly agreed a price and delivery of a weaner. I heard them thank him for his time and for the help he'd given me, and told him I'd thank him myself as soon as I was well enough.

With Mum's approval, Nan was able to give me a larger than normal-sized dinner to keep my strength up. It was certainly unexpected, and appreciated.

It took Dad three-quarters of an hour to complete all my regular jobs. He knew they had to be done, and there wasn't anybody else, so he got on and did them. He didn't complain or appear to be very concerned even though he was unable to do any of his own work.

On several occasions during the evening Mum hinted how convenient my accident was for me. I wondered what she meant. Nothing was said at first until Dad asked, "what are you talking about Babs, Robin's convenient accident? I don't understand!"

"Well, look at him sitting there like Lord Muck. I wonder if it really was an adder or just a grass snake. Even the doctor wouldn't know yet; there's not the slightest sign of any symptoms. Perhaps he's just telling a story to get off doing some work; maybe it wasn't an accident. He looks very comfortable; he's lapping it up."

I was horrified. How could Mum think, or say, such a thing. I couldn't speak and felt as if I'd died inside.

"You're so wrong Babs," Nan almost shouted, "sometimes you don't even attempt to think of anybody except yourself, do you? Are you worried you may have to get involved and actually do something yourself?"

"That's enough, now stop it, I don't want to hear another word." Dad loudly instructed, glaring at them both in turn. Then looking at me he continued, "don't look so worried Robin; try and forget what Mum said. She didn't mean it, did you Babs? Tell him," he shouted glancing in her direction. There wasn't any response whatsoever; the only sound was a nightingale singing its heart out. There was comfort after all above the noise of the verbally erupting thunder.

An hour or so later Dad began to give me quick glances, asking how I was feeling. I told him not to worry; I was okay, and felt fine. I wondered if he was beginning to believe that the terrible remarks Mum had made could be correct. I was so concerned by the thought that I went to bed. Nan came to bed a short time later, and we chatted for a few moments before she fell asleep almost immediately after saying her usual last words of the day to me. "Good night, God bless, Robin, and don't forget to say your prayers."

Years beforehand, at various times, I'd thought Aunt Kit, and then Aunt Meena was my mother. Nan was so kind and caring towards me that if I hadn't known otherwise, I'd have thought the same about her. I wondered if Mum had ever realised how fortunate she'd been to have a mother like Nan. Probably not, I thought; she expected to be looked after by everyone.

The next morning, Dad tethered Judy in the woods, dealt with the chicken and then stacked enough logs by the two fires to last the day. As it was a Saturday he intended to work on the bungalow. However before he could start he had to carry and stack enough bricks to last the day. When he'd finished dealing with the bricks, he had to mix the cement, and carry it to the site.

Dad came indoors late in the afternoon for some refreshment and to enquire how I was feeling. I told him I hadn't any discomfort and was still feeling okay. "Well the sooner you get better, the happier I'll be," he said speaking very firmly. "Do you know, it took me nearly two hours this morning doing your bloody jobs, before I could even lay the first brick?"

"Yes Dad, I know exactly how long it takes, because I have to do it every day! I'm sorry I can't help! I wish I could," I lied.

"There's nothing wrong with you, as far as I can tell," Dad muttered.

Mum appeared in the doorway and interrupted saying, "your father won't have time to collect any milk from Mr Rose. You go and fetch it; there's no reason why you can't do your jobs. It won't kill you; if it did, it'd serve you right, and be your own stupid fault. Your father and I agree; there's nothing wrong with you. All you need is a good hiding you little sod; that'd soon sort you out. You certainly deserve one; you've made a fool of us long enough."

It wasn't the familiar low stuttering hooting sound of an owl, or the heart-warming song of a nightingale that awoke me in the early hours of next morning. Something did, but what? I lay still and listened; everything seemed normal. I turned over onto my side in the small gap left between Nan and the wall, and then closed my eyes to continue my sleep. It was then I felt it; the right side of my chest, shoulder, and arm felt rigid. Every muscle became seized in an agonising cramp, as if paralysed. My mouth fell open as I instinctively took a deep gasp of breath to relieve the pain. I wasn't even aware I'd called out in agony; but Nan was! The next I remember was two Tilly lamps, hissing and shining a bright light in the sitting room where Dad must have carried and placed me in the armchair.

By Monday morning it felt as if every muscle in my body had seized rigid. Nan eased my pain by gently massaging my limbs every few hours with horse oils, over the next three days. Whenever I shivered with the cold she'd cover me with the blanket to keep me warm. Whenever my blood pressure or temperature rose, she would wipe the sweat away with a wet cloth. My wrist had turned black and had become so swollen the cut had burst open tearing the stitches out. Nan snipped through the thin twine with the nail scissors, removed the short lengths, and then bathed the wound with Dettol.

During the first week, Dr Wood visited me every day and generally spoke to Nan about my condition. He'd soon realised she was the main person who nursed me and looked after my welfare. Initially I'd expected Mum or Dad to help me; in particular because of their wrongful accusations, but they didn't. They'd never consider they could possibly be wrong and frequently reminded me that I probably wouldn't die. But, as I'd been told, if I did, it'd be my own stupid fault!

By the beginning of the second week the muscle cramp had begun to ease and the agonising pain slowly faded away until I was able to begin to move about without feeling faint or dizzy. Within three weeks of being bitten, the summer holidays had finished and I was back at school. I was also back doing my normal jobs every day, including stacking bricks and mixing cement for Dad.

Chapter Fifty-three

When I was able, I visited George at the pig farm and thanked him for his help and for probably saving my life. He was pleased to see me and we joked about what'd happened. We'd become, and remained good friends, for years to come.

The second thing I did was considered to be serious business. Dad had told me to take the wheelbarrow, a sack and an envelope for George containing a note and money for the weaner piglet I was to collect. George and I chose and caught a piglet without too much difficulty. When it eventually stopped squeaking, we put it inside the sack, tied the top and placed it into the wheelbarrow.

George looked serious as he said, "I expect you'll be the one to feed it twice a day Rod, come rain or shine?"

"I don't expect so George! I know so."

"It's a pity you haven't got any brothers or sisters to help. You'd be able to share the jobs then, wouldn't you? It'd certainly make life a bit easier."

"Yeah," I answered, "like most of my mates have. But it's too late for me now. Anyway I'm used to it; I've had to be."

We eventually said our goodbyes and I moved off towards home pushing the wheelbarrow. With the very first step I took, there were two loud squeaks. I took another four or five steps. It was the same; there were two squeaks to every step I took. I stopped to the sound of George's laughter. We looked at each other wide-eyed, and speechless in disbelief; the more we looked at each other, the more we laughed.

We realised the loud squeaking was caused by what appeared to be two simple identical sounds each one following the other to perfection. When we eventually controlled ourselves after realising where they were coming from, I set off towards home once again. The sound of our laughter was drowned by the noise of the squeaking.

In the peacefulness of Ifold the only sounds to be heard would normally be the wildlife of the countryside. With every step I took, the wheel of the barrow loudly squeaking could possibly be heard two hundred yards away; but with the addition of the piglet loudly squeaking alternately with the wheel, it became a loud shrieking noise, which probably echoed a good quarter of a mile away.

At first I had a slight feeling of guilt for disturbing the peace and tranquillity, but it didn't last long. Listening to the noise of the piglet, and wheel squeaking in perfect time very soon had me laughing until my stomach ached again.

As I reached Chalk Road, Dad came walking towards me. I stopped in the middle of the road and waited. "What the hell is that terrible noise?" He demanded and then added, "we could hear it from home, but now it's suddenly gone quiet. Why?"

"I'll show you, Dad." I answered pushing the barrow about six paces. "What can you hear now Dad?"

He stood speechless, his mouth open, then burst into laughter. He thought it was hilarious and told me if he hadn't seen it for himself he'd never have believed it.

While I put the piglet into its sty Dad probably told Mum and Nan the same story about the squeaking three or four times, each time he told them he made the story a little more comical. They all thought it funny and, more importantly; Mum and Dad were both in a good mood.

They didn't ask too much of me for a couple of weeks. As long as I did my normal jobs, plus any others asked of me, they'd be quite satisfied to give me a few hours off at weekends. Because I'd been able to keep my own stock, I was able to save hours fetching cigarettes for Mum! It had proved a good and beneficial idea, particularly as it was one of the best times of the year for food. Moorhens, mallard and other birds laying edible eggs were beginning their second clutch: fish were plentiful and Eddie had grown a garden full of far more fruit and vegetables, than he'd ever need. Without even fixing any snares there was an abundance of good free food. I very soon got my full strength back again.

One evening following their departure to Canada, I told Mum and Dad the story of Tommy and his family and why they'd emigrated. I also told them he'd given me his fishing rod as a farewell gift. He knew I'd enjoy fishing as we'd talked about it on many occasions.

"How'd you know you'd enjoy fishing? I've never taken you," Dad remarked. "Fact is I've never been myself. Wasting time, doing nothing, catching nothing. I'm not that stupid you know, but obviously you must be!"

"Uncle Bert used to take me whenever he could" I quickly replied. "He told me nothing felt more relaxing, or gave more contentment than fishing. He said it helped to clear his mind and it often helped solve many problems by thinking with a fresh and clear mind. I'd only just begun to understand what he meant."

Dad looked at Mum and in a half-laughing tone said, "hark at the little sod, Babs. From the way he's talking, you'd think fishing could solve all the problems in the world."

Mum grinned at me for a moment, then in a giggling tone said. "Tell me Robin! What's the difference between somebody standing on the bank fishing, and somebody who's standing on the bank watching and looking like an idiot?

In a flash my thoughts turned to my most important reason for fishing. It was the necessity for food; the more fish I caught, the more I'd eat. I always enjoyed the contented feeling I got when overcoming my food problem, with a simple logical thought.

Being uncertain of what Mum meant I replied, "I don't know the difference, what is it?"

"It's a very thin line," Mum answered; she was still grinning.

"Oh," I said, then added, "which thin line do you mean Mum?"

"What thin line do you think I mean, you idiot? The fishing line; the one on the reel of course, there isn't another thin line is there?"

"Oh." I said again, "I wondered if you meant the thin line of thought you can sometimes get crossed in the mind."

"Are you trying to be funny? What do you mean, thin line of thought?" She blurted out.

"I'm not trying to be funny Mum! Anyone could think they're looking at a pair of idiots doing what appears to be nothing; it doesn't necessarily mean they are. Perhaps one's enjoying fishing and the other one's enjoying watching him. Perhaps they're both lucky and smart enough to be enjoying the peacefulness of mind and the feeling of contentment and tranquillity. Depends which way you look at it, or the way it crosses your mind. You know what I mean; don't you?"

"Yes, I know what you mean." She said, with a dismissive attitude, as if completely unaware or disinterested in what I'd meant; or in anything I'd said.

Dad changed the subject completely by telling me about the many deliveries expected by the weekend. He'd then show me exactly what I'd have to do, which would take several weeks to complete.

Chapter Fifty-four

Early on the Saturday morning, I'd tethered Judy out for the day and was about to start on my next daily job, when Dad called out and beckoned me to join him. He was standing near the bungalow inspecting the new deliveries.

I'd no sooner reached his side than he said, "right then Robin. First I'll tell you what my job will be, then I'll tell you yours; but remember, it's only to be done when all your normal jobs have been finished. They must still be done as usual, do you understand?"

"Yes Dad, I know what my daily jobs are." I paused for a moment, and then added, "I always do them without fail! Well except when I got the adder bite."

"The least said about that the better", Dad muttered, "just make sure they're done every morning and evening as usual and you'll have no problems. Now listen carefully, this will be the toughest job yet"

Dad told me I'd still need to mix the cement and stack any bricks needed every day as before. He would work on each of the seven rooms one at a time until the bricks reached damp-course level. It was at that stage that my job of preparing the floor of each room ready for the concrete and cement screed would begin. In addition to the other deliveries, there were two separate enormous piles. One of rubble and brickbats, of all shapes, sizes and colours; most were split, cracked or distorted as a result of overheating in the brick kiln. The second pile consisted of large lumps of black shiny lightweight clinker; it needed to be broken into smaller pieces before use, but it was lighter and more manageable than ballast.

"I'll place levelling pegs into the ground of each room as I finish the brickwork," Dad explained. "You put the brickbats and rubble inside each room until the void is filled level with the top of the peg. When you've done, smash the clinker into smaller pieces, then shovel it into the gaps so the whole floor is flat and even. You'll be able to smash the clinker with the mattock, that'll be easy for you, but you'll need the club hammer to smash the bricks."

Knowing exactly what he wanted doing, Dad continued, "next week we'll have a delivery of sand, cement, and ballast. It'll take you too long to mix all the concrete and screed by hand, so I've hired a concrete mixer. Now for the biggest job of all," Dad said speaking more slowly, "as I finish each room, you take over; as you finish each room, we'll both take over. You mix the concrete; I'll fill the barrow and tip it. Then we'll both spread the concrete level and lay the cement screed."

Dad had explained what was expected of me and as far as he was concerned there was nothing more to say. For a moment or two there was complete silence. I could sense he was waiting for me to say something. It was as if it was my turn, but I needed to be careful.

"You're right Dad; it is a tough job and it's going to take a long time." I looked up at him saying, "the problem is the nights are drawing in and within a few weeks it'll be dark by the time you get home from work."

Dad looked thoughtful for a moment before saying, "you should still be able to do at least an hour's work most days. If necessary we'll both have to work all day at weekends until the floors are finished."

I couldn't help smiling as I jokingly said, "if we had spare Tilly lamps and it wasn't raining, you could lay bricks any time; day or night."

Dad looked thoughtful, "what a bright idea Robin." He stopped talking and grinned as he realised what he'd said. "In fact it's a brilliant idea, do you get it? Tilly lamp! Bright! Brilliant!" He paused, "oh never mind; I thought it was funny, forget I said anything."

Dad was pleased he'd been able to make a witticism; it wasn't very often he did. I was pleasantly surprised and answered, "very funny Dad. Ha Ha! I thought I'd shine some light on the subject, that's all," I jokingly replied.

We both enjoyed the silly joke and expressed our feelings with laughter. I was completely unaware it would be the last joke, laugh, or even smile shared between us until the job had been completed.

The concrete mixer arrived by the following weekend. Nevertheless, I continued to mix any cement needed for the brickwork of an evening by hand. It was easier than starting the mixer engine, and throwing shovels of sand and dry powdered cement, plus buckets of water into the air about four feet, to land in the revolving mixer drum. Due to frost, and the cold wind and rain, it wasn't possible for Dad to lay any bricks of an evening. I helped him all day every weekend by continuously replacing used bricks and mixing fresh cement as required. I was told that despite any cold or wet weather conditions, it'd make no difference to whatever I had to do. Providing it wasn't raining too hard, or blowing too strongly for the Tilly lamp to stay alight, rain or shine, I had no choice but to continue the strenuous work every day.

Week after week, every evening, when all my regular jobs had been done, I'd wheel load after load of brickbats or clinker and tip them within the appropriate room. When I'd filled a floor to the required level, I'd smash the brickbats into smaller pieces, and fill the larger voids; I'd reduce the clinker to almost a powder, and prepare the floor area ready for laying. The sitting room and the main bedroom were the largest of the seven rooms. It often took Dad and me three days to lay the concrete and the cement screed in each room.

Due to the amount of work expected of me, I found it impossible to spend any time finding myself additional food in preparation for the winter. I needed to buy essentials urgently, and there was only one way I could get the money; I didn't have any choice but to begin snaring earlier than I'd expected. Dick and the other friends I'd made since the end of the last rabbiting season never let me down; they bought every bright-eye I caught. I hadn't time to cook any fish or bright-eyes for myself, but I never missed the opportunity to take giblets home for Wendy and Jet. They were able to enjoy them most days. Fortunately for me, the money I earned was sufficient to purchase any food I needed.

It may have been because of my determination to survive, and overcome the difficult and often intentional obstacles life would throw at me, that like my dumb animal friends I'd succeed in our God given life.

I could have sold every field mushroom I picked but I took most of them home. We all enjoyed them although Nan and I were waiting for the first of the year's wild mushrooms. What a feast they'd be! When I collected the milk one evening, I gave a bag full of the freshly picked mushrooms to Mr Rose. He was delighted and reminded me how much he'd enjoyed them last year and gave me a box lined with dry grass containing a dozen or so eggs to take home. I cracked open two, and then mixed them with milk in the metal lid of the milk churn. They tasted good and were filling.

A couple of days later, I also gave Amy Lucas a freshly picked bag full. Her thanks, as far as she was concerned were instinctive; but to me, her gratitude meant a lot more; her warm caring smile of appreciation gave me a feeling of comfort and acceptance worth more than all the thanks in the world. It was then I realised her wonderful serenity.

The nights had drawn in and it was dark shortly after I arrived home from school each day. The trees, completely bare of leaves, looked as if they were all standing upside-down with their bare roots smooth, yet twisted and misshapen, tapering upwards towards the cold grey clouds. The wind felt as if it drove the white frost into my body from every angle; my short trousers were no defence and most days my legs were blue and numb with the cold. Most evenings I'd sit around the tortoise stove enjoying the heat until bedtime; when, as if she were a great big hot water bottle, I'd cuddle up to Nan's back to keep warm for the rest of the night.

Eventually, the unforgettable moment arrived; it was at twenty past two on the last Sunday in November that Dad made the last and final levelling trowel stroke. It was just inside where the front door and hallway would eventually be built. As he stood up I noticed his shoulders slightly drop as he visibly relaxed. Then casting his eye over the large smooth floor area spread before him, he smiled for the first time in weeks. He'd been right when he'd told me beforehand it would be 'the toughest job yet.' I'd felt so weak and exhausted on several occasions, I'd had to force myself to continue the task, but I'd been determined not to give in.

Chapter Fifty-five

My normal daily jobs and any others needing to be done were still expected of me, but seemed easy compared to the hard work I'd been doing during the last three months.

To some extent I was gratified I hadn't been able to spend more time indoors of an evening, because if I wasn't there I could neither say nor do anything wrong. More importantly I couldn't be made the excuse for anyone's rush of bad temper! Nan told me Mum and Dad could often hear me smashing the brickbats of an evening and would remark to each other on what a good job I was doing. I knew Nan was pleased I hadn't been shouted at or told to keep my opinions to myself; what's more, I hadn't been given the stick for two months. Nan and I were both aware it couldn't possibly last!

The weather had changed drastically and the temperature now plummeted to below freezing every night and most days. It wasn't worth the risk of laying any bricks because of the severe damage caused by the frost. Everywhere I looked, the woodland and fields had been turned as white as snow, but it was far too cold for any possibility of that happening.

In the next couple of weeks I was able to find time to go fishing; I caught my first fish for about two months. I cooked and ate a strange and unattractive-looking mixture of fish, egg, sugar beet and walnuts, all washed down with a drop of

Judy's milk; it all tasted wonderful! From the unmistakable excitement reflected by Wendy's wagging tail and the continual purring from Jet, there was absolutely no doubt they'd also appreciated their unexpected treat.

The small piglet I'd collected from George, now aptly nicknamed Squeaky, had grown large enough for its intended use and had been collected by the butcher. To see it taken away gave me the same feeling of sadness I'd had the year before. Nevertheless when it returned as bacon, I soon forgot any sentimentality.

On the Saturday before Christmas, arrangements were made to make the regular yearly visit to various members of the family in London and for Nan to stay with her daughter Doss for a couple of weeks or so. All the while she'd be away I'd miss her terribly; but I knew, because of the amount of work she did, her rest was essential. She'd worry I'd work too hard and wouldn't be getting enough food and I'd worry if she'd be getting enough rest.

They were about to leave and as I took Nan's case to put it into the car she very quickly whispered to me, "don't say anything to anyone but when we've gone, look in the bottom draw of my dressing table! There's something for you wrapped up in a pair of your socks. Don't spend it all at once." Then with a cheeky-looking grin on her face and speaking a little louder so she could be clearly heard added, "don't forget while I'm away to do as you're told and keep your opinions to yourself, alright?"

"Oh! I shall Nan," I jokingly replied, "would I dare to think or do otherwise?"

"No! You'd better not either," Mum said in a sharp tone, "you can do whatever you want today, but I don't want to return home to a freezing cold place like we did last year;

make sure the fires are kept alight and the kettle's on! As your father and I told you, there's no reason for you to come with us today. You might just as well stay here and make yourself useful."

I waved as Dad drove the car away and then around the bend at Foxbridge Farm entrance and out of sight, knowing it'd be two or three weeks after Christmas before I'd see Nan again. As I returned to the wagon, my friendly red robin appeared, tweeting and watching me through his pinhead-sized black eyes. He'd stop every few yards, then look back twittering and chirruping rapidly, much louder than normal. It was as if he was telling me to hurry up and reminding me, I had the day to myself. I quickened my pace.

Entering the wagon, I went directly to Nan's dressing table where I found my old sock, exactly where I'd been told. From the weight and the feel, I realised it contained a lot of money; kneeling by the side of the bed I emptied the contents of the sock onto the eiderdown. I stared at the coins in pleasurable disbelief; there were farthings, halfpennies, pennies and a few three-penny pieces, totalling three shillings and seven pence.

After stacking the fires up as high as I dared, I completed my regular jobs, made myself a sandwich then set off to put the money into my tin and collect the fishing tackle. Wendy had been at my side all the time we were out and seemed to shiver in time with me, especially when we were sitting by the side of Ifold Lake or the river while fishing. Nevertheless we soon warmed up and the cold was forgotten when we later sat under the beech tree around the fire, cooking the catch.

Mum and Dad arrived home in the evening; the smile on their faces reflected their approval of the warmth throughout the wagon and the kettle boiling away on the stove. After Mum had made a mug of tea for herself and Dad, she told me they were tired and they both went to bed. I wasn't told anything about their day in London or asked anything about my day. I sat close to the fire for warmth, with Wendy stretched out at my feet fast asleep; her legs and paws were twitching furiously as she made heavy breathing noises and the occasional high-pitched squeak. I thought from the speed her legs were jerking that whatever she was chasing in her dream must have been running very fast.

The next morning, I looked closely at the remaining stack of cordwood. From the amount we'd need during the winter and early spring months, I estimated we only had enough to last until midsummer at the latest. We'd need at least as much as I'd previously used to last while the bungalow was being built.

Dad could purchase cordwood from one of the local farmers; most of them even supplied it already logged at very little extra cost. If Dad bought the cordwood ready-logged it'd save me hours of hard work every week, rain or shine. I was sure he'd agree it was a good idea, as it would allow me to spend more time helping him work on the bungalow. During the evening I explained to Mum and Dad the situation regarding the cordwood and the benefits of buying logs as opposed to lengths. I thought it was a logical idea; but according to them, I was wrong.

Dad stared at me for a few moments, and then in a raised and furious-sounding voice stammered, "I'm getting fed up with telling you to keep your opinions to yourself. Even Nan reminded you to behave yourself before she went away." He paused and glaring at me said. "Are you trying to get away from doing a simple job? Or are you getting lazy? Maybe you just want to waste money, you little sod."

I was fully aware that, no matter what I said or did, Dad would always think otherwise. He'd called me the word I dreaded most of all, 'sod.' Knowing he'd blasted his final shot and aware of exactly how it would end, I kept very quiet.

During the evening, while the stinging on the back of my legs was gradually fading, I was called from the kitchen into the sitting room. As I entered the room Dad glanced at me and spoke softly in an unconvincing tone, "neither your mother nor I enjoy you getting the stick Robin. It hurts us, as much as it hurts you; believe you me, it does." I noticed what I thought to be the tiny hint of a smile on Mum and Dad's faces; both appeared to have a nonchalant attitude, Mum had even continued reading her book. Glancing at them expressionlessly, I remained silent. I thought it was an absurd remark; almost laughable. Did they really expect me to believe them?

"Now pay attention, I don't want to have to tell you again. This is what you'll do in future and I don't want any backchat, okay?"

"Yes Dad, whatever you say," I answered. Somehow I knew I wouldn't like what I was about to be told, and lowered my head concealing any sudden expression of disapproval.

"The cordwood from the oak trees that were on this land when we first got here has lasted a long time, and there's still enough to last until the summer, so you tell me. Nevertheless, if you think for one minute I'm going to buy some when it's finished, you'd better think again. You can travel for miles around here and everywhere you look the whole area is covered in woodland, even on our own doorstep. All we'll need to keep the fires going every day is decent sized birch and oak; to find the right-sized tree, cut it down and bring it home should take you less than half an hour a day. You're lucky; there's plenty around just for the taking. If you want logs delivered to the door you can bloody well buy them yourself; I'm certainly not going to and that's that."

Despite Dad's thoughts on the matter, I kept to my original opinion.

Chapter Fifty-six

By Christmas morning the temperature had risen considerably. It felt definitely warmer but although there hadn't been a frost, the clouds looked heavy and dull, giving a flattened miserable grey tone to everything.

When I'd completed my regular morning jobs, I was told to select one of the chickens and prepare it for the oven, as I'd done the year before. Once I'd selected the unfortunate bird it didn't take me long; it was a job I didn't like and was made worse as, in complete silence, my friendly red robin watched as I plucked every feather.

My Christmas present from Mum and Dad was a pair of baseball boots, and a very welcome long-sleeved woollen jumper. The present Nan had left for me comprised sweets, biscuits, two pairs of hand-knitted socks and a pair of thick woollen gloves. The gifts were unwrapped and spread on the table. I didn't ask why they weren't parcelled and labelled! I'd seen the parcel Nan had left for me previously and wondered why it had been opened.

Mum gave me a half-crown piece to buy Dad his Christmas drink and told me I could keep any change as I'd done the year before. I was also given a bowl of porridge for breakfast; but as expected it'd been made much earlier and was stone cold. I politely reclined the offer making the excuse that as I normally only had one meal a day it would spoil my Christmas dinner.

Shortly after midday, having given Dad the half-crown piece to pay for our drinks, I stood outside the Onslow Arms with a glass of ginger beer and a packet of crisps while Dad was inside the pub with his pint talking to some of the locals. I looked across the river towards the school and the church; the area was in a dip and the shining icy frost still lingered on the buildings and trees. The silence was so noticeable it held my attention as if it were a loud noise.

The floodgates at the old mill had recently been opened and the water level had dropped considerably. A thin layer of ice had previously formed on the water's edge along the side of the river. It had become attached to the mud bank and protruded flat and clear from each side reaching almost a quarter of the way across. It was like a wide thin glass shelf laying level above the water, leaving a gap of about three feet. Between the edge of the water and the underside of the ice, I could see the flat footprints left by an otter and several wading birds, as they sheltered from the cold and worked the edges of the soft mud bank in search of food. The wafer thin ice covered the whole length of each bank as far as the eye could see before becoming obstructed by a bend or overhanging trees.

I looked in awe at the beautiful sight spread out before me as large floating flakes of white snow enhanced the view. I'd never seen anything like it before, and wondered if I'd ever see such a sight again.

I was sheltering from the snow by standing under the porch of the pub when Dad opened the door and told me I could go inside and wait in the warmth of the bar. I was shown to an old wooden stool where I sat unobtrusively, and kept quiet. From where I sat I was able to watch three old men sitting around the fire; each often holding his beer mug between both hands as if keeping his hands warm.

They talked incessantly as if they hadn't seen each other for years. Whilst talking one of them heated a poker. When the tip got red hot and glowed, tiny bright white sparks made a snapping sound as they spat from the brightly heated tip. They kept dunking it into their big pewter beer mugs containing their drink. The heat caused the beer to hiss and foam and the froth overflowed down the sides dripping on to the old oak stained wooden floor.

There were small groups of men either watching or playing dominoes, cribbage, or darts. Everybody, including the local bobby, still in uniform, seemed to be laughing, joking, and enjoying themselves. Mr Humphreys, the local barber who used to cycle to all his customers' homes to cut their hair was there and I overheard Dad ask him to visit us and cut ours every four to five weeks.

Dad had spent the half-crown; there wasn't any change, but it didn't matter. It'd been a year since he'd talked, joked and enjoyed the company of having a pint or two with other men. As I sat watching the festivities, the smiling faces, and the sound of the incessant laughter, it made me feel happy just watching everyone else.

On the way home, the car slid from one side of the road to the other as the tyres tried to grip the smooth surface. The snow was heavy and, settling much faster than expected. Nevertheless, Dad kept going, driving slowly and carefully through the undisturbed gleaming white surface, leaving behind narrow wavy wheel tracks all over the road until we reached home.

Within ten minutes of getting indoors, Mum and Dad sat down to their Christmas Dinner. Mine was also served, but then put on a plate in the stove to keep warm. Due to the bad weather conditions it would get dark earlier than usual and therefore although it was only mid-afternoon I was told, while I waited for dinner, I should get on with my normal jobs. Long before I'd finished, Mum called me for dinner. I knew they'd have eaten theirs and gone into the sitting room. Mine would have been put on the table getting cold, but I didn't care, it was good and filling food, and the place was warm throughout.

It was early evening when I awoke. It was dark and the fires needed to be made up. I lit the Tilly lamps, made a pot of tea, and then gathered some logs from outside the kitchen door; it was still snowing heavily. As I squinted between the large falling snowflakes into the darkness, I felt uneasy; something seemed unnatural. I gawped deeper into the darkness. Two small bright lights glittered directly at me from no more than ten yards away. At first they were motionless, then moved a short distance upwards; they seemed to hover in mid air side by side separated only by a few inches. Then together, as if joined, they slowly moved to the side until they'd completely disappeared. As I stared through the darkness they reappeared, this time closer to the ground before suddenly shooting upwards again, only to slightly move in conjunction with the sound of a soft labial. I'd heard the sound before; it solved the mystery. In a split-second I realised they were staring eyes, reflecting from the bright light of the lamp. My mixed feelings of concern and inquisitiveness instantly disappeared into a wide smile and I spoke into the darkness, "I wish you'd made a noise earlier Judy; you almost frightened the life out of me!"

I took a Tilly lamp into the sitting room and made the fire up. Mum and Dad awoke from their doze and I gave them both a mug of tea before returning to the kitchen. There was plenty of boiling hot water on the stove and knowing I'd be told to wash up the pots and pans I got on with the job while they quietly chatted.

It was about an hour later when Dad called me to join them. On entering the room I was told to sit and listen carefully to what I was told. Naturally I agreed. Wendy sat at my feet with her chin on my knee looking directly at Dad; it was as if we were both waiting for him to begin. He leaned back in his chair, looking completely comfortable and spoke clearly and slowly as if reading aloud. "You worked very hard last year and did very well; much more than most boys of your age would have been able to do! I'm very proud you've done a good job." I stroked Wendy then looked at Mum, I didn't know what to think; something was coming; but what?

Dad continued, "next year I'm packing up my job to spend all my time working on the bungalow. If you have every Monday and Tuesday off school I'll have four days a week of your help. You can mix the cement; stack the bricks and breeze blocks every day, while I lay them! Weather permitting of course." He hesitated then added, "we'll have the roof on by this time next year."

I knew it would be hard work, but thankfully not as hard as previously preparing and laying the floors. Dad appeared pleased and watched my face looking for any sign of my reaction. I glanced at him with a look of approval and then spoke. "We'll get it done, no problem; we'll finish it with time to spare. It's going to be a lot easier than my last job; of that you can be sure." I fervently believed in what I'd said. How wrong I was!

"Due to the snow we'll be unable to work for a few days so tomorrow morning I'll explain everything I want done over the next year. It may not be that easy Robin so don't get excited, you don't know exactly what's to be done yet."

I felt a little concerned but what else could I be expected to do? I didn't realise until the next morning, how shocked I would be when I found out what was expected of me.

Chapter Fifty-seven

The following morning, the snow had virtually stopped. In most places it lay knee-deep in small sloping and wavy soft drifts; in others the light breeze had blown shallow clearings, exposing the cold surface of the mainly bare ground.

Dad told me to join him at the building site of the bungalow. At first glance, his smile made me feel at ease, as he began his explanation of the work expected of me during the next year. After a few minutes I thought he was joking! Within half an hour I realised he wasn't.

After we'd made our way through the snow, we stood next to the piles of building materials, with our backs to the road and looked at all the work we'd previously completed. "This is what I want you to do Robin. I'll tell you now so you'll know what I expect you to do."

I shrugged my shoulders and let out a deep sigh; it was an instinctive reaction I couldn't control as I muttered, "okay Dad."

"I want you to stack the sand-faced bricks in layers of four and eight high. If you stack those about six feet apart all the way around the outside they'll be within easy reach," then quickly glancing at me, he added, "you understand don't you?"

"Yes Dad," I replied, "of course."

"Good, as long as you're sure," he responded; then said, "I also want you to stack piles of breeze blocks the same distance apart as the bricks, on the screed all the way around the inside of the walls. They're much larger so only put eight in each pile. Okay so far?"

"Yes okay so far Dad, it sounds easy enough to me," I said, trying to make a joke of my answer.

"Every day you're away from school, your first and most important job will be to replenish the piles of bricks and breeze blocks ready for use. Then, make sure the spot boards are in the right place and I've always got plenty of cement mixed ready for use." He sighed then added, "that's not all, there's more Robin, a lot more. I'll drive levelling pegs into the ground on the outside, along the whole length of the front, the side, and back of the bungalow to make a pathway along the three sides." He paused and looking at the enormous piles of brickbats and clinker continued, "we'll lay shuttering on the outsides with boards four feet apart around the three sides. Your other job will be to fill and level the space inside the boards with hardcore, rubble, and clinker. Depending on how much you've completed, we should be able to concrete every three or four days. It'll be the same as you did for the floors."

I quickly glanced along the three sides where the path would be situated and immediately realised the area I'd have to level was approximately the same total floor size as the whole bungalow. "How long do think it'll take me to do that Dad?" I asked, dreading his answer.

"I don't know Robin," he paused, "three, maybe four months; it doesn't matter, you'll be helping me for the next year anyway."

"Apart from always keeping the piles of brickwork and mixed cement ready for you, there isn't anything else I'll have to do is there Dad? I've still got my regular jobs to do. There isn't much more I can do, is there?"

"Oh yes there is," he answered. "Now listen, while I finish telling you what I want completed during the forthcoming year."

"I'm going to build a greenhouse on the right-hand side of the bungalow. Then, about eight feet to the right, I'm going to build a double garage with a small workshop. From the garage to the edge of the road there'll be a concrete drive." He slightly lowered the tone of his voice for a moment, and then added, "we'll put all the levelling pegs and the shuttering in place as soon as the thaw sets in. Then I want you to lay the hardcore; I expect you'll need to smash some of the larger brickbats and clinker as before. When you've prepared a decent sized area, you can mix and tip the concrete. We'll level it together."

Mixing the cement, stacking the bricks and breeze blocks every day was one thing; but this was an enormous job for me. Nevertheless I didn't have a choice; I'd have to do it. I was horrified at the thought of it all, as we stood in complete silence side by side, the fluffy lightly falling snow settling on our heads and shoulders. My legs and knees, completely bare between the bottom of my short trousers and Wellington boots, felt stiff in the cold breeze. Dad remained silent; I knew he was waiting for my reaction. When I managed to utter a response there was a distinct and uncontrollable quivering tone in my voice as I stammered, "all that amount of work will definitely take me a year to finish won't it?"

"It'd better not," he quickly answered, "you should be finished by the autumn. By December I'll expect you to have dug the cesspit and drains. I'll have to help you with digging the cesspit because of the depth." He paused for a moment, then wagging his finger in my face to emphasise his seriousness he continued, "I've got all the bricklaying and other building work to do. When I've finished building the walls, I've got to get the wooden trusses for the ceiling joists, the rafters, and battens fixed. When that's done, I'll arrange for a tiling company to finish the roof; I'll also need some glaziers to supply and fit the windows. Do you think you're the only one who's got to work? Because if you do; then you'd better think again. At least it'll be the last of the big jobs you'll have to do. I'll need to employ skilled tradesmen for the plumbing, plastering, and electric work. I should be able to manage the rest. Wherever your help is needed I'll tell you."

There was no consideration for my age, schooling or the amount of time I would have to spend on such exhausting work. I remember the feeling of weariness and shock his instructions and attitude gave me. He walked away a short distance towards home then stopped. Turning towards me we looked at each other, eye to eye, in complete silence. Physically I'd remained perfectly still and expressionless like a statue, yet my mind was racing uncontrollably with thoughts of the pain and anguish I'd undoubtedly encounter within the months to follow. Then I heard him call.

"Have you got anything to ask me?"

"No, Dad."

"Do you understand everything I told you?"

"Yes, Dad."

"Well be sure to remember it all; I don't want to have to tell you again, okay?"

"Okay, Dad."

"Right then, finish your jobs off, I'm going indoors for some breakfast." Then as if it were an afterthought he nonchalantly said, "I'll ask Mum to get something for you" then turned and continued his walk.

I didn't tether Judy outside on account of the deep snow, but left her inside her shed, out of the cold, and fed her bran and pellet food. As I went to feed the chicken, I noticed from a distance that Charlie had left deep tracks in the snow all around the enclosing run, where he'd crept along the edge of the wire netting looking for a way to get inside. Fortunately, the wire run was secure; but for their own safety, after feeding the chicken and geese, I left them locked up inside the run. Charlie was out of luck this time.

By the time I'd finished, the gentle breeze, which had created the whirling snowflakes and small undulating drifts, was slowly but gradually becoming a cold wind. I was about to take protection under the lean-to when Mum called me indoors. "I've made you a cooked breakfast and it's on the table." She paused, and smiled, then continued, "when you've finished, clear up all the dirty crocks and come into the sitting room; your father and I want to talk to you."

As soon as I'd finished clearing everything away, I went into the sitting room, sat down and waited for whatever it was Mum and Dad wanted to tell me.

Chapter Fifty-eight

Sitting back in his armchair, Dad crossed his legs and giving a light cough to clear his throat. He just about smiled as he looked at me and spoke. "Your mother and I realise how much walking you do, so to save time we've bought you a push bike; it's second-hand, and it'll be delivered next week." His smile was still barely visible as he asked, "what do you say to that? Are you pleased?"

I was delighted, yet had the feeling everything wasn't quite right. I knew I should be cautious and not get too excited. "Oh, thanks a million! Even if I only use it for school and nothing else, it'll save me hours of walking every week. Thanks, it's the best Christmas present I've ever had; you've no idea how much it means to me."

"Wait a minute Robin! Just wait a minute," Mum quickly blurted out in a raised voice, "you're not to ride your bike to school, not ever. If you think it would be safe outside all day unattended, then think again my boy. You're definitely not to ride it to school, and that's final. Do you understand?"

I lowered my head and heard myself answer, "yes, but nothing is ever stolen around here. Nobody even bothers to lock their doors or windows when they go out. I'd have thought the bike would be safe outside the school; we're in the country; not in a big town where you need to be more careful."

"I said, no, not ever! Are you deaf? Stupid? Or simply voicing your unwanted opinion again, you ungrateful little sod?" Do what you're told and keep your opinions to yourself. You really are your own worst enemy."

I looked down to avoid any eye contact with either of them and quietly answered. "Yes Mum. But I'm not deaf or stupid. I just thought I'd be able to ride to school. I was obviously wrong; I'm sorry."

"It was a natural mistake," she abruptly muttered; "the best thing you can do is to keep out of the way for the rest of the day. If I were you, I'd get outside! Now!"

"There isn't anything I can do in this weather, is there Mum?" I asked.

"Yes there is! What's more it'll take you a long time," she paused briefly, as if thinking of what instructions to give me. "Take your shovel and clear all the snow away from outside the door, around the chopping block, and Judy's shed. When you've finished, clear a pathway up to the road. That way you'll be able to check if Sid's delivered any post without trudging through the snow every time."

I thought to myself; she's gone mad! Why would I need to check for non-existent post? To me it didn't seem logical. I spoke with an intentionally polite and courteous tone. "Do you really think its worth doing Mum? Nobody's been on the road since Dad and I got home yesterday. There isn't a footprint or track in the snow; the surface is completely smooth and untouched. Sid can't ride his bike in this weather and he certainly won't be delivering any post until the thaw has set in." Neither made any comment, so I continued, "it'll take me nearly all day to clear a path and by the time I've finished, it will have all drifted back again. It'll soon be covered up; it's snowing again now, and the wind's getting stronger. It'll be a waste of time."

Dad leapt to his feet. With one hand he grabbed me firmly by the collar while pointing towards the door with the other. Then leaning forward to within two or three inches of my ear shouted; it was deafening. "You've just talked yourself into the stick again. You've already had it once this week for voicing your opinion when it wasn't asked for. I'll save this one, but don't think I'll forget. Now do as your mother said. Get outside and clear the snow. Now!"

Previously, on several occasions, for reasons beyond my comprehension, they'd both been in inexplicably bad moods. I knew I had to get out as quickly as possible. Within a few minutes I was wearing my Wellingtons, raincoat and school cap; I'd collected the shovel and started clearing the immediate area around the wagon before tackling the pointless task of clearing a pathway all the way to the road.

By mid-afternoon, there were only a couple of dozen yards left to clear. I'd almost finished when the snow, which had been fluttering gently in the air, like small cabbage-white butterflies, stopped. The weather suddenly worsened to almost blizzard conditions; the wind became stronger every minute until it drove the increasingly heavy snow sideways and upwards from all directions. Because of the rapidly flickering and moving white background that surrounded me, I could only identify the outline of the pathway I'd previously cleared. Cursing under my breath, I headed back to where I'd started, hours beforehand.

On arrival, I took shelter under the lean-to, where within minutes I'd removed my wet clothes and was sitting on the log pile for a short rest. Mum, who'd apparently seen or heard me arrive, opened the kitchen door and looked out. Squinting through the gusting snow at my rapidly disappearing work she turned and glared at me. I knew immediately from her expression, and the manner in which she spoke, that she was livid with me. "You were right about the weather! We hoped you wouldn't be; we hoped it wouldn't stop you working either," she paused briefly. "Your father and I are about to have dinner; I haven't done yours yet, I'll give you a call when it's ready. You're all right to wait here; you're in the dry and out of the wind! Don't go away," she laughed, as she closed the door.

With my coat around my shoulders, I made myself comfortable sitting on the logs, trying to keep warm by rubbing my hands on my cold bare knees. I could only sit and wait until I was called. I looked up towards the roof and was amused to see a pair of blackbirds, and several blue tits drowsy eyed and nodding half-asleep perched on top of the log pile. They all appeared completely relaxed and quite unconcerned at my close proximity while they sheltered from the weather. My friendly red robin was perched in his normal position silently watching me; within a few inches his mate sat snug and warm with only the tip of her tail and beak visible. He was the only bird to move; by taking short hops and flutters he gradually drew closer and closer, not taking his eyes off me for a second. Then, as if it were a normal occurrence, he casually made one final hop and perched on the back of my warm hand, which was still placed on my knee. We sat, studying each other in silence, face to face. He knew he was safe, and I could only smile while he began to trill and chirp non-stop. Despite the fact that we were completely different types of creatures, we both instinctively shared feelings of caring, friendship and contentment in each other's presence.

The feeling of suspicion I'd had about the benefits of a bike inexplicably returned. Why? Surely a bike would only help, not hinder me. I'd need to re-think the situation thoroughly to ensure I was right; I sat and thought deeply.

If I couldn't use the bike for school, then what was it for? Slowly it became clear to me; it was obviously for errands and shopping only. By using the bike I'd only take a fraction of the normal time, hence giving me more time to work! The horrifying consequence concerned me deeply. I shuddered; but not with the cold; it was worse! For at least the next year, it wouldn't be possible for me to catch any fish to cook and eat. I'd lose about half the amount of milk, vegetables and other food I was normally given at Turpins Farm. I couldn't lay snares if I couldn't guarantee I'd be able to check them; therefore I'd be unable to catch any bright-eyes to sell for extra food. I realised all the additional work, plus the difficulties the bike would bring me, could only result in a tough and hungry time for me during the forthcoming year.

Regardless of the weather, new daily jobs would include finding suitably sized trees for our own cordwood, cutting them down and dragging them home to stack. I was to clear the area where Dad had been working and clean all the tools and spot boards; check and where necessary, replace any bricks or breeze blocks required and mix the cement ready for use. When all that was done, my next most important job was to lay the hardcore by smashing the bricks, breeze blocks and clinker to the necessary size, then level to the required height; to mix and tip the concrete when required every three to four days until all pathways, the driveway and garage had been finished; only then I was to start on the digging work.

I wouldn't have the time to sit under my beech tree very often and I certainly wouldn't have time for cooking anything;

Wendy and Jet would also go hungry. It wouldn't be possible to go out mooching or scrumping with Dave or Michael, or swim in the river with friends; I knew I wouldn't have any spare time. At least Dad had given me a little comfort after he'd told me he'd need to employ tradesmen to finish most of the remaining work.

Sitting on the logs trying to keep warm, I mulled over several events in the past. I'd successfully overcome various problems I'd experienced of one type or another by simply assessing the situations and options. I'd begun to learn from my mistakes, and importantly those of other people; particularly when they weren't even aware themselves. I'd learnt to fight against failure, and hardship. I'd learnt to have confidence in myself and knew life could only get better. I knew I had to try hard to succeed; even if I failed, it was far better than not trying at all and becoming a complete failure.

Chapter Fifty-nine

Two days later the snow stopped. It lay about three feet deep in most places, but reached a depth of over five feet where it had drifted with the wind against the hedgerows and woodland. A large old Fordson Major tractor fitted with heavy iron purpose-made spiked wheels for gripping soft surfaces, travelled along the road from Plaistow to Loxwood, leaving double sets of wide tracks in the snow. I knew it wouldn't be long before I'd be walking along them to Loxwood for a replacement accumulator and shopping. Dad would travel in the opposite direction to collect water from Spring Hill.

Within a week the thaw had set in, turning the snow into soft slush. It slid from the wet shiny branches of the trees making loud plopping sounds where it melted into clear trickling water that ran from the land into the ditches and eventually flooded the stream and river.

Dad and I finished and level-pegged all the shuttering work to enable me to start laying the hardcore. Despite being unable to lay even one course of brickwork because of the damage the severe frost at nights would cause, I'd stacked and piled materials in readiness for whenever Dad could start.

Due to the bad weather conditions my bike was eventually delivered two weeks later than expected. It was full-size, and even though Dad lowered the saddle I was only just able to sit on it and reach the pedals. There was no doubt in my mind that I'd be increasing the wear on the seat of my trousers until I'd grown a couple of inches. I guessed what my first errand would be; Mum proved me right!

During the third week of January I spent almost a whole day cleaning and tidying everything inside the wagon before Nan returned home. Her homecoming was always heart-warming for me and as usual we greeted each other with a big welcoming smile and a kiss on the cheek. Within half an hour of being home, Nan was already working; she'd made a pot of tea and was preparing vegetables for dinner. Mum and Dad had taken their tea into the sitting room while I sat talking and watching Nan work. "Nothing ever changes, does it Robin?" she said grinning, gently shaking her head.

"No; of course not; it'd be too much of a shock for you if it did," I laughingly replied.

We both smiled at each other as I softly said, "welcome home Nan."

When I'd finished my day's work and eaten my dinner, I was permitted to join the others to sit around the fire in the sitting room and listen to the 'Dick Barton' programme on the wireless. When we'd finished listening they all began talking together while I sat in silence and listened; I knew it was the best thing to do. Nan, talking casually to Mum said, "I notice you've bought Robin a bike. I bet he's pleased; it'll save him hours of walking to school and back." She paused briefly, then jokingly continued," if he'd had one before perhaps he'd be taller by now!"

"He's not to use it for school," Mum quickly answered, sounding obstinate as she muttered her answer through clenched teeth. "If it's left outside all day it'll probably be stolen."

"Don't be so ridiculous Babs; surely it's the main reason for getting him a bike? It's not only for getting your shopping and cigarettes, is it?" There was a long pause before Nan spoke again: "It is, isn't it? I'm right aren't I? Please tell me I'm wrong?"

Mum looked directly at me while answering Nan. "No I can't, because you are partly right. It'll save a lot of time, which he'll be able to spend on the new jobs he's been given."

Nan glared at Mum; she was furious. "Oh dear," she replied, smiling in a blatantly sarcastic manner, "tell me more Babs, I'm sure you can make it sound intriguing."

Everything that was expected of me during the next year was explained in detail. As if it was a second thought, or perhaps to pacify us, Mum quite casually told Nan I could attend the Magpie Shoot this year, if asked, providing I'd be paid with good wholesome food as before; I'd also be given sufficient time to collect wild mushrooms in the autumn. I noticed Nan's hands clench and slightly shake; her prominent gnarled knuckles turned white while her lips quivered momentarily as she tried to conceal her fury.

She sat upright in her chair, then leaning forward and pointing her shaking finger directly at Mum's face, blurted out in an accusing and angry voice. "What about his schooling and general education Babs? This is probably the most important time in his life; you'll take it away from him. What about the friends he's made? What about all the many different things he's learnt? They're all an essential part of growing up and building his character. He won't have any friends left; he'll end up a loner. The only time he'll be allowed out will be to walk to school and back; not three times a week, as you've said, but probably twice a week at the most. I expect the only other time will be to collect your shopping because you can't be bothered to get it yourself. As usual you're being selfish; you infuriate me."

It was as if time stood still; there was silence except for the sound of the clock ticking. In my imagination the ticking became louder and louder but suddenly, the noises within my mind were abruptly quelled.

I was startled, as Nan suddenly and unexpectedly continued in a loud and dominant voice. Her anger with Mum was obvious as she lent forward again, staring directly into Mum's face. "To save Bern a lot of valuable time and effort, you bought a bike about a year ago to help fetch the fresh water from Spring Hill, didn't you?" There was no answer, as Nan paused for a moment in thought, then added, "well Babs, to be honest you have; but on only about four occasions within the last year and I'll tell you why, it's because you can't be bothered! You'll always get someone else to do it if you can. Why can't you use the bike and get your own cigarettes or shopping? Because you can't be bothered! What's more, I'll bet this place was like a tip before I got home; I bet you didn't clear it up, did you? No, you got someone else to do it; you always do, and always will. I'm not wrong, am I?"

We all sat dumbfounded. Nan was right; we all knew it and waited. Would she say more? Dad and I quickly glanced at each other, while pondering over Nan's accusations.

Nan was determined to make it quite clear to us what she knew to be true; and in what she fervently believed and thought. She didn't hesitate or waiver for a moment when she continued, "as a child and being the youngest, you always expected to have everything done for you. Originally the family called you Baby, but you got worse, not better as you got older. We couldn't continue calling you Baby so we called you Babe. The new nickname lasted until you left school but your selfish attitude never changed, so we changed it once again and called you Baby Babs for a couple of years, which finally became Babs. Even now you're still a baby and expect everything to be done for you, don't you? If you didn't, I'd be living with one of your sisters, taking life a little easier at my age; but Robin's still young and he needs all the help he can get, particularly during the next two or three years. I'll be here to help him. You won't: you're unable to; you can't even help yourself!"

Nan had only been home a few hours and she certainly hadn't expected this unpleasant homecoming. She'd travelled a long way and was tired but not too tired to tell Mum a few home truths.

All the while Nan had been talking; I'd watched Dad's expression change while he listened intently. At times he was agog, his eyes and mouth wide open. At other times his eyes and mouth were closed as if forcing himself into silence. I never noticed any sign of agreement or disagreement with anything Nan had said. I felt certain he'd say something; instead, he seemed to practise what he preached by keeping his opinions to himself. Why? I thought. Was it because he didn't want to upset Nan? I knew he appreciated the importance of her hard work within the home; or was it because he didn't want to upset Mum? If he did, it could only result in bad feelings and unpleasantness between them; he'd want to avoid that at all cost.

The atmosphere was heavy and unpleasant as Mum glared at Nan but said nothing. Then turning her attention towards me, I noticed the flushed expression on her face; for once, she looked embarrassed. "This is all your fault you little sod," she shouted. "If we hadn't bought you the bloody bike, none of this would have happened. You cause nothing but trouble, now get out, and stay out until you're called."

Dad quickly reacted. "For goodness sake Babs, it's the dead of winter, its pitch dark and freezing cold. You can't send him outside in this weather!" From the tone of his voice and the expression on his face, I knew he was surprised by her accusations. Glancing toward me he quietly continued, "the best place for you Robin is bed, and don't worry; despite what you may think, you haven't done anything wrong. I'd get out of the way if I were you; off you go."

I wished everybody goodnight, but Mum didn't answer; she stared at the floor. As I lay in bed I thought I'd be sure to hear raised voices or shouting and arguing, but not a word was spoken; there was complete silence. Although I wanted to stay awake and thank Nan for trying to help me, tiredness and sleep ended my day.

Chapter Sixty

As I returned from tethering Judy the next morning, I noticed Dad sitting on the chopping block, which was unusual. He looked pensive; I wondered what he could possibly be thinking. Looking down at Wendy I had an idea, which would at least show me what frame of mind he was in. I knelt at her side and placing one hand on her back to steady her I pointed at Dad with the other. Immediately upon seeing him, she began wagging her tail. I held her still for a few moments, then in a playful tone, whispered, "fetch him! Go on! Fetch him!" She darted forward; Dad saw her coming and opened his arms as she leapt onto his lap, and began wriggling herself up his chest while franticly trying to lick his face at every opportunity.

Taking her in his arms to control her excitement he laughed aloud; the expression he showed was a picture to behold. At first, he showed signs of surprise and helplessness, which quickly gave way to pure delight and enjoyment; even if he hadn't been in a reasonably good mood, he certainly was now. Holding Wendy with one hand, he gently stroked her head with the other. Then glancing up at me from his sitting position said, "they say a dog is a man's best friend Robin; unlike humans they'll never let you down. I'd say Wendy and Nan are your two best friends. You're very lucky; always try to keep your friends, and those you can trust; you never know when you may need each other. It's very easy to make an enemy out of a friend, but it's very difficult to make a friend out of an enemy. It's worth remembering; keep your friends and they'll never turn their backs on you."

"I've got several mates who are good friends Dad. I shan't fall out with any of them because I shan't be seeing much of them for ages."

"The big job ahead of you won't last for ever you know! It might seem like it now, but it's got to be done, no matter how long it takes. There's plenty of time to see your mates when you've finished."

Sliding Wendy from his lap he slowly stood up, then looking directly into my face said, "there are a couple of things you should know. Remember them both and don't ever forget them."

"Yes Dad, whatever you say."

"Good! Firstly as you know, your mother and I won't live forever; nobody does. When we've both gone, everything in our Will shall be left to you. It'll be all yours; you couldn't have worked any harder, and you've earned it." He hesitated for a second then said, "you won't worry about all the work you've had to do then, I'll bet!" He laughed.

I didn't know what to say. Although I was aware I should do something to show my gratitude, I couldn't think of anything!

"Well, haven't you got anything to say Robin?" Dad asked.

"I don't know what to say Dad; I've never thought of it before. But if the boot was on the other foot and it was you who'd just been told, I know exactly, what you'd say."

"Oh, do you; and what would that be?" He asked in an enquiring tone.

I looked at him with a smile as I answered. "You'd say; you hadn't thought about it because there's plenty of life left in the old dog yet."

"Yes, I suppose you're right," he chuckled.

"Thanks anyway Dad. I'll never forget; it's not the kind of thing anybody would. Anyway it's easy to remember; I only hope the second one's as simple?"

"It is," he replied. "Just remember it's very important you never mention anything Nan said about Mum last night. Promise me you'll never, ever, mention it to anybody. If you did and your mother found out, she wouldn't stop moaning at me until I gave you the stick. Forget everything you heard! Whether you think Nan was right or wrong to say what she did; don't even think about it, okay?"

"Yes Dad I promise," then following a short pause I added, "I wouldn't even think of telling anybody, I'd feel too embarrassed!"

Dad's expression quickly changed; he suddenly looked sad as he answered, "I know exactly how you feel."

Neither of us spoke as we walked to the bungalow site to start the day's work. It wasn't until I'd taken the shovel from the sand pile; ready to mix the first batch of cement of the day that Dad broke the silence. "Leave it for the time being, we've got another job to do first which should make life a little easier for you. It may work, it may not; we'll have to wait and see."

Pointing towards the large pile of various building materials, he smiled as he said, "there's an old damaged scaffold board somewhere over there; find it and saw a piece off the good end, roughly about five feet long. When you've done it, get my brace and bit, then drill a half-inch hole about a foot from one end; then find one of the large nuts and bolts we use for fixing the corrugated iron together. I'm going to see Mr Beatle who lives up The Drive; I've been told he sells various bits and pieces of second-hand materials and junk." As Dad began walking towards the car he turned his head and speaking over his shoulder said, "I shan't be long; by the time you've finished, I should be back." As he got into the car and drove off I wondered what he'd gone to get, and why he wanted a scaffold board with a hole in it. I was completely bemused!

Within fifteen minutes of finishing what I'd been told to do, Dad arrived home. After he'd parked and opened the car boot, he called me to look inside at what he'd bought. "Do you know what we're going to make with these?" He asked, as he lifted out two metal rods each fitted with a pram wheel at each end.

"I haven't got a clue Dad; it's certainly not a pram, not at over five feet long" I jokingly answered.

"Well as it happens, you're not far wrong," he smiled, slowly nodding his head. "We're going to make you a cart!"

"What on earth for Dad? Mum doesn't smoke so many cigarettes that I need a cart to carry them all," I joked.

"Thank goodness for that," he replied; "you'll find it very useful for carting the firewood, you'll see. Instead of dragging each length home one at a time, you'll be able to cart about six at a time; it'll be much easier for you. All you need to do is cut and trim the trees, drag them to the lane, stack them on the cart and pull them home; it'll be much easier and quicker for you. You can't say I'm not thinking about making life a little easier for you, can you?" He'd noticed my look of uncertainty as he finished talking and he looked uneasy.

"Certainly not Dad! It'll save hours every week!" I paused, and then added, "think of all the extra time I'll have." I only had to wait a second for his answer and dreaded his response.

"Yes of course; I hadn't thought about that; it means you should be able to finish all your work on the bungalow easily within the year. You'll probably be able to help with something extra; I'd never given it a thought."

I knew the cart was simply an excuse to give me more time for work; it certainly wasn't to help make my life easier.

It only took half an hour to make the cart and during the whole time nothing was mentioned about its use. Dad realised I knew the real reason for the cart and had seen through his deception. With the exception of being told what to do, the next job was also completed in silence. Between the two of us, we drove four long poles into the hard clay to form a square. We then tied four other poles around the top edge and formed a roof by covering the whole of the top area with a canvas sheet secured with ropes.

It hadn't taken long to build, from start to finish; and as we both stood looking at it, Dad spoke, "there you are; it's all yours! Can you guess what for?"

"Not really." I paused for a moment, and then said, "maybe to keep the cement and the tools dry; that's all I can think of."

"Not quite Robin; it's to keep you dry when it's raining and you're breaking the brickbats into smaller pieces. Because it gets dark early this time of year, you'll also be able to hang the Tilly lamp inside whenever you need it."

"You've thought of everything Dad. Was it your idea, or Mum's?" I asked.

"A bit of both really," he answered; "like the cart, it'll make life easier for you."

I kept silent and wondered if he and Mum really believed it would.

My next job was to mix a pile of cement and put it on to the appropriate spot-boards. When I'd finished I was told to spend the rest of the day cutting down trees and to bring them home on the cart. To enable me to judge the amount I could comfortably manage at any time, I started the first trip by carting four, eight foot lengths. When I eventually reached home with my load one and half hours later, Dad had used all the cement I'd previously made and I needed to mix another load. Dad waited indoors until I'd completed the job.

During the rest of the day I carted three more loads of small trees, and decided five ten foot lengths was about as much as I could handle at any one time. I'd also mixed two more loads of cement and spent the last hour before darkness alone, breaking brickbats and laying the rubble. By the time Nan called me for dinner I was famished and tired; it certainly wasn't for the first time, and with life-threatening results, it certainly wasn't to be the last!

Chapter Sixty-one

The last snow of the winter fell during mid February, although the heavy frost and bitterly cold winds continued until the end of the month. March blew in with two weeks of almost non-stop gales and torrential rainstorms. It'd been the coldest and worst winter anybody could remember.

The decision on whether I went to school, or stayed at home and worked, was entirely dependent on the weather conditions. I was only sent to school on days when it wasn't possible to work, because of the severity of the rain or wind. Despite only passing through Turpins Farm once or twice a week and seldom seeing Dick or the other dairymen, I was always expected to help myself to a large beaker-full of milk. The only cattle fodder grown on the farm during the winter was kale; because it was raw it tasted bitter, but I didn't have a choice, I'd eat the large green leaves whenever I had the opportunity.

During the autumn months, I'd enjoyed the bulbous roots of the rat-tail plants, the wild nuts, mushrooms and blackberries. What seemed to be nature's special treat, were the rose hips; the bright red berries and green leaves of the hawthorn, known as the bread and cheese plant, and sweet ripe sloes. Best of all were those Nan had used in her home-made sloe gin: because they'd been soaking in alcohol for months, I was never allowed more than six a day; they tasted wonderful. But now it was winter; nothing grew and everything was cold and bare.

Although it appeared instinctive, it seemed incredibly unnatural to see Jet frequently drag part of his catch home to help feed Wendy. I'd never have believed such a thing would have happened if I hadn't seen it with my own eyes on most days since I'd become unable to obtain any additional sustenance for either of them or myself.

Mr Rose was quite happy for Jet to work his land to hunt for food, even when he roamed around, or between the young chicks and hens. Naturally they'd scamper out of his way; and he knew Jet wouldn't harm them, not for food and certainly not for fun. Having experienced severe injury and the severity of the pain a gin trap could inflict, he always kept clear. Wire snares were a different type of holding trap; virtually no harm or pain is inflicted providing the captive animal doesn't frantically try to pull free. Unfortunately, the majority of trapped animals would instinctively try to escape capture, and would end up severely damaging themselves in the process.

Jet was no exception; he'd been trapped in a snare while hunting for bright-eyes. During his frantic struggle for freedom he'd ripped off an inch wide strip of fur and skin in a complete circle around his neck; he'd learned another painful hunting lesson. Fortunately he was found and released by Mr Rose only a day after the snares had been set. Within a few weeks the wound had completely healed and the snare left its mark in the form of a wide snow-white strip of fur. The white fur looked a little comical against his smooth, shiny, black coat as if he was wearing a white boot and a white collar, but nothing hindered him in his quest to catch sufficient food for himself and Wendy.

The morning frosts, which had previously been so heavy and severe turning everything snow white, gradually became lighter allowing the new growth of the ground cover and trees to shine in the early morning sunlight. The stillness and silence of the ice cold winter mornings had passed for another year.

Spring arrived with the sound of birds singing and tweeting continuously as they flitted from one hazel tree to another. My friendly red robin joined in the excitement with the others; despite reminding them they were trespassing on his territory by either displaying his large red breast or giving a light peck to those getting too close to his nesting area. Larger birds such as crows, rooks and occasionally Jack heron, floated and drifted in ever increasing circles so high in the clear sky they often became barely visible. Occasionally the chicken would lower their heads and straightening their necks, make short running bursts around the run, flapping their wings and clucking with excitement for no apparent reason. They looked as if they'd all gone completely mad!

At the crack of dawn each morning, Judy would bleat until I'd tethered her out on the edge of the woods for the day. She enjoyed the first warmth of the spring sunshine and the new tasty plant growth. Her milk yields gradually increased day by day until I was able to a sneak an unnoticeable amount of the precious nectar for myself. It was necessary; as was the importance of learning to become self-reliant and completely independent, if and when necessary.

As April arrived and the weather got better, I spent more and more days working. Mum told me my education could wait; I'd always be able to catch up at any time. Nan didn't agree, and would question whether the amount of work I was expected to do and the amount of food I was given would affect my health. Regularly and strongly voicing her concerns and objections was to no avail. It always ended in an argument; nothing changed and it was pointless even trying.

Despite Mum believing the amount of food I was given once a day was sufficient; occasionally either Nan or I would be able to persuade her to allow me a little extra. Unable to get any natural food for myself, I'd no choice but to become completely reliant upon my evening meal. At the end of every day, regardless of whether I'd gone to school or worked at home, I'd feel very hungry and weak.

Dad became extremely proficient at brick-laying with the result that by the end of May, I'd spent much more time stacking bricks and mixing cement than either of us expected; laying the ballast and mixing the concrete for the appropriate areas took second place. Nevertheless, I was expected to complete the work in the allotted time. I didn't have any choice; therefore I worked late most evening after having completed my regular jobs.

Although there didn't appear to be a visible wound of any type, the outside of my right leg below the knee began to swell and become painful. I showed Mum a few days later when the swelling had got larger and the skin had turned red; it was so hard it had become smooth and shiny. I wasn't surprised in the slightest at her comments.

She told me that because there wasn't a head to the swelling, it couldn't be as bad as I made out. As expected, I was accused of trying to skive off work and wasting time. I was told to forget all about it and it'd go away.

Three days later, the pain was excruciating and kept me awake all night. Nan, who'd regularly inspected my swollen leg, before and after my day's work, took a close look the next morning. With a hint of sarcasm in her voice she spoke to Mum and Dad, who were sitting at the kitchen table.

"I'm sorry to disturb your well-earned breakfast, but I think you should have a look at Robin's leg. He needs to see a doctor, and soon!"

"It's not that serious, is it?" Dad asked.

"Yes it is," Nan replied, "it's swollen as tight as a drum and it's red hot and throbbing. Worst of all, there are two red lines under the skin, which are beginning to move up his leg. You know what that means don't you? Blood poisoning," she said, answering her own question. "It's got to be dealt with, now. If you don't get him to the doctor, then I shall; I don't know how, but I will, somehow or other."

"You can ride your bike using one leg can't you Robin?" Mum asked.

"Yes, I remember doing it before when one of the pedals broke off."

"Good," she answered, "problem solved. When you've seen to Judy and the chicken, take your time and ride to the doctor. I expect your Dad's got plenty of bricks and he'll easily be able to mix the cement for himself, until you get home."

"Oh! That's all there is to it; is it Babs? You've got everything worked out. Bern can mix his own cement and continue working. Robin can see to Judy and the chicken. Then despite the fact he could either be taken in the car or you could cycle to the doctor and ask him to call in during his rounds, Robin's got to struggle to the doctor himself. Well thought of Babs! You don't have to do anything do you?" Then added, "as usual!" The three of us looked at Mum wondering if she'd answer. But she didn't; she couldn't, we all knew it was the truth.

Within an hour and a half Dr Wood was thoroughly inspecting my leg. He looked concerned and called Dr Vine for his opinion. After a quiet discussion, they had decided on the best course of action. Dr Wood explained to me what needed to be done, and that it needed to be done as soon as possible either there and then, or at the Guildford Hospital. I didn't need asking or telling twice, I made my decision; there and then.

I sat on the examination couch and leant against the half-raised back with my legs in front of me resting on the black, smooth vinyl surface. Dr Wood gently cleaned the swollen area with cotton wool, which he soaked from a bottle. The liquid although clear, was cold and stung my leg. Dr Vine removed a cloth from a white enamelled dish and selected one of the implements it contained. I recognised it immediately, as being the same type of surgical knife he'd used to lance my wrist to release the last of the poison from the adder bite I'd received. It had been painless; therefore I wasn't the slightest concerned and sat upright for a better view.

The combined weight of the scalpel and the doctor's hand was sufficient to gently pierce the tightly stretched skin with the sharp tip of the blade. The abscess burst open, releasing the thick green and yellow fluid to shoot several inches high. Without abating, it continued to pour from the small incision and down my leg for several minutes, dripping on to the cloth placed beneath. Both the doctors pressed down onto my leg one from below the knee, the other from above the ankle, gently working anything remaining towards the erupting cavity. Eventually, as much of the poison and congealed blood was squeezed out; the agonising pain I'd suffered gradually disappeared, although I felt slightly dizzy. I was given a Penicillin injection and my leg was tightly bandaged. Having been given a sealed letter for my parents, a few kind words of encouragement and told to rest for the next couple of days, I set off towards home.

Chapter Sixty-two

On arriving home, Dad followed me indoors where I explained what had happened. On passing the letter to Dad, he opened the envelope and silently read the contents. When he'd finished he looked to be deep in thought as he handed it to Mum. Within a few seconds, she'd glanced through the contents of the note, rolled it into a ball and thrown it into the fire. The expression on her face had changed to a glare: she was furious. I couldn't understand why, although I very soon found out. "You little sod," she blared, "you've told the doctor you don't get enough to eat and you work too hard, haven't you?"

"No Mum; I didn't mention work, or what I had to eat, honestly," I answered.

"Well then, why does it say in the letter you need additional nourishment and rest? I'll teach you not to lie to me you sod! You're due for a good hiding and you've just earned it." Glancing up towards the stick over the doorframe she added, "now get outside and cut yourself a fresh stick; now!"

There was complete silence, which seemed to last for ages although it was only a few moments later when Dad spoke. "I can't hit him while he's got that bad leg Babs. Do as the doctor says, let him rest it."

Mum looked thoughtful for a fleeting second before speaking. "Okay, he can rest until it's time to do his regular evening jobs. If he's fit enough to get to and from the doctor today, he's fit enough to work tomorrow; you can give him the stick then."

Mum had made her decision. It was final. Nothing had changed.

Sitting in the kitchen later that evening after my meal, I cleaned and bathed my leg; the pain had completely faded away. I soon began to feel warm, then drowsy and went to bed. No sooner had I pulled the blankets and eiderdown up to my shoulder, I fell into a deep sleep.

I didn't know how long Nan had been in bed when we were both woken by a high-pitched spine-chilling scream that came from somewhere outside in the darkness. We both sat bolt upright in bed, shocked, and startled. The horrific screech was frightening, and echoed around inside my head, jarring every nerve in my body.

Through the thin partition wall dividing the two bedrooms within the wagon I heard Dad's voice, followed by movement and the sound of the Tilly lamp roaring into life as it threw bright light around the kitchen. Dad's silhouette slowly moved along the wall as he crossed the room and went outside. He'd barely had time to close the door behind him when the horrific noise stopped. For a while the only sounds to be heard were the incredibly melodious and comforting song of the nightingale, an occasional soft bleat from Judy, and the roar of the Tilly lamp, which was turned down to the familiar faint hiss upon Dad's return indoors.

Within fifteen minutes, the nerve jarring screeches started again. The only time they stopped were for a short period whenever Dad got up and went outside. In the early hours of the morning he gave up: it was pointless; there wasn't a clue as to what the noise was or from where it came. It wasn't until dawn it stopped.

Dad decided that when I'd finished my regular daily jobs, my second task of the day would be to find out the cause of the hideous noise that'd kept us awake; where it came from, and what we could do to quell it. Because of the direction the noise seemed to come from, I decided my first call would be to Eddie. I hadn't seen him that year although I knew he'd been about, due to the amount of preparation he'd done in the vegetable garden. He wasn't there and, from the condition of the freshly dug clay, the surrounding grass and vegetation he hadn't been there for about two weeks or so. After checking everything was secure and safe, I headed off to make my next call. I didn't feel any discomfort from my leg; the wound had stopped weeping and had dried enabling it to heal. The job I'd been given gave me a feeling of freedom; it'd been a long time since I'd had that feeling and I knew it might only be short-lived. Simply being able to wander about again with Wendy at my side gave me the relaxed and comfortable feeling I'd missed so much; it made me feel good.

There were only about eight properties within a quarter of a mile radius and nobody I spoke to had ever heard such a nerve jarring screeching. Neither Mr Rose nor Michael's dad, Frank knew the answer. I wished they did; but it wasn't to be. Later, when I told Dad nobody had any idea what had caused the noise, he appeared dubious. He told me someone must have known the answer and I should have found out instead of wasting time.

Dad had rested and was ready for his day's work. I was to mix the first batch of cement of the day, then replenish any additional bricks, or breeze blocks required. When I'd finished the job he said, "I want you to go out into the woodland and look for whatever could have caused the terrible screeching last night. Something's out there somewhere; try and find it! Take the billhook; you've got to cut yourself a stick for later anyway, so you may as well do it now."

I wasn't concerned as I walked to the chopping block for the axe. I needed a fresh stock of sticks from this year's growth in any event; the sooner the better.

I searched a large area of the woodland but all I found were a few deer tracks and some paw prints, left by Charlie. I'd previously heard the loud grunting and high pitched barking noise of deer when rutting; I'd also heard the terrifying loud screech, similar to a baby crying, made by a vixen at night to attract a mate. Both made loud frightening noises, but it was neither a buck nor a vixen. Eventually, rightly or wrongly, I decided it wasn't an animal; there wasn't a single track anywhere. Perhaps it was a bird; but what kind of bird would make such a terrifying noise? I thought hard to no avail while I cut and trimmed six suitable sticks. I took one home for Dad to use on me that evening and hid the rest within a short distance of the wagon.

Having worked until dusk, I was given six painful lashes with the stick; given my daily meal and sent to bed. I was shattered; I felt weak and needed to sleep. I don't know how long I slept for; it felt like only a few minutes, when the horrific noise started again. Everyone was woken and shocked, Dad rushed outside with the Tilly lamp and we all heard him shout out loudly, "who's there, who's there?" There was silence; not a sound could be heard above the hissing of the lamp. From the window, I could see the glare of light reflecting off the trees as Dad walked around the wagon then up to the bungalow before returning indoors. The nightingale began to trill again; everything was peaceful, but not for long. We all found our own way of obtaining a little sleep. The others simply snatched an hour or so during the day, but for me it was a case of going to bed and getting as much sleep as possible directly I'd finished everything for the day.

Over the past few years I'd become accustomed to Mum or Dad losing their temper with me for no apparent reason. But now because of their tiredness, their aggression towards me gradually got worse until they didn't know what to ridicule me for next. Both of them would become so annoyed and furious over such trivial matters that they'd begin to rant and rave at each other for the most ridiculous reasons. They didn't realise they were giving each other a taste of their own medicine; Nan and I thought it hilarious and couldn't help but laugh to ourselves.

On the fifth night, when the screeching once again shattered the silence of the night, I was startled by a loud bang, from somewhere outside. It sounded like a small explosion, followed by complete and utter silence; it could only be one thing! Then my thoughts were confirmed as the sound of the lead shot from a 4.10 gauge shotgun began clattering like heavy hailstones onto the thin corrugated iron roof of the wagon.

I guessed it must have been a Saturday and Eddie had come down for a peaceful weekend, or so he'd thought. The screeching must have become as unbearable for him, as it was for all of us. Nevertheless he had the answer; he wouldn't take a chance, he must have known exactly what he was doing! The target must have been small and close to him and he'd decided there was no need for the larger 12-bore shotgun; the 4.10 gauge would suffice.

I listened to the pandemonium in the sitting room increasing, as Mum excitedly asked Dad what possibly could have happened. Listening to some of the random guesses I couldn't help smiling to myself. For a while I listened to the drone of their voices, then relaxing and keeping my opinions to myself, I fell asleep.

After I'd finished my first jobs the following morning, Dad told me that if at all possible, I was to find out what had happened the night before. As I approached Eddie, he looked up from digging his garden and smiled. "I've been expecting you Rod. I'll bet you've come to see the great big wild animal I shot last night."

"Wild animal! What kind of animal?" I shuddered at the thought of some type of large creature creeping through the woodland at night.

"I'm only joking. It wasn't an animal at all; it was a stark raving mad man!"

I was aghast. My mouth fell open; I was speechless.

Eddie immediately realised I was horrified at what he'd said. "Don't look so worried, I'm only joking. It's hanging in the shed. I thought you'd like to see it because you'll probably never see another one. Come on I'll show you."

The door of the old wooden shed was half open and various garden implements and other tools either hung or lent against the walls. On the top of the small workbench I noticed a pull-through, together with oil and a rag in preparation for cleaning the shotgun, which lay nearby. As soon as we got into the shed, Eddie pointed to one of the timber roof supports above and behind the door. "There it is," he said, "the culprit that's been keeping you all awake all night; but not any more. I arrived yesterday and last night was enough for me; I can't understand why you've put up with it! I'd have thought you'd have done something about it by now; you know how to use the gun, and you know where I keep it hidden."

"But I didn't have a clue what it was and nobody I spoke to did. Besides, Dad doesn't know I can use a gun; he wouldn't let me use one even if he did."

I looked at it closely; I'd never seen a bird like it before. It hung from its feet, allowing the dark hawk-shaped wings to drape wide open, revealing a few white flecks. "I've never seen a bird like it before; it's as big as a full-size crow. What on earth is it?" I asked.

"It's called a 'nightjar.' I've only ever heard one before and that was years ago. They certainly live up to their name; perhaps that's why they're becoming rare. I was surprised to hear it."

"So was everyone else. Nobody had a clue what it was; they'll all be pleased you did. I'll see you later, if I get time; if not whenever I can."

Chapter Sixty-three

Spring arrived with the beauty and sight of wild primroses, anemones and violets growing within and around the woodlands. The tiny blue tits seemed to be the most excited of all the birds as nests were built or repaired in readiness for the first clutch of eggs of the summer. I felt as if the pleasantness gave me strength; it was comforting and inspiring to me as I continued my daily work.

One morning, as I was shovelling cement on to a spot board for Dad, several loud shots rang out from the direction of Foxbridge Farm. I didn't stop what I was doing or look up. Within a few moments two more shots echoed across the clear sky followed intermittently by more short bursts of fire. I guessed what was happening, but remained silent.

I'd begun staking bricks when I sensed Dad looking at me. "What on earth is all the shooting for Robin?"

"It's the local farmers' annual Magpie Shoot, Dad."

"Well for goodness sake, why aren't you there doing the pick-ups? I told you it would be okay to have the day off."

"I haven't seen Dick at Turpins Farm for ages. If I can't go to school I can't see him; if I can't see him he can't ask me, can he Dad? It's the same with Prince Tom; I haven't been to Foxbridge Farm for nearly six months. I haven't seen anyone."

I'd told the truth and waited for Dad's reaction. I didn't have to wait very long.

"Well, we'd have enjoyed the farmhouse food that's for sure, but you've got work to do and that's far more important. You can go shooting any time once you've finished."

As the spring weather got warmer, I frequently volunteered or suggested reasons for going to Loxwood to either purchase cigarettes or any other shopping that was required. They unwittingly believed I was being thoughtful and considerate because of the fear I had of them. The true reason for offering to undertake any errand was simple. If I rode fast, I'd have about fifteen minutes to spare at Ifold Lake where I could have a quick dip or wash while collecting a good meal for myself of moorhen or duck eggs. I'd never have time to cook them but it didn't matter; they were equally as tasty and good for me eaten raw.

While learning to become independent, I'd taught myself to appreciate even the smallest of comforts, particularly those of nature's incessant natural beauty. The two mute swans, which had occupied the lake throughout the winter, had built an enormous nest. One half floated on the water, whilst the remainder was securely attached to a clump of bulrushes. It was in a position safe from any predators and was large enough to house and bear the weight of a large brood of cygnets.

The cob and pen always shared their parenting equally from building and repairing the nest, to participating in the incubation period and teaching the cygnets how to survive. Either parent would attack any potential intruder with frightening ferocity, having the capability to break a man's leg with a single blow from its enormous wings. Charlie always kept well away, regardless of how hungry he might have been.

On the day I first saw the family of swans, the parents glided effortlessly across the reflective surface of the lake, with both large white wings arched high above their backs. I'd never realised the immense strength, even in their slow leg movements, as they surged forward with such ease. I knew I'd never forget the wondrous sight, which literally took my breath away. Frequently I smiled to myself as I watched the small golden coloured chicks furiously paddling their tiny webbed feet, trying to keep up and follow in line with the leading parent. Initially, I thought there were only six chicks, until I noticed four little heads popping out from underneath the feathers and arched wings of the leading parent; they were keeping snug and warm while getting a free ride.

I laughed softly to myself but the swan following up the rear heard me and stopped. Straightening its long neck it turned and looked directly towards me. I stood perfectly still, wondering if it would make a dash across the surface of the lake to attack me; or stretch out its enormous wings whilst making a fearful sound to frighten me away. Instead it opened its large orange bill and hissed loudly, warning me to keep away.

I watched them, enthralled by nature's undiluted beauty for fifteen minutes before leaving; I'd not given a thought to either collecting eggs as food, or having a dip to wash myself; I knew I'd regret it later, but at the time I was in awe of what I'd witnessed.

During the afternoon, and whatever work I did, my mind would drift back to the morning and the unforgettable sight of the swans with their cygnets. I cherished the experience.

A few days later, while selecting the brickbats to use, I was sheltering under the tarpaulin sheet from the hot sun when I heard Amy Lucas call my name. As I approached her I noticed a look of concern on her normally smiling face. She spoke softly. "As you know, my father looks forward to seeing you every day Robin. He tells us how hard you work from first light in the morning, to last light in the evening. You've never met each other and he would dearly like talk to you, would you come indoors, and say hello?"

"I'm a bit dirty and sweaty, and I'll have to ask Dad first," I answered.

"That's alright you've been working in the heat of the day. We also know your Dad's in the wagon having a rest. He won't be out for some time yet but if he does come out I'll speak to him, so don't worry."

I walked parallel to the fencing until I reached the road where Amy directed me to their bungalow. Her mother and sister greeted me and told me how pleased they were I'd come to see Mr Lucas and how he looked forward to seeing me wave to him every day. You've never forgotten, have you Robin?" Cathy asked.

"No; if it brings happiness, I don't think it should be forgotten," I answered.

"You can't see from outside but he always tries to wave back. He can't help dozing off," she smiled and added, "so let's hope you have time for a nice chat."

As I was shown into the room I immediately noticed it was large and bright as if filled with sunlight, and the atmosphere was inexplicably soothing. The French windows were enormous and provided a panorama, which encompassed every detail, not only of their well-manicured garden, but of almost the whole of our land. The wagon, the bungalow the half-dug cesspit even the animal sheds was clearly visible. I felt pleased I'd waved to him every day; even though I hadn't been able to see him, he'd seen me. The wallpaper was a pale green and covered with a soft yellow, blue and pink flower pattern, which was so lifelike I could almost smell the sweet aroma. It had all only taken a split-second for me to notice as I glanced towards Mr Lucas.

He sat propped upright in his bed against lightly-starched crisp white pillows and matching sheets, which were covered by a patchwork quilt, made up from brightly coloured woollen squares. At first he didn't speak but simply held out his thin frail hand for me to hold. His face was gaunt and the same colour as the bed sheets. His white hair looked like thin strands of cotton, which had been combed to one side to cover the balding top.

Although he did his best not to let it show I instinctively realised that whenever he managed to talk a little, he suffered terribly. He was a brave man, with an active mind and I sensed he knew what would soon happen, but was unable to do anything about it. Although the thought of being compos mentis lying and waiting for the last breath of life horrified me, I thought it was probably better than having a healthy body with a dead mind.

Our short conversation was difficult for him and although we were both pleased to have met each other and wanted to continue, he gradually got more and more tired. Eventually we had no choice except to finish the visit and say goodbye and God bless to each other.

Two days later the curtains, which covered the large French windows, were drawn together, and remained closed for the next three days. I believed he knew we were never to meet again.

Chapter Sixty-four

By the end of June, I'd filled and levelled all the paths, driveway and garage area needing concrete. Once Dad and I had laid and smoothed the final screed together, apart from restocking the materials and mixing the cement every day as and when required, I was left with only one more major job. Or so I thought!

Dad had built the bungalow to a height where he needed raised scaffold boards to reach above the brickwork level. All I needed was the strength to dig deep trenches in the hard clay from the kitchen to the road in which to lay the expected mains water supply and two sloping ditches to the cesspit for the main drainage pipes. I'd been told my final job would be to dig over and level all the ground in front of the bungalow in preparation for a garden and lawn.

Although I initially thought it was intentional; on reflection I realised it was simply coincidental. It seemed every time I became completely exhausted through breaking up the heavy clay with the mattock then shovelling it out of the trench and badly needing a short rest, Dad would call me for more cement. Within a few weeks I could feel myself getting more tired and weaker by the day.

I'd felt a slight pain in my ear whilst tethering Judy out early one morning. It didn't bother me much until the afternoon, when it began to throb and I mentioned it to Nan who suggested waiting and seeing how it felt in the morning. If it didn't feel any better she'd tell Mum and suggest I go to the doctor. During the evening the throbbing pain became excruciating; there wasn't any possibility of sleep and I paced the kitchen all night for some form of relief. Nan got up during the night on several occasions to try to help me, but it was to no avail. We could only wait for the morning to ask Dad it he'd take me to the doctor.

In the morning, shortly after first light, I started the first of my regular daily chores. I thought the pain might become a little more bearable if I could keep my mind occupied. My assumption was correct, until I began swinging the axe to split the logs. The action of chopping raised my blood pressure rapidly, which pumped around my body causing the agonising pain to throb heavily in time with my heartbeat. It was too much to bear and I had no choice but to stop and return indoors.

Nan was explaining to Mum and Dad about the pain I'd been suffering; she suggested it could be a mastoid and that I should see a doctor. Mum said she knew I'd been outside working, so there couldn't be much wrong with me. "He may have some hard wax or dirt in his ear; I'll soon sort that out with some drops, although it's more likely he's trying to get out of working," she said, turning towards me. "Go and sit at the table Robin, while I get the drops."

"What are you going to give him Babs?" Nan asked.

"I know what I'm doing; leave it to me, and just carry on with what you were doing please," Mum replied.

Sitting at the kitchen table I waited while Mum went into her bedroom; she shortly returned with cotton wool and a bottle of liquid. I sat with my head tipped sideways to enable the fluid to be tipped into the ear. When the cavity was completely full Mum tightly rammed the ear full of cotton wool.

Within a couple of minutes a warm feeling began to take over from the excruciating pain and for a moment I relaxed. I barely had time to take a breath when I realised the warm feeling was getting hot. Within seconds I began to feel a burning sensation within my head as if the ear had been filled with boiling water. The agonising pain that ravaged through my head made me gasp as I sank to my knees holding my head screaming with the pain.

Three hours later, Dad eventually went to the doctors' surgery at Loxwood and finding them both out on calls, left a message for one of them to visit me urgently. Several hours later Dr Wood called, to be told by Mum that she'd given me some drops to clear any wax from the ear. Having spent most of the day curled up, holding my head for some kind of relief, I forced myself to sit upright for the doctor to examine me. Using a pair of tweezers, he was eventually able to clear all the tightly packed cotton wool from the passageway of the ear. While Nan held a shallow dish to catch the cleaning fluid, the doctor gently used a syringe to clear and sterilise the inside. "There" he said, "that feels better doesn't it? You had a mastoid, but its burst and all cleaned out. I'll have a quick look but you'll be okay now."

"It's still burning, and I can't hear you very clearly in that ear," I answered.

Using his auriscope, he looked inside for only a few moments before he stopped, and staring at Mum whispered in a horrified voice, "what on earth did you put in his ear? It's blistered so terribly his eardrum has been perforated. He could be deaf in this ear for the rest of his life; what did you use, for God's sake woman?"

We all stared at her; she looked embarrassed and uneasy as she answered, "Peroxide! It cleans thoroughly and kills germs; anyway it was all we had."

She knew what she'd done; the guilt showed clearly on her face as she went into the sitting room, slamming the door behind her!

The doctor rinsed, cleaned and dried the ear passageway, gently without causing any additional pain, then packed the void with a gauze bandage soaked in thick ointment. The complete lobe was folded forward and sealed tightly with several layers of wide sticking plaster. Sighing as he looked at Nan he spoke softly as if apologising. "I'll give him a penicillin injection; there's nothing else I can do. Keep the wound dry and leave the plaster on for at least two weeks. Hopefully, the damaged skin of the eardrum will heal together; even so his hearing will always be impaired. If you have any problems let me know." Then turning to Dad and staring him fully in the face he said, "as I mentioned in my letter to you a few weeks ago, you must make sure he has enough to eat; he needs to keep his strength up. I'll see myself out Mr Davis; I'm sure you'll tell your wife anything she may be interested in. Good day"!

By the next day the pain had completely gone and within three weeks Nan removed the sticking plaster and bandage. I could still hear, although not quite as well as I had previously. Mum was the only one never to mention what had happened or ask how I felt.

Dad knew I'd lost a considerable amount of strength from my leg infection and I was now even weaker. He thought if I did something less strenuous and different for the day, on the principle that 'a change is as good as a rest,' it would give me strength, thereby solving any problems labouring for him. I knew a few good meals would have sufficed.

By midday I'd cleared out the chicken boxes, the inside of Judy's shelter and the pigsty. Then cut sufficient armfuls of ferns to replenish the entire floor area of each. It seemed a long time since Wendy and I had walked side by side to see my friend George, the pig farmer at Hogwood. Now I was able to collect six magpie eggs on the way; they'd be good sustenance. I began to enjoy the freedom and feel relaxed until I was halfway along the track, which passed the roughly cleared field where I'd, encountered the adder. One quick glance was enough to remind me of the suffering I went through and to send an icy cold shiver through my body. I quickened my pace unable to look back.

George had always spoken to me as an adult, and we often sat chatting like a couple of old women for what seemed ages; eventually we got round to discussing the main reason for my visit. Could he sell me a piglet again this year? Unfortunately he couldn't; there weren't any spare he explained. He'd been very disappointed with the breeding results, to the extent he'd need to buy some himself. He told me I only had one chance and explained one of the sows had produced a runt in her litter. As he wouldn't have the time to nurse it properly it was a foregone conclusion it wouldn't survive. He offered me the runt free of charge, telling me it would grow as big and strong as any of the others born of the same litter, providing it was well nurtured for the next few weeks. I agreed immediately.

I hadn't taken the wheelbarrow with me for transporting the piglet, as I didn't expect to make the deal with George that day. We laughed aloud when jokingly suggesting the various methods of getting it home. It would be cruel to carry it in a sack over my shoulder or in my arms; but without the sack it would wriggle and squeal constantly until it got free. The thought of me chasing it through the woodland trying to catch it calling out "piggy, piggy, piggy," was too much to stop us laughing.

Following lengthy deliberations, we agreed that unless I walked all the way back for the wheelbarrow, probably the easiest way of getting it home was to use a blindfold and a short leash to keep the piglet completely under control. When I was ready to go, I gave the leash a gentle tug to lead the way but the piglet had other ideas; it sat and wouldn't move. I bent down and firmly gripping the small corkscrew-shaped tail, lifted the hindquarters until it stood upright. We walked no more than a yard before it sat again; having lifted it by the tail again, we were able to walk another yard before it sat again. I didn't relish the thought of this happening all way home! George solved the problem by simply tying a piece of twine around the base of the tail. Every time the piglet sat, I tugged with my left hand and it stood up. Then with a tug of the leash with my right hand it walked on. With both hands fully occupied I shouted out goodbye to George and set off.

As I neared home, a car passed slowly and I noticed the three occupants laughing hysterically. They must have thought I was taking a dog and a blindfolded pig on a lead attached each end, for a walk. How ridiculously funny I must have looked as I smiled and laughed back.

Dad was so pleased I hadn't paid anything for the runt that he gave me the afternoon and the whole of the following day off from labouring and digging. Instead, I was to take the bow saw, the billhook and the cart to find sufficient small trees to restock the log pile. Felling, trimming and carting timber were much easier than digging the clay trenches. Nevertheless, it was hard work and took a full day longer than expected. For some reason I wasn't surprised to be accused of skiving and malingering; I thought I was due for the stick, and this was as good an excuse as any.

Chapter Sixty-five

Within a few weeks of regular feeding, the runt had begun to grow into a good-sized healthy pig. Whenever there was a lack of fodder, I'd often feed Judy with high protein food pellets. The runt was fed the same and benefited enormously. I'd previously tasted the hard dry pellets and found them barely palatable. It was the same for Wendy and Jet; we'd only eat them out of necessity.

By autumn, with the exception of the large double fireplace and chimney, which separated the sitting room from the kitchen, nearly all of the main interior and exterior structural brickwork of the bungalow had been completed. Most evenings, I'd hear Mum in the sitting room describe to Nan how, with each new course of brickwork Dad had laid, the outline of the building was taking shape. In one-way or another she was always complimenting Dad on how hard he was working!

Then one evening, I was unexpectedly invited to join them, providing I kept quiet, and only spoke if spoken to. I'd only been in the room a few minutes when trying not to look or sound bored by Mum's repetitious comments on Dad's hard work, Nan lent forward in her chair and then looking at both of them in turn said, "Babs, I'm not blind. I know exactly what goes on and who does what," then glancing quickly at Dad added, "so do you Bern." I felt uneasy and looked down as I put my hands on my muddy knees. I could feel two pairs of eyes staring into me as Nan jokingly, but sarcastically, continued, "I suppose every single brick and breeze block Bern lays must have been carried and stacked for him by the fairies. They've mixed every shovel full of cement Bern's used and spent months digging trenches for the drains, and they haven't finished yet by a long way. It took them months to smash and lay the brickbats. Did the rain, the wind, the early evening darkness stop them? No, of course not. But it would always stop Bern, wouldn't it Babs? How he got the fairies to work like that I'll never know. They must be invisible, because I've never seen them!" Nan pretended to giggle and smile as she added, "it couldn't possibly be anything to do with Robin could it? Oh dear me no! He wouldn't have time would he, only being allowed to go to school half a dozen times during the past eight months. Do you want me to go on? I can you know."

Nan stopped talking and sat back in her chair. It was very obvious by the look on her face, that she was furious. In her own way Nan was only trying to help me but I wished she'd stop before I became the centre of attention and was accused of being the instigator of any argument. I knew if that were to happen, the end result would be a foregone conclusion.

"Very funny," Mum answered sarcastically, "Robin's doing what he's told to do. So he should if he knows what's good for him. There's work to be done, and someone has to do it. We can't afford to pay anyone, so why shouldn't Robin do it? We know its hard work but he doesn't do much otherwise. He should consider it as a way of earning his keep and be thankful to have a home anyway." Mum quickly glanced at Dad and then me, before gazing into the fire. I briefly wondered what she meant by her last remark but soon dismissed the idea of it containing any hidden meaning.

"But Babs, you and Bern both know it's too much for him, he's only a young boy. You also know he's started to have nose bleeds two or three times a week; it's not normal, give him a rest for goodness sake; look at him, he's as thin as a rake. Or don't you care at all?" Nan asked with a pleading tone in her voice.

Mum's answer sounded very matter of fact. "He won't give it a second thought, when Bern and I have gone and it's all left to him, he'll own everything. You're getting as bad as he is! Please keep your opinions to yourself because I'm not prepared to discuss the matter any longer. As far as I'm concerned the subject is closed."

Dad looked directly at me and looking a little sad he said, "do you have anything to say Robin?"

"No Dad," I answered.

"If you had something to say, would you say it?" Dad asked.

"No Dad," I repeated.

"You mean, 'yes' don't you?"

"I mean I haven't got anything I'd like to say, or dare to say Dad."

"Good I shouldn't think so either," Mum interrupted, and then added as if it were an afterthought, "you've been the instigator of enough trouble for one day. Now get to bed before you cause any more."

Again Nan had tried to help me, but to no avail.

During the next few days, on several occasions whenever I was alone, I'd laugh when visualising dozens of fairies dashing about stacking bricks, mixing cement and digging trenches.

Within a fortnight I was having a nosebleed without fail every day. Initially I wasn't the slightest bit concerned, as Dad had told me it often happened to boys of my age and was a sign of growing up. By the end of the third week I began having two nosebleeds every day and began to feel weaker and weaker all the time. Mum agreed with Dad it was all part of growing up and didn't seem interested as long as my work was on schedule.

Nan's attitude was completely different. She was worried I bled so much that I might be becoming anaemic. Something was definitely wrong with me; she told Mum I should see a doctor as soon as possible. Whilst her opinion was unwelcome and ignored she never gave up.

On the following Monday, Dr Wood visited to enquire about my health, to Mum and Dad's amazement. Mum asked who'd called him, to which he replied casually, that somebody had left a message stating I was unwell, and would he call in; he didn't remember who had written the note. On the previous Saturday, unbeknown to any of us, Nan had arranged with the deliveryman from Loxwood Stores to ask the doctor to visit me. For Mum and Dad it was indeed a mystery, whoever could it have been? They never found out.

Within ten days I'd been admitted to Guildford Hospital, where an operation to cauterise a vein within my nose was performed to stem the bleeding. Two days later I was back home. I'd been given a letter from the specialist containing a list of the essential foods I should be given, together with strict instructions that I was to convalesce for at least two weeks.

Mum and Dad weren't at all impressed with the fact that I shouldn't be allowed to work for two weeks. However they were relieved at the thought of me not losing any more time by having nosebleeds.

Within a week Mum told me I appeared and looked fit enough to work and there wasn't any reason why I shouldn't. She'd also said the operation I'd had together with the entire contents of the letter I'd brought home were unimportant and no longer applied. I wondered how long it would take before it was me who became totally unimportant and no longer applied. What would happen then?

Chapter Sixty-six

As expected, towards the end of autumn, the weather slowly but gradually began to deteriorate. Dad wouldn't work in adverse weather conditions, although I was expected to continue with my work unless the rain or wind was particularly severe, in which case I'd be able to attend school. I didn't give a second thought to getting wet or cold on the days I went to school. I was too pleased at having a day away from the exhausting work expected of me at home. It was always worth the long walk alone, simply for the refreshing and nourishing beaker of milk from Turpins Farm and the natural food I'd be able to gather along the way.

Miss Rees never queried the explanations given in the note from Mum as to why I hadn't been able to attend school. She and all my schoolmates knew the truth; there was nothing anybody could say or do to change the situation. In a way I was pleased; it was my problem and nobody else's. With the exception of feeling so weary, I'd learned how to deal with almost everything expected of me, as I grew to become more and more independent.

Dad had underestimated how long it would take us to complete our respective jobs but he wouldn't admit it. Instead, the excuse he made for not being on schedule was obvious;

the delay had occurred because I'd been unwell and unable to work.

I couldn't imagine reaching the end of digging the trenches. The heavy yellow clay gradually changed colour the deeper I dug until it became tightly compressed grey and blue layers like sheets of slate. The only way to break through was to smash it with the mattock; the work was exhausting.

As in previous years, I hoped to be given a rest on Christmas Day. I expected to visit the Onslow Arms with Dad to buy him his Christmas pint. I also hoped I'd be given a good meal before I washed-up and cleared away; Nan was in London for her well-earned rest. Apart from my normal jobs I'd then be excused work for the remainder of the day while Mum and Dad slept. I desperately needed a good meal and a rest, but it wasn't to be; the weather had remained dry and mild for some time and I needed to catch up with our work schedule. Consequently my visit to the Onslow Arms wasn't forthcoming, neither was my Christmas Dinner, nor a rest.

I'll never forget that while I was digging, and without a word being spoken to me, I watched Mum and Dad set off in the car at lunchtime to return two hours later. When I'd finished work for the day, I went indoors to be confronted by a table covered with dirty plates and other utensils. From the remains, it was obvious they'd eaten roast beef and vegetables for their Christmas Day dinner. When I'd cleared everything away and washed up, I cut myself a large helping of fresh boiled bacon, bread and pickles, and ate my fill. There wasn't any sign of Mum and Dad; they'd retired to the sitting room; from the sound of loud snoring and the smell of alcohol, it wasn't difficult to guess where they'd been.

I vaguely remember Nan returning home; I also remember reaching the stage where virtually all the digging was completed. The weather was very wet, windy, and cold. It was probably about March or April when I first began to feel dizzy. I soon became so weak I couldn't cut any fresh firewood or swing the axe to split the previously prepared logs. I dared not mention it for fear of the consequences. Nobody was aware of how seriously unwell I was until I collapsed and fell into oblivion.

Although for only short periods at a time, I gradually became aware of the sound of voices and the sudden sharp pain of an injection. I never knew how long they continued because they were always followed immediately by nothingness. Eventually my mind stirred sufficiently to give me a feeling of total worthlessness and a feeling that death was so close I could reach out and touch it. I remember thinking; why not? Why should I stay, when it would be so easy to slip away into solitary eternal darkness? I was about to grasp it, when in my subconscious I saw a shred of light. I don't know why, but I grabbed it with both hands. It shook and jerked violently, as if trying to shake me off; I hung on gripping so tightly my fingers moulded into the glow. Psychologically the struggle became a battle. Regardless of how long it continued, I knew I desperately needed to find the strength to win.

Gradually the increasing light became brilliant and so intense with various colours I imagined I was encapsulated within a rainbow. I began to feel the blood gently pumping through my body and realised that somehow I'd won the battle for survival. It wasn't until I slowly gained my mental and physical strength over the following weeks that I realised God had given me life again; it was for the third time.

It wasn't until mid-July that Dr Wood told Nan and me how serious my illness had been. He explained it had been caused by the lack of essential food containing vitamins, proteins and iron to keep me healthy; combined with the manual work my body had virtually given up and closed down. Dr Wood made regular visits and liased with Nan to ensure I was receiving the prescribed iron tonic, the M&B antitoxin tablets, and Brands concentrated essence of various meats. He'd realised long beforehand she could be trusted never to let me down. She never did.

Apparently, after careful deliberation, the doctor had insisted, due to the seriousness of my failing health and the paramount importance of undisturbed rest, I should occupy Mum and Dad's bedroom throughout the entirety of my illness. Nan was not to be inconvenienced; she also needed her rest. As my health improved, they regularly made perfectly clear their dissatisfaction at having to sleep on chairs in the sitting room; they couldn't understand why I couldn't have stayed in the other bedroom; they'd even suggested it would be a better idea if Nan slept on the chairs at night; they would have their own bed and I'd have a bed to myself! The doctor's answer was that he considered their suggestion to be selfish and outrageous; he'd refused to discuss the matter any further.

Nan had nursed me every day throughout my illness. It lasted for months but she never gave up; she was always there for me. I dread to think what would have become of me if she hadn't been there. I also remember Wendy barely leaving my bedside day or night. Now I was stronger, she lay by my side where she was often joined by Jet. I was often able to sit up and watch my friendly little red robin as he perched on the windowsill peeking and chirping at me. Nan told me he'd visited me several times each day since I'd first become ill, as if to check on my progress.

Because of the shape of the wagon and the manner in which the windows were fitted, it was only possible to look out straight ahead; very little could be seen to the left or right. By sitting up in bed and looking straight ahead it was easy to see that Dad had finished all the brickwork. All the unused bricks and rubble had been removed and replaced with a large stack of various sized timbers and an enormous pile of roof tiles. The drains had been laid in the trenches I'd spent months digging and the heaps of yellow, grey and blue clay used to back-fill and completely cover the pipes. All the remaining ground, with the exception of the open trench prepared to accommodate the mains water supply had been levelled and rotovated. The work was on schedule and it looked good. Dad had obviously employed someone to carry out the work. He couldn't possibly have done it all himself. Due to my inability to work, a labourer or possibly more than one at some time or other had definitely replaced me.

My sixth sense told me that something outside had changed drastically. Something was very different; something I wouldn't like and something that would give me a different opinion of something, or someone. I tried without success to imagine what it might be. Nan avoided answering my questions, but I knew something had changed; I'd just have to wait and see for myself.

The next morning, I sat on the edge of the bed for an hour or so before getting dressed and sitting in a chair looking through the front window for the remainder of the day. At last I was feeling well and inquisitive and I desperately wanted to get outside.

On the second morning, following a good breakfast, which had become a regular occurrence, Nan helped me slowly from the bedroom into the sitting room. It was the first time I'd been able to leave the room for five months and now I received my first shock. I could feel the heat from the fire, which was burning brightly, although there wasn't a log to be seen. Then looking to one side I noticed two buckets; one contained coal, the other coke. I'd always been told that we'd never use it because it needed to be brought from Billingshurst and was too expensive.

In the kitchen next to the tortoise stove stood a bucket of coke. It was all it ever needed. When I got outside, there wasn't a log to be seen under the lean-to; the large pile had been used and replaced with sacks of fuel. The only familiar sight was red robin's nest on the top ledge. I smiled to myself; one thing at least hadn't changed. I very soon realised it was about the only thing that hadn't!

As I glanced towards Judy's hut I was horrified; it wasn't there! It'd gone, as had her collar and tethering chain hung on a branch of the chestnut tree; she'd also gone. I began to shake with anger as I looked around; the chickens had also gone; their hutch and wire run, together with the pigsty had all been dismantled and removed. It seemed that to limit the additional work for Dad, everything had been cleared away as if it'd never existed. I'd thought something was wrong, but why this? Surely Mum could have done something, even if it were only to tether Judy out and feed the chicken? It was beyond my comprehension, particularly when I learned it was Dad who collected the milk every day from Mr Rose. Mum couldn't be bothered; she certainly lived up to her nickname.

Chapter Sixty-seven

For a few weeks, I was regularly given breakfast and a cooked meal every evening, with a mug of the water in which the cabbage or other green vegetable had been cooked, to ensure an iron sufficiency. I rapidly gained strength and weight, when for no apparent reason, my breakfast ceased completely, and everything reverted back to one meal a day. As usual, whenever I ate, I'd sit alone in the kitchen to eat within full view of the hazel stick lying between the brackets above the door; nothing had changed, or had it?

Despite the seriousness and length of my illness, Mum and Dad's attitude towards me had deteriorated even further. They'd unexpectedly had to pay for someone to complete the work I'd been unable to do. I was fully aware that very soon there wouldn't be any jobs I'd be capable of doing; then I'd become of little use and be considered an encumbrance. Once again the future concerned me although it wasn't insurmountable. I was fit and strong once again and determined to survive successfully with or without the help of others. I'd had to care and fend for myself before; I could do it again. Most importantly I'd have the time.

Although I'd previously been told the months I'd spent digging the trenches would be my last job, Dad had since decided otherwise. I was now considered fit and with the experience I'd gained using a saw; he thought I'd be quite capable of cutting the ceiling joists, rafters and batons etc. It would save him time, as he'd then only need to fix them. My reward would be to have weekends off.

Although it'd been a long time since I'd seen Dave or Michael, I soon realised time hadn't changed our friendship; only my aim with a catapult. It was too late in the summer for eggs or fruit, although thankfully there was a plethora of other wild nutritious delights. Once again I was able to enjoy being able to catch and cook fish, and watch the obvious signs of excitement from Wendy and Jet, as they sat with me by the fire, under the beech tree waiting for their cooked tit-bits.

Without expending a vast amount of energy, it only took about a month of steady work to complete the timber frame and battening; the preparation work for the men who'd fix the roof tiles was completed. One man arrived to stack the tiles on the roof a day prior to the arrival of the others. I fervently believed it would be a really tough job carrying all the tiles up on to the roof. How wrong I was; he made it look so easy and simple, I was filled with awe. He wore an old cloth cap stuffed tightly with paper, which created a flat surface giving a protective cushion effect. He'd stack the tiles in pile; then balance them on his head, climb the ladder, then the roof and place them in strategic positions ready for laying. By mid-afternoon he'd finished his day's work. The next morning two more men arrived and began tiling. It didn't take them long to finish and within three days the roof on the bungalow had been completed. It was a job well done; what's more it looked good. Despite all the fuss and praise Mum gave to Dad, as if he'd done all the work by himself I didn't care. I'd eventually completed my final job at long last. At least that's what I thought until the next morning.

Dad had made it abundantly clear that he and Mum considered my health fully recovered so there was no reason why I shouldn't continue to help with anything I was capable of doing. As so many times previously, I had no choice but to listen to their instructions. The only time I'd dare speak, was to say 'yes' or 'no' at the appropriate time and in the appropriate place.

Because the roof had been completed, everything inside would be kept dry. My first job was to help Dad fix the window frames. The only reason I was required soon became apparent; Dad would measure the size of the frame then mark the timber where it needed to be sawn. It took him three hours to measure and mark the frames. It took me a full day to cut them to size. After which it took him four days to set them into the walls. A glazier was employed to complete the job.

When the windows had been installed, my next job was to help fix the lightweight ceiling boards in each of the seven rooms. It was to be the easiest and least stressful job I'd done; the large thick lightweight beaverboards required very little effort to hold up to the ceiling joist with the use of the bristle end of a broom. Then whilst standing on a pair of steps, Dad simply slid the boards into position, temporarily fixing them with clout nails. Within a week sufficient boards had been fixed to allow a plasterer to commence his work whenever he became available.

A local man from Ifold undertook the rendering and plastering of the necessary walls. He never employed a labourer, as he would usually mix the cement and plaster himself. However, if someone else did the mixing he'd no need to stop working and a considerable financial saving would be made; it was the third job expected of me. Nobody except the plasterer, realised how continuously mixing the sand and cement, then the plaster, on demand every day for weeks, would test my fitness to the very limit.

Coal and coke, which had been temporarily used during my illness, would no longer be used. I wasn't surprised in the slightest when I was informed of my next job. It was to collect sufficient appropriately sized trees to ensure there were enough logs to last throughout the winter months. Because I'd completed everything expected of me and providing I'd collected any milk, eggs and other shopping Mum required, I could continue to have weekends to myself.

As I was able to virtually fend for myself once again having regained my strength, I found little difficulty in felling and carting the required amount of trees for logging. My health and capability made the job easy. With Wendy at my side every day and with red robin fluttering within an inch of me twittering and watching my every move as I cut, then stacked the logs under the lean-to near his nest, I felt completely at ease. I couldn't remember feeling happier. Little did I realise very soon my lifestyle would change for the better.

It was close to midday, as I pulled my cart laden with timber along The Ride towards home, when a car passed going in the same direction. Within a few feet it stopped and a tall man stepped out holding a piece of paper and walked towards me.

"Is your name Rodney Davis?" He asked, in an inquisitive voice.

"Yes," I replied.

"Do you live at 'Vi-Bern' on the Plaistow Road?"

"Yes."

You must be fit and able to pull a cart along loaded with that amount of timber. I'm glad I've seen you first. I'm on my way to meet your parents; I'll also need to talk to you, so get yourself home, as soon as you can."

I was speechless as he got back into the car and drove off. Who on earth was he, I wondered; he'd certainly sounded bossy.

I pulled the cart past his car, which was parked behind Dad's and began unloading the timber. Nan came out of the wagon and called me to her side. "When you've finished what you're doing, don't come indoors Robin. I think it would be better if you stayed outside."

"Am I supposed to have done something wrong Nan?" I enquired. "I know someone's come to see Mum and Dad about something or other. I met him earlier, who is he?"

"He's the man from the School Board and about time as well if you ask me. Don't worry; you're not in trouble, in fact the opposite."

"I don't understand Nan. What does he want?"

"He wants to know why you've hardly been to school for almost two years. He knows you were very ill and also knows why. He's very cross indeed." Nan hobbled to the chopping block and sat down before continuing. "Apparently you've missed your 11-Plus examination, which means you shan't be going to Loxwood School anymore. Depending on their examination results, some of your friends now go to Horsham Grammar School while the others go to Wisborough Green Secondary School. That's where you'll be going."

Nan returned indoors while I waited outside for the unexpected meeting to finish. Fortunately my mind became preoccupied when I noticed my friendly red robin whose feathers were all puffed up to keep him warm. He looked like a fluffy ball of wool as he squatted on the ledge next to his mate. She, as usual, was snuggled up in the nest with only the tip of her beak visible.

Eventually the door of the wagon opened and the tall stranger stepped out, closely followed by Mum and Dad. I stood up expecting him to pass but he stopped, then smiling he looked directly at me and said, "Master Davis, tell me; what would you say if I told you you'll be going back to school within the next week. Would you be pleased?"

"Yes," I answered, "I'd be very pleased sir."

"Good, I'm pleased as well. I'll see you when I visit your school next. Bye for now."

He turned his back and walked toward his car without glancing at or speaking a word to Mum or Dad. From the way they looked at me I knew I'd need to be extra careful and wished I could just simply disappear for the remainder of the day.

Chapter Sixty-eight

Having been ordered to remain in the kitchen until told otherwise, I sat alone in silence. The only sound was from the wireless and the low inaudible discussion, which filtered through the wall from the sitting room. Eventually I was called into the room; Mum abruptly told me to sit down, keep quiet and listen.

"As you know, you'll be going to school next week. At least you've finished the work we expected of you; that's one good thing I suppose. The worst is we've got to buy you completely new clothes. Most of the money we thought you'd saved us by labouring will now have to be spent on you." Mum was staring at me. Her lips went tight and barely moved as she continued talking at me through almost clenched teeth. I cringed as she told me my usefulness was virtually finished and I'd very soon become a burden on them. The tradesmen were expensive to employ and most of the money had been spent. The only solution left was for Dad to get himself a part-time job. To make matters worse, they were expected to pay for me to have school dinners. They didn't like the idea very much, but they didn't have a choice. I almost smiled when I was told this, but very soon became disillusioned when Mum informed me that one good meal a day would suffice. Everything was to continue as before. I should keep an ample supply of logs and collect any shopping as and when required. Nan stopped knitting; there was complete silence; we knew she was about to say something, but what? We all looked at her and waited.

"You'll expect Robin, summer or winter, regardless of the weather, to go all the way back to where he's just passed to get your cigarettes? You've got a bike and you're at home all day; if anyone has time to get them, you have. You certainly know how to live up to your nickname Babs!"

"He'll do as he's told, won't you Robin?" Mum snapped. "He's of little other use to us now anyway."

I remained silent, uncertain whether to speak, "Well answer me Robin, or have you gone deaf?"

I'd heard enough and stood up. Whatever the consequences I decided to speak my mind; neither of them could hurt me any more than they had.

"Where do you think you're going?" Dad asked, "answer your mother."

"I'm going to answer Mum. I'm also going outside to cut a stick Dad; do whatever you like with it. I don't care."

"What on earth are you talking about?" He shouted.

"Mum just asked me if I was deaf. The answer's 'no' although if it had been left up to her, I would be; thank goodness it wasn't. Why doesn't Mum go shopping herself? The answer's simple; she can't be bothered! Why should she? It's easier to send me. The tyres on her bike have been flat for at least a year and she certainly wouldn't ever consider walking. At least a meal at school every day will be more than I normally get; if I'd had one every day in the past I would never have been so ill. If Nan hadn't nursed and cared for me, I wouldn't be here now, but don't worry, as if you ever would," I laughingly joked, "I know how to look after myself. I've had plenty of experience.

I'm going outside now for a stick; I'm certain you'll find a way of agreeing how much I deserve it."

As I trimmed a previously-cut hazel stick, I thought it was time I cut a fresh stock; little did I realise it wouldn't be necessary, as it would be the last time I'd ever be given the stick.

Dad struck the back of my legs alternately with such force and frequency I initially found difficulty in controlling any expressions caused by the excruciating pain. I clenched my teeth and tightly gripped the back of a chair for any relief and support I could get. If I hadn't, I'd have dropped to my knees with my legs buckling under me. Nan rose to her feet and stood facing Dad, screaming at him to stop. "Look what you've done to his legs Bern. I've never seen you hit him so hard before. You should be ashamed of yourself. Everybody's entitled to his or her own opinion; regardless of whatever Babs or you think. I'm only too pleased he told you what he was thinking; he's done the right thing and I agree with him completely." She paused, long enough for them to consider what she'd said. "How will you keep his wounds covered until they're healed? If you don't, everybody at his new school will very soon realise what's happened."

"Don't give it a second thought," Dad answered, "nobody will see them. He won't be wearing short trousers, once he's got his new clothes and started school."

"Thank goodness for that," I said, not meaning to speak aloud.

"Why?" Mum snapped loudly, startling us all.

"Because Dad can't give me the stick if I'm wearing long trousers," I answered shrugging my shoulders.

The room fell into silence for a moment or two. I could see they were all pondering over what I'd said. Mum was the first to speak by way of instructions to Dad. "He's right Bern, you can't give him the stick again, but what we can do is simple. I'll keep him in line by giving him a clip around the head or perhaps a slap across the face, as and when necessary. Don't bother about it any more; I'll deal with him. Mind you, the first time I hurt my hands will be the time you take over from where I've left off. Okay?"

Dad's answer was simply to nod his agreement.

Whilst cutting and stacking the winter stock of logs the next morning my mind frequently flashed back to what was said and done the evening before. I'd often wondered how long Mum could wait before trying the effectiveness of her hand on me. I knew she'd never need an excuse. Eventually I decided that no matter what I did, it was pointless trying to please either Mum or Dad all the time; it couldn't possibly work. Instead, I'd keep out of their way by avoiding them as much as possible; hopefully out of sight and out of mind. I'd sit in the warmth of the kitchen whenever possible, and enjoy the preferred company of Wendy and Jet. I knew Nan would agree.

Mum and Dad came out of doors together. Dad walked passed me towards the car without speaking but Mum stopped, and stood directly in front of me. Then putting her shopping bag down, watched as I picked up the next armful of logs.

"Stand up and listen to me," she said in an unusually soft tone, "your father and I are going to Horsham shopping to get your new shoes and clothes for school. Is there anything in particular you'd like?"

I couldn't believe my ears; something had changed her attitude, she sounded so pleasant and considerate. "No, thanks very much Mum," I heard myself say.

"Never mind, I've got something in particular for you anyway," she said smiling.

I was surprised and for a second or two wondered what she had for me. I very soon found out as the first hard slap landed across my cheek. The strength behind the unexpected blow knocked my head sideways directly in line with the second vicious slap, which landed directly across my mouth drawing blood. Instinctively dropping the logs, I raised my hands to protect myself, taking the blows that followed, either on my arms or painlessly on the side of the head. Mum soon realised the element of surprise had passed; there wasn't any point in continuing.

She stood for a few moments staring me up and down. Then her mannerisms and expression reverted to normal as she spoke. "Consider that your punishment for speaking to me the way you did last night. You can expect the same again every time you do something wrong. It wasn't too bad was it?" She said smiling, "it didn't hurt a bit. Did it?"

"Yes it did Mum," I answered, wiping my bottom lip.

She smiled again, and then almost laughing picked up her bag. "Well I didn't think it was too bad. In fact I didn't feel a thing," she said walking away.

Chapter Sixty-nine

The weekend soon passed and the time for my first day at Wisborough Green School arrived. Feeling a little overdressed, having donned my long trousers and new clothes I set off on the long walk to Flitchfold Pond at the junction of Loxwood and Plaistow Road to catch the school bus.

Several hundred yards along the road I passed an area that had been cleared of all the oak and hazel trees. The work had been undertaken over a period of several months. Bricks and breeze blocks were stacked in piles and two men were digging out the foundations for a building of some sort on the land. It would become only the seventh building before reaching Ifold Stores about a mile further on.

As I passed the entrance to Turpins Farm I realised how few times I'd seen Dick and my other friends during the past year. They'd undoubtedly have made it their business to know exactly what had happened to me and that I'd be starting at a new school. They'd also know I'd be seeing them as soon as I could. Nothing relating to the past year would be discussed in the slightest; everything would continue as normal as if I hadn't been away. A large beaker of milk would be readily available; rabbit snares would be hanging up, ready for use. I'd be given all relevant information regarding wild mushroom, toadstool and walnut quantities.

Whilst I waited at the roadside on the edge of the large pond, watching the dozens of farm ducks noisily quacking and splashing about, I noticed another boy walking towards me from the direction I'd come. As he drew close, I recognised his stature and long, lolloping strides. From the way he hunched his shoulders and drove his hands deep into his trouser pockets, I realised it was Douglas Cooper-Pullen or Dougie as he was called. We'd met at Loxwood School; it was good to see someone I knew.

As he drew within earshot, he put his arms above his head and waving to attract my attention yelled out, "hi Rod, long time no see. Are you ok?"

"Hi Dougie; yes I'm fine thanks, it's good to see you," I called back, walking towards him. During the fifteen minutes we waited for the school bus, Dougie had so much to tell me that he barely stopped talking. He told me everybody knew I'd been very ill, and the reasons why. He explained they'd all have helped if they could, but it was family business and therefore nothing to do with anybody else. Dougie went on to tell me how pleased he and my friends would be to see me again, particularly looking so fit and strong. I felt happier than I had for a long time; it felt especially good to have the dinner money in my pocket.

Whilst we'd been talking, another boy about our age and two girls had joined us to wait for the bus. When Dougie finished and was about to introduce me to the three strangers, the boy spoke to me, before Dougie had a chance. "You must be Rod; we heard you'd be coming back to school soon," he said with a wide grin on his face.

"Who on earth told you that?" I asked ignoring his initial remark.

Dougie quickly interrupted before the boy could answer. "Brian and his sisters have only lived here a few months Rod; they've obviously met the delivery man from the village stores. Is that right?" he asked the boy.

"Yes that's right. He told me we only live about a mile apart. He also told me you've had to work hard with your Dad and you've been very ill."

"Well, well! Surprise, surprise! Who'd have thought it?" I joked. "My Nan, bless her, has obviously kept him well-informed, and he's passed it on to everybody else." They all smiled in agreement. "Whereabouts do you live Brian?" I asked.

"In the cottage at Little Headfoldswood Farm. Our Dad's got the job of head farmer for Captain Moore. Mum's also got a job; she does the cooking, and cleaning in the big house. We've been there about four months now. It's nice!" It became obvious his sisters were elated with their new home; having smiled in agreement they began talking excitedly and incessantly. Dougie, Brian and I didn't have any choice but to stand in silence and look at each other while listening to the girls' non-stop chattering. I couldn't possibly recall the amount of times in the past I'd envied my friends for being able to confide in and share any problems or work with a brother or sister; by the time the school bus arrived I wasn't so sure!

As the old Bedford bus slowed to a stop, the high-pitched screech of the brakes made my teeth tingle. The large cloud of black engine smoke, which was emitted from the exhaust dispersed in the light breeze and I recognised several of my past schoolmates waving and smiling at me through the windows. During the journey of about four and a half miles to Wisborough Green I was briefly told about the general routine at school, the teachers and in particular the likes and dislikes of the headmaster. Donald Kitchener, one of my schoolmates from Loxwood, voiced his disapproval and finished by saying he was as bald as a coot, with about as much brain. Margaret from the Post Office added, "some people say you don't get grass growing on a busy street."

We all thought for a moment before Dougie made us all laugh as he jokingly said, "but you don't need thatch on an empty barn!"

The school was much larger than I expected, having two playgrounds. One was specifically for infants, the larger for those up to the leaving age of fifteen. After one of the teachers had rung the bell to indicate the beginning of lessons, everybody went to their appropriate classes. I was directed to the headmaster's office to be informed of the school protocol. During the trip to school, I'd been told the headmaster's name was Donkesley; it was easy to guess his nickname although I should remember to only call him 'Sir' to his face.

I realised exactly what was meant, when I was called into his office and met him for the first time. From my first impression, he was very much a weakling; he certainly wasn't physically a very strong man. His bald and shiny extra large head, thin protruding nose and large prominent ears, supported thick, heavily rimmed glasses. Fortunately, as he began to speak I'd instinctively directed my eyes to look past him and, as advised, called him Sir at the appropriate time. If I hadn't, I'd have easily smiled, particularly every time I'd thought of the comments made about his baldhead, or his nickname. Although he was aware of my long absence from school he didn't appear to be the slightest bit concerned about my past or future academic education. He told me my future upon leaving school would probably involve either working on the land or in the building industry; living in the country,

I wouldn't have much choice, unless I was very fortunate. When he explained my daily routine, I very soon realised that preparations for both occupations were a natural part of the school curriculum.

I was to spend the whole of the Monday afternoon period with another ten or so boys working in the headmaster's enormous vegetable garden. It was situated on the other side of the road behind a large wooden shed, which was utilised by the top class. Row upon row of every conceivable vegetable was planted; all the teachers plus the local village shop owners thought they were the only ones to enjoy the benefits. How wrong they were!

Because Brian and I lived close to each other, we were teamed together to learn farming. Once we'd had assembly every Tuesday, the two of us would buy local-made meat pies, rolls and chocolate with our dinner money before setting off to walk about six miles back towards Ifold. Despite the severest weather conditions, we looked forward to the long walks, mainly because we simply enjoyed the countryside, the wildlife, and most of all, the freedom.

Each week, we were told which one of four chosen farms to stop at and work. The majority of the farmers and their workers treated and taught us well; a few of the others treated us as free labour and didn't attempt to teach us anything about farming.

It became a foregone conclusion which of the regular farm workers would always leave us the unpleasant tasks of either painting the farmyard buildings with tar, or mucking-out the cattle stalls and pigsties. We'd spend the spring and summer days on such jobs as filling sacks of new potatoes from the field or alternatively climbing ladders and picking apples from the tops of the trees which the paid women apple pickers couldn't reach from ground level. The vast orchards contained thousands of apple trees of various types ripening at different months throughout the summer.

Every Wednesday afternoon all the boys were collected by the school bus and taken to Billingshurst School for carpentry classes. Several of us soon became enthusiastic and enjoyed the thought of being able to turn a plain wooden board into an attractive or useful object. Quite a few of them would seize the opportunity of being able to work with their hands, which hopefully might form the basis of an occupation. Others thought differently, while a few couldn't even think for themselves at all and were, as Mr Rose would say 'twelve loaves short of a baker's dozen.'

Thursday afternoon, regardless of the weather or time of year, was sports or recreation of one kind or another. The picturesque sports ground surrounded by horse chestnut trees was enormous and occupied the entire centre of Wisborough Green village. With the occasional audible light hammering sounds that came from the traditional blacksmith's forge midway between the two typically old English pubs positioned at opposite ends of the green, it was a beautiful sight, once seen, never to be forgotten.

Because the combined out-of-classroom activities accounted for two and a half days in every week there was insufficient time allocated for all lessons. It became important to keep up with what little we were taught or otherwise fall behind never to catch up. Everybody tried his or her best. I tried as hard as I could to catch up with my lost schooling knowing how important it was; but it would be difficult for some to fully succeed, although nobody appeared very concerned. Many mistakenly thought there was no alternative but to accept a life, which had previously been planned for them.

I never realised the consideration and kindness I'd receive from so many of the local people I'd meet over the forthcoming years. Instinctively they always tried their best to help, and give me good sound advice, which taught me so much natural awareness. It was because of their unequivocal guidance, that I unwittingly began to form my own decent foundations on which to conduct my life.

Chapter Seventy

When I first met Brian's father, he'd told me that if I'd like to avoid the mile walk on schooldays, it would be perfectly safe to ride my bike to the farm and leave it there. I told him I appreciated his consideration but that I knew Mum wouldn't give me permission. From his expression it was the answer he'd expected so he changed the subject completely. Initially I was surprised, but it soon became abundantly clear he'd met and spoken to someone from either Turpins or Foxbridge Farm. He was well aware of all the land I was permitted to snare and he told me that if I'd like to include Little Headfoldswood Farm, I'd be welcome to do so.

Access to an additional four square miles of land in which to set snares on the way to and from school was indeed a bonus. The majority of the catch I'd sell to Dick and the rewards were plentiful. With the combination of school milk and dinner money to buy additional food, plus freshly caught fish, rabbits, and various types of eggs every weekend I never went hungry; neither did Wendy or Jet.

Within a short time Brian and I became good and trusting friends in the same manner I'd shared with Dave and Michael for such a long time. Whenever I was at home Nan was always a comfort close at hand for me. The antics of red robin, always gave me a smile. My life had changed to such an extent, that most evenings I'd look forward to the next day.

The idea of keeping a distance from Mum and Dad was working. Providing I did my regular or any other jobs whenever told, life became more bearable. Mum's often unprovoked slaps across the face didn't hurt much as I'd learnt to ride with the blows, unlike the unexpected slap across the ear which came from around the back of my head. Even then I was far more bothered as to why I was slapped without reason.

One evening, whilst Nan and I sat alone in the warmth of the kitchen, I told her how much I enjoyed the school dinners, and being able to sit with others when having a meal. She told me I'd appeared much more content ever since I'd started back at school; I'd even gained a little weight. As she continued, I couldn't help noticing the smile on her face, and the manner in which she raised her eyebrows. I sensed she had some idea of what I'd been doing to feed myself.

Whether or not she'd been told, I decided to tell her everything. I explained the land I covered and the various methods I used; the types of food available throughout the year, and how I'd learnt to cook over an open fire under the beech tree close by in the woods. I told her Wendy and Jet were once again able to sit with me watching and waiting for titbits. Nan became so enthralled, her eyes and mouth widened in awe. Speaking in low tones, to avoid being overheard by Mum or Dad in the adjacent room, a stream of inquisitive questions reflected her enthusiasm.

When I'd answered all the questions she asked, Nan made it perfectly clear how pleased she was with the way I'd become self-reliant and my ability to care for myself; reminding me she'd always be there for me should I ever need help in future. I immediately seized the opportunity to suggest it might be possible for me to help her for the very first time. Initially she looked thoughtful and surprised, although it wasn't long before she began to smile as I explained my idea to her. I reminded her it'd soon be Christmas and she'd be going to stay with her daughter for a couple of weeks' rest. It was when I suggested that she should stay with her daughter for a longer well-deserved rest that her smile gradually became a wide grin and I sensed a glint in her eye as she nodded her agreement.

It soon became obvious she was elated with the thought and after a while decided she'd go to her daughter Doss two weeks before Christmas and not return until the end of January. I told her I was pleased for her and wondered what Mum's reaction would be. Nan's lengthy answer came as a complete surprise, which left me shocked and speechless for several minutes.

"I don't care what she says, or what she does; I'm going. What's more, I shan't be going only two or three time a year in future; I'll go four or five times, whether she likes it or not, I don't care! You're at school every weekday, and when you get home you've still got to do your daily jobs; you won't have time to do anything indoors. Your mother will have to do it instead of leaving it all to somebody else. I could have lived with one of my other daughters years ago, but I stayed because I wanted to be certain you were cared for and treated properly. It was a good job I did! But now you don't need me so much. You've done well Robin; you can fend for yourself, you're completely independent and what's more, you're now fit and strong."

Half an hour or so later when Mum came into the kitchen, Nan confronted her with the length of time she'd be away. Mum's reaction was short-lived when she realised Nan was adamant about going. I knew from previous experience that the only difference it would mean to Mum was that she'd have to cook.

When the day arrived for Nan to go to London, Dad took her to catch a bus from Horsham instead of driving her and Mum to see the family. Although it had become customary, there wasn't any point in making the trip this year. The excuse being, there wasn't any joint of bacon to give them as a Christmas present because for various reasons they'd been unable to keep a pig. Nan and I knew the real reason was because I hadn't been able to do the work.

When I'd finished preparing the vegetables on Christmas Day, Mum gave me a half-crown to buy Dad his Christmas pint of beer. I welcomed my present of a thick woollen long scarf. The unusually dry autumn had turned to a cold and windy start for the winter and I'd noticed the first of the low dull and heavy snow-bearing clouds gathering as I climbed into the front seat of the car next to Dad for our annual trip together. Dad looked so deep in thought; I decided to sit in silence until spoken to. We'd travelled approximately half the distance towards Loxwood before he spoke, slowly and quietly. "Do you remember me telling you one day, that all Mum and I own will be yours? It'll be left in our Wills and it'll all belong to you Robin?"

"Yes I remember Dad," I answered, "although I've never given it another thought."

"Well, you don't have to think too much about it now," he paused; "it's just that," he paused again, and remained silent. The only sound to be heard was the low tone of the engine.

"It's just what Dad?"

"Well it's just that now you'll only get half. You'll have to share it with a brother or sister. Your mother's going to have a baby; I wouldn't have thought it possible, I've always been so careful, and always taken precautions."

He alone couldn't understand how it could have happened; not wanting to dwell on the subject, I replied to the best of my ability in a relaxed and humorous tone, "I'd expect to share everything equally Dad, it's only natural surely. Unfortunately, any help has come a bit too late for me now; all the hard work's done. There'll be nothing for him or her to do. I'd have liked a brother or sister ten or eleven years ago. By the time they'll be old enough to help me everything will be finished. I'll have left school and be going to work. Can't you send it back?" I said laughing, "I'm used to being alone."

Dad didn't show the slightest reaction and we remained silent in our own thoughts for the duration of the journey.

Chapter Seventy-one

It was early in February when I arrived home at dusk and found Nan sitting in the warmth of the kitchen waiting for me; she looked well and completely relaxed. From our first glance it became abundantly clear how happy we were to see each other. Because I wasn't sure what Nan's reactions would be when I told her the news, or whether she already knew, I purposely avoided the subject of Mum being pregnant as we sat around the stove talking. We talked for ages; Nan about the friends and family she'd met and her enjoyable rest. I talked mainly about school and wandering about with my mates over the Christmas holidays.

It was when I'd finished talking that I realised Nan knew about Mum's condition; she asked me what I thought about having a baby brother or sister. I explained it wouldn't make much difference to me. I was more concerned about the additional work she'd get involved in again. There wasn't any need to get concerned for her, she'd told me; Mum would breastfeed the baby and would nurse it herself for at least the first two years.

The winter evenings were drawing in earlier each day making it only possible to set my snares on the way home from school on fine light days. Although on a good week I'd capture up to five or six bright-eyes, I had so many customers who enjoyed rich and warming rabbit stew that I could have easily sold twice as many.

It was when I noticed my friendly red robin and his mate preparing their nest for the first hatch of the year, I realised how quickly spring was approaching. As usual when the time was right to protect any bright-eyes' kittens I'd cease snaring for a few weeks. Within a month, as planned I stopped, completely unaware I'd never restart. I'd sufficient savings to purchase any additional food required for the anticipated duration even though I was a little concerned as to how I'd make up my deficit in earnings. I needn't have worried as within a day, completely unexpectedly, Mr Rose gave me the chance to continue earning money in a most surprising and unusual way. I took the opportunity, which led, from one easy and profitable job to another.

We were standing close to his chicken run casually chatting, which was normal while collecting the milk and eggs, when I saw three rats creeping around the corner of the goat shed. Looking at them in disbelief, I stopped talking, as I pointed them out. Then noticing movement to one side I realised there were two others a few feet away entering the small orchard from the boundary of dense woodland. Mr Rose was well aware of the situation and explained his dilemma as the infestation of rats was gradually becoming out of his control.

The adjacent land, the bungalow and about five acres of Strudwick Farm land had recently been sold. Several newly erected small outbuildings were utilised for the mass production of hundreds of chicken, all of which were caponised and fed a special high protein diet to enable rapid growth. The giblets and general food waste had initially encouraged a few rats. They in turn had thrived and rapidly multiplied becoming serious pests for Mr Rose. I understood his concern; not only did they steal enormous quantities of chicken and goat pellets, but more seriously, valuable eggs and young chicks. He was in a quandary, and unable to utilise the gin traps to their best advantage, as the rats were so numerous; the pests were virtually uncontrollable.

I automatically withdrew my catapult, and then loading with a stone from the driveway, quickly aimed and fired. The one I'd aimed at dropped lifeless, the only brief movement being the slight twitching of nerve ends in the feet. The remaining four stopped in their tracks, looked, then turning within a second, scampered so quickly I didn't have a chance of reloading.

For a moment or two Mr Rose looked pensive, then looking at me he smiled as he spoke. "You've found the answer to my problem Rod; I'd never have thought of using a catapult, well done! How would you like to earn yourself some money?"

"I'd like to, in actual fact I've got to. I've stopped snaring for a few weeks; somehow I need to find some other way to earn money. But what?" I asked.

"I think I've got the answer. I know what you just did wasn't a fluke. I know you're a good shot. So here's the deal," he said, in a very matter of fact manner. "For every rat you can stop I'll give you three pence. Hopefully they'll eventually get the message and stay away for good."

I could barely believe my good fortune when within minutes we mutually agreed a deal which was to continue on a regular basis. Our agreement not only included a beaker of raw egg and milk, but was also the instigation of many other unexpected benefits for me.

Good fortune seemed to be on my side when, within the week, I'd made the same arrangements with Dick and Prince Tom, for keeping their farms as clear as possible from rats and other pests. I'd also gratefully accepted the invitation and arranged to help at the annual Magpie Shoot in three weeks' time. Then to top it all, Prince Tom offered me part-time work; initially helping to herd and prepare the cattle for milking. Soon I was shown how to help in the care and feeding of the large stock of pigs; later I'd be taught how to drive a tractor, which would enable me to undertake various jobs about the farm and on various apple orchards summer or winter. His offer was generous, with no particular days or hours specified. I could work any evenings, weekends or school holidays to suit myself. Although I gladly accepted the opportunity, I remained open minded on whether or not I'd automatically be expected to become a farmer.

To everyone's delight the rat population at all three farms had noticeably dropped to at least half by the day of the annual shoot. The routine remained the same as previously; I was given a lift on the trailer and travelled with the other farmers and their dogs from Foxbridge Farm for the beginning of the shoot at Dick's. Upon arrival I was given my instructions for the day during the short wait for the others from Little Headfoldswood Farm.

By mid-afternoon the enjoyable day's work was finished and we all sat on bales of hay inside one of the barns, talking, and sharing the free food and drink. When everyone was rested, having walked around all the fields on the three farms they began enjoying themselves even more by laughing, joking, and watching the antics of the dogs.

Prince Tom thanked me for my help and presented me with a large parcel of farmhouse produce, plus the money each of the men had given. Everybody was silent and I noticed they were all looking at me. I'd previously thanked them all, what more should I do? I began to feel embarrassed and found myself looking at Dick; he was smiling, and then I noticed, so was everybody else. Thank goodness, I thought! Dick moved to another bale a few feet away, then speaking in a soft voice, although loud enough for everybody to hear said. "Prince Tom spoke to your friend Mr Rose this week Rod, and providing you agree, the three of us have decided to do you a favour, and of course, ourselves at the same time." He paused, but I felt too embarrassed to speak. "We're all aware of the good job you're doing by keeping the vermin down on the three farms. However, we all know the rats are getting crafty. They are watchful all the time; as soon as they see your whole body standing perfectly still, face on towards them, they know you're going to shoot, and they scurry for cover. The problem is that's the only way to aim your catapult accurately; you can't hide behind something and shoot while your body is hidden around the corner. Its not as if you had an air rifle; is it?" He asked.

"No." I answered. "You can hide anywhere with one of those and still shoot, but I haven't got one, as you know."

"Yes you have," he said grinning. Then reaching behind the bale of hay he took hold of an Under Lever Air Rifle and held it out towards me, "what do you think this is then?"

"My goodness, it's not mine, is it?" I dared to ask. Then, hardly believing my eyes, I looked at the other men; they were all still smiling. It was then I realised why; they all knew what to expect.

"It's a virtually new BSA Air-Starter and yes, it's yours; providing you agree with our conditions."

"Yes of course," I immediately answered, "what are they?"

"You'll be well paid, as usual Rod, for any pests such as bright-eyes or wood pigeons you get, but that's all. In exchange, and on a regular basis, you'll be expected to check our three farms are as clear as possible, from any other pests. The gun is very powerful, so you must be careful. Nevertheless, never shoot at a Charlie because if you wound one it'd only suffer and we wouldn't want that to happen. That's the deal. Take it; or leave it; the decision's yours."

I smiled and felt a twinge of emotion as I replied, "I don't know what to say, except thanks very much. I don't have to give it a second thought Dick, it's a deal; probably the best I've ever had. I'll take it, no problem."

Dick handed me the rifle, which balanced perfectly and felt comfortable lying over my forearm in the carrying position. "Looks as if it was made for you," he said. "We'll get a 12-bore for you one day; we'll make a gamekeeper out of you yet."

When I got home and Mum saw the size of the large food parcel I'd been given, I wasn't surprised by the warm reception she gave me. What did surprise me was the unexpected casual comment, when she asked why I couldn't go shooting every day. For a moment I was shocked.

Later, during the evening, when we were alone, I told Nan of my good fortune. She was pleased for me and jokingly commented about getting as fat as a barrel. She reminded me how important it was to remember not to mention to Mum or Dad about the money or food I'd earned in the past. I knew she was right; I'd be expected to take part of my catch home, my school dinner money would cease, and I'd be expected to fend for myself entirely.

Within a week I'd learnt how to adjust the sights on the rifle to enable me to shoot with pinpoint accuracy up to thirty yards away. From that day onwards my snares and catapult, upon which I'd become so reliant, became virtually obsolete.

Chapter Seventy-two

During the second week of May, Mum was admitted to Horsham General Hospital where on the thirteenth she gave birth to her baby. Dad collected them both four days later when Nan and I first met Carolyn, my baby sister. Nan was delighted with her new granddaughter, making strange cooing sounds while rocking her and tickling her under the chin. The three of them were all smiling, making silly noises and saying how lovely she was and how much she resembled Dad. To me she appeared to be nothing more than a tiny, wrinkled, ugly and extremely noisy baby. I could only wonder what all the fuss was about, and how long it would be before she was old enough to help me.

Within twenty-four hours, Nan realised her thoughts of only being a little involved in the initial upbringing of the new baby were futile. Although she was right in her assumption that Mum would nurse the baby for the majority of the day, she hadn't expected to get up alternate nights and attend to Carolyn because Mum made the excuse of being too tired to get up every night of the week!

Carolyn was no different to any other infant; we were all woken every time she cried which was intermittently throughout the night, every night, for weeks. I wasn't permitted to help; I was too young; although Mum considered me old enough to take over the responsibility of washing the daily pile of dirty napkins whenever Nan was away.

Dad arrived home one evening with an enormous pram strapped to the open boot of the car. When he'd untied the straps and stood it upright I could barely believe my eyes. The spokes and rims of the wheels were chromium-plated trimmed with white rubber tyres. The two front wheels looked to be at least twelve inches high; the two at the rear were even larger. The gleaming black carriage with a metal name label saying 'Silver Cross,' supported a frilly-edged collapsible hood at one end, with a wide shaped white pushing bar at the other.

Being occupied with various thoughts, which were racing through my mind, the sound of Dad's voice startled me.

"Well; what do you think of it Robin?"

"I don't know what to think. It's a bit posh isn't it? Where's Mum going to go with it? There isn't anywhere except Ifold; and that's too far for her to walk; she never has yet."

"You know what she's like. You tell me! No doubt we'll find out sooner or later. I'll tell you one thing Robin; you'll never see me pushing it. Don't worry, I'll make sure you don't have to either; I promise."

"Thanks Dad, I must admit the thought had crossed my mind."

The following morning I was told Mum's plan was to walk around Ifold with Carolyn in the pram. I was to smarten up my appearance and escort her. I was also expected to give as much detail as possible on the occupants of each property we passed. I should act and be very proud to introduce everyone we met to Mum, then I was to remain quiet and speak only when spoken too, she'd do the talking.

Under normal circumstances I'd have completed the tour of Ifold in just over an hour comfortably, but time was of no importance to Mum. Oblivious of looking ridiculously overdressed in her finery, whenever possible she'd try to give the impression of her superiority and fool the few people we met into believing how hard she'd worked with Dad building the bungalow. It wasn't until we were almost home that she realised she hadn't fooled anyone, except herself.

It was three hours before we eventually arrived home. Barely able to walk another yard Mum virtually collapsed into her armchair exhausted. After a short rest Dad asked her if she'd enjoyed herself. Both he and Nan were interested in her impression, and the response she'd received from the local people.

Mum expressed her disapproval of two of my mates, Dave and Frankie by saying they looked scruffy and simple-minded. She'd ignored them completely as they grinned at each other for no apparent reason. I'd felt embarrassed, knowing everyone we'd met could see through Mum's façade and would find it highly amusing as she assumed her air of importance while pushing a posh pram along a roughly made-up lane in the heart of the country. Unfortunately Dave and Frankie's expressions, had said it all.

We listened intently as Mum spoke of her disappointment in what she described as a wasted trip. Within minutes her voice level got higher and higher as she virtually screeched her words out with increasing anger.

"We saw three people on push bikes, apparently on their way to collect water from Spring Hill. None had the common courtesy to stop and speak; all they did was to say hello to Robin as they passed."

"Didn't you see anybody else Babs?" Dad said frowning.

"Yes we did; for what it was worth," Mum sneered.

"What do you mean, for what it was worth?" Dad asked, still frowning.

"I only met eight people to talk to. Three of them were in Ifold Stores; they all said 'hello' when Robin introduced me. That's all they said, except one old man who added,' "pleased to meet you." It was as if I wasn't even there; I was virtually ignored. No one had the slightest interest in having a conversation or to pass the time of day with me. Strange don't you think? Particularly when they all had time to talk to Robin. All I heard from them was, 'hello Rod! Nice to see you Rod! How are you Rod?' I've never felt so embarrassed in my life. They were all so rude and ignorant. Not one of them even bothered to look into the pram. It was a waste of time and I'm fed up with it."

"Well, to be honest Babs, you were a little over-dressed, to say the least; it was obvious to anyone you were trying to impress them. You should remember we're in the country; there isn't any reason for people to dress up. I would imagine anybody who saw you, would have had a bit of a shock. I'm surprised nobody took the mickey out of you and I'm not in the least surprised they all spoke to Robin; they all know him. I'll bet his two mates didn't look any scruffier than Robin does when he's been either mooching about or bird nesting."

Dad tried to conceal the chuckle in his voice and the grin on his face by turning away to look at Nan. It was too late he realised, as his eyes briefly met Nan's and they smiled at each other in agreement. It was enough to infuriate Mum. "That's it, I've had enough, and you're as rude as the locals; I'll never bother with any of them again. Don't sell the pram; just get rid of it, as soon as you like. You can give it away or break it up; I don't care, I've finished with it, I'll never use it again. I've tried my best; if they don't want to meet me, it's their loss not mine." Mum refused to comment on her decision and as expected considered the matter closed. Dad remained silent, knowing if he didn't he'd get into a slanging match with Mum, which she'd win; she always did, because Dad always gave in.

About two weeks later, as I was pulling a large load of timber home for logging, I met Dave and stopped for a chat. We'd only talked for a short time before he looked down at the cart and the lengths of wood strapped along its length. "Is that a new logging cart you've got Rod?"

"Yes, Dad helped me make it last week," I answered. "It's two scaffold boards wide, and six feet long. Do you like it?"

"Yes, particularly the large chromium wheels with the white rubber tyres. The two larger ones at the back are even better. It looks very posh to me," he joked.

"If you think the wheels are posh; what do you think of this?" I asked as I moved aside lengths of timber to reveal the two large shining words I'd fixed to the front boards.

Initially I only smiled, but very soon found myself laughing with Dave as he kept repeating aloud the two words he'd read, 'Silver Cross.'

Chapter Seventy-three

The summer became so hot and stuffy, red robin, like the majority of other birds, spent most of the daylight hours motionless and silent; perched on shaded branches in an attempt to keep cool, their wings and beaks half open to catch any breeze.

The work on the site I passed most days on my way to and from school soon became recognizable as a bungalow. As temporary accommodation for the new residents, a small wooden building with a corrugated iron roof had been assembled and connected to a large caravan. Within a few days I had the opportunity of meeting the Bartletts. The family of four included two boys; Barry, the eldest, was about the same age as myself; his brother Ian was about two years his junior.

During the following weeks I tried hard to befriend Barry and his brother, but they didn't appear interested in me, my mates, or any of the normal things boys of our age enjoyed doing. Whenever I visited, Barry's father would ignore me completely. His mother always made me feel uneasy by asking me why I'd called, and what I wanted. She reminded me of Mum, by always giving the impression of being better than everybody else, but like Mum she wasn't.

In a final attempt at friendship, I asked if they'd like to join Dave, Michael and myself at the annual Plaistow Fete. I told them it was worth going as the local squire always presented a deer from his private estate; the venison, cooked in front of you, on the spit, then sliced into fresh rolls, was given away free to all the local residents. I thought we'd all enjoy the time out together, but to no avail. They did go to the fete; although not being expected to walk their father had driven them, and like him they completely ignored us. It didn't take long before I decided not to bother. About four years later the action I took against Barry ensured my decision would become irreversible.

Whenever I'd time available I'd work on the farm for Prince Tom. Some of the work I was expected to help with wasn't very pleasant. In particular; mucking-out the pigs and cattle; participating in the unpleasant performance of castrating the young piglets and, when needed, assisting with any farm animals experiencing difficulties delivering their young. Nevertheless, I was paid well, and no matter what the work involved, we always ended up having a laugh and joke, particularly on the memorable day I first drove a tractor.

It was a Sunday morning when Prince Tom took me in his car to a large field about three miles away towards the village of Kirdford. The grass had previously been cut and dried where it lay; a Fordson Major tractor, fitted with a large wire hay-turner had been left on the side of the field ready for use. My unforgettable fun day was about to begin.

I positioned myself on the driver's bouncy metal seat feeling quite important. Prince Tom swung the starting handle three times before the engine roared into life, pumping a thick cloud of white smoke into the air from the tall exhaust pipe. Then, climbing onto the tractor, he balanced himself behind me on the large back axle. When he'd hung a large canvas bag within my reach on the wheel arch at my side, he took hold of the steering wheel in his left hand. With the movement and adjustment of several levers and knobs, the tractor lurched forward at a set speed with the wide hay turning equipment rotating at the rear. Everything was working and leaving rows of freshly turned hay behind us.

Within five minutes, having been told not to touch any of the control levers and shown how and where to steer, Prince Tom was satisfied I was in control of the situation. He told me the job would probably take me about five hours to complete. All I was required to do was to steer the tractor; nothing could go wrong, and he'd return before I'd have time to finish. He told me I was to help myself and enjoy the surprise refreshment in the bag he'd hung by my side. Then agreeing we were both content with the situation, he jumped clear, gave me a thumbs-up sign and walked away.

I soon realised, that because the field was perfectly flat and level and the steering wheel so stiff, the tractor would travel a considerable distance in a straight line, without correction. The morning drew on and within an hour the heat had increased steadily, and I began to feel thirsty. Wondering what type of drink would be inside the refreshment bag; I placed my hand inside and felt a large bottle, which I immediately withdrew. I'd been told to enjoy the refreshments, which contained a surprise, but a quart bottle of beer was more of a shock than a surprise, although not as much as the other things I found. The next was a large lunch box containing two enormous beef and horseradish sandwiches, tomatoes and sticks of celery. What a feast I thought, and what a welcome surprise. Eagerly I plunged my hand into the bag again. A box of matches! What on earth would I want those for I thought? Then as I withdrew the last item I realised; they were for lighting the twenty Dunhill cigarettes! What kind of day is this going to be? I knew I'd eat and enjoy the food, and it seemed obvious I was expected to have a beer and a cigarette; I decided perhaps I should give them a try.

By mid-afternoon I was nearing the middle of the field and within half an hour I'd reach the centre and the end of the job. I felt a little dizzy and wondered if either the beer or the cigarettes had caused it; perhaps it was both, but I didn't care, I was merry.

When there were only two rows of grass remaining, there wasn't any sight of Prince Tom. My mood changed; I did care, and didn't feel so happy. Instead I began to feel concerned. How could I stop the tractor? Everything had been set to avoid accidental use and I'd been told not to touch anything; I tried to move some levers, but they were ridged and I couldn't. In desperation, I tried to kick the gear lever into the neutral position; but it wouldn't move. I pulled the large hand brake on as hard as I could and stood upright with both feet on the foot brake; all to no avail, the tractor didn't even slow down.

As I drove the last few yards, I realised there was only one option left open to me, which without time for a second thought, I put into operation; the effect was immediate. Driving as before, with the front wheel in the same position between the rows of cut grass I'd previously turned, I drove in the reverse direction towards the outer edge turning the hay for the second time with the original side upwards. It didn't matter and I was relieved to realise the additional aeration would give a quicker drying time, yet wouldn't cause any problems with the baling procedure, which would follow another day when the hay was completely dry.

When I'd reached about a third of the distance between the middle and the edge of the field, the tractor engine began to spurt and splutter as it slowed to a halt before falling into silence, as it ran out of fuel. Climbing down with the refreshment bag, I sat on the hay and leant against the enormous back wheel. There wasn't anything I could do, except wait. I ate, relishing the last of the food and the last swigs of beer. Then relaxed and enjoying the peace and tranquillity of the countryside, I fell asleep.

The sound of Prince Tom's laughter awoke me, as he stood looking down at me. My head was throbbing, and I could guess why! I couldn't remember getting in to the car or the drive back, although I do remember arriving at the farm. We all laughed when Prince Tom told the three other farmers and myself that he'd accidentally set the speed of the tractor engine to run much too fast which was why I'd finished early and had no choice but to turn most of the hay back over to its original position. He couldn't help laughing himself when he told us he'd also mistakenly given me his bag of refreshments; my bag had contained beef sandwiches, cake, and lemonade. The jokes about me, a young boy, getting paid for going around a field the wrong way, smoking expensive cigarettes and getting drunk, while Prince Tom secretly preferred cake and lemonade as refreshments, were to keep us all amused for many weeks!

The next day, while working in the school garden, Dougie asked Brian and myself if we'd help at his father's annual cider-making day on Sunday. If we helped pick the various quantities of apples required we'd be given food and drink, plus a large container of last year's cider to take home. We both readily agreed. Nan was away for a rest, and as I washed the nappies during her absence Mum or Dad wouldn't object. I'd be out of the way; and they'd get the cider.

The following Sunday I set off for my first experience of cider making. It wasn't long before Brian and I entered the opening opposite Turpins Farm and were walking the quarter mile narrow mud track through the mixed woodland of Headfolds Wood. Because it was only accessible either by tractor or on foot, the majority of deliveries to Orchard Cottage where Dougie lived on the small isolated farm were impossible.

The small attractive old farm cottage, which appeared alive with hundreds of free-range chicken, was partly surrounded by fruit trees and various sheds. Several of the local men stood at the side of two large oak trees which were growing about ten feet apart. Four long square beams joined the trees together; two at head height and two at knee height fixed either side with thick hand-forged iron straps. The top beams supported various cogs from which hung a long thick steel screw with a large steel plate fixed to the bottom, fitting perfectly inside an oak container supported on the two lower beams. It was the cider press.

During the morning, everybody joined in picking bushels of apples in equal quantities of sweet, cooking and the essential wild crab apple. The large container of the cider press held a full box of each type, which was screwed down by the men using fence poles as levers. The fruit was squashed under the immense pressure and the juice poured from the channel in the box into buckets. The full buckets were in turn emptied into barrels; fine yeast was then added and the lid tightly fitted before they were rolled into the cellar of the cottage where they were left for at least a year to mature.

When the work was finished, Brian and I were given a good meal. We were given two shillings each, and the cider to take home. A few of the men drank a couple of glasses of strong cider before eating their food; most of them ended up lying on the grass asleep and drunk.

Chapter Seventy-four

Brian and I often enjoyed the odd cigarette, making our own by rolling the tobacco left in any dog ends we found. When money was available, we'd forge notes from our parents, to purchase cigarettes from Ifold Stores. It was a terrible mistake to make, but no one at the time knew the health risks and long-term damage caused by smoking. The only thing we considered was the good hiding we'd get from our parents, if we were caught!

One particular Saturday as we entered Loxwood village, we noticed the Post Office telephone engineers had rewired all the lines, leaving the replaced copper wire lines rolled up into loops at the base of each telegraph pole. After we'd bought a pack of cigarettes on the pretence they were for Mum, we set off on our return home.

Within minutes we were on the outskirts of the village and about to pass the Onslow Arms when we noticed the local bobby's push bike leaning against one of the posts supporting the front porch of the pub. Having noticed a roll of wire lying at the base of a telegraph pole a few feet away, we looked at the push bike again, then the post it leant against, then each other. It was obvious from our exchange of smiles, we both had the same idea; the prank would give us a laugh and be quite harmless; or so we thought.

Unobtrusively, we took a small roll of the telephone wire, which we hid between a barrel containing flowering plants, and the wall of the porch. While Brian twisted one end of the wire around the post, I secured the other end under the saddle of the push-bike. Then ensuring the wire was concealed, we ran across the road into a small field. We watched while hiding behind the hedge, trying to keep our laughter to a minimum and waited.

Frequently, during the next hour or so, the men who'd been drinking came outside and went to the gent's toilet at the back of the building. Mains water hadn't been installed in the toilets as yet, which were only flushed clean when it rained. Any rainwater or thawed snow would run from the roof, into the guttering, and then through strategically placed down pipes to wash the floor and the wall of the urinal, then into a clay gully, which ended at a roughly dug soak-away pit, several yards away in the woodland. The foul stench had become so strong on account of the heat of the dry summer; it must have been noticeable inside the pub. Despite the fact we were hiding a reasonable distance away, the smell was awful.

It was about half past two and we were beginning to wonder if our little prank would really be worth waiting to see, when we heard the pub bell ring and the landlord calling time; we knew it wouldn't be long now before everybody left.

Within ten minutes the policeman had come outside and while talking to the men, first put his helmet on and then his bicycle clips, as we waited in silence. Brian and I assumed he'd swing his leg over the saddle, and then sit on the seat, before gradually peddling away. The wire would tighten, stretch, and then break under his weight. At a slow speed, he'd get a sharp jolt and everybody else a laugh. It wasn't to be.

Having said his farewells he took hold of the bike by the handlebars and put his left foot onto the left pedal. Then, firmly pushing off with his right foot, the bike quickly rolled forward as he lifted his leg over the saddle. As he was holding tightly to the handlebars, his body balancing perfectly horizontal above the bike, the wire pulled tight. Unexpectedly the wire didn't break; instead there was a loud twang as it tightened, causing the bike to stop instantly. For a moment, it remained in the upright position, motionless, while the policeman appeared to hover over the bike, before flying headfirst and crashing several feet away. We could only watch open mouthed in horror as we heard the sound of a loud crack; the policeman landed facedown on the hard gravel, his helmet tumbling then rolling in semicircles and skidding away.

Men ran to his aid, lifting him to a sitting position where he slouched, gently groaning. With his grazed head bent forward resting on his chest, he was bleeding profusely from the nose and forehead. His left arm lay motionless at an unnatural angle across his lap, bent in half, midway between the wrist and elbow, broken.

Gradually he regained his faculties, and began to look around. Holding his arm while the blood was wiped from his face, he realised what had happened and began cursing and swearing. As he was helped half staggering back to the pub we heard him babble that whoever was responsible would probably still be close. He was right.

Within minutes, one of the men suggested they split up to find if whoever was responsible for the accident could be hiding nearby. The field we were in was to be included in the search and two men came towards us.

The river was only a few yards behind us, to our right; it passed through the bridge and under the road. We were cut off on three sides and hadn't realised the situation we'd put ourselves into. A small bungalow with a garden reaching to the edge of the river on our left was our only escape route. Having no choice, we kept our heads below the hedge line level, and made a dash towards the garden using the greenhouse and tool shed as cover from the bungalow.

We'd hoped to creep unseen around the edge of the shed; making our getaway by jumping over the fence, then scampering across the garden into a small wooded area for cover, but it wasn't to be. The shed we'd used as cover had hidden our view of a man digging a vegetable plot. We didn't have time to think; our reactions were instinctive, scared, and aware the men would be looking over the gate of the field any second; we couldn't wait.

Scurrying like a couple of squirrels, we reached the bank of the river and slid over the steep edge into the chilly water. Standing chest high in the slow current, our heads being several inches below the level of the field, we couldn't be seen. Feeling safer, we held on to roots or tufts of grass growing from the high mud bank; then in silence, hand over hand, we gradually worked our way along the edge. When we'd waded about a hundred yards we'd passed the bottom of the garden. We could hear voices, but we'd reached cover from the overhanging branches of the woodland and safety. We stopped, rested, and listened.

Two men were giving the gardener their exaggerated description of the policeman hovering in mid air like a bluebottle, before crashing downwards headfirst like a sack of potatoes. Brian and I didn't join in their loud laughter; we simply looked at each other dreading being caught, or found out. Goodness knows what the local policeman would have done if he'd ever thought we were responsible for causing the pain and embarrassment he'd suffered. Realising the further we got away from the area the safer we'd be, we continued wading along the edge of the bank until we were completely out of sight, having rounded two bends in the river.

Brian listened intently while I explained the two different ways home; one was to follow the disused canal, but it was open countryside for about a mile to the footbridge and Ifold Lake. We could be seen; it was too risky. Alternatively, we could swim across the river; from there we could walk under cover, across the length of Turpins Farm emerging at Ifold Stores. Brian would virtually be home whilst the remainder of my walk would be through the woods and fields of Foxbridge Farm.

There wasn't any need for discussion as we simultaneously faced the opposite bank and quietly began swimming the twenty or so feet across the deep water. As soon as we'd hauled ourselves from the water we dashed to the cover of the trees and relaxed. Despite being completely soaked through and the food I'd bought, the matches and cigarettes all ruined, we saw the funnier side and made jokes of what we'd seen and done. We eventually thought it all so hilarious and laughed so heartedly that our eyes watered and we needed to sit down to control ourselves.

During the long walk to Ifold Stores we'd dried out completely; nobody would guess we'd swam the river, or what we'd been up too. We'd experienced a day of mixed feelings, certainly a day to remember.

Chapter Seventy-five

Before I realised it, the remaining weeks leading up to Christmas had passed and all the delicious berries and fruit, which were so important to me, seemed to have finished. For my own use, I'd collected and stored as many nuts as I could; the harvest of Cox's Orange Pippins had been carefully picked, wrapped in paper, for preservation and then stored under the bed. As usual a large quantity of edible mushrooms threaded on a cotton line, hung in rows from the kitchen ceiling to dry.

Many creatures, ranging from squirrels to lizards, hibernate with the approach of winter, whilst a large percentage of the bird population migrate to warmer climates. As in previous years, for protection against the oncoming cold winter winds, red robin and his mate had strengthened their nest under the lean-to. As to be expected, the hen bird would occupy the nest while her mate would perch level with the top row of logs only venturing outside for food. Eventually the countryside barely moved with wildlife, gradually getting quieter and quieter. No living creature had to look for death; it was always there, summer or winter. Self-protection was imperative and affected everything and everybody one way or another.

Within a few weeks I was once again waiting outside the Onslow Arms, having been given a half-crown to buy Dad his customary Christmas Day drink. Although the sun frequently broke through the gaps between the high puffballs of cloud, reflecting on the heavy white frost like masses of shining mirrors, my ears and nose became numb in the strong ice-cold wind. It was the first Christmas I hadn't waited for Dad in the snow, unaware it would be the last time I'd ever wait outside any pub for Dad at Christmas.

Whilst waiting I recalled the previous day. It was a well-known fact that as it was the last postal delivery of the year, Sid was expected to find and then join the addressee in a Christmas drink. Apparently he always enjoyed the chat, and in particular the drink; consequently he was always unable to finish his job. Three years in succession I'd seen his wife driving the small horse and cart towards Loxwood looking for him. When found, he'd be put into the back of the cart, with his bike, where he'd be covered over with a couple of sacks to keep warm while his wife continued delivering any letters during the long trek home.

I recalled what had happened to the local policeman only a few feet from where I stood under the porch. Initially I'd felt sorry about what happened, but the more I thought about it, the more I began to smile. Virtually everybody knew and joked about what had really happened, although according to him, he'd apparently broken his arm by accidentally falling off his bike. Brian and I often found it difficult to remain silent, as we were the only ones who knew the whole truth.

In preparation for the installation of the mains water supply, by mid-spring the Water Board had stacked small piles of 4-inch cast iron pipes several yards apart along the complete length of Plaistow Road. Whilst two workmen, each operating large mechanical excavators, dug a deep trench along the side of the road; four others connected small valves at regular intervals to accommodate stopcocks. When the large hydrants were fitted to control the water flow, the heavy pipes were joined together and tested. When any leaks had been rectified, they were lowered into the trenches and backfilled. Working a normal 48 hour long week, the workmen planned to have the mains water installation finished along the entirety of the main road by early autumn; they'd then start installing the supply throughout Ifold.

On the 13th May the workmen reached the halfway mark and at long last our mains water was connected; the same day other workmen arrived and began fixing a large pole behind the bungalow, which was to carry the mains electricity supply.

During the evening, Mum unexpectedly called me into the sitting room where, smiling, she beckoned me to sit: I didn't feel at ease; something was wrong.

"Tell me Robin, did you know its Carolyn's first birthday today?" she asked smiling.

"Yes Mum, I did know," I answered.

Looking surprised she sat up and stared. She was annoyed; it obviously wasn't the answer she expected. "You're lying, why didn't you say anything then? You forgot didn't you, admit it?"

"No I didn't forget Mum; in fact I thought you had. If you had and I'd reminded you, you'd have got cross. That's why I didn't say anything."

Her hurtful answer was instantaneous, "I might forget yours, but I wouldn't forget Carolyn's birthday, I never will. We've arranged for her christening in a couple of week's time. I thought you should know, that's all." Her voice seemed to echo in my head and I looked away from her glare, waiting for whatever was to follow.

Mum then directed her attention to Dad reminding him, that as it wasn't necessary to collect water from the well at Spring Hill anymore, he'd have more time to spend on the bungalow. The tone in her voice sounded like instructions when recommending that the electrical requirements should be completed post haste. We were all aware the long trench I'd dug for the installation of the water supply, had filled with rainwater and needed to be emptied. It was to be my responsibility and first priority; then I was to cut and thread the piping for the plumbing system and when completed, was to backfill the trench, ensuring I raked the ground level in preparation for a lawn. Although I'd miss three or four weeks of school, the work, once again, was considered more important.

Although Dad's annoyance at Mum's attitude showed clearly in his face, he remained silent. The work wouldn't bother me, although the thought of not getting a school dinner, or not having sufficient time to catch any food could be a problem.

Dad installed temporary lighting to most rooms within three days; the same time it took me to empty the long trench and help connect the water supply into the kitchen on 1 June, only two weeks later. Even though only half completed, the addition of the services and the transformation they made, gave me encouragement to finish the work. I'd expected and prepared myself for a busy full day's work when Mum told me it was Carolyn's Christening Day and she'd decided I should become involved.

By mid-morning we were all ready. With the exception of Mum, who had the excuse to dress in her finery once again, the rest of us could only wear the cleanest of our old clothes. Dad drove us to the majestic and beautiful old church at Loxwood, which stood high above the pine trees, which were scattered between the lawns and bunches of fresh flowers which had been placed in various jars and containers at the resting places of many loved ones.

I'd peered inside the church on several occasions before, although I'd never ventured inside. The vicar met us at the entrance to the church and showed us to our positions. I felt myself relax from within the depth of my soul, as a sensation of peacefulness flowed through me. Initially I was mystified why, but it would soon become clear, thanks to Amy Lucas.

Standing at the font, Mum passed Carolyn to the vicar who performed the short ceremony. When he ended naming, blessing and crossing her forehead with holy water he was about to pass her back to Mum but she hesitated and declined to accept her. Instead, smiling at us all individually, she opened her hand and directing it towards me said, "would you pass my baby to her brother please; I think it would be nice if he carried her." Nan and Dad looked as if they believed her; I didn't, not for a split second.

On the journey home I asked Mum when and where I was christened. "I don't know, we didn't have you christened," she answered abruptly.

"Oh, why not Mum?" I asked feeling disappointed.

"Because I didn't see you, there was so much going on at the time," she said rushing her words. A few moments passed, and then as if an afterthought added, "It was on account of the war, and we were far too busy."

"Well I'd have thought you could have had me christened today, at the same time as Carolyn?" Too late, I realised my mistake! I'd voiced my own opinion!

Dad turned his head slightly and briefly towards me and then shouted so loudly for me to keep quiet that we all jumped.

He then loudly continued to answer the question I'd asked Mum. "Your mother and I don't know if you'd been christened before you came to live with us; we simply don't know!"

"Surely it wouldn't matter if I'd been done again anyway?"

"No, you couldn't Mum snapped. "It's too late now anyway so forget it. We've got enough to do without thinking about a christening for you."

Nan squeezed my hand in a gesture of comfort as we sat silent in the back of the car, both keeping our opinions to ourselves.

Chapter Seventy-six

By mid-June all the electrical and plumbing work was completed. The small Ideal boiler, installed in the kitchen, which only supplied hot tap water, would be kept alight constantly with coal or coke. The same fuel would be used on the fire in the sitting room. After all the trees I'd cut down, the thousands of logs I'd split, I couldn't believe I'd never be expected to cut, split or cart any logs again. What a relief!

Despite the tremendous amount of work still to be completed, Mum was ecstatic with the installation and completion of the mains services. For a couple of days she'd frequently praised me for my efforts and been so nice, I felt as if I couldn't do anything wrong. I certainly hadn't done anything special to earn such praise. Had she genuinely changed her attitude towards me for the better? Why the niceties now? What was she up to?

I pondered for several days, feeling uncertain and uneasy, until one evening Mum called me into the sitting room where I was directed to stand opposite her. Nan and Dad, although looking surprised, remained silent. Likewise I remained silently thoughtful wondering if I was about to learn whether Mum's pleasant attitude towards me was genuine or false. I didn't have to wait long for her first question.

"Do you know what's special about today Robin?" She asked glancing at me momentarily. She'd remembered it was June the 24th I thought, giving me the immediate impression that her pleasant attitude towards me was sincere. I felt myself relax, and then half-smiling, I answered, "yes Mum, it's my birthday!"

"Oh is it?" She mumbled. "Why didn't you tell me?"

I looked at her in disbelief, thinking she must be having a joke, I grinned at the three of them individually before saying, "I thought you'd remember. You did remember didn't you Mum?"

"No I didn't; it's not important. I forgot your birthday; I normally do, so what?"

"Because you asked me if I knew what was special about today."

"Yes that's right," she said smirking, "it is the 24th June, Midsummer's Day, but never mind that. The reason I called you, was to tell you to start back at school tomorrow. I've written a note for your headmaster telling him you've been unwell."

On my return to the kitchen, instead of feeling mortified at Mum's intentions to upset me, I smiled to myself. I'd previously realised some lessons in life could only be learnt from experience. My doubts on the sincerity of Mum's pleasantness towards me had been automatic, and proved to be correct. Dad had remained silent throughout, as if frightened to speak, which confirmed my belief in his weakness. Nan's expression and sly wink, showed her approval of my ability not to show any sign of emotion. I'd learnt another important lesson in life from my previous experiences.

I hadn't seen any of my mates for several weeks and was pleasantly surprised the next morning to find Dave waiting for the school bus to Wisborough Green: having moved from Ifold to one of the houses close to the edge of the recreation ground on the Plaistow Road he no longer came under the Kirdfold schooling area.

No sooner had I begun to settle back into the routine at school when we broke up for the summer holidays! I was sorry in some respects, although in others I was pleased, because I'd have plenty of time to work, for which I'd be paid. Virtually every week or two, furniture, mainly old and second-hand, would be delivered for use when we moved into the bungalow. Dad envisaged we could move in at about Christmas-time, when the sitting room, kitchen and bathroom would be completed. The other rooms could be finished later, one at a time during the winter months.

Within a few weeks, the kitchen and sitting room were nearing completion. It was a normal Friday; Dad had gone to work and I was about to get ready for school when Mum told me to stay at home. She told Nan and me that she'd had a brilliant idea and made a decision on the spur of the moment, which would mean an important day's work for the three of us. To start with, I was to bring the wheelbarrow and timber cart to the kitchen door; Mum had decided it was the day we were to move!

The move was exhausting; no sooner had I carted one load of furniture or fittings to the bungalow emptied it into the appropriate room and returned, the next load was ready; it took hours. The mattresses and metal bases of the beds were the most difficult to balance but fortunately nothing was particularly heavy.

By midday, red robin who'd flitted around me all morning finally perched on an overhanging branch, where he spent the remainder of the day preening and singing. Wendy who'd followed me into each room as I carried in the furniture gave a single bark as if of approval as I placed each piece of furniture in position.

By mid-afternoon everything had been placed in the appropriate rooms. Nan's large room, similar to Mum and Dad's, could benefit from the warmth of the kitchen and sitting room whenever the door to the hallway was left open. My room, which was only accessible by passing through Nan's, was attached to the back corner of the bungalow. The three exterior walls were open to all weather conditions throughout the year and the wind could be heard howling through the gap between the sloping ceilings, fixed only six inches away from the bare roof tiles. It was the coldest and smallest room of all but despite barely being able to contain a single bed, a small three-drawer cabinet and one chair, I didn't care. It was my own bolthole with lighting; it was mine!

By early evening, despite the warmth in the sitting room and kitchen, each room looked bleak. The darkness outside caused the lights to reflect brightly on the uncovered cement floor and knowing the amount of work still to be completed it didn't give me any feeling of home-comfort or contentment.

I'd placed the kitchen table with four chairs in the middle of the room, assuming I'd be included at meal times. Surely I wouldn't be expected to eat alone in future; although on reflection, I thought perhaps it might be better if I did. I'd wait and see; knowing Mum could always think of a reason why I shouldn't. Nan had started preparing dinner when Mum made the excuse that because I was always out at meal times; it was my fault I ate alone; therefore, it wouldn't make any difference if we continued as normal. Then, as if previously decided, I was told to remove one of the ordinary chairs from the kitchen table and replace it with Carolyn's high chair. Mum's expression was of annoyance; she'd obviously expected me to be surprised and upset. I wasn't. Mum's excuse confirmed my second thoughts and doubts.

Whilst I'd learnt the hard way to keep my opinions to myself, I believed there were undoubtedly occasions when you should voice them, making your thoughts justifiably and clearly understood. Regardless of the consequences, I decided this to be one of those occasions and answered Mum's remarks by telling her we couldn't possibly believe what she'd said was true.

I knew I was taking a risk, but to satisfy my own conscience I had to speak my mind. Keeping as calm as possible, I reminded her of two reasons why I didn't join them at meal times. One was because the table in the wagon was intentionally placed against the wall, not allowing enough room for us all to sit around it. Secondly, as I wasn't expected to be present whenever meals were served, I'd become accustomed to keeping out of the way. Only when they'd finished their meal and retired to the sitting room, was I usually permitted to have mine. I finished by reminding Mum that whenever Nan was away, even though I might not have been given a cooked dinner, I was always expected to wash up their dirty dishes.

Nan and I watched Mum as she stood in front of me, her arms folded, remaining silent, deep in thought. We waited, trying to imagine what she was thinking, or what she'd say or do. We didn't have to wait long.

I'd normally expect an open-handed hard slap across each side of the face or back of the head, but not this time. Mum's folded arms were level with my face and for the first time she unexpectedly lashed out to strike me across the face with the back of her hand. I barely had time to duck my head and soften the blow when it landed. The loud snap of breaking bones was followed by Mum's scream of agony as she clenched her hand close to her chest, her eyes filling with tears of pain. Mum frenziedly lashed out with her feet, from all angles, trying to kick me; I had to get out of sight for a while and quickly dashed for the door. Wendy, head and ears drooped, and tail between her legs followed close behind. Nan obviously thought the scene so hilarious she couldn't control her sudden outburst of laughter. After I'd relaxed outside, I also laughed when I thought how ridiculous Mum had looked!

On his return from work, Dad realised from the blaze of lights that we'd moved into the bungalow and stormed indoors, his mouth open with a look of disbelief and horror. Mum, arm in sling, didn't explain why she'd suddenly decided to move home; instead her priority appeared to be the news of how she'd broken her hand. Dad didn't show any concern, but reminded her she'd originally agreed to stop once she hurt herself; now she had, she shouldn't try it again. I could see Dad was furious as he led Mum into the sitting room, leaving Nan and me in the kitchen. Having eaten my sandwiches, I decided to keep out of the way and go to my bedroom. Wendy, who must have felt confused, followed me to the room, where to my surprise I found Jet sitting, meowing outside on the windowsill. Within ten minutes I fell asleep to the sound of Dad shouting at Mum; although I didn't have the warmth of Nan's body next me, Wendy was curled up on the bed at my feet and Jet had curled up against me under the covers.

Chapter Seventy-seven

Despite his full-time job at Dunsfold Aerodrome, Dad had prepared himself to complete the interior work gradually in the evenings during the winter months. He never forgave Mum for her inconsiderate and unforeseen decision, which had ruined his plans; the completion being suddenly and unexpectedly brought forward left him with no other choice but to work weekends and evenings, virtually non-stop, twelve hours a day. He soon began to look tired; the long hours and hard work were obviously too much for him. He became very quiet and solitary, becoming miserable and very short-tempered, particularly with Mum.

On Christmas Day, I expected to go to the Onslow Arms with Dad for our annual drink. At midday Mum gave me the customary half-crown to pay for the drinks, telling me I could keep any change, which should be considerable, as I'd be going alone. Dad would be staying home, as it would only take two or three hours to completely finish the work on the bathroom.

Having received Mum's instructions for the remainder of the day, I began by setting off to the pub. When I arrived I waited outside, hoping somebody would help me get a drink. I hadn't waited long when I was invited into the bar; on the condition I'd keep out the way. The majority of the locals chatted to me and exchanged Christmas greetings; it was pleasing to be included in their casual conversation. Although I felt a little nervous when the local policeman enquired, "why on earth didn't your parents let you ride your bike instead of walking? It must be all of two miles each way."

"I'm only allowed to use it for shopping, when it's only left alone for a few minutes at a time. I think they're worried it may be stolen." I answered, shrugging my shoulders.

His response was immediate. "Rubbish; I'm the law around here and you can tell them from me there's never been a bike stolen from the Loxwood area yet. In fact, you could safely leave it unattended anywhere on my patch for days on end. It wouldn't get a second glance, let alone be touched."

I could barely believe my ears as my mind flashed back, remembering the sight of him flying through the air, head first, over the handlebars of his bike and crashing into a heap only a few feet away from where we sat. In order to control the inevitable outburst of laughter I quickly put some crisps into my mouth and took a large sip of ginger beer, but the action didn't wipe the sight out of my mind. The uncontrolled eruption from my mouth was fortunately mistaken as choking, which he quickly tried to help clear by patting me firmly on the back. I could barely believe my luck, and was convinced from his attitude he couldn't have suspected or connected Brian or me with the embarrassment he'd suffered.

Being Christmas Day the pub closed early, but as I'd been told not to return home until dusk, I'd no choice but to wait about in the ice-cold wind. I'd then be able to have all the warmth of the kitchen to myself.

Once indoors I stood shivering in front of the boiler, gradually warming myself, looking at the dirty pots and pans stacked on the draining board and table, ready for me to wash up. It was to be my last job of the day; washing of a different type taking priority.

The wet paint in the bathroom smelt strongly; an old towel lay on the floor in place of a mat and a clothes line stretched high over the bath. It was the third room to be finished. I'd completed my first job of the day by keeping out of the way; my second job lay in front of me. In preparation, Mum had filled the bath with dirty nappies, which were soaking in warm water ready for me to wash. When they were finished, I was to continue with the enormous pile of all our dirty clothes, which we'd worn over the last two weeks.

Three quarters of an hour later when I'd finished; I took my burnt Christmas dinner of roast chicken from the hot oven. Unable to cut into the crisp meat or potatoes, I used my fingers and crunched into the ruined tasteless meal; I was hungry.

By the time I'd finished washing-up the crocks and stacked them away, it was eight o'clock. Sitting close to the boiler in the warmth I could hear Mum and Dad in the sitting room talking, whilst listening to the wireless; I hadn't seen them since I was sent to the pub. As Mum hadn't bothered to check if I'd finished my jobs or if everything was okay, I didn't bother either! As well as Nan being away it hadn't been a good Christmas.

Despite feeding myself adequately and being able to buy myself special little treats, I gradually accumulated spare money, which I'd earned as a result of pruning, grafting and various farm work. The more I saved, the more I wanted, hoping when I decided the time was right, I'd have sufficient to leave home and build my own future in life.

In a bid to increase my savings, I told the boys at school I was thinking of selling my collection of birds' eggs, whereupon several of those with a regular supply of pocket money showed a genuine interest. Having laid the various shells on beds of sawdust inside cardboard boxes, I took some to school each day, and over a short period of time I sold every one. The easier the eggs were to collect the less the value; which fluctuated from sixpence to a shilling each. Naturally the rarity of an egg, the higher the value; which often ended in a mini auction earning me five shillings for a nightingale's egg; one pound for a heron's egg and an unbelievable two pounds for a cuckoo's egg, which I agreed could be paid over a period of time.

I covered my savings with sawdust inside a disused egg box, and put it under my bed, safely out of sight. I thought that the possibility of my savings being found was remote.

During mid-spring when Wendy came on heat, and as we didn't want her to have any puppies, she was put into the sitting room each day and only released, under my control, before and after school. Although she never tried to get away, Bonzo the only other dog in the area was never far away, waiting for the opportunity to mate with her. Neither Mum nor Nan admitted to leaving the window open, which allowed Bonzo to enter the room; when they were found together it was too late!

About three months later, as Wendy neared the end of her gestation period, she began to whimper at regular intervals. From the experience I'd gained from various farms, I was aware she'd undoubtedly have difficulties giving birth; which I estimated to be within two or three days. Wendy was in pain, which I knew was getting worse; something was very wrong and I feared the worst. I knew something had to be done quickly. I'd met and voluntarily helped the local vet on many occasions in the past, but didn't know where he lived.

Prince Tom did! What's more, he had a telephone, he was a friend and I knew he'd willingly help.

Within minutes of explaining the details of Wendy's predicament, he was on the phone talking to the vet. When the conversation had finished Prince Tom told me the vet was due to make his regular visit to check the livestock at the farm; despite tomorrow being Saturday, when he normally undertook emergencies only, he'd agreed to combine the two visits, calling to inspect Wendy first.

Shortly after eight o'clock the following morning, Dad answered the knock on the door and then, followed by Mum and Nan, showed the vet into the kitchen. Under watchful eyes I lifted Wendy onto an old towel I'd laid over the kitchen table then held and stroked her head while the vet gently and methodically began his examination.

Within a few minutes he lifted his head and looked into my eyes. "You know she's in pup don't you Rod?"

"Yes I do; I think she's about ready to have them but something doesn't seem right. As you can see she's discharging very heavily and I thought it might be too much. She's also in a lot of pain, that's why I thought you should see her."

"Well you did the right thing; she's definitely suffering. How old is she?" he asked, removing the stethoscope from his neck, and then folding it to put away.

I anticipated his answer and looked down closely at her as I softly fondled her silky smooth ears. "She's only about ten or eleven; that's not too old is it?" I asked, dreading his response.

"Yes Rod, I'm afraid so. All the pups are dead, which would normally mean I'd have to operate and remove them. Unfortunately I can't; Wendy's heart is so weak it wouldn't withstand an operation or allow her to give birth naturally. I'm sorry, but the kindest thing I can do is to put her to sleep; it's the only way to stop her suffering, otherwise she'll certainly die in pain. I know you don't want that, do you Rod?"

My answer was so instinctive I hadn't realised I'd answered him until I'd said "No! But I want to stay with her while you do it."

Within seconds everyone had left the room, leaving the vet and me with Wendy. Within a minute I was left alone with Wendy and five minutes later, I was walking through the woodland to Eddie's. One part of my mind remembering the happiness and companionship we'd shared and now lost forever, the other part wondering why it had ended so sadly. My feelings of anger, sadness and confusion overtook my sense of judgement as I began to plan my revenge on Bonzo who, I'd come to the conclusion, was entirely to blame for my loss.

Upon entering Eddie's shed, the first item I took was an old half-sack. Then reaching under the wooden bench where it was hidden from sight I slid out the double-barrelled 4.10 poachers' gun. After I'd slid two cartridges inside the open breach I folded it in half and rolled it up inside the sack, out of sight, and set off through the woods to the junction of Chalk Road and The Ride.

Within ten minutes I was hiding at the crossroads close to the edge of the track, camouflaged by the hazel trees and ferns watching Bonzo sitting in the morning sun, on the path to his home, scratching himself. One short whistle and call of his name was all he needed to come looking. The short distance between us was the last he ever walked; the call I made to him was the last he ever heard and to this day no one has ever mentioned the name Bonzo, or what happened to him.

Chapter Seventy-eight

It was a warm summer morning as Brian and I strode from school through various woods and across fields towards Dounhurst Farm; one of the better farms chosen for our weekly farming lessons. We had emerged from a thicket into a small grazing area when, without warning, came a deafening explosion from directly overhead causing shockwaves which vibrated violently through the air, shaking the ground and trees. We stopped dead in our tracks ducking, as if for protection from we knew not what. The surrounding wildlife fell silent, and motionless with fear. Although it was only a matter of seconds, eventually after what seemed ages, bright-eyes, squirrels and birds began dashing about screeching in fright. We'd experienced for the first time the strident blast of an aircraft breaking the sound barrier.

When we'd overcome our shock and almost reached the middle of the field, we were surprised to notice several bright-eyes; some squatting motionless low to the ground with their heads facing downwards, others hopping around in small circles. It didn't appear right, and we knew something was wrong; it wasn't natural for them to remain exposed without constantly checking their safety. We assumed they were still scared and clapped our hands loudly, in a bid to scare them into bolting for cover. Nothing happened; they remained completely still. Following Brian's witticism of them, 'not turning a hair,' we ran towards them shouting and waving our arms in a bid to frighten them away. Again nothing happened; they didn't take the slightest notice; it was as if we weren't there.

As we reached them we looked closely and were horrified at what we saw. Their eyes had swollen to such an extent they were completely closed; the bright-eyes were blind. The lips, nose and the inside of the ears were so badly enlarged it was impossible for the poor creatures to eat, smell, or hear anything; they were among the first of many thousands to become infected and die from Myxomatosis.

This disease that is transmitted by the common rabbit flea is incurable for those in the wild. Originally imported into France by a wealthy landowner to control the rabbit population on his estate, the disease had spread out of control; local farmers knew it was only a matter of time before it reached our country and they dreaded the consequences. Their decision in dealing with the situation was, without exception, final; any bright-eye found suffering from the fatal infection, was treated with care, before being put out of its misery, as humanely, and quickly as possible, thus avoiding the expected 7 to 10 days wretchedness before death came.

Without exception, the various farm jobs we were normally expected to do were cancelled. Our priority was to search the fields and hedgerows looking for any bright-eyes suffering from the killer disease. At most farms we were loaned air guns or 4.10 shot guns to shoot at point blank range to end the misery. We hated and dreaded the job; even more at some farms, when we didn't have a gun. Although we knew a correctly delivered rabbit punch was as painless, quick, and deadly as a shot, we hated doing it, but didn't have a choice.

Although it was an accepted fact, that Charlie was cunning and clever in the manner in which he hunted his quarry, and despised for over killing simply for the fun, he now unwittingly became an asset. He and his cubs were probably responsible for terminating the suffering of more bright-eyes than any humans possibly could. Silly Charlie certainly lived up to his nickname by hiding behind any available cover, before creeping and slowly crawling flat on its stomach toward a defenceless deaf and blind creature completely unaware of his presence. The end would have been virtually instant and painless.

Any farm cats, which were only kept for controlling mice or rats, seen tormenting or thought to be cruelly treating any bright-eyes, were to be shot, without hesitation. By late summer, the bright-eye population had been drastically reduced. Those fortunate enough to survive had found their natural defence was to live above ground level in the cold, where fleas couldn't breed as easily as within the warmth of an underground burrow. Uncertain of the effects of the disease on humans, almost everybody became cautious and abstained from eating them and gradually the population began to grow again.

The months of culling were sickening for Brian and me; we couldn't wait for the time when eventually we'd be able to stop the killing and walk the farms without any signs of the terrible disease. I'll never forget when it eventually came; it was during the first week of September 1953. The majority of bright-eyes had gradually developed a natural immunity, whereby some would overcome the disease; others couldn't fight it off and we continued to stop the suffering of those we'd find, but the worst was over. From that week onwards, I stopped hunting them, never to kill another.

It was also the week when, for the first time in over a year, the daily tests breaking the sound barrier ceased. Neville Duke had broken the world speed record, and the countryside slowly began to return to normality.

The third reason I have for remembering the week wasn't as pleasant. Within half an hour of Dad arriving home one evening, I was summoned to the sitting room; I was in trouble. The unexpected had happened, for which I was so unprepared; I hadn't even considered any possible consequences. Mum had found all the money I'd earned and saved hidden safely, or so I thought, under my bed.

I'd never have dreamt Dad could look so furious as he stood in front of me, demanding to know how I'd acquired so much money, why I'd tried to hide it, and what I intended to use it for.

I eventually overcame my initial shock and thinking it would be for the best, I decided to tell the truth, as honesty was always the best policy. Or was it? Keeping as calm as possible and feeling certain they'd understand, I explained in detail how I'd earned the money from jobs on various farms; pruning, grafting, the sale of my egg collection and, of course, my weekly orders for bright-eyes.

"You lying little sod!" Mum snarled, pushing me closer to Dad." You must have been stealing out of my handbag for ages. Why else would you hide it?"

Being wrongfully accused of stealing was too much; my heart sank, and I felt devastated, impulsively shouting my answer in return. "I hid it from you because I thought you'd take it if you found it." I paused, having spoken my thoughts; knowing I was now in deep trouble; nothing I could do or say would make any difference. I continued, "I was saving the money for when I am old enough to leave home, as you call it.

I don't expect to spend it now because as you've found it I bet you won't give it back; you'll keep it for yourself, won't you?"

Mum stood up, a glare of disbelief on her face at what I'd said and prodding me in the chest shouted, "of course I'm keeping the money; its mine, you stole it from me, you're a lying little thief." Then with a demanding tone to her voice and looking at Dad she snarled, "you know what you must do Bern; teach the little sod a lesson." Dad's response was instantaneous. I never expected anything so drastic to happen; not until I was looking upwards from the floor, dazed. I hadn't seen, or even suspected the punch.

"Your mother's right; you're a thief, and if you're ever suspected of stealing again, you can expect the same again, but next time twice as hard."

Mum looked down at me expressionlessly, then speaking softly said, "don't worry yourself about leaving home Robin; when the time's right, I'll help you. You never know; it could be sooner than you think."

Chapter Seventy-nine

With the exception of the weekly delivery of Dad's football pools coupon, there was often a gap of several weeks between Sid leaving any letters in our post-box. Then unexpectedly, over a period of several weeks, for reasons which neither Nan nor I could fathom; at least one letter would arrive each week bearing either the postmark of Hamble or Winchester. Apart from exchanging several sealed letters between Mum and Mr Donkesley at school, half a dozen were also received from the education section of the Petworth Borough Council. Despite Nan regularly enquiring the reason from Mum, she was always told to wait and see, as we'd both find out in good time.

Having taken a letter to school one Monday and waited, as expected while it was read, I was shocked to be told what was expected of me that day. As I'd been unable to take my 11-plus examinations, through no fault of my own, I'd been given the opportunity to take the standard Technical School examination that afternoon. I didn't have any say in the matter. If I passed I'd go to a Technical College and be taught a trade of my choice, or so I was told and fervently believed.

Never having taken any form of exam in the past I dreaded the spelling, arithmetic and other questions which would be asked as I very nervously opened the front page. I'd begun reading the first section, which detailed the rules and conditions of the project, when Mr Donkesley's unexpected instructions stopped my anxiety instantly. He walked towards me, then bending down, spoke softly no further than a few inches from my ear. "You don't realise it yet and it's none of my business, but I'll tell you, this could be the most important opportunity you've ever had or you'll ever get. If you want my advice, take it; you can always change your mind later. Don't worry what it says at the top of the paper about how long it takes to finish; in your case there's no time limit. If you get stuck on any of the questions just tell me and I'll help you."

The questions on the examination paper were of general knowledge and not as difficult as I had expected. Within two hours I'd finished, everything was checked and the exam papers marked. I was given a sealed letter for Mum and the rest of the day off school.

As I walked home feeling reasonably content I repeatedly found myself trying to comprehend why everything had happened so quickly without any prior indication. However, I felt convinced the contents of Mum's letter had instigated the day's events, but I was in a quandary as to whether or not the procedure, which had been followed at school, was correct.

When I arrived home, Mum expecting me to have the letter for her, snatched it from my hand on sight. Ripping the envelope open and reading the letter inside, she smiled, first at Nan and then at me saying, "well done Robin! You've passed your examination; there's only one more thing to be done and we'll do that next week."

Nan, who like me, had been completely unaware of what would take place during the day, looked confused as she spoke. "What examination Babs? And what are you going to do next week? Why all the secrecy?"

"Robin's passed the test, which enables him to attend Technical College," Mum answered. "I'll take him for an interview next week, which I'm sure he'll pass. I've decided what's best for his future. I'll explain it to you both when everything is settled."

Wearing polished boots, clean-pressed trousers and jacket with some of Dad's Brylcreem smeared on my hair I felt distinctly uncomfortable as Mum and I waited at Horsham Station for the train to Chichester. My feelings towards my first train ride were of some excitement, but my feelings regarding the interview were mixed. I was to call the teacher Sir, speak only when spoken to, not to ask questions and keep my opinions to myself. I'd be given a general knowledge test and a medical; all of which should only last about three quarters of an hour at the most.

When we arrived for my interview, nearly two hours later, I was surprised it was within a block of offices, as opposed to a school. I was also surprised when I met the teacher, who appeared to be wearing some sort of uniform. His smart dark blue double-breasted suit was adorned with two vertical rows of bright brass buttons, matching epaulets and three gold stripes around each cuff, the top one being looped.

A nurse performed the medical examination, which lasted no longer than five minutes, whilst Mum and the teacher looked on quietly talking. Apart from a little concern shown relating to the scar on my eardrum, I was considered fit and healthy. Following an eye and colour-blind test, I was asked ridiculously simple questions to satisfy the teacher I knew my full name, my age and date of birth, my address and Mum and Dad's names. I was shown various pictures of landscapes, each supposedly containing a hidden number moulded within the scene; in all cases the numbers were prominent and blatantly clearer than the picture itself.

Half an hour after arriving I was told I'd completed and passed the tests, but not what would happen next. I knew Mum would only tell me when she was good and ready. Sitting in silence on the train home, my mind raced until it ached trying to comprehend the reason for the medical and the examination, and what the eventual outcome of the day would bring, but all to no avail.

When we arrived home, Mum went straight into the sitting room to join Dad. I explained to Nan everything that had happened during the day. We were confused and tried our best to fathom out what was going on, wondering how long we'd have to wait before being told, when Dad called us to join them. He looked at Mum as we entered the room and said, "shall I tell him?"

"No" Mum answered, "I'll tell them both together. If either of them has anything to say we can get it over with now, it will save any arguments later."

Nan and I stood side by side in the middle of the room, her gnarled hand of comfort on my shoulder. We both knew from the smirk on Mum's face that whatever she was about to say to me would be bad news. There was a short pause, then gazing towards Dad she spoke. "Now then Robin, you remember the money you stole from me, which I found hidden under your bed, don't you?"

"He didn't steal the money Babs; you know only too well, he worked for it. He had to, he didn't have a choice and you know why." Nan shouted in fury.

"That's irrelevant as far as I'm concerned," Mum answered, looking towards Dad. "It's the reason why he was saving the money that's the crux of the matter." Mum turned her head in my direction and continued. "You told me you were saving the money for when you were old enough to leave home, didn't you Robin?"

I did; furthermore I'd meant it. I wasn't sorry for what I'd told her; there wasn't any point in denying it. "Yes Mum" I answered, "and when I'm old enough, I shall."

Mum slowly sat back in her chair, her expression changing to a beaming smile, her eyes sparkling brightly as she softly spoke. "Well I've good news for you Robin. You won't have to wait any longer; you're old enough now! In about a month's time you'll break up from school for the Christmas holidays and would normally return in the New Year. Not any more; you'll be going to a Training College. You'll be leaving home; you've got what you wanted and so have I!"

"Surely he won't need to leave home Babs. Is it really necessary for him to stay away from home? Or is it because it suits you better if he does?"

Mum shrugged her shoulders nonchalantly and then calmly responded to Nan's question. "The College is miles away; it's too far to come home except during the holidays. Anyway, he's of no use around here anymore; he only costs us money. He'll be out of the way; what's more, he'll learn a trade."

"Why so far away? Where on earth are you sending him Babs?"

"Either of you can say whatever you like; it won't change a thing, not one iota. Everything is agreed and arranged between myself, his headmaster, the County Council and the Training College he'll be attending for the next two years."

"What bloody College?" Nan shouted in frustration.

Mum directed her short, but certainly not sweet, answer at me, staring wide-eyed into my face. "Robin, you'll be going to the Training Ship *Mercury*, which is based on the

River Hamble, near Southampton. There you'll be trained to become a sailor. When you've finished your training you'll have enough experience to join the Royal or Merchant Navy, whichever you prefer."

Nan and I stood dumbfounded; our mouths open in shock and disbelief. My first reaction was to look at Nan; her eyes were full of tears and I felt terrible. Dad hadn't looked in my direction since I'd entered the room; he sat staring into the fireplace; he hadn't moved, not even to glance at my reaction. Mum, straight-faced, continued staring at me waiting for my expected response. There wasn't any point in holding my feelings back and I blurted out my immediate response. "I don't want to be a sailor Mum. I don't want to be confined to spending week after week with the same people inside a ship with only the length of the vessel to get away and walk. Can you imagine how I'd feel whenever I looked over the side of a boat? Only water and sky as far as the eye can see. You know I'm a country boy Mum; it's where I've spent most of my life. I love the wildlife and woodlands, the fields and wild berries and fruit. I've enjoyed the eggs from birds; fish from the lake; bright-eyes and pigeons; they've all kept me alive, in more ways than one. I'm part of it all, it's me, and it's what I am. How could you want to send me away? How could you be so cruel?"

"Like it or not, you'll do what you're told. You've only got a few weeks left before you go; I'd make the most of it if I were you. That's all I've got to say on the matter, you can go back into the kitchen now and leave your father and me in peace."

Chapter Eighty

Three days after the New Year I was driven to Horsham, where for the second time, I stood on the railway station platform waiting for a train. As soon as the enormous steam engine ground to a halt, Mum opened one of the carriage doors, then ushering me to enter, spoke to me for the first time since we'd left home. "Remember what you've always been taught and you'll get on fine. Speak when you are spoken to and keep your opinions to yourself. Oh, by the way, you won't be called by your nickname any longer; you'll be called Rod or Rodney your proper name. Goodbye Robin."

I didn't even consider answering her and although Dad gave me a manly handshake, he looked embarrassed. I said nothing to either of them as the door closed and they walked away.

I sat in the warmth of the compartment listening to the chuffing of the engine as it occasionally jerked before smoothly pulling the carriages out of the station. It wasn't long before I began enjoying the journey and forgetting my concerns about what the future might hold. I was to disembark when the train eventually stopped at Southampton, where I'd be met and taken onwards to the *T.S. Mercury*.

A couple of hours later, I stepped from the train into the ice-cold wind; presuming I was the only person to be met, I looked along the platform for somebody who seemed to be expecting my arrival. To my surprise, at least twenty boys dressed in naval uniform with kitbags slung over their shoulders had alighted in small groups from various compartments at the front section of the train. Within a couple of minutes, they'd all left the platform, boarded a coach and were driven away.

Waiting close to the 'Way Out' sign were four other boys all dressed in sailor's uniform. One was holding a blackboard above his head inscribed with the words, 'Training Ship *Mercury*, New Recruits.'

Ten minutes later, having had our names called and checked, to find there were two absentees, twelve of us were sitting in a wooden seated coach beginning our noisy, bone-shaking route to *T.S. Mercury*. The boys who'd come to collect us chatted non-stop between themselves; the remainder of us sat in silence, deep in our own thoughts of what we'd left behind and wondering what to expect.

As we passed through the village of Hamble, one of the uniformed boys stood up and spoke loud enough to be heard, above the incessant rattling and loud roaring engine noise. "When we've rounded the next corner, to your right, you'll be able to see the *T. S. Mercury* for the first time. Take a good look; you'll either love or hate what you see. Either way it doesn't matter because for a couple of years she'll be your home. Regardless of the worst weather conditions imaginable, you'll row to and from her every day. It's where you'll sleep every night and scrub the decks every morning, good luck shipmates."

Within seconds, the impression I'd concocted in my mind of the ship's appearance, was shattered. Moored several hundred yards from the bank of the tidal River Hamble was the most hideous sight I could ever have imagined. The bottom half was an enormous wooden hulk; the only resemblance to a sailing ship was a barely noticeable and insignificant figurehead. The top half was covered with hundreds of vertically hung corrugated tin sheets containing dozens of odd shaped windows. The dull grey painted top, matched the low snow-laden clouds perfectly, while the barge-shaped black base was reflected in the darkness of the icy looking water. With the corrugated roof partly covered with the droppings of hundreds of incessantly screeching enormous seagulls, it wasn't just an ugly hulk, which turned my stomach; it was a monstrosity.

We arrived at the training ship's base within five minutes; my first impression of the many buildings, of various shapes, sizes and materials, was another disappointment. This was supposedly where I'd be educated in nautical basics.

We were taken into the mess room, divided into sections, shown our seating positions and given a mug of tea. For the next hour or so the door opened frequently admitting boys, all appearing to be between fourteen and sixteen years old. Most were in uniform, returning from Christmas leave. Some looked happy to return and having joined their friends, were very soon laughing and joking. Others didn't look so happy and simply greeted each other saying very little else. The remainder, like me, were obviously new recruits, easy to identify, not only from their attire, but also from their look of disorientation.

Shortly after being directed to my designated table, I was soon in conversation with the other boys. Of all those who passed behind me, looking for their place to sit, for some uncanny reason, I looked to my side, then upwards, directly into the face of Barry Bartlett. Simultaneously, the unexpected sight of each other caused our mouths to fall open in shock and disbelief. Eventually, following the lengthy silence, Barry was the first to speak, his voice quavering. "Rod, what on earth are you doing here? I didn't have a clue you'd be here as well, or that you wanted to be a sailor."

"I didn't have a choice; like it or lump it, I was sent here. I certainly don't want to be a sailor, you can be sure of that." I paused a second and then added, "I don't think so anyway. We'll have to wait and see."

"I've got to sit somewhere over there." He said pointing towards the end of the mess. "I'd better do what I'm told, I'll see you later Rod."

"Yes okay; we're in a different section to each other, nevertheless see you about." I answered as he walked away looking for his table number.

By late afternoon a total of about a hundred or so boys had arrived, each joining his nominated section of about twenty boys. All new arrivals were taken by an officer along a dimly lit path to the washrooms where we were shown our lockers. We were each given items for washing, including a toothbrush; the first I'd ever owned. For everyday use we were issued with navy blue canvas trousers and matching shirt. Flat canvas shoes with rope soles alleviated the possibility of damaging any wooden floor or decking. Once the Officer had decided which size uniform would fit us, we were told that despite a lack of hot water, we were to undress and take our first communal shower.

Virtually everyone felt embarrassed; some even appeared horrified. A few were so shy they stood facing the white-tiled wall with their backs towards us. Most of us didn't care, at least not until the water was turned on. The dozens of showerheads suddenly burst into an ice-cold torrent with the force of a powerful hosepipe. Everyone gasped for air and within seconds were all laughing at the effect the coldness had on the naked, rapidly shrinking private parts of their bodies. Those who had initially felt shy or embarrassed laughed the loudest. We all ended up the same; shivering with the cold, with painfully sore shoulders and all feeling much smaller and less manly. We weren't allowed to leave the shower until told; whereupon we were to dress only in our newly issued underpants, then return to the mess.

Upon entering the mess, we were instructed to stand facing four officers dressed in their uniforms, sitting along the side of a long table. The officer I'd originally thought was a teacher when interviewed was the only one to speak.

"My name is Commander Bradley; you'll address me as Commander and all the other officers as Sir. You'll do exactly what you're told, when you're told. If you don't, you'll be punished." There was a lengthy pause while he casually glanced at us individually before continuing. "When I call out your name, come forward and state your full name and date of birth. I'll then give you a number, which from then onwards shall be used to signify your identity. Do you all understand?"

Some boys aware, even pleased at becoming a number answered, "yes, Commander." A few of us, completely unaware and dismayed at loosing our name to become a number, stood silent in disbelief.

The Commander appearing satisfied with the response continued his instructions. "Upon my command you're to repeat your number to me, then drop your underpants, raise your arms above your head and cough upon my instruction. When dismissed, about turn, pull up your underpants, return to the washrooms, get dressed and wait for your shipmates."

When we'd all dressed in our issued clothing and were waiting for our first meal, we talked quietly among ourselves exchanging our names and serial numbers, mine being No.

220. Whilst there'd been silence during the embarrassment we'd all endured being gawked at whilst standing naked in front of four officers, we each had plenty to say when asked our opinion as to why, and if it was really necessary.

Eventually, having collected my dinner of the day, I sat at my nominated table to eat. Firstly I cut into the boiled potatoes, which were only partly washed, peeled and half-cooked. Although the cold, half-cooked vegetables were edible, the meat in the stew was as tough as leather, and difficult to chew.

When we'd finished the meal we were directed to a large rowing boat and rowed slowly away from the pier, into the freezing cold darkness towards the *T.S. Mercury*.

Chapter Eighty-one

Once on board, the majority of the boys quickly dispersed to their sleeping quarters. The rest of us waited on deck for the remaining new recruits to arrive. When Barry was aboard, we joined each other for our first conversation in ages. Our main discussion was about our surprise meeting, which neither of us had the slightest inkling would take place. Eventually unable to find any answer to our unforeseen situation, we accepted it to be purely coincidental.

Whilst waiting for the others to arrive, we stood shivering in the dim light, our teeth chattering in the bitter cold under the masses of icicles hanging from the thin corrugated tin roof. By the time everybody had assembled, Barry had told me how much he was looking forward to beginning his training and exciting new life as a sailor. He'd also told me he hadn't needed to get the train because his father had driven him to the *T.S. Mercury*. He sounded cocky until I told him I didn't need to waste Dad's time; it had been my decision to catch the train, and mine alone; I certainly didn't need mollycoddling. My little fib had the desired effect.

When taken to our sleeping quarters, which were at water level, the temperature was so low our breath turned white in the freezing still air. Stretched tightly from the sides of the ship were rows of thick wire cable. Regularly spaced on the scrubbed wooden deck were small piles of canvas and rope; our first lesson on lashing a hammock, was about to begin.

We were taught the correct method of tying the ropes, laying the blanket the entire length of the hammock, and folding our clothes to act as a pillow. By hanging onto the cable we were shown how to swing our body high enough to land flat on our back in the centre of the canvas.

Shivering, my nose and ears stinging with the cold, I eventually swung into my hammock folding the bedclothes over me. Lying on my back in a curved position made it impossible to turn over. However, I soon began to warm up and realized that being wrapped in the hammock was warmer than my bed at home. I relaxed, as pictures flashed before my closed eyes, filling my mind with pleasant memories of Ifold; it felt comforting. My first day at *T.S. Mercury* was ending; a bugler played the 'last post' - it was such a soft, slow tone, which echoed throughout the ship, that I fell asleep before it finished.

The following morning, the sudden, almost deafening screeching of a bugler playing 'reveille' shocked everyone awake. Most of us sat upright looking around dazed, others lay motionless too confused to move; it was 6.00 am. During the night ice had formed on the heavy wire cables and rope lashings which supported each hammock. The deck on which we stood in our bare feet whilst dressing was frozen hard, almost thick enough to skate on.

Within five minutes of being woken, we had lowered buckets and drawn water from the river, which we poured over the top and lower decks. Every boy within the Ship's Company, many so cold they were barely able to move, joined in scrubbing, mopping, and then finally wiping dry the white tightly fitted wooden decking. Regardless of the enormity, we knew it was the first job of the day.

I hadn't noticed until we rowed ashore, how the river had risen with the tide. The water had covered most of the mud, leaving only the top of some mounds exposed, and creating dozens of small islands dotted along the edge of the river.

On reaching the training centre we began the next daily routine. Each section was to shower, on a daily rotation basis. The heated water was only sufficient for two sections, resulting in each section having cold showers for three successive days. It was tough on us all, and although it brought tears to the eyes of a few, nobody took the mickey out of them; we were all equally upset.

Breakfast for most of the boys would normally have been the most important meal of the day. It wasn't any longer, and was referred to as pig food; nevertheless they ate it. To me it didn't matter; being unaccustomed to a regular breakfast I didn't even want to try one, being more than content with two slices of bread and jam.

Within a fortnight the majority of the boys had written home explaining how much they appreciated the wonderful opportunity they'd been given, and how well they'd settled into their new life. Most of them were sincere, although each of them had mentioned, as if by chance, the poor and virtually inedible quality of the food. Naturally it was a ploy, which worked so well, it prompted their parents to send weekly food parcels. Thankfully many of the boys often gave treats to the few of us, who knew any letters we wrote home would have remained unanswered, therefore there wasn't any point in trying.

Having previously decided on a career in the navy, the majority of the boys looked forward to their training. Some felt proud to continue the family tradition, and connection with the sea; others, whether from orphanages, broken homes, or simply unwanted, considered themselves fortunate at being given a home, with friends and the opportunity of a future of which to be proud. The exception was a handful of us, who'd become accustomed to making our own decisions and now found ourselves in a dilemma. Should we continue to remain autonomous, or take the easy way out by changing our ways completely, becoming totally dependent upon others? We'd be unable to choose our own mates, only shipmates. I wanted to be certain I did the right thing; I didn't want to be impetuous. I decided I'd comply with what was expected of me for three months; by then I'd be as certain as possible of making the correct decision.

Various daily lessons on seamanship, most of which I found exceedingly tedious soon became routine and so repetitive they became monotonous. Nautical training naturally took precedence over everything. The priorities consisted of signalling in Morse code, semaphore and navigation, which even included learning the thirty-two points of the compass backwards. These lessons were followed by gunnery, and general drill. The lack of availability of classrooms restricted lessons in the 'three Rs' to a minimum.

Additional scrubbing and mopping was the norm for the smallest misdemeanour. More frequently, punishment was either a hard slap around the head or a kick in the pants.

Well within the three-month period, which I'd allowed myself to think carefully on my future, and whether or not to make a career in the Navy, I'd made my decision. I'd tell Mum and Dad of my intentions during my first leave, which was due at the end of March. Each day during the week before leave was to commence, the travelling details of those going home were displayed against their number on the notice board in the mess room. The majority would be taken to the station to catch a train; others would be collected and driven home by their parents.

During the afternoon of the day before leave, the final information was displayed next to each boy's number. The only information written next to my serial number and that of three other boys read, 'No details available.'

By ten o'clock the following morning, the boys, dressed smartly in their uniforms stood in ranks, kit bags at their feet, talking excitedly while awaiting collection. For various personal reasons the remaining four of us felt envious and saddened, as we stood in silence, watching as the rows of boys diminished.

As the last coach left for the station, the only officer who'd stayed behind informed us that within reason, we could do, as we wanted. We could use the kitchen and be responsible for cooking our own food. To alleviate the difficulty of rowing out to the *T.S. Mercury* every day we were to sleep ashore in the gymnasium, where hammocks were available.

As we made our first brew we began chatting. Initially I was apprehensive about how the other three felt about not receiving any details of home going. It soon became apparent that despite our varying backgrounds, we'd each learnt how to care for ourselves. Openly sharing our experiences, we turned even the saddest of memories into jokes and laughter; we enjoyed our leave.

Although the winter had been exceptionally cold and windy, we'd only had two short flurries of snow. The spring was slow in coming and the small amount of green countryside was slow in growing; the wildlife, which I'd normally have related to particular surroundings, was virtually non-existent.

Time seemed to drag on very slowly, until eventually the third Friday of July arrived; this was the day compulsory summer leave commenced and *T. S. Mercury* would close completely for three weeks. This time, everybody stood in rows on the parade ground, each dressed in uniform, holding their tightly packed kit bags. Having exchanged what most believed to be their temporary farewells we all eagerly waited our arranged collection.

Barry was one of the first to be collected, rushing to greet his father as the car came to a halt. Within seconds they'd given each other a quick hug and stood face-to-face, smiling and chatting to each other. As they were about to get into the car, Barry turned towards me about to wave goodbye, but then stopped. He bowed his head briefly before looking up again, directly at me; except for a deep frown on his forehead, he was expressionless, but I could see him thinking. Turning to his father and pointing in my direction he spoke. They both looked at me while speaking to each other and I returned their gaze with a smile and a wave. It was apparent to me that Barry was asking his father if he'd give me a lift home but his father's decision was obvious. Barry was directed into the car and speedily driven away.

Chapter Eighty-two

By one o'clock, when my long journey had ended, I was walking along the narrow road towards home taking in the breathtaking smell of the countryside. Once again, the sight and sound of the birds singing and flitting from tree to tree filled me with awe. Some stopped, briefly cocking their heads to one side watching me, their beaks full of food for their fledglings.

Nothing had changed; tracks made by Charlie, and deer, during their regular nightly patrol were still prominent, leading into the woodland cover at each side of the road. As expected, lizards and slow-worms lay basking in the warmth of the sun on bare patches of clay and the tops of disused ant-hills; the only movement was the craning of their necks towards me as I passed.

On the top bar of the gate was the best welcome home I could have ever wished for. Perpetually running, hopping and wildly flapping the entire length, red robin welcomed me in his own extraordinary way. Eventually he stopped and perched on top of the disused post-box where he began chirping incessantly and looking inside the opening to attract my attention. He certainly did, and upon peering inside I received my next surprise.

Unperturbed by my presence, the hen bird, looking content, and at ease, squatted on her newly built nest. As she raised her body I carefully slipped my finger under her partly splayed wing expecting to count her eggs; instead I felt the warm wrinkly skin of chicks, only hours old, their black bulbous eyes still closed. Exhausted and scarcely moving after hatching out, they rested, gaining strength in the warmth and comfort of the nest.

Red robin was excited and so was I. What a welcome back to Ifold; I was home! But would Mum and Dad welcome me? They hadn't written once. Did they know I was here? Did they care? I'd soon find out.

As I walked through the open back door into the kitchen, Nan turned from the sink and greeted me with a quick hug followed by compliments of how well and smart I looked in my uniform. Carolyn, who'd grown considerably, sat at the table scribbling in a drawing book with coloured crayons while reciting a nursery rhyme.

Within a couple of minutes and having overheard the chatting, Mum entered the room. She stared at me expressionlessly. "Hello Mum, it's good to be home. Is everything ok?" I asked cheerfully encouraging a welcoming response. But it was to no avail; my pleasant attitude was ignored.

"You're late Robin!" I expected you long ago."

"It was a long train journey Mum; even when I got to Horsham I had to wait over an hour for a bus; everyone who passed seemed to gawk at me dressed in uniform."

"Well there's nothing I could do about that, you should have expected it; you don't see many sailors in the countryside. When does your leave officially end anyway?"

"Officially I'm supposed to be back by four o'clock, three weeks today."

"Well, although you don't live here any longer, I suppose we're expected to keep you for nothing. And do your washing."

"Not exactly Mum; I knew I wouldn't get something for nothing as you've told me enough times. So I've regularly saved most of my weekly allowance, knowing it'd be better if I could pay my way; and I can. Because of Nan's arthritic hands, whenever I can, I'll help her with any washing, as before. Don't worry Mum; I shan't be an encumbrance to you."

"Good; at least you've learnt how to stand on your own two feet."

"Robin learnt how to do that years ago Babs," Nan interrupted. "He had to, he never had a choice."

Mum continued to speak, completely ignoring Nan's remark, without as much as a glance in her direction. "First of all, get yourself changed and unpacked. Then go for a meander or wander or whatever. Get back about 7 o'clock, not before. By then we'll have had dinner; yours will be in the oven. You may as well wash-up when you've finished, it'll save Nan a job. When you've finished you can come into the sitting room and tell your father and me all about *T.S. Mercury.*"

Once I'd changed my clothes and called in to say 'hello' to Amy Lucas and her family, I was on my bike peddling off to find Michael and his Dad, or so I hoped.

Leaning my bike against a birch tree at the entrance to the white brick bungalow, I unknowingly strode towards my first disappointment of the day. Couch grass, brambles and ferns, which had grown in clumps to a height of about three feet covered large areas around the building and land. Tall weeds grew where the beehives and ferret cages had stood. Everything had gone; the large area once housing the chicken hutch and run was flat and barren. I was flabbergasted and saddened. Where'd they moved to and why? I kept asking myself. The more I thought about it the quicker my disillusionment faded. I knew I'd soon find someone who'd know where they'd gone. They'd been locals for many years; they wouldn't have moved far away. Or so I thought at the time, completely unaware I'd never see or hear from them again.

Sooner than expected, I was on my way to see Brian at Little Headfoldswood Farm to experience the second abysmal disappointment of the afternoon. When I reached the yard, I knocked on the cottage door and waited. A deeply sun-tanned man appeared from the open barn a few feet away. "If it's work you want son, I've got plenty, part-time, and full-time, which do you want?" He asked smiling.

"Well neither thanks all the same. I only came to see if Brian was in."

"Who do you mean, Brian Hunt?"

"Yeah, I've been away six months and he's one of my mates."

"Not any more son; his Dad got himself another job and they've moved away. I took over about six weeks ago. Sorry I can't be of more help." Bewildered, I explained my prior experience when visiting Michael's home and now the disappointment of losing a second mate. He listened intently, making it easy to talk. By the time I cycled off to find Dave, I'd forgotten my dismay.

When I called at Dave's he was out, having got himself a job with the local builder from Loxwood. He was in work, the type he wanted; he'd been lucky. Leaving word with his mother that I'd call back, I rode off, hoping find Bill. He had been lucky in getting work on a farm, which despite the long hours was the type of work he preferred. Although I was pleased for him I wondered when we'd have time to meet.

Once I'd visited and chatted to most of my other friends, I headed home to arrive at an acceptable time, the kitchen being empty. Within half an hour I'd eaten my meal, washed up and cleared away, feeling as if I'd never been away. I knocked on the sitting room door and entered.

Upon entering the room, Dad remained seated while Mum beckoned me to stand between them. Question and answer time was about to begin, and knowing they wouldn't get the answers they'd be expecting, I wondered how they'd react once I'd had my say.

Dad's first comments made it clear how they felt about me being home. "We were just getting used to not having you about, and then you turn up. Never mind, it's only three weeks before you go back, isn't it?"

"No Dad."

"It is! That's what you told your mother, isn't it?" He asked frowning.

"No Dad," I repeated.

"Yes you did you little liar. I asked you when your leave ended and you said at four o'clock three weeks today," Mum said, sounding horrified. Looking confused, she turned to Dad and said, "Nan was there Bern, ask her yourself, she'll tell you."

To avoid Nan's involvement or any confusion I quickly interrupted Dad before he could say anything. "Yes I did say that because Mum only asked me when my leave officially ended. She didn't ask when I was going back; otherwise I'd have told her; I'm not. You got me into the navy not because I'd have a worthwhile secure future, but because it was the quickest and cheapest way to get rid of me wasn't it? You tried to get shot of me because my usefulness had run out. There wasn't any more work to do and I'd become an encumbrance. Well I'll tell you now. Whatever you say, do, or threaten, I'm not going back, not ever!"

I kept talking, managing to control my collywobbles and giving the impression of calm decisiveness. They sat motionless, their mouths open; they were dumbfounded and unable to comprehend what they were hearing. Their expression of shock and disbelief made me smile to myself before continuing. "Any one of my farming friends would give me a job tomorrow. Also, from the labouring work and experience I've had I could probably get a job with the local builder. I'll pay weekly rent and I'll do my own washing. You needn't concern yourselves about me getting in your way. When I'm home I'll stay in the kitchen; you'll never know I'm here." Nobody moved an inch, or uttered a sound; it was as if they'd been frozen in time. Initially I'd felt nervous, but not any more. I'd had my say; it was now time I went. It was done! My future was in my hands, nobody else's, and that's how it would stay. Turning slowly I calmly walked out of the room, somewhat surprised at my composure.

Chapter Eighty-three

From that evening onwards, I was virtually ignored by Mum and Dad. Their attitude confirmed my perception of their feelings towards me; they didn't care. But they didn't have an inkling that I already knew, and I didn't care either.

The next evening Nan came into the kitchen chuckling. "What's so funny?" I asked.

"The way your mother asked me to give you a message. From the tone of her voice I think she's too anxious to tell you herself. Mind you I'm not surprised after your performance last night. Without beating about the bush, you certainly told them what you're determined to do. They were both so taken aback neither of them spoke for ages. Well-done Robin! Do what you think is best for you and remain resolute; you should decide your future, and what's best for you, nobody else."

"I shall, thanks to your help over the years. There's no going back now, not ever. Now then," I said smiling, "what's this important message Mum's too anxious to give me herself?"

"Well I think it's a bit hard, but the best thing is to grin and bear it, if I were you."

"Surely it's not that bad, is it Nan?"

"No not really, but your Mum wants you to get a job as soon as possible. Your weekly rent will be half of your wages. In exchange you'll get two sandwiches and a bottle of tea to take to work, plus an evening meal." Nan shrugged her shoulders then quickly added. "You'll have to get your own evening meal at weekends."

"You're right Nan I'll have to grin and bear it; I've done it before, I'll do it again."

Within a week I'd started work as a labourer for George Catlin and his only other employee, Cyril Ray, an experienced general builder. The hard work I anticipated never materialised. Regardless of how large or mundane the job, they'd both help. Every task was explained to me until within a few weeks I was able to participate in some building work. Enjoying my freedom, the work and a weekly pay packet, life began to feel meaningful.

With the exception of the local pubs, and occasional special events or a function in the village hall, evenings in every parish within about a ten-mile radius were silent and lifeless. Dave and I wanted more and agreed whenever possible, despite the distance, that each Saturday, we'd cycle to a cinema, a dance, or whatever took our fancy, at either Cranleigh or Horsham. Regardless of the lengthy ride it was undoubtedly a decision neither of us ever regretted.

It was the last weekend of September and the end of the season for the small funfair on the green opposite the Onslow Arms. Realising it'd be for the last time that year, Dave and I decided to join in the amusement with the village locals and our old school friends. By nine o'clock, having participated in the majority of the events and laughed ourselves hoarse, we needed refreshment. Because we weren't old enough to go into the pub, we gave the money to Dave's elder brother Arthur, who offered to get us a ginger beer while we waited outside watching the merriment. The nights were rapidly drawing in and the light had faded giving way to the bright lights of the fairground; laughter and music filled the air.

We didn't have to wait long before Arthur returned, a large mug in each hand. "I thought I'd treat you both to your first pint of King and Barns Festive Bitter," he smiled. "If you like it and I'm sure you will, I'll get you another but that's the lot; it's very strong and two of these will be enough. Now get round the corner where you can't be seen, I'll come back and see how you're getting on later."

Dave and I dashed around the side of the pub, barely able to believe our luck and slurped and relished our first pint of beer. We'd only been enjoying ourselves a short time when one of the locals appeared around the corner on his way to the toilet, just as I raised the mug to my lips. Momentarily he stopped and stared. Oh no, I thought; now I'm in trouble. But I was wrong. Firstly he smiled as if to himself, then sniggered and laughed quietly. "Aha caught in the act; well don't worry Master Davis, I was about your age when I had my first pint," he said grinning as he passed. "You get it down boy; it'll do you good, cheers!"

Within an hour of drinking our second pint we were both being uncontrollably sick when the same local came back to the toilet area. "You okay boy?" He asked, resting his hand on my shoulder.

"Yeah I'll be okay thanks."

"Well," he answered, "you get it up boy, it'll do you good."

"Make your mind up; first you tell us to get it down, then you tell us to get it up," Dave jokingly said.

"It makes you feel good either way doesn't it?" He laughed.

We had to agree.

Chapter Eighty-four

One Saturday evening, a village dance had been arranged at North Hall. As it was an unusual occurrence Dave and I decided to go; if only for the laugh and knowing we'd meet some of our old schoolmates. Within half an hour of arriving I'd met a number of friends I hadn't seen for years. The laughing, joking, questions and answers we shared were thoroughly enjoyable. I was with a small group of pals sharing their jokes when I looked towards the entrance door to catch sight of the last person I'd expected to see! Barry stood in the doorway, almost to attention, fully dressed in his uniform, looking around the hall for somebody whom he might know; there wouldn't be many. Eventually he saw me, his only movement being to nod his acknowledgement, which I returned before continuing in the group chitchat.

It was still early evening when Bill and another couple of friends merged with the group telling us Barry had spoken to them. "I've only met him a couple of times before, I hardly know him," said Bill.

"What did he have to say for himself?" Dave asked.

"He was telling us about Rod," Bill replied, turning towards me. "Why did you really leave the Navy Rod?"

"You all know why. I didn't want to go in the first place, but I didn't have a choice, so I thought. When I was absolutely certain I didn't want to be a sailor at any cost I decided; regardless of the trouble I'd cause at home, that I wouldn't be forced into a way of life I didn't want. I decided to leave; I'm glad I did. As far as I'm concerned it was the right decision then, and still is. Why do you ask?"

"That's not what your mate Barry says. He says you were chucked out of the *Mercury* because you missed your family and were homesick.

"Did he really say that?" I stuttered.

"I wouldn't lie about it Rod, it's the truth."

I glanced at the two others, who had been with Bill at the time. "Did either of you hear him say that?"

"We weren't the only ones; there were a few others as well, and we all heard him."

I quickly looked around the circle of faces, "did any of you believe him?"

"We know you certainly wouldn't have missed your Mum and Dad or been homesick Rod," Dave laughingly commented. "If you were chucked out, so what? It doesn't make any difference to us; you're back where you belong, that's all that matters."

"No it isn't Dave; not as far as I'm concerned. He's making it sound as if I'm a liar. I'll soon put an end to that." I was furious.

Trying to give the impression of remaining calm and collected, I strode the few yards across the hall and grabbed Barry by the arm. The fact that he was in conversation didn't make the slightest difference to my intention. "I want to see you outside Barry, right now." I said pulling him by the sleeve so hard; he had little choice but to follow.

As soon as I stepped outside I swung him around and pushed him backwards against the building. Standing face to face about two feet apart, I hollered in an exasperated voice, "why have you been saying I was chucked off the *Mercury,* when everyone knows I left of my own accord? Why have you been saying I missed my parents and was homesick, particularly when it was the complete opposite?"

He appeared unresponsive, remaining silent until I repeatedly prodded him in the chest telling him to answer me.

He looked with embarrassment at the gathering of boys, and then shrugging his shoulders he lowered his head and said, "quite a few of the boys don't return. Everybody assumes they get homesick. I do; quite a few of us do; but I always go back at the end of leave. If you don't you're automatically discharged."

I was furious, unmindful of clenching my fists as I spoke and feeling my pulse quicken. "I'm not surprised you get homesick; you're spoiled and mollycoddled. Even so, I'd stay in the Navy if I were you. If you play your cards right you'll never be expected to make a decision. You could even end up being wet-nursed for the rest of your life. You'd like that; it would suit you down to the ground; it's what you're accustomed to, isn't it?"

Goaded by the shouts of encouragement from the small group of onlookers, to hit Barry, I threw my first hard punch low into the pit of his stomach. Doubling up with the pain, his knees buckling, I grabbed the back of his uniform collar, holding him half-upright. When I'd powered four or five uppercut punches into his ribcage, I gripped him in a headlock and half-dragged him across the driveway. There I knelt on the grass, and tightened my grip on his head while pounding his face until he became motionless. Initially the small crowd, which had gathered to watch, cheered, then fell silent as they noticed my concern as I looked at Barry laying face down.

We were all apprehensive, as we watched and waited for positive signs of movement; fortunately the wait was brief. Within a few minutes he was kneeling on all fours, and unable to walk crawled away into the darkness groaning with pain.

The remorse I'd initially felt for the hurt I'd caused Barry soon faded following the ego-boosting remarks I received from my mates. By the time I reached home later that evening, the incident had practically been forgotten.

The following morning, while I was chopping some hazel into short lengths for fire lighting, Dad appeared at the back door and called me to the sitting room. Wondering why I'd been called, I was very soon confronted not only by Mum and Dad but also the local bobby. "Good morning Master Davis, I've a couple of questions I'd like to ask you," the policeman said, resting his cup of tea on the arm of his chair. "Is that all right with you?" He smiled, taking a notebook from his top pocket.

"Yes of course," I answered. Surely after all this time, it couldn't be anything to do with the prank Brian and I'd played on him when he broke his arm.

"I understand you had a disagreement with Barry Bartlett last night outside North Hall. Is that right?"

"Yes," I said, breathing a sigh of relief, "he said things about me which weren't true and it made me cross."

"You lost your temper and punched him several times, didn't you?"

"Yes; so would anybody else, he deserved it."

"Tell me," he said crossing his legs and scribbling in his notepad, "how many times did he hit you?"

"He didn't hit me; he didn't have time, he was hurt too much."

"Okay, now let me get this straight. You hit him, but he never hit you at all. Is that right?"

"Yes of course; I wasn't going to stand there and let him hit me, I'm not daft."

"Thank you Master Davis; that'll be all for now. I'll be back tomorrow with your statement for you to sign; then you'll be charged."

"Surely you're not going to charge him over two boys having a fight for goodness sake; most boys have a fight at some time or other," Dad said in a raised voice.

"Ordinarily no I wouldn't," the policeman answered rising to his feet and preparing to leave, "but this time I've no choice because young Bartlett's in hospital with two broken ribs; he's also suffered severe damage to some nerves in his face which has caused his cheek to drop. Let's hope it gets better, he was hit very hard."

Mum saw the policeman to the door as Dad took a hefty swing at me, hitting me on the side of the face. The shock of the unexpected hard blow caught me off balance. "What have I done wrong now? You've always told me to only fight to win. I won; or can't I win, no matter what I do?"

"You did right, but never say you threw the first punch; you're admitting you started it, and you're to blame for whatever happens. Now you're in trouble."

At Petworth Magistrates Court I was found guilty of Actual Bodily Harm and fined. Within three months Barry's family had moved away and I never saw any of them again.

Chapter Eighty-five

Nan was the only one who'd foreseen my reactions to being largely disregarded and treated like an unwanted relation for the majority of the time. From the day I paid my first week's rent, I made it categorically clear I'd refuse to get Mum's cigarettes or any other shopping following a day's work.

Although Dad tried his utmost to persuade Mum to either ride her bike or walk to the shops, she was adamant it was too far to even consider the possibility; besides, he had transport and it was easier and quicker for him to drive. The words 'transport' and 'drive' gave Dad an idea, the result of which materialized a few weeks later.

Upon returning home from work one Saturday morning Dad, wearing a beaming smile on his face, asked us all to go outside to see the surprise he'd bought Mum. We looked about but couldn't see what he meant, until eventually we were directed around the corner of the garage. There it was, the like of which I'd never seen before, leaning against the side of the garage. "What's that?" I heard myself say at the same time as I heard a sudden deep gasp of air from Mum and Nan.

"It's a Corgi motorbike, Robin," Dad replied, "they were made during the war for the paratroopers. They'd fold the handlebars and seat flat when parachuting from an aeroplane. It's strong enough to take the weight of a soldier, with all his equipment; it's low enough to sit on with your feet on the ground. It has one gear with a top speed of about twenty miles an hour. It's simple and safe to drive and ideal for your mother to get any extra shopping. Isn't it Babs?"

Mum looked horrified, then putting her hands up to her face quietly muttered, "I don't know if I could ride it without falling off."

"Don't worry, you won't fall off," Dad smiled. "There's no time like the present; I'll explain how it works, and then you can have a practice ride. You'll be all right; a child could ride it."

Unobtrusively I watched and listened to Dad explaining the simple instructions while watching Mum's expression change from disinterest to vacant. Considering her lack of enthusiasm for doing anything for herself I rightly anticipated Mum's response following her test ride, but had no idea of the excuse she'd use.

Within a very short time Mum slowly pulled away at a speed equivalent to a fast walking pace. Within seconds we realized the ease of controlling the bike as it slowly drew further away, straight and upright. Hearing the noise from the engine slightly increase; the bike picked up speed before disappearing around the bend towards Chalk Road.

Dad turned to look at Nan. "Thank goodness she can drive it," he sighed, "Babs can go shopping locally wherever and whenever she wants without involving me. It means I can actually come home from work without being asked to go out again. If the money the bike cost was twice as much it'd still be worth every penny."

Nan who'd moved close to my side gently tugged my sleeve as she whispered, "I'll bet you two shillings your Mum comes up with some ridiculous excuse as to why she's unable to ride it."

"I'm not that daft Nan, it's a foregone conclusion; but what excuse will she use?" I quietly replied.

"Oh you can bet she'll think of something Robin. She always does."

The three of us stood listening to the purring sound of the engine coming from around the bend while waiting for Mum's re-emergence. We didn't have to wait long for her to reappear, casually strolling along muttering to herself. Dad's face dropped, his mouth falling open, his eyes widening, before becoming fixed in disbelief at what he saw. "What's the matter Babs, where's the bike?"

"I'm okay, no thanks to you. I fell off the stupid thing when I tried to turn round. I told you I wouldn't be able to ride it; are you satisfied now?"

"I can't believe it; you started off so well, and it was easy, so simple. How could you have possibly fallen off?"

"I don't know and I don't care. It suddenly went from under me, out of control. It went into the ditch and as far as I'm concerned it can stay there; or you can take it back from where you got it, I don't care."

From the expression on Dad's face and from the tone of his voice he was furious. "I can't take it back; I bought it cheap from a bloke at work who needed the money."

"Bern, I'm going indoors; I've just had a frightening experience, and I'm shaking inside. You'd better get used to the idea that I'll never ride it again. That's my final word on the matter."

As Mum walked away, Dad moved closer to my side where for a while we stood in silence with our thoughts. "Robin, I know we don't always see eye to eye but I'd appreciate it if you'd go and get the bike out of the ditch for me. I don't feel like doing it myself, not at the minute anyway. When you get back, stand it behind the garage and cover it over out of my bloody sight."

"Yes, okay Dad; I know how you must feel. Welcome to the club, as they say. Life isn't always a bed of roses is it?"

"You're right it isn't, although it must be for Mum; she hasn't as much as a scratch or graze after her fall. Strange don't you think? No! It might be better if you don't answer that," he quickly added.

The sound of the Corgi engine and a quick glance at the straight narrow strip of flattened fireweed plants directed me to the bike. Leaning unscathed against the side of the dry weedy ditch it only took one attempt of combined driving and pushing to get it back onto the road. I wondered how the bike had entered the ditch pointing in a forward direction, on the wrong side of the road. A considerable amount of freshly made footmarks had disturbed the clay soil, and many of the surrounding wild plants had been trampled. If Mum had fallen off the bike her body weight would have flattened a larger area. There wasn't any variance in the trajectory of travel; something didn't appear quite right. Then within a few moments of pondering it became blatantly clear. Mum hadn't fallen off the bike. Instead she'd ridden to the roadside and dismounted, then leaving the engine running pushed it over the verge into the ditch.

The short ride back stirred my enthusiasm to such an extent that I began to work out a plan to persuade Dad to let me have use of the bike.

One evening about a week later, I was permitted to enter the sitting room, to explain an idea I'd had. "Well, what's this so-called brainwave you've had then?" Dad asked half-laughing.

"It isn't a brainwave Dad; it's commonsense." I paused hoping he and Mum would agree. "As much as I enjoy working with Cyril and George, if I don't begin to learn a trade soon I'm going to end up being a general builder's labourer for the rest of my life."

"Oh you've got some sense after all," Mum sneered, "you should have thought of that before you left the *Mercury*."

Paying no attention to Mum's remarks I continued. "When we built the bungalow, I learnt enough about plumbing and electrical work to possibly get a start as an apprentice in one or the other.

"Yes, you'd earn a lot more money as well, but where are you going to get a job around here?"

"When Cyril and I were working in Cranleigh last week, we met a Mr Thomas who's about to start his own plumbing business. He said he needed an apprentice and he offered me the job if I want it. The wages are about the same and I don't have to work Saturdays."

Dad's response was as I'd anticipated, "that's good, but there's one problem. How are you going to get to all the various jobs? They could be anywhere; even if they were all in Cranleigh, you couldn't cycle that distance every day could you?"

"No not really; I was hoping you'd let me use the Corgi, Dad; it'd be putting it to good use."

Mum's immediate reaction was negative, but Dad's response was slower, and I realized he'd need prompting into making the decision I desperately wanted. "If I had full use of the bike it would be beneficial to all of us Dad."

"What do you mean all of us?" Dad enquired.

"It would help Mum because whenever she wanted any shopping I could get it for her. After all, that's what you got the bike for in the first place. It also means you wouldn't need to go out again after you got home from work, would you?"

"You're right, I wouldn't; thank goodness. I think you've earned yourself a bike."

Within three weeks I'd taken the job and became a plumber's mate. A large percentage of my time was spent cutting and threading galvanized pipe or cutting holes through walls. Even so I didn't have any problem handling the work. I was getting a good wage, and learning a trade.

Chapter Eighty-six

During the first week of September, Nan became noticeably weaker, going to bed earlier each night. I became concerned; asking her on several occasions to tell me if she felt unwell, or if she needed any help. Her answer was always the same. She'd laugh and tell me not to worry, she was perfectly okay; besides at eighty-four years old; she'd inevitably feel a little tired every now and then.

Arriving home one evening during the second week in September, I was surprised to find Mum alone in the kitchen preparing dinner. "What are you doing Mum, where's Nan?" I asked.

"She's in bed, she's been there all day; she says she's too tired to get up." I heard Mum answer above the clattering of empty pots and pans being thrown into the sink.

"I'll go and see how she is, and if she needs anything."

"No leave her alone; if she wants anything she can get up and get it herself." Mum gruffly instructed, then as if an afterthought added, "she's probably asleep anyway; wait until tonight when you go to bed. In the meantime go and see one of your mates or whatever; just get out my way and let me finish the dinner."

By nine o'clock, having washed and cleared away the dinner utensils, I'd grown bored of sitting alone in the kitchen and decided to see Nan as I passed through her room on my way to bed. Nan lay on her side, her knees bent, only half-covered by the eiderdown, which was pulled up to her neck for warmth. Her thin white hair drooped partly over her pillow and head, covering her ears and the deep creases in her forehead. Her breathing was shallow and silent, but sensing my presence, her eyes opened. She was awake and managing to half-smile. I gently slid the bedclothes forward to cover her knees and back tucking them under the mattress and around her shoulders. "Hello Nan, is there anything I can do, or get you?"

"No thanks Robin," she answered softly, "I'm just so tired, I feel as if I could sleep forever."

"Well don't worry about anything, you rest while you can. Give me a call if you need anything, otherwise I'll see you in the morning Nan. Good night, God bless."

"Okay and don't forget to say your own prayers. Good night, and God bless Robin." Nan whispered her last words as she closed her eyes.

I returned to the peacefulness of the tiny cemetery of Loxwood Church during the late afternoon of Nan's funeral and knelt beside her grave and silently prayed. I felt saddened beyond belief; yet blissful of the love; faith and confidence Nan had freely given and taught me. What would have become of me if it weren't for her?

A variety of headstones adorned the majority of the three hundred or so graves. Nan's had nothing; not even a wooden cross or stake driven into the freshly dug clay, not a marker or number, only the mound of freshly replaced turf marked the spot. I wondered what people might think, seeing an unmarked freshly dug grave. I felt embarrassed but there was nothing I could do. I knew the exact spot where Nan lay; I'd always be able to find her. As I knelt by her side I sensed a deep urge to leave something for her, and reached into my pocket to take out whatever suitable possessions I had.

Within a matter of seconds I held three items in one hand while with the other I removed a fresh turf from the head of Nan's grave. Firstly, having scraped a small recess in the clay, I laid a smooth shining brass disc the size of a penny, around which I placed a short ornamental silver chain. Both of these I'd found and carried with me, considering them to be lucky charms. Finally I gently pressed my most cherished possession into place; the slightly curved dark rosewood handle of my pruning knife was smooth to my touch, while the hooked wide blade reflected the light for the last time. When I'd replaced the square clod of earth to cover the only offerings I had to give, I dabbed away the moisture from my eyes before finally whispering, God bless Nan, and thank you.

Chapter Eighty-seven

Mum's incessant griping about her responsibilities and how much time she spent doing the housework very soon became monotonous. Within a month, Dad became so jaded he dared to overcome his vulnerability by insisting that Mum's non-stop whingeing cease. It did, but so did practically all the household chores. Dad ended up humiliated once again; making the best of what little Mum did. Fortunately for me, not being reliant upon either of them, it didn't make any difference.

Dad's sullen behaviour towards Mum became apparent; not for the first time I noticed his change of mood. Gradually over the following weeks he began speaking to me more frequently until one Saturday morning while cutting firewood he joined me. "Stop what you're doing; I want to ask you something Rod."

"Yes okay, fire away so to speak; but before you do, tell me; why don't you or Mum call me Robin any more?"

"Mum says it's only a nickname Nan gave you and we're to call you Rod, your proper name in future."

"And of course you do everything Mum tells you, don't you Dad?" I laughed as if joking. "I'm only pulling your leg Dad," I lied, "what were you going to ask me anyway?"

Dad looked at me long and hard, frowning as if uncertain whether to believe me or not. Eventually he spoke, "I'll tell you, only if you promise not to mention a word to your mother."

"That's an easy promise to keep; Mum scarcely speaks to me anyway."

As if rehearsed, Dad spoke clearly and methodically. His initial questions and statements, which left me feeling very confused, soon became clear and logical. He needed my answer to be positive and, by co-operating he got the answer he wanted. Yes, undoubtedly I'd go to Australia and start a new life with him. I'd work on isolated sheep farms if necessary and because of the lack of prompt medical support I'd even be prepared to have my appendix removed beforehand. I'd arrange to have my passport photo taken in Cranleigh and give it to him as soon as possible. I promised I wouldn't change my mind or give the slightest inkling of the discussion and alliance between us. I was to forget our conversation in its entirety at least until such time as everything was organized and Dad was ready to break the news.

One Friday evening several weeks later after Carolyn, who now occupied Nan's bedroom, had been tucked up for the night, I was unexpectedly called into the sitting room. Mum looking dauntingly at me, and as usual, indicating with her finger where I was to stand, spoke directly to me. "Your father has something to tell you."

"Is everything alright Dad?" I asked.

"It depends on you; as far as I'm concerned it is. I only want to tell you I've eventually finalised a deal today and earned a lot of money."

"What deal was that?" I enquired.

"A deal on this place, our home; I've sold it. Take a look at what's on the sideboard."

My mouth fell open in disbelief as I stared at the large neat stacks of five-pound notes.

"Good grief," I half-whispered with surprise, "how much is there Dad?"

"You're looking at two thousand, five hundred pounds; a small fortune by anyone's reckoning."

The issue, most frequently in my thoughts, was rekindled. In anticipation of Dad reiterating our secret agreement I asked the prominent question, "What are you going to do with the money Dad?"

"We're going to Australia."

"When Dad?" I half-smiled.

"By the end of the month. The cabins are booked and all the paperwork completed; all that's left to do is pay for the tickets."

"That's a nice surprise Dad. How many of us are going?" I asked anticipating his answer to be only the two of us.

Dad paused, giving Mum the opportunity to interrupt; "how many do you think are going? We're all going; you're still our responsibility until you're eighteen."

"Dad," I said in a probing tone. He remained silent; I knew nothing more would be forthcoming when, ignoring my look of disbelief, he turned away to stare out through the window into the darkness. Why hadn't he told me what was going to happen? Was he too embarrassed to mention anything to me? Or perhaps, as he lost most altercations with Mum, he was too apprehensive to mention anything, fearing even greater loss of esteem.

"It was a bit of luck you were vain enough to have your photograph taken recently. It's come in very handy; we've used it for your passport. Here, have a look," Mum said, passing it to me. She was obviously unaware of the arrangement Dad and I had made.

I glanced at it briefly, confused and not particularly concerned, "yes it looks alright," I answered fleetingly before looking at the mirror-image of the entire room and Dad's solemn face reflected in the black glossy window.

"I've also got a copy of your birth certificate. I'll hang on to them for safekeeping and give them both to you shortly before we leave. I've also got something from Nan to give you. She left the money to buy this for you; it's to remember her by," Mum added, passing me a small pack the size of a matchbox.

Having placed the passport on the table, I gingerly opened the small heavy box, to reveal a sight, which made my heart beat fast with excitement. Breathless with emotion, I removed the smooth shiny remembrance gift and slid the largest gold signet ring I'd ever seen, on to my finger. "It fits perfectly; I'll never take it off. She always gave me so much, now this. I don't know what I can say except, thank you Nan wherever you are, and God bless."

Mum's lack of sentiment was instant. "As we won't be here much longer you'd better start saying your goodbyes to your mates. Now give me the passport back and you can go."

"You said you also had my birth certificate Mum."

"Yes that's right; so what?"

"Well, could I see it please? You did say you'd give it to me with my passport when we leave."

"I suppose so, but there's nothing much to see," came the nonchalant answer as I was handed the document.

Upon opening the half-size sheet of paper, I glanced at the red printed and partly handwritten information. The printed heading read 'Birth Certificate'; the bare minimum of details that followed showing my full name, date of birth and, surprisingly, Chelmsford as the place my birth was registered.

"This is only part of a birth certificate, haven't I got a full one?" I asked. "The ones I've seen before were almost three times the size showing lots of information. Parent's full names and address; the place of birth, even mother's maiden name, and the father's occupation."

Neither of them spoke and an uneasy silence encouraged me to look from one to another while waiting for some form of response. The silence became so tense I felt I should say something a little more congenial. "I never had a clue we lived in Chelmsford, Mum; it wasn't for very long was it?" I said enquiringly, in a futile effort to break the silence. Dad remained silent and motionless while Mum, who'd been staring at the floor as if deep in thought, slowly looked up into my face. Pausing momentarily, the flicker of a grin showed on her face. I felt uncomfortable looking at her smirk; completely unaware I'd soon be receiving soul-shattering news beyond comprehension, the effect of which would stay with me for the rest of my life.

"You think Nan was your grandmother, don't you?" Mum said calmly, almost leering at me.

"Well of course I do; she was," I answered, thinking to myself; what a silly question! "You also think I'm your mother, don't you?" She added staring into my face.

"Yes I know you are, because you all told me so after Dad collected me from Mannings Heath after the war."

"Well have I got some news for you. Nan and I hadn't even met you until your father brought you to Dorking. Naturally we knew all about you, but we'd never met you before then. Nan wasn't your grandmother; you weren't related. Neither am I, because I'm not your mother; it also means Carolyn is only your half-sister."

For a moment, I didn't believe a word Mum had said, until I noticed the glint in her eyes. Distraught and shocked by the revelation, I had no choice but to listen as she continued, "now the cat's out of the bag, so to speak, I'll answer your question. Your birth was registered in Chelmsford because your father and mother had recently separated and she was living with her parents in Ingatestone near Chelmsford. Your father visited you on several occasions, eventually taking you away to London. After that your mother apparently joined the Air Force."

"Why wasn't I told before, when we first met? Why has it been kept a secret all these years?"

"You weren't told because, not being your mother, I thought you might not do what I told you to, without making a scene. I made Nan and your father promise not to tell you. It was only because your father was so insistent that I agreed to have you in the first place. Anything else you want to know?"

"No nothing; everything's beginning to fall into place. Now I understand why you treat me as you do. I was sure, one of these days I'd have the answers to the questions I've pondered over in the past."

I glanced at Dad who'd remained silent and motionless, gazing all the while into the blackness of the night. He appeared disorientated; full of guilt and shame as he stood with closed eyes, his arms raised and folded over his head with fingers firmly interlocked tightly gripping the back of his neck. As my utmost thought was to ignore their presence; I shrugged my shoulders and, without the slightest sign of agitation, I slowly walked out of the room.

Jet remained curled up in a ball as I slid my hands under his top and bottom end and lifted him, still purring, onto my lap as I sat on the chair next to the boiler where he'd been sleeping. "Well Jet," I said, as if he were human. "I've had two aunts who treated me as if they were my mother. The third has reluctantly pretended to be my mother for years and now I've got a fourth mum; what do you think of that? Mind you, I've still only got one father. But then again, over the years Mum's changed his attitude towards me; he's certainly not the same caring man he used to be, that's for sure."

Why hadn't Dad told me about my mother before he took me to Dorking? It would have explained so much, particularly the meanness and often cruel attitude he and Mum had developed towards me. Within a couple of minutes everything became apparent to me. Mum, Dad and Carolyn were a complete family and I was the odd one out; I'd become an encumbrance, which I realised was the reason I was sent to the *Mercury*. Unbeknown to anyone, Nan had prepared me well for this day; so well I began to feel unconcerned and to some extent relieved.

I sat for a while deliberating on my present position and admiring my glittering gold ring. My response soon became apparent and I decided there were only two ways to handle the situation. One was to try and become the flunky of the family; a family unit which didn't particularly want me and who'd treated me harshly for many years. The second was to remain independent and build my own personality; biding my time until I'd decided what to do with my life. It wasn't long before I came to a decision; I'd bide my time.

I only vaguely recalled my early days and being driven away from the place I was living, never to return. It was then that the unexpected thought suddenly hit me. The pretty blonde lady dressed in, what I now realise, was a uniform; the lady who looked at my scarred forehead, who knelt in front of me, with her arms around me; the lady with tears in her eyes who kissed me; the lady, who wouldn't answer my calls of goodbye, but continued walking away without even glancing back, was my mother.

Although Dad never mentioned how the decision regarding Australia had evolved it was easy to guess why. I dismissed any thought of asking him, knowing he'd evade any questions.

In what seemed hardly anytime at all, Amy Lucas and her family were caring for Jet and virtually everything we'd owned had either been sold or given away. The saddest days I could ever remember were when I said my farewells to Amy and my friends. The longest goodbye was in total silence, and motionless, as red robin and I gazed at each other, for the last time. But would it be the last time?

Chapter Eighty-eight

A tiny percentage of the passengers were wealthy tourists simply holidaying, and enjoying the cruise. All the other hundreds of passengers travelled under the Government Assisted Emigration Scheme; whereby they paid an inclusive fare of only twenty-five pounds each. We were the only exception; Mum wouldn't consider being subsidised, I heard her tell Dad one evening weeks beforehand. It was belittling she'd told him and insisted they pay the full fare.

As was normal, and certainly not unexpected, she gave the impression of being important and distinguished. The first class luxury cabins Mum had insisted upon were situated on 'A' deck. They were indeed sumptuous; being so expensive that the cost of the trip including the masses of new clothing for Mum amounted to a huge chunk of their money. Money, which had been earned and worked so long and hard for, only to be frittered away to satisfy Mum's egotistical whim.

To ensure the minimum of contact between us, Mum had arranged for my enormous twin berth cabin to be at the opposite end of the first class section. Likewise the dining table I was allocated was at the far end of the restaurant and well away from theirs. Nothing had changed; it was what I was accustomed to. It suited me particularly well because to keep up her authoritative upper class impression Mum felt obliged to ensure I also had ample money to spend.

Within a couple of days, I stood alone and fed up on the upper deck of the enormous P & O Liner *Strathaird*. As the ship skirted around the rough waters of the Bay of Biscay en route to Australia, I made a decision, which would change my forlorn approach towards the voyage completely.

Because I thought I'd feel more at ease in their company, I decided to use the standard tourist decks, returning to first class only when necessary. It certainly paid dividends and I immediately made friends with several boys about the same age as myself as well as their families. The majority of the wealthy passengers I met, particularly the ones I joined at meal times, very soon sensing my difficult family situation, befriended me, treating me as one of them. Nan's lessons in etiquette had become natural to me and very soon I began to relax, enjoying the company at mealtimes more than I'd imagined.

Due to the blockade of the Suez Canal, the ship continued on a straight course down the Atlantic Ocean, crossing the entrance to the Mediterranean, towards West Africa. Docking at the Canary Islands, my newly found friends and I found ample time to tour around Las Palmas; the first visit any of us had made to a foreign country. Initially enjoying the experience, we soon became bored, agreeing the one-day stopover at the quiet capital had been long enough.

Dakar, in French West Africa, was the next scheduled stop; it was also the most interesting. Several small rowing boats came out to welcome the ship's arrival, each containing young black boys who dived and swam around the ship, collecting any loose change thrown in the water by the passengers. Dozens of the black community gathered at the edge of the dock hoping to sell their wares of fresh fruit and various memorabilia; others offered tours around the town by rickshaw. Almost immediately after getting ashore we realised due to the language barrier, we were unable to communicate with anyone. However, we soon discovered that simple sign language was the answer and it didn't take us very long to agree that a tour around the town by rickshaw was well worth the cost. Three tall black men dressed like Zulu warriors, with enormous headdresses of flowing white ostrich feathers, masses of smaller feathers and bracelets of bells around their arms and legs, lifted up the front of the carts and ran the half-mile trip around the town at a steady pace.

When we'd each made our payment by giving them either a John Player or Senior Service cigarette each, they showed their gratitude by making gestures to shake our hands. This they did, at least half a dozen times each.

Noticing four white people sitting outside a small hotel close by the Docks we also sat down at a table in the shade and ordered a drink by making drinking and bottle gestures to the waiter. Within minutes he returned with a bottle of beer each, and a price list handwritten in French.

"I've only got English money," one of the boys declared.

"So have I. We all have, haven't we?" I asked, placing a handful of loose change on the table.

"Don't worry about it," a white man with an unusual English accent sitting at the adjacent table smiled. "The waiter may not be able to speak English, or read and write, but when you're ready to pay your bill, he'll charge you the right amount, and give you the correct change in French francs, you wait and see."

Having thanked the man for his helpful information we joined into casual conversation. He told us he was a crewmember on a French cargo ship, which called at Dakar every month. He began telling us about the local people, and their customs, when he began to smile. "What's so funny?" One of the boys laughed.

"As you've undoubtedly noticed," the man answered, "the majority of the black population live under cover of tin sheets, cardboard, and sacking. Unfortunately, because there isn't any sanitation, they have no alternative but to use the verge of the road or any open land as a toilet. Not having a choice, they don't give it a second thought; it's their accepted way of life."

"Yes, we've certainly seen some sights in the last couple of hours," one of the boys jested. "We could barely believe it; barely being the operative word."

"I know what you mean," the man continued, "but my smile was in anticipation of the expressions you'll show when you see what the bloke coming towards us does. He's the local butcher; watch what he's about to do; you have to see it to believe it!"

A scantily dressed native leading a mule stopped within a few feet of where we sat. Lengths of cord hung over the back of the frail-looking creature, attached to which were large lumps of meat. The mule stood motionless, the bright red blood from the bulky raw chunks dripping from its underside and running down its legs.

With his bare feet, the butcher, completely undeterred, set about clearing an area within the fly-infested human excrement and filthy litter. When a large enough space had been cleared in the refuse, the heavy load of meat was transferred from the mule into a pile on the edge of the road. Within minutes people began arriving to purchase lumps of meat from the butcher, who sat by the side of the pile with a machete hacking off lumps to the required size.

"Well, I was right about your facial expressions," the man smiled.

"That's disgusting; I'd never have believed it. The thought of eating it knowing where it's been is repulsive. We've certainly seen some strange and unusual things today." One of the older boys remarked.

"What other strange things have you seen?" The man asked, "I've got accustomed to them."

"Well," the boy continued, "why do most of the men walk about together holding hands? They're not all, you know, that way inclined, are they?" He said shyly.

"No not at all, far from it," came the answer. "It's customary in this country for natives to hold hands with their friends; it's a way of binding their friendship I suppose. It's the same as you shaking hands with a friend, or putting your hand on his shoulder."

"Oh well, we certainly got the wrong end of the stick there," I said smiling. "It's probably a good job none of us speaks the language. Who knows what we'd have said?"

We told him the saddest sight we'd seen were the numerous cripples who had no choice but to become beggars. We listened intently; shocked into silence and revulsion as he explained that their legs had been intentionally paralysed by being permanently tied under their bodies from infancy until adolescence. By being able to fold the skeletal limbs under themselves, and squat balanced on a small square board fitted with tiny wheels to push themselves along; they were able to move about, begging from passing ship passengers or crew, to guarantee their livelihood. He told us it was an accepted occupation here and that the proud parents were often considered to have been attentive to the future needs of their child. To my mind and to others like me, it was the most horrific and poignant act imaginable.

When it was time to leave, we placed our money on the table and watched the waiter produce a sheet of paper, which he placed upon the table. Initially confused, we glanced at the writing and varying sized circles each containing a different number. Very soon we realized someone had used English currency, placed it in order of worth upon the paper and carefully drawn around each coin. The waiter simply took our coins one at a time, placing them onto the matching size circle until the value of our coins matched the cost of the beer. It was all so simple.

Within minutes of leaving Dakar the following morning, several sharks were following the ship, waiting to feed on waste food discharged into the sea from the kitchens. Alongside, glittering flying fish frequently skimmed two to three feet above the surface of the sea at such a rapid speed, they out-manoeuvred any predators.

A week later, everyone joined in the celebrations for the crossing of the equator ceremony. Very soon I realised, regardless of being virtually ignored by my own family, the camaraderie I shared with many others. Setting off to start a new life, in a new country, gave me a feeling of contentment.

Later that evening we were informed that the sick woman passenger who had boarded at Dakar suffering with a high fever, had passed away during the night. Due to the unexpected death and its perplexing circumstances, the ship slowly came to a halt. I watched with others, as the body, wrapped in canvas was tightly stitched from the feet upwards, the final stitch being through the nose to ensure total inertness. Weights were tied around the enclosed body, which was lifted by four crewmen onto a wide plank at the edge of the railings and completely draped with the Union Jack. Two short prayers were read aloud by the Captain, and then one end of the plank was lifted to allow the body to slide down from under the flag, some fifty feet to its watery grave. Within five minutes, the burial at sea having been completed, the ship was under way again.

Within twelve hours, as a precautionary measure, every passenger on board had received a smallpox vaccination. As expected, within two days everybody's arm had swollen often causing excruciating pain due to the side effects of the medication. Everybody's, with the exception of mine! The ship's doctor couldn't understand why my vaccination hadn't taken. He waited another couple of days, then somewhat mystified, decided to give me a second dose!

Three days later, we sailed into the beautiful metropolis of Cape Town, which spread across sandy beaches below the majestic sight of Table Mountain. For hundreds of years, Cape Town docks, being halfway between the Western world and Asia had been used to replenish food and water stocks for the crews of passing ships. The result showed in several of the native population, who bore the colour or appearance of mixed nationality.

When we realised we were in an English-speaking community, with English currency and cigarettes once again being of prime value, the small group of us certainly got the best we could from the two-day stopover! Bus rides took us to the spotlessly clean city centre, beaches, and bars. The most exciting trip was the cable car ride to the top of Table Mountain; the most surprising, being invited to join Mum and Dad to visit Stellenbosch Wine Growers Co; the most unusual, seeing a male with facial features comparable to the black African native, but who was an albino with skin as white as mine and with tightly-coiled blonde hair. But most striking of all were the pink pupils of his piercing eyes; they were so scary, I only looked once!

Shortly after we'd left Cape Town and begun steaming across the Indian Ocean towards Fremantle, I was called to the Medical Quarters. Two doctors gave me a brief examination and informed me that my smallpox vaccination hadn't taken for the second time. They concluded I was immune to the disease and should consider myself very fortunate, which was good news. But there remained the problem of possibly being a carrier of the disease and unwittingly passing it on to others; to ensure I was clear of infection, I'd no choice but to stay in the medical quarantine cabin for tests.

For several days, although bored beyond belief at looking out of a porthole at nothing except sea and sky, I ate well, read well, and rested well; even so, it didn't stop Mum claiming a refund against my reduction in facilities from first to second class. Time dragged on until I was eventually given a clean bill of health and released to enjoy the company of my newly found friends.

It was now the opposite; time seemed to go so quickly it wasn't long before we docked at Fremantle and were saying our farewells. The last leg of the trip was over for some of us; others would go on to Melbourne or Sydney as we all wondered what our new life and future would hold for us.

Chapter Eighty-nine

Within fifteen minutes of leaving the ship, we travelled by taxi to a large rambling wooden halfway house on the outskirts of Perth. Dad left us at reception, and within minutes, set off again in the taxi to buy a car.

Having completed a questionnaire, Mum was called into one of the offices. Several minutes later she reappeared, accompanied by a young man. I was asked to follow him outside to the back of the building where I'd be temporarily staying. Twenty or so wooden buildings, some no bigger than a garden shed were scattered around the area. Having been taken to my temporary accommodation, which comprised of a room large enough to house a single bed, wardrobe and dressing table, I was shown the communal toilets and showers before returning to the main building.

Dad had returned; it hadn't taken him long to purchase a large pick-up vehicle into which he'd loaded all their cases. "You won't be very impressed when you see where you'll be staying," I said, "they're sheds, and very bleak sheds at that."

"We shan't be staying in any shed," Mum grunted as she got into the vehicle with Carolyn. "We'll be staying in hotels until we find a house to rent. There's no point in all of us going. You'll be all right here; it shouldn't be for long. Your father will visit weekly to pay your rent as well as giving you enough money to buy food." Dad had remained subdued while Mum spoke; I'd remained mute and motionless only able to look on as they drove away without a goodbye or backwards glance.

The dozen or so other immigrants, who had also stayed in the temporary accommodation, were gone within a few days. I soon became bored spending weeks doing nothing except sitting about feeling lazy, lethargic, and unfit. From the age of six, I'd been made to work hard, often non-stop for long hours. By the time I was thirteen years old, I was as strong as the average man, but now I could feel the decline in my strength and not relishing the feeling, decided to do something about it.

Having purchased a pair of shorts and plimsolls, I'd alternately jog, and then walk, the distance between telegraph poles for an hour each morning. Within three days, whilst I continued to walk the gap between two telegraph poles, I'd trebled the distance jogging. During the day I'd spend a minimum of one-hour weight training in the small, unused gymnasium, although within a week I'd increased the weight-lifting sessions to twice a day. Within two weeks I'd restored my strength and physique.

Despite being told Dad would visit me, he didn't; instead the rent, including sufficient money for my food, was posted to reception every week. I wasn't left a message or visited until the day Dad came to collect me, two months later. It was a Friday and I explained to Dad that as I'd thought I'd seen the last of them, I'd got myself a job, starting on Monday. I'd also made arrangements to move into a room I'd rented closer to Perth and suggested he told Mum he couldn't find me, saying I'd moved out of the halfway house weeks ago and nobody knew of my whereabouts. He completely disagreed with my suggestion; telling me to keep the job, but that on no account would he allow me to leave home. I was to return with him to the furnished bungalow he'd rented; he categorically refused to leave without me.

The journey to our new home was the first time Dad and I had been alone since he'd furtively first mentioned Australia. Despite my efforts to generally chat, Dad, probably concerned at the questions I might ask, kept any conversation to a minimum. Having difficulty in finding time and a suitable place to live was the only explanation I was given for the lack of communication. In any event, I felt sure he hadn't bothered because he knew I'd be able to care for myself.

When we reached the small town of Kalamunda, Dad drove to a white timber bungalow situated on the edge of a small orange grove. As with all the properties we'd passed, the garden was lush and green from regular watering from a sprinkler system. The corrugated roof, which like most others reflected the heat of the day, bore patches of red rust caused by the soaking from the hosepipe it received most days to cool the interior.

Noticing the large dry areas of the woodlands and open spaces, I realised that the old saying that the grass on the other side is always greener, wasn't true; far from it! The wildlife didn't appear very prolific, but then again, I wasn't certain where to look, being unaccustomed to the habitats of the unfamiliar creatures. Nevertheless I felt confident I'd quickly settle into my new life.

When Dad pulled up at the front of the bungalow I stepped from the vehicle to the sound of Carolyn, who'd been sitting with Mum on the veranda, waving and calling out her greetings to me. I smiled waving back as she stood and stepped towards me. It was the only step she took, before

Mum grabbed her by the arm telling her to sit down and keep quiet.

"Hello Mum, it's good to see you again," I lied through my false smile, watching her expression closely for a response to my greeting.

"Did he behave himself coming home Bern?" Mum asked, ignoring me completely. "Nothing seems to have changed then," I said softly, but loud enough for Dad to hear.

Ignoring my remark Dad answered, "yes, no problem, he kept quiet for most of the time. We didn't have much to say, just idle chat."

"Good; as long as you weren't quizzed by any embarrassing questions. Perhaps he's realised its all water under the bridge and he'd be wasting his time asking anything," she said.

"There are a couple of things I'd like clarified Mum, but don't concern yourselves; I won't ask either of you any awkward questions. You've both unwittingly answered most of them by your attitude, and the way you've hidden the past from me. I'll find the answers and the truth for myself; regardless of how long it takes me, you can be sure of that."

"That's enough," Dad interrupted. "Now come with me and I'll show you around the place and where you catch the bus to take you to work. At least you've got a job; that's more than I have."

Mum's facial expression changed instantly to a smile; "oh that's good, at least you'll be able to pay your way." The smile disappeared as quickly as it'd appeared as she continued, "but don't forget whenever you're home, you're to carry on as before. Don't expect to be mollycoddled, and don't forget to give us our privacy. On account of the heat you'll only need to make yourself a salad of an evening. If you want anything else, do what you did before; get it yourself during the day."

"As you said Mum, we'll carry on as before. I wouldn't expect anything else, or want it any other way; it suits me fine."

The job I'd got as an electrician's mate in the maintenance department of Atkins (W.A.) Ltd was interesting and paid well, with plenty of overtime if I wanted. Within a week, initially to keep out of the way, I'd joined a gymnasium close to work. Weight-lifting classes held by experienced instructors, very soon became my favoured sport. Training hard each working day, I was proud of becoming gym leader within my weight inside three months.

Dad wasn't so lucky, only being able to get the odd job now and again, making it necessary for me to hand over the majority of my wages to help pay the household bills. Very soon, the money we had arrived with began to dwindle and it became necessary to move to a less expensive bungalow in the town of Northam. Continuing with my job, and now only half the distance away, I earned a pay rise, which allowed me to save a small amount each week.

Friends became plentiful and weekends were mainly spent surfing, swimming, sunbathing or partying. I knew I'd always remember the good and bad times of my life in Ifold, but this life was good all the time, and I lived it to the full!

No matter how hard he tried, Dad couldn't find suitable full-time work and over the following months gradually became depressed and bad tempered. The thought of Mum helping out financially by getting a job, even for a few hours a day, was inconceivable. Dad didn't have the nerve to suggest such a possibility; he knew he'd be talked down.

Carolyn reached the age when she should have started school, although Mum had no intention of taking her because it was a fifteen-minute walk away. Mum, very soon began complaining of being homesick, and questioned how much longer the money they had left would last. Dad understandably became more despondent as the weeks passed. I kept well out of their way; whenever possible by going out with friends or to the gym, enjoying everything my new life had to offer.

As I was leaving for work one Monday, Mum followed me to the front door and said in a casual attitude, "wait for your father, he'll take you to work. When you get there give notice to your employers that you'll be leaving at the end of the week. We've decided that while we still have enough money to pay the fare, we should leave; arrangements have been made for us to return to England next week. Your father's adamant that you can't stay here by yourself, so he'll be taking, and collecting you from work every day this week. You're not to go out of an evening; you're to stay at home in case you get any ideas to the contrary and decide to sod off. I don't expect you agree with the decision, but that's too bad; you'll just have to put up with it! So will I."

Mum had once again, for the umpteenth time, smashed my dreams and hopes to smithereens. My new future, had gradually been taking shape; I'd decided what to do, and when to do it. But it would take time; the one thing I didn't have. My plans were in ruins, everything was lost.

Chapter Ninety

As the medium-sized, part-passenger, part-cargo Italian ship *SS Toscana* slowly cruised out to sea heading due north; I looked back at the slowly diminishing buildings and beaches, recalling how much my life had changed within the last year and a half since Nan had gone. I could only speculate on my future, or how it would have turned out, had I been able to stay in Australia.

My cabin was small and hot, nevertheless it was above the waterline and I could open a porthole for fresh air; unlike the sweltering four-berth cabin beneath the waterline, which Mum had unwittingly booked!

Within a couple of hours I'd befriended the other three boys on board and we agreed to join one another during meal times and on any trips we made ashore. Having reached Indonesia, we passed between Java and Sumatra into the vast seas of the Thousand Isles; the most beautiful, breathtaking sight ever imaginable. Countless islands, with bleached white sandy beaches rose from the clear pale blue sea; some so small they reminded me of the cartoon of a shipwrecked survivor leaning against a solitary palm tree waiting to be rescued by a passing ship. Some of the islands took a few minutes to pass; others took half an hour or more. The picturesque islands, the different species of spectacular multi-coloured birds and watching the strange stunningly decorated fish in the clear water, were awe-inspiring.

Java was our first port of call; we spent two days loading various cargos and it was the longest stop we made. The other stops in this intriguing part of the world, at Sumatra and Colombo, where we took freight aboard, lasted half the time.

By the second week, the ship had docked at Aden and from there we travelled through the Red Sea, stopping at the Port of Suez. With the money I'd saved, I'd been sightseeing at other ports of call, but this one was special. The first part of the trip inland was to Cairo, then on to Giza to see the pyramids, through the sweltering heat of the desert. The enormous manmade structures, over two thousands years old, very soon rose high above us. Everybody's reaction was complete silence as we gazed at the amazing sight and splendour of the enormous pyramids and the Great Pyramid of Khafre.

Until that day, the most unusual ride I'd experienced had been in a rickshaw, but plodding steadily along in comfort on a camel's back was enjoyable and even more rousing than driving the Corgi had been on that first occasion.

The next day we continued along the recently reopened Suez Canal to Port Said where freight was loaded for the last time. At Bari on the eastern coast of Italy, our penultimate stop, it took two days to unload part of the freight before finishing the trip and disembarking at Venice.

As we had to wait several hours for our journey to continue by train across Europe, I walked alone around the beautiful City of Canals. New and intriguing sights filled my mind with wonder as I gazed at the houses built on stilts above the water of the many gondola-strewn canals separating the islands, reachable by magnificently hand-built arched bridges. It wasn't long before I found myself marvelling at the captivating domes of St Marks; the stupendous oil-painted figurines adorning the ceiling, the golden façade, the statues of bronze and marble; all unforgettable sights, once seen, never to be forgotten.

Sitting in the railway compartment for many hours in virtual silence with Mum and Dad, as the train thundered across the Continent towards London, our final destination, was the closest and longest I could recall having been in their company. It certainly wasn't exciting! By the time we reached England it was light. Being unable to bear the silence any longer, I went and stood in the corridor; I immediately realised how much I'd missed the fragrance, and variation of the lush countryside and wildlife.

When the journey eventually terminated at Waterloo Station, the enormity of the building, the number of platforms and the amount of people astounded me. What amazed me next was Mum's categorical refusal to board another train. She insisted we got a taxi to Dad's parents' home in Peckham, even if it cost their last penny. It didn't quite cost all the money they had; they were left with five and six pence! It wasn't much to show for the years of toiling I'd experienced at Ifold.

Chapter Ninety-one

Dad had hoped we'd all be able to stay temporarily with his parents, but as there wasn't enough room for all of us, I was fortunate and stayed in the house next door with one of my aunts and her husband. Not only was I was warmly welcomed into their home; I was treated as one of the family. During the evening, the three of us were chatting about our lives in general, when I asked if they'd tell me about my early childhood. The response from my aunt was instantaneous. "I don't see why not Rod; everybody has the right to know the truth, and we all believe you should have been told years ago. However there's one thing we won't discuss."

"Oh, what's that?" I asked feeling a little concerned.

"Babs, and what she did to break your mother and father up once she got her claws into Bern," came the instant reply. "If I were you, whatever you are told, keep to yourself, until you decide whether it's worth mentioning or not."

During the course of the evening, I found out how and when Dad first met my mother and how many years they were married, living only a few streets away. All my questions relating to my mother were answered; I was told all the family had considered Dad very fortunate to find such a loving and caring person. Whilst I clearly remembered being cared for by Aunt Kit, I certainly wasn't aware she actually was my mother's sister. When I asked for clues to help me trace my mother or the other half of my family at some time in the future, I was surprised to be given five addresses, all within a two-mile radius of where we were!

The next day, Mum and Dad came round and having bluntly conveyed the depressed state of their financial position to me and despite my objections, took the keepsake Nan had left me. Supposedly to temporarily borrow urgently needed money; it was to be taken to a pawnbroker. They lied to me, and despite their promises they sold my ring, never to be replaced.

Within a week, I'd met nearly all of Dad's close relations and was taken aback by the number of aunts, uncles and cousins I'd never known I had. I met my cousin Roy, a qualified electrical engineer, who arranged with his employers to give me a job as his apprentice. Roy, who was about six years my senior and I not only enjoyed working and joking together but we soon became good and trusting mates.

Within three weeks, Dad had rented a partly furnished house in the next road. Carolyn started at her first school, which was a short unaccompanied walk from home, while Mum did what she was best at every day – nothing!

As I'd become accustomed to not feeling part of the family, I wasn't perturbed in the slightest to be told I was expected to comply with my usual routine and generally look after myself and keep out of the way.

Initially, although I'd have preferred living in the country, there was so much to see and do; I began to enjoy living in London. Within a month I'd been accepted and taken up membership of Pullens, a renowned professionally organised weight-lifting club in Camberwell Green. Within six weeks, along with two others about the same age as me, I became a bouncer four nights a week at one or other of two

Marsdens Dancing Schools; one in Peckham and the other in Kennington. Staying out of an evening very soon became routine and didn't create a problem at home in the slightest.

By the time I was eighteen and a half I'd met, and grown fond of a girl named Jean, who regularly went dancing with a few other girls at the Peckham club. From the time we first met, on a day trip organised by the club, we enjoyed each other's company, and started going out together. I'd always walk her home, from the club or wherever we'd been out to together, often being invited indoors to chat with her parents and brother John.

It was late one Sunday evening, when I got home to find a note left for me on the kitchen table. It was short and simple, asking me to leave my front door key on the mantelpiece in the morning, as Dad wanted to have a spare cut; the front door would be left unlocked whenever I went out during the week. Putting my key where stipulated I never gave the matter another thought until Friday.

On Friday evening, finding the front door locked when I returned home from work, I knocked on the letter flap and waited; there was no response, although I could hear voices. I knocked again, and then a third time before Mum eventually opened the door. Her expression was absurdly smug as she pointed towards the kitchen. She followed me closely into the room where Dad sat at the table reading the paper.

"Did you manage to get my door key cut Dad?" I asked.

"No," Mum interrupted, "we've decided not to bother to give it back to you."

"Oh, why not? I don't get home until late most nights; surely you're not going to get up and let me in at any hour, are you?"

"No, we're most certainly not," Mum sneeringly replied.

"What do you mean? I don't understand. How am I going to get indoors then?"

"You're not coming indoors, it's as simple as that," she answered, her face beaming as she continued, "did you notice a suitcase in the hallway as you came through?"

"Yes, but I'm not concerned about that; I'm more concerned about my front door key."

"Well you should be concerned about the suitcase, because it's yours."

"What do you mean, it's mine?"

"Exactly what I said," she smirked, "it's yours; all your clothes and everything else you've got are packed inside. We've made our minds up; you're leaving home, and you're leaving now. All you need to do is pick the case up, and get out."

Directing my question at Dad I said, "I'm not ready yet, can't you at least wait a few day's until I've got somewhere to live?"

"Do as your mother says." He spoke quietly, looking down to avoid eye contact.

"Please don't ever say that again. If I ever meet you again, that is."

"What do you mean?" He quietly asked, turning a page of his newspaper.

"You referred to Mum as my mother. She isn't; please don't ever refer to her as my mother again, neither to me or anyone"

"That's right and don't ever forget it. I never wanted you in the first place; I've only ever put up with you because your father was so emphatic and obstinate, now get out," Mum screamed, slapping me across the face.

Carolyn grabbed me by the belt and began kicking me repeatedly in the shins over and over again shouting in a shrill voice, "Mummy said get out, get out, so get out."

Dumbfounded at her actions and attitude, I wondered if Carolyn had shown her true feelings towards me. Was she siding with her mother? Or was she trying to keep on the right side of her? I'd have to wait to find out; only time would tell, and it did. I left in silence; my only regret being that Mum had got in before me.

Chapter Ninety-two

My instinctive reaction was to head for Marsdens Club where I hoped to get advice on any possible flats to rent. As it was to no avail, I was offered, and thankfully accepted, the facilities of the club until such time as I could find suitable accommodation. Later in the evening I met Jean and having explained the situation, which had arisen a little earlier than expected, was a given a list from her and her friends of local shops which often advertised properties to rent. Early the following morning I eagerly started looking for a suitable place to live, little realising I'd experience so much disappointment and frustration.

After a full day travelling around the southeastern area of London, I only found three suitable flats; unfortunately, none of them was local or within easy access to the area I wanted; they were also all unfurnished and not available for immediate rental. I'd welcomed the comfortable and adequate facilities within the club, although it clearly wasn't a place I could, or would want to stay indefinitely. I realised I'd need to place my own advertisement for a room to rent in some of the local shops. Jean agreed it was probably the best thing to do and offered to type the details and take them to appropriate newsagents.

It had just turned midnight on my second night at the club when the doorbell rang. Initially I didn't take any notice; not until it rang continuously. Reluctantly I got up, partly dressed, and went to the entrance. "It's gone midnight for goodness sake, who on earth's that? And what do you want?" I shouted through the sturdily built door.

"It's George," came the answer, "is that you Rod?"

"Yes it's me, but George who?" I called.

"George Waters," came the answer, "you know me, I'm Jean's Dad. She told Rose and me what's happened and I've come to take you back to our place. We can't let you stay here mate, come home with me; we've got room enough for you."

I opened the door; completely unaware that this would be the start of an extraordinary and fascinating life, which any man could be proud of.

Within three years Jean and I were happily married, and remain so to this day. I traced and was reunited with my mother and another half-sister; none of us ever mentioning the past. Although I was delighted to have qualified to compete in the Weightlifting finals of the 1962 Commonwealth Games, I declined, being determined to catch up on my lack of education. I was well aware my long-term future was far more important than the possibility of winning any short-term glory.

Grateful to Roy for everything he had taught me, when the opportunity arose I joined another company becoming an electro-mechanical engineer. Within four years I became the Chief Engineer of a company and personally responsible for the design, manufacture and installation of the first British and European automatic barriers, parking and toll equipment, controlled by coded security cards, or coins.

By my-mid thirties I'd qualified and held the Technical Sales Manager position in a prestigious manufacturing company. I was also the nice; or not so nice man, who sold the first parking meter in Britain. Well, I suppose somebody had to!

I experienced Sir Ronald Bennett's 21 day residential Business Management Course, reputed to be the toughest in the world. As a result of which I became an Executive of a large and infamous Public Company, with sole responsibility for sales as well as entertaining Government Officials and other potential clients throughout Europe and many countries beyond for almost 20 years; my business experience qualifying me to become a Fellow of the Institute of British Management.

One of my most unexpected experiences was to share a bottle of 12-year-old Malt Whisky with Edward Heath, the then British Prime Minister and my boat-builder friend John Martland. Another was spending months in India looking for viable business opportunities; as was being flown by helicopter from Bombay to inspect many oil rigs in the Indian Ocean and the Arabian Sea.

Later for business reasons whilst in South Africa I became involved in the Angolan war. The South African government became aware of this and paying for my silence, deported me with a warning; never to return.

How this, little old country boy grew up to live such an unpredictable and exhilarating life is all a story for another day, or two. Until then, "Good night, God bless, and don't forget to say your prayers."

ISBN 1425158781

9 781425 158781

Printed in Great Britain
by Amazon

43705752R10274